HOW THE
GOVERNMENT
BREAKS
THE LAW

HOW THE GOVERNMENT BREAKS THE LAW

Jethro K. Lieberman

STEIN AND DAY/*Publishers*/New York

For Susan, of course,

and Jessica and Seth

Acknowledgments

MANY PEOPLE aided in the development of this book and I gratefully acknowledge their help. Sandor Frankel and Marc L. Fleischaker read the entire manuscript and made many valuable suggestions and corrections. Senator William Proxmire and his legislative assistant Thomas van der Voort helped me greatly in pursuing with the Comptroller General the issue of civilian control of the military. I recall with pleasure numerous enlightening conversations with John H. Stassen (especially in connection with fund impounding and civilian control of the military) and with Salvatore A. Romano, Denis M. Neill, Joseph Sahid, James P. Mercurio, and Donald M. Barnes. Many of the attorneys for Lloyd Eldon Miller, Jr., provided details of that case. I am grateful to my father, J. Ben Lieberman, and to Jon M. Van Dyke, for discussions concerning scope and emphasis. Mary Solberg was a subtle and discerning editor, and Maureen McFeeley's cheerfulness in the face of my typing requests was awesome. Thanks are due also to many others, some in the Government, who would not care to be named, who have answered queries large and small.

Special thanks are due my wife, Susan E. V. Lieberman, for perceptive criticisms, bountiful all-purpose aid and comfort, and stoic patience at the newspaper clipping service that seemed to take over our home.

Washington, D.C., April, 1972   J.K.L.

Preface

GOVERNMENT IN the United States is at a critical point. People at all social and economic levels are saying that Government is functioning poorly. Many people believe that it is not functioning at all. A Gallup Poll in 1971 found that "nearly half of the American population believes that current unrest is so serious that 'a real breakdown in this country' may be in the offing." *

The American people can cite example after example of scandal, corruption, and fraud; of impotent policies chasing after misguided goals; of indecision, ineptitude, and unintelligence; of a monstrous proliferation of paper and rules; and of a dramatic decline in the Government's ability to deliver. Crime, inflation, unemployment, poverty, war, pollution, environmental decay, racism, consumer fraud, monopoly—all are evils on a large scale, and the Government seems unwilling or unable to combat them.

The despair of the victims has turned them increasingly to violence. But the response of government officials throughout the land has been only a simple-minded asking for a return to law and order and for belief in the credibility of the "system." These officials do not discuss their own role in the breakdown, their own contribution to America's crime problem. It is time they were forced by public opinion to do so.

Government lawlessness is very old. In democracies, government is supposed to be controlled by checks and balances. But to the oppressed the belief in this abstract system is as comforting as the belief in the long-run operation of the law of supply and demand was to the unemployed during the Great Depression.

* Citations for quotations and other authorities throughout this book are collected in the Notes and References section, beginning on page 281.

"The law" is supposed to be a device that assures that people of passion and prejudice do not ride roughshod over the rights of others, nor destroy the whole society. But the law does not—and cannot—assure its own survival. It takes people to enforce the law, and it is axiomatic that officials can fail or refuse to enforce it or can even violate it directly. Law exists everywhere and everywhere is violated. Democracies are no exception to this rule. Especially not the United States. The people in a democracy need to know this, so they can protect themselves.

Hence this book, a description of some lawless acts of our contemporary Governments, and some short prescriptions for restoring legal order.

This book was written during a time of serious debate about whether the United States had committed a variety of war crimes in Vietnam. The book was concluded in the shadow of the President's attempt to enjoin newspapers from publishing information not favorable to his and earlier administrations.

When unlawful powers are asserted on a broad enough scale, many people can be found who believe that the powers are legitimate, and who neglect smaller illegal acts altogether. It is the purpose of this book to remind the ordinary citizen that our officials are only human and that crime is not, therefore, solely a product of the private sector. It is to be hoped that some of the frustration of our time can be turned to positive actions to reduce government criminality, and thus reduce a major cause of injustice.

Contents

In a government of laws, the existence of the government will be imperilled if it fails to observe the law scrupulously. Our government is the potent, the omnipresent, teacher. For good or ill, it teaches the whole people by its example. Crime is contagious. If the government becomes a law-breaker, it breeds contempt for law; it invites every man to become a law unto himself; it invites anarchy.

—Mr. Justice Brandeis, dissenting,
Olmstead v. *United States* (1928)

Self-discipline on the part of the executive branch will provide the answer to virtually all legitimate complaints.

—Mr. Justice Rehnquist, then
Assistant Attorney General (1971)

1

A Healthy Contempt
for the Law

LET'S PUT CRIME in perspective and openly admit that we couldn't get along in America unless we were all willing to break the law. Despite gloomy ruminations over the sorry state of things in this most apocalyptic of centuries, we Americans do remain steadfastly cheerful about at least one thing—the life of crime. That unremitting moralist, Senator Strom Thurmond, spoke for every American when he tongue-lashed a policeman who was dimwitted enough to attempt to arrest him for running a red light. Senator Thurmond did not deny the crime; he merely reminded the officer that a Senator cannot constitutionally be arrested for committing traffic violations when the Senate is in session. "He didn't understand the system," the Senator later complained of the hapless cop.

In pursuing our way of life, Americans generally share Senator Thurmond's healthy contempt for the law (if not always his immunity). When we have wanted to do something that disturbs our moral sense, we have seen to it that a law is put on the books and have then gone right ahead anyway, secure in the knowledge that we have discharged our moral duty. And we all break laws, those of us who decry the breakdown of law and order no less than others.

When morality is on the books, it is accounted for. Fornication and adultery are crimes, but Americans—even law-abiding Americans—are guilty of them nonetheless. There were tens of thousands—maybe millions—of drinkers during Prohibition, but Congress refused to authorize adequate funds to permit the alcoholic ban to be enforced. Drug laws and children aren't what they used to be: if some unlucky individuals are convicted of smoking marijuana, most are not—by mutual consent of the police and the governed. Congressmen don't like other people to accept bribes; but they are more equivocal when it comes to judging their own behavior, and eager officials in the Justice Department would rather not indict until the candidate has lost. You're a sucker if you think the Internal Revenue Service will spot every bit of padding, and you are not supposed to jaywalk or speed, but everyone does. A free nation of activists need hardly be deterred by restrictions everyone knows were never intended to be enforced. It is the pact we Americans have made with ourselves: condemnation without injunction. So many laws and so little reason to abide by any of them. Even more than baseball or professing self-righteousness, law-breaking is the national pastime.

To be sure, some among us profess disgust with crime. Some even deplore the "crime rate" and its inevitable, drum-rolling increase. Candidates of most persuasions, suburbanites, depraved city dwellers, and even some honest folks have expressed alarm at the rape and robbery index. The Governments of the United States pour out torrents of statistics to show us how worried we should be. But surely many of our esteemed citizens are joking, for they own guns and glorify bad men by paying high prices at movies to be nourished by violent deeds. Surely these protestations of innocence are merely the subtle jokes of a people more sophisticated than most suspect. But perhaps not. For the crime statistics measure only "hard" crime, and the lawbreaking in which most Americans indulge is "soft" or "petty" crime, not usually measured because it is rarely detected. So the irate citizen who takes a few office supplies home for his personal use or pads an expense account is not necessarily inconsistent—and may be innocent in outlook, if not in deed—when he decries the steady increase in larceny.

This "soft" lawbreaking would be inconsequential and scarcely worth noting, except that it establishes a moral climate conducive to a grander form of lawbreaking. Petty thievery is obviously a business expense; speeding, of itself, hurts no one; "nickel-and-dime" cheating on a tax return hardly affects the size or operations of the federal Government. So none of these incidents of lawbreaking causes any general crisis in confidence about America itself. They do, however, provide the foundation for our tolerance of the most serious threat to law and order: "official" lawbreaking by the Government itself.

Nowadays when Presidents of the United States and other officials of high rank—like Kings and Premiers—exhort their citizenry to obey the law, the implication is obvious that the governments they head are virtuous upholders of the law of the land. It is, in fact, more than an implication: every President likes to say that his administration will enforce to the limit all the laws, without fear or favor, equally and without discrimination.

Thus, President Eisenhower at a news conference in 1954 shortly after the Supreme Court ruled public school segregation unconstitutional, said: "The Supreme Court has spoken and I am sworn to uphold the constitutional processes in this country; and I will obey." * And President Nixon, similarly asked of his policy with regard to the Supreme Court's decision in 1969 ordering immediate school desegregation, said: "To carry out what the Supreme Court has laid down. I believe in carrying out the law even though [I disagree with the Supreme Court decision]. . . . But we will carry out the law."

It was not always so. Years ago kings were not wont to disguise their conceits: *"L'état, c'est moi,"* said Louis XIV, and no one supposed a public would react to the belief with an overbearing display of moral indignation. Kings were above the law, not of it. Since they made it, they scarcely were required to abide by it. In our time, even Mao Tse-tung has proclaimed his empire a "People's Democracy." Though the conceit may be the same, "democracy" has made its claim so strong that few would seriously support another name. It means, no matter how dazzling the rationalization may sometimes be, that governments are creatures of the law.

We should not be fooled by the claim. Unhappily, not all governments today abide by the proposition that the state is subservient to law. In the Soviet Union, for example, it is a commonplace that Russian citizens are subject to a rule of men. Suspects of suspect crimes are locked up on bureaucratic whim, sentenced to long prison terms for abusing the freedoms of speech and press which the Soviet Constitution purports to grant. Secret police monitor the activities of the citizenry. Thirty-five years ago, millions were murdered during bloody purges. Torture was countenanced. Nations were illegally invaded on trumped up charges in the name of threats to security. Some would contend these things happen still in Russia.

Nor is the greatest ideological foe of the United States the only nation to which an accusing finger can be pointed. Brazilians and Greeks and Pakistanis know torture. In Italy, people can be detained in prison without charges for months, on the flimsiest of grounds; Italian law makes American "preventive detention" seem a polite interlude in a civilized proceeding. In China, there is massive slaughter in the name of revolution. In South Africa, people are detained without cause, placed under a house arrest that continues for years without charges ever being preferred, and political prisoners are tortured and some are killed. Throughout the world repressive juntas, cabals, dictatorships, and elites are commonplace.

The orthodox view is that it doesn't happen here. This is not merely the official line; it is the unblushing opinion of sincere citizens through-

* When asked three months later whether he had given any thought to seeking legislation from Congress to back up the Supreme Court decrees mandating integration, President Eisenhower said: "The subject has not even been mentioned to me."

out the nation that the Government is a doer of good and that our good will should be accorded it.

There are dissenters. Professor Joseph LaPalombara, a political scientist at Yale University, has charged that the foundations of modern America are sunk deeply into crime and corruption. This, he asserts, is not merely true, it is inevitable: corruption is a necessary mechanism in the development of backward societies, our own not excluded, and our AID officials ought to stop feeding pap to local missions about how to organize and manage pure and sincere development programs. He urges our administrators not merely to tolerate but to appreciate the existence of a little hanky-panky. Professor LaPalombara thinks that in twentieth-century America there is still need to blink at a few honest examples of corruption and official crime.

Just as the private citizen must commit crime to get along in this modern world, the argument runs, so the Government can hardly be expected to sit back and obey the laws which some Puritans among us forced into enactment. The double standard is un-American, and therefore the Government must break the law in a thousand ways; it must break the law in as many ways, in fact, as there are reasons to do so.

When a man is fired from his job for telling the truth to Congress about the scandal in his federal office, his boss has broken the law (but other employees have learned a lesson).

When young children are forced into slavery by the wardens of reformatories, no one can doubt the law has been at least politely overlooked (but someone gets free labor).

When a judge increases the sentence of a convicted felon because the criminal wants to appeal his conviction, the Government has broken the law (but it has forestalled troublesome proceedings).

When the police raid your house because they don't like the discussion that is taking place, the Government has broken the law (but it has warned others against quarrelsome conversations).

When the Defense Department forges documents to be given to a Congressional committee, the Government has committed a crime for which ordinary mortals, unloved by Congress, have been sent to jail (but luckily the federal officers cannot be imprisoned, since they were clearly politically motivated).

When the Government decides that some polluters, but not all polluters, ought to be prosecuted, the Government as well as the polluters have violated the law (but the laudable ends are obvious).

When the President of the United States appoints a man constitutionally ineligible to hold a seat on the Supreme Court, and the Senate confirms the nomination, and the man takes that seat, the Government has merely flouted a silly rule in the Constitution.

When a major general is permitted to hold a job that he may not legally hold, and a lieutenant is told he has forfeited his commission under similar circumstances, the Government has breached the law (but the general is protected).

When a high Government officer changes official policy to suit the needs of a prized campaign contributor, bribery has occurred (but the official gets re-elected).

When a prosecutor puts into a case evidence he knows to be false, the Government has committed an illegal act (but it has upheld the "rights" of the public).

The President breaks the law when he commits the United States Government to policies not submitted to the Senate for ratification as required by the Constitution (but he thereby gets policies he might not otherwise have got).

When judges declaim from the bench, as they occasionally do, that they know the law is other than they say, they have broken the law in the name of the state (but the conviction is secured, at least temporarily).

When state legislators, knowing that their constitutions require them to apportion their seats in accordance with a scheme that would not suit them politically, do suit themselves by failing to reapportion for more than seventy years, the legislature has engaged in a willful and continuing flouting of law (that unfortunately has led to federal control we all naturally detest).

When the governmental agencies choose to disregard their own regulations, on the theory that if you make them you can break them, they have violated law (but they do not undermine confidence in the administrative process—if no one finds out).

When clusters of governments, agencies, boards, and bureaus choose to weasel around clear policies against discrimination, they have degraded themselves and disgraced principles for which American constitutional law stands (but they do keep the blacks out a few years more).

And when the Government requires soldiers to obey orders that it may well be unlawful to obey, and condemns these soldiers for obeying the same orders when it becomes clear that they were illegal, some think the Government's lawbreaking skirts visible national disaster, whereas it is perfectly clear that the Government is simply trying to uphold freedom in a time of turbulence, if only the people would let it alone, shut up, and forget about it.

Of course, the Government is merely an odd assortment of people paid by the public treasurer. The "Government" in the abstract does not break the law. Men and women do. When ordinary private citizens break the laws against murder or robbery or extortion, we call them "common criminals" or "thugs," depending on their body weight and resemblance to a Nordic ideal of physical beauty. When extraordinary private citizens (those with higher salaries or better connections) break the laws against bribery or price-fixing, we tend to call them "corrupt" or "misguided," depending on the number of times they have been divorced and whether we believe in their product.

So with politicians and officials on the take: he who accepts a bribe or a favor or a suspiciously large campaign contribution has been corrupted, and that is too bad, and a little depressing, to be regretted and condemned; but the fault is peculiar to the criminal and should not reflect on you or me (so long as it is not too widespread a phenomenon; so long, that is, as we don't know about it). Because nothing much hinges on it, the petty corruption of elected and appointed criminals is not new and is rather boring, except around election time when a man can suddenly be simultaneously a despicable hound and a martyr the likes of whom has not been seen since Giordano Bruno was burned at the stake.

Certain people would have us believe, however, that when public officials break the law for and on behalf of the Government, and not on their own account, crimes of a different order and consequence have been committed. It is said that a democratic society can tolerate random lawbreaking by robbers, rapists, murderers, and even self-styled revolutionaries, but that it cannot avoid serious damage, or even survive, in the face of sustained "official" criminal activity. Historically, the argument is nonsense, since the Government has been breaking the law consistently during the past two centuries and we have not collapsed yet. Rhetorically, however, the argument has a certain surface plausibility: Government lawbreaking, our theorists conclude, is fundamental to the ills of society, for nothing can be more conducive to the breakdown of law than the Government's own willful disinclination to obey it.

The full argument runs something like this: when citizens become criminals on their own account the community has a way of rallying around the agents of "justice." There is little resistance to the notion that those who violate most classes of prohibitory laws are to be condemned, and even among those who advocate "civil disobedience" there is a strong undercurrent of belief that those who break the law for higher ends must be prepared to accept the consequences. Socrates's willingness to accept capital punishment is still generally regarded as a moral act of the first magnitude.

When the Government breaks the law, however, the psychological reactions are far more complex. The community is split. No one need defend a criminal, but "our Government" (as opposed to "the bureaucracy") must be sustained and defended; illegal activity, when committed by the Government, quickly becomes fuzzy and political, thus salving the conscience of some, since staunch and "sincere" political beliefs are highly prized. And when the political activity is illegal, it can put even the most fair-minded citizen in a terrible dilemma, for he is part of the citizenry that nurtures the Government. Thus, whenever the Government takes some action, part of the populace—whether a larger or smaller part depends on the issue—will automatically support it simply because it is action taken in the name of the Government. The resulting ambivalence of individuals and antagonisms among citizens of different political opinions can tear society apart.

At first blush, the foregoing argument may seem to have intrinsic appeal. Indeed, the logic is inescapable but for one glaring assumption —namely, that the laws are all perfect expressions of social policies to be enforced or carried out. And obviously, this assumption is fallacious. Laws are often wrong, or sloppily worded, unclear, troublesome, or even dangerous.

Look at the laws that are supposed to protect the consumer and the environment. Look at the laws that are supposed to protect us against fraud and highway accidents. Look at the laws that are supposed to give us good public education and medical services. Doctors have apparently found it easy and profitable to rob and cheat under Medicare. Should we expect greater honesty from the Government?

A Government cannot be expected to obey laws that are inconvenient or unsuited to the needs of the times, for what good is governmental power if it cannot be used? If social illness from Government crimes is the price we must pay for law and order, we ought to be willing to bear it. No less than the common man, the Government must have a healthy contempt for the law if it is to govern at all.

That is the composite answer to the argument against government criminality. More ingenious and narrow answers are made whenever

The President of the United States,

The Army,

The Navy,

Other military services,

The Attorney General,

Other Executive officials,

Prosecutors,

Judges,

Congress, and

The police

break the law. They all have their lawyers. This healthy contempt for the laws, without which society would probably collapse from the strain of trying to remember, much less abide by, the entire rulebook, is a subject that scholars and popularizers sorely neglect, except in bits and pieces, now and then. To illuminate this heretofore dark byway of social science and American mores, the following discussion will chart the ways by which the Government comes to grips with the law—and defeats it.

It is not ordinary to think of the Government as a lawbreaker, though it is quite usual to berate it for stupidity, cowardice, and folly. Yet in modern times, charges against the Government have taken on a new dimension—not mere hardship born of unwisdom, but rank oppression sired by blatant violations of the law. Hear the rollcall: Mylai, the Panthers, Kent and Jackson State, Attica. Scandal that came to light once in a while and merely titillated or mildly shocked is now a torrent rushing forth, and it horrifies.

But back off. The Government is no citizen, though it is run by citizens—and even the citizen is conceded to have the right to disobey certain laws whose complete depravity convince the Supreme Court of their unconstitutionality. The Government is an instrument designed to bring order out of social chaos. Should it be bound by formalistic legalisms? That is the counterargument, but it will not wash.

Proponents of civil disobedience often point to the moral necessity of disobeying particular laws, while adhering to a belief that "the law" or "law" must continue to be respected, even revered. "The rule of law," they say, has a value intrinsically superior to that of any particular law, moral or immoral, wise or unwise. Though they may break a law to protest it, they will suffer the consequences.

Less conservative advocates of civil disobedience contend that it is a prime fallacy to say "that the rule of law has an intrinsic value apart from moral ends." A law student, in a book review lauding a series of radical essays on law, summed up one extreme view when he recommended that the book "top the reading list of all lawyers who think humanity might be more important than the law."

At the other extreme, of course, some people deny there is ever a cause to disobey any law.

The debate is a fundamental one because it concerns the nature of human freedom—if people are free only as they obey their own laws, what must they do about laws that deprive them of freedom or are otherwise unjust? Can we be free without law? Can we be free with unjust laws? The debate continues to rage wherever it is conceded that people are ends in themselves, and not means to other ends.

The argument is altogether different, however, when the question is whether the government must submit to "the rule of law." For the government is surely a means to an end, not an end in itself. Moreover, it is a means created by law and endowed with great power, which, untempered by the charter of its existence, becomes irrational and unreasoning armed might. The government's disavowal of the rule of law —exemplified by its violation of particular laws—is far stronger than the citizen's protest against a particular law: the citizen will be forced to stand the consequences of his act, whether or not he should morally be required to do so; the government will rarely be rebuked in ways that count.

This book is devoted to the government's violation of the rule of law. Some examples are of how the government breaks particular laws; others are instances of the government's failure to enforce particular laws. But this is not a book about particular policies; it is not a book about raw injustices; it is not about unwise acts; it is not even about bad or harmful laws, except insofar as they may be unconstitutional. It is not a book about the injustice of racial conditions in the United States (except insofar as they are the reflection of government criminality), nor about the injustice of poverty, war, or inequality; again, except insofar as these conditions spring from the disobedience of government to the rule of law.

Of course, the most clearly seen goal can be thwarted by the awkward fuzziness of reality. "The law" is rarely clear, and therefore, what is unlawful is not always easy to discern. The legal profession has thrived in Western culture for more than five centuries because of that plain fact.

The lack of clarity and certainty in law not only creates confusion for the citizen; it spawns political institutions of vast and ill-defined powers. A government of many and diverse powers and its attendant bureaucracy, created to control the infinite variety of private crimes, undesirable practices, and acts of moral turpitude high and low, carries with it an amazing degree of discretion. Statutes creating administrative agencies are always vague. The laws allow to the administrators, and even their clerks and assistants, a wide latitude of possible moves. If this is an evil to be deplored, it inheres in the nature of things. Regulatory authority cannot be clear-cut. If the aim is to put an end to discriminatory and shady business practices, a clear definition of what is prohibited would permit any moderately intelligent lawyer to show his client a dozen ways to avoid the law. So it is said.

Bureaucracies are not the only governmental agencies with the power of discretion. All law confers some degree of discretion. Judges who apply the laws of ordinary crimes, of contracts, and of fiduciary responsibility must be guided by their sense of equity and by their own judgment, for these laws talk in terms of "reasonableness" and "substantiality," terms that give those who must judge room in which to wander. Thus, much of what a trial judge decides will not be upset on appeal even though the higher judge thinks it wrong, because the law permits the trial judge the leeway of discretion, and often only clear abuses are reversible.

On final analysis, this is as it has to be. Decisions must be made in life, and people have to know they can rely on what has been decided.

A course of conduct that calls for a decision to move this way or that cannot forever be held in abeyance because it is subject to being second- and third-guessed. This is true of personal life as well as public life, and mistakes should be tolerated because there is no realistic alternative. The code of law that dispenses with all discretion is and always will be an impossibility.

Unfortunately, this fact stands obstinately in the way of controlling —even judging—both undesirable and unlawful government behavior. If it is imperative to grant the Government discretionary powers, it is correspondingly difficult to block their usage. The result is that the Government takes actions that are immediately denounced by partisans as being unwarranted, unwise, or unlawful.

Legality is a slippery concept. Like most complex abstractions, it is subject to daily abuse. The temptation is often overwhelming to denounce what we despise as not merely wrong, misguided, or evil, but as actually unlawful or even unconstitutional. "They can't do that," we say. The capacity to distrust Government and to be discontented by what it does is nearly infinite; the United States, we like to remind ourselves somewhat mistakenly, was founded on just that distrust and skepticism.

Lack of agreement does not convert otherwise lawful action into crime, however. Though there can be nearly unanimous agreement that some laws are unwise or unjust, it will not wash to describe actions taken pursuant to such laws as illegal. The oil depletion allowance is condemned by many people, conceivably even by a public majority. You can say the allowance is unwise and unjust. Yet deductions taken pursuant to it cannot therefore be regarded as unlawful. Neither can the Government's refusal to grant deferments to those young men who conscientiously object to certain wars be branded as unlawful, though you may deplore the spirit and the reach of the Selective Service Act, which allows draft boards to deny such requests. Even obvious Government oppression is not necessarily illegal, though the dividing line between lawful oppression and unlawful acts is often extremely difficult to discern.

For the most part, governmental actions explored in this book can be tested against the standards of the laws. One agency will give us trouble: the Supreme Court of the United States. For just as a king might be perplexed to know how he could be bound by the law that he fashioned and could unfashion, so it is difficult to contend that the Court can act unlawfully when it interprets the Constitution or other laws. As Justice Robert Jackson once said: "We are not final because we are infallible, but we are infallible only because we are final." This is not to say that the Court has not made some outrageous decisions; everyone agrees it has. It is only to say that we will have to proceed with some caution in alleging errors in measurement against the holder of the yardstick.

Because the Court is likely to change the meaning of the Constitution at unpredictable times, it is sometimes unfair to charge that an official agency has acted unconstitutionally before the Court has so characterized the agency's activities. While the supremacy of the Court's constitutional decisions is unquestioned here, they will for the most part be used to test the legality of governmental action prospectively. To take an obvious case, racial segregation of public educational institutions, while regrettable and oppressive in 1953 and before, was not unlawful in states that had laws permitting it, because the Supreme Court itself had sanctioned the practice in 1896. In 1954, however, after the Supreme Court ruled such practices unconstitutional, further adherence to the policy became blatantly illegal. (There are, however, occasions when it is clear that a Supreme Court decision should be used to test the legality of Government activity retroactively, for the Government frequently acts in ways never judicially sanctioned.)

The test for illegality is not easy to apply, though the extent of governmental illegality is widespread enough to make for easy pickings. Often a law will be clear enough on its face that anyone who denies the violation is saying merely that "no" is "yes," a definitional process that happens more often than it should. More regularly still, owing to the fact that courts must interpret the muddy sentences of legislatures, judicial decisions make it unmistakably clear that the law means that the Government may not do what it commonly does. In response, the Government will sometimes simply remain silent. Occasionally, Government will attempt to shift the focus by accusing its accuser of crimes. Most often the Government, caught with its pants down, will attempt to create a haze of justification and block from view those delicate sights sure to cause it and its admirers embarrassment. That the technique of law-avoidance requires the government to assert that what is a crime is not, that it is really just some routine, discretionary, managerial, executive function, ought to fool no one. Painting a leaky ship will not prevent it from sinking, even if those who believe the defect has been remedied stay aboard.

2

Crimes Against the Individual

THE INDIVIDUAL citizen—as an individual—can be victimized by a democratic Government, but the range of unlawful encounters is not large. Modern life is usually too complex and modern Government too bureaucratic to bother individuals randomly and outside their groups. In fact the Government rarely confronts the individual directly; we are a society of groups and organizations and our Government deals with us accordingly.

This is one of the chief complaints about bureaucracy: that it is incapable of making individualized decisions tailored to particular persons. Bureaucracy reacts to recurring patterns and groups, to the "typical," not to the atypical, particular, unusual, or unique. In many respects, of course, the lack of ability to pounce on the individual is a blessing. Unless particularly aggrieved, the bureaucracy is unable to point a discriminating finger at the individual and do specialized harm. One computer number is the same as any other—or should be.

Nevertheless, the Government can discriminate against individuals not identified as members of particular groups. Such discrimination, in the form of knowing deprivation of legal rights, is most likely to occur when Government officials come into direct contact with the person. These contacts are most often with the Government as employer, prosecutor, judge, and policeman.

The criminal activities include:

¶ Dismissal from jobs or prosecution, to coerce or force the individual to desist from lawful activity or in retaliation for revealing governmental corruption;

¶ Prosecution of individuals under laws not enforced against other violators;

¶ Manufacturing or suppressing evidence to secure convictions;

¶ Devotion of resources and time to investigation and prosecution of individuals for "crime" that is not the real object of social disapproval;

¶ Denial of procedures guaranteed by law; and

¶ Unlawful sentencing or other unlawful deprivation of liberty.

EMBARRASSING TRUTHS

The Case of A. Ernest Fitzgerald

A section of the federal criminal code makes it unlawful for any person—including Government officials—to threaten, influence, intimidate, impede, or injure a Congressional witness, either before or after testimony is received on Capitol Hill. The maximum penalty is a $5,000 fine and a five-year jail term.

In Congress in 1968, the Joint Economic Committee's Economy in Government Subcommittee began an investigation into questionable practices in the negotiating and awarding of military weapons contracts. From evidence developed in a number of hearings, it was discovered that the Air Force C–5A Galaxy program would require $2 billion more for completion than originally contracted for. Though many disputed the Pentagon's methods of arriving at contract costs, no one disagreed that the C–5A cargo jets contract with Lockheed would result in the $2 billion "overrun."

The cost overrun figure came originally from A. Ernest Fitzgerald, the Deputy for Management Systems, Office of the Assistant Secretary of the Air Force for Financial Management. Fitzgerald was asked to testify by the Committee's chairman, Wisconsin Senator William Proxmire. Normally witnesses before Congressional committees are required to prepare written statements for advance submission. Senator Proxmire asked Fitzgerald to submit one hundred copies of a written statement one day before his appearance. Fitzgerald's superiors in the Air Force directed him not to prepare any statements. Nevertheless, Fitzgerald was permitted to testify and on November 13, 1968, he did so, with telling effect. No one from the Air Force disputed the figures supplied by Fitzgerald; Secretary of Defense Melvin Laird later declared that "Mr. Fitzgerald's position on the C–5A has been correct." A Pentagon spokesman who accompanied Fitzgerald to the hearings assured Senator Proxmire that Fitzgerald was free to answer any questions put to him by the Subcommittee.

Two weeks after his testimony, the Air Force revoked Fitzgerald's job tenure, awarded him only three months previously. The official explanation was that the tenure had been erroneously decreed by a computer in the first place and that the "revocation" was but a ratification of the computer's original error. The Air Force admitted that the computer made errors only once for every five thousand employees. The tenure notification had been signed by the chief civilian personnel officer of the Air Force.

On December 24, the Subcommittee received a supplementary state-ment from the Air Force. Proxmire had requested Fitzgerald to supply certain cost data on the C–5A. The Christmas Eve package was labeled "Insert for the record, testimony of A. E. Fitzgerald." Unfortunately the cost data provided therein was not the same as Fitzgerald's. Contacted by the Subcommittee, he denied that the figures were his. Asked why Fitzgerald's figures were not correctly stated, the Air Force responded that the "total Air Force position" was assumed to be what the Sub-committee had wanted, and so the Air Force had thoughtfully pro-vided it in Fitzgerald's name. The proper data was subsequently supplied.

One month later, in January 1969, just prior to the inauguration of Richard Nixon and a new management for the Air Force, Senator Prox-mire came into possession of a remarkable memorandum from the Ad-ministrative Assistant to the Secretary of the Air Force. The memo-randum was a discussion of three ways by which Fitzgerald could be severed from the Air Force. The memorandum follows in part:

January 6, 1969

Memorandum for Dr. Brown
Subject: Background Information Relating to
         Fitzgerald Case.

As an employee in the excepted service under Schedule A, with Vet-eran's Preference, Mr. Fitzgerald has certain rights, which can be grouped in two categories:

(1) *Adverse Actions.* Chapter 752 of the Federal Personnel Manual applies to discharges, suspensions, furloughs without pay, and reductions in rank or compensation taken by agencies against employees of the United States Government. Mr. Fitzgerald's rights are:

(*a*) Adverse action may not be taken except for such cause as will promote the efficiency of the service;

(*b*) He must be given at least 30 full days advance written notice, identifying the specific proposed action, stating the reasons supporting the proposed action, including names, times and places;

(*c*) The notice must tell the employee that he has the right to reply both personally and in writing and to submit affidavits in support of his answer;

(*d*) Normally he must be retained in an active duty status during the notice period;

(*e*) Full consideration must be given to his reply and if the decision is to effect the action originally proposed, or some action less severe, he must be given a dated and written notice of the decision promptly after it is reached;

(*f*) The notice of decision must inform him of the effective date of the action, of his right to appeal the adverse action within the agency and to the Civil Service Commission and of the time limits and procedures for making the appeals.

(2) *Reduction in Force.* In the event his job is abolished, Mr. Fitzgerald is in Tenure Group I in the Excepted Service and has the right of full application of all reduction-in-force procedures insofar as "bumping" and "retreat" rights *within his competitive level grouping.* However, since he is the only employee in his competitive level grouping and since he did not progress to his position from other lower grade positions, the net result is that he is in competition only with himself. He could neither "bump" nor displace anyone.

These are the rights involved should charges be preferred or should his position be abolished. There is a third possibility, which could result in Mr. Fitzgerald's departure. This action is not recommended since it is rather underhanded and would probably not be approved by the Civil Service Commission, even though it is legally and procedurally possible. The Air Force could request conversion of this position to the career service, utilizing competitive procedures, and consider all the eligibles from the Executive Inventory and an outside search. Using this competitive procedure, Mr. Fitzgerald might or might not be selected. If not, displacement action would follow.

When Mr. Fitzgerald was appointed in September 1965 by Assistant Secretary Marks to fill the vacancy created by the departure of Mr. J. Ronald Fox, it was with a mutual understanding that this was to be a Schedule A appointment of *two or three years duration.* There is nothing in official records to support this understanding. Dr. Flax contacted Mr. Marks by telephone on January 2, 1969, and verified this understanding and reflected the conversation in his memorandum to the Secretary of Defense, a copy of which is attached. We have carefully screened all files and records and can find no formalized confirmation of this understanding.

If you desire additional information or more detailed specifics, I have the complete files available.

John A. Lang, Jr.
The Administrative Assistant

That spring Fitzgerald's responsibility as deputy for management systems—meaning, oversight on weapons systems—was terminated. Intead, he was directed to look into the costs of operating mess halls and a bowling alley in Thailand. Chided about what certainly seemed to be a demotion of the beleaguered Fitzgerald, the new Secretary of the Air Force, Robert Seamans, retorted: "Proper cost control of recreational facilities is not a matter to be taken lightly." That is true, as could be seen when the revelations concerning widespread corruption in the Army's PX system began to surface, but the answer was scarcely satisfying. Proxmire called it a "cynical effort to cover up the truth."

The demotion did not seem related to Fitzgerald's competence. In 1966 Fitzgerald was the Air Force candidate to compete with other career civil servants throughout the federal Government for the Civil Service Outstanding Performance Rating. In 1967 the Air Force, in recommending he receive the Air Force Association's Citation of Honor, cited his "exceptional contribution to the development, installation and utilization of improved management systems tnroughout the Department of Defense." In November 1969, shortly before the Air Force fired him, Secretary Seamans said: "Mr. Fitzgerald's work, along with the efforts of many other civilian and military personnel, has resulted in a substantial improvement in the data-gathering part of the weapons procurement financial control system."

In May, 1969, Secretary Seamans had asserted in the course of testimony before the House Armed Services Committee that Fitzgerald had released classified documents: "It is interesting," Seamans said, "that in the testimony in front of a number of committees documents keep appearing, some of which are confidential, that were obtained from Mr. Fitzgerald." That was untrue. Fitzgerald wrote his superior, the Assistant Secretary, denying the imputations and requesting a meeting with Seamans. No answer was ever forthcoming. The following November, however, one year after Fitzgerald's original testimony, Seamans appeared before Proxmire's Subcommittee and recanted his prior perjury: "I will say categorically now that Mr. Fitzgerald has not to my knowledge violated national security."

But Fitzgerald was clearly becoming a tiresome nuisance to the Air Force. In January, 1970, therefore, Fitzgerald's job was abolished (as recommended in the memorandum one year before) and he was dismissed. The Air Force cited "economy" as the reason for the job's abolition. Reasons of economy, however, did not deter the Secretary from hiring a special consultant at the rate of $107 a day to continue doing part of Fitzgerald's job. Seamans's testimony that Fitzgerald was not fired at all was greeted with loud laughter during the Senate hearings. Spencer Schedler, Seamans's Assistant Secretary and Fitzgerald's former boss, privately told Congressmen at the time that Fitzgerald was fired because he failed as a "team player." (A week later, however, Schedler said he "could not remember" these remarks when questioned by incredulous Senators.)

To Proxmire, the year-long train of incidents concerning Fitzgerald included clear violations of the law prohibiting harassment of Congressional witnesses. "In my view," the Senator said, "the existence of [the above-quoted] memorandum coming into being shortly after the Fitzgerald testimony and unrelated as it was to any economy action or office reorganization by the Secretary of the Air Force shows that Air Force officials were contemplating the ultimate obstruction of a Congressional inquiry by injuring a witness, which ultimate course they in fact followed . . . when they fired Mr. Fitzgerald. . . . For months, from May to November, he lived under a cloud as a violator of security. He has suffered from a charge which the Secretary of the Air Force has finally declared to be wholly false. If this does not constitute harassment of this witness, what does?" Senator Proxmire called the Attorney General for an investigation and prosecution.

The Attorney General of the United States does not relish prosecuting members of the President's official family. The Justice Department promised "priority treatment" and then buried the file. Six months after Proxmire first wrote the Attorney General, a laconic letter from Will Wilson,* Assistant Attorney General in charge of the Criminal Division, stated that the Department was awaiting Civil Service Commission action on an appeal Fitzgerald had made concerning the abolition of his job. When that appeal was concluded, Wilson wrote, it was conceivable that Fitzgerald might be reinstated. "In order to insure fundamental fairness to Mr. Fitzgerald in connection with his present appeal, further comment, or action by the Department at this time, is believed inappropriate," Wilson said.

Fitzgerald took his case to court after the Civil Service Commission refused to permit a public hearing on his appeal for reinstatement. Two years after he was fired the Government was appealing a federal district court decision that he had the right to air his case in public. The Government wasn't saying what it was afraid of, but Fitzgerald's appeal to the Commission had yet to be heard. The Government's stalling tactics were believed prompted by the hope that Fitzgerald's witnesses would leave the Air Force and thus be beyond the Commission's subpoena power.

So much for priority treatment and, of course, Fitzgerald's appeal had little or nothing to do with Robert Seamans's violation of Section 1505 of Title 18 of the *United States Code*.

In 1951 a newly-elected California Republican named Richard Nixon took the Senate floor to condemn the Truman Administration for harassment of Congressional witnesses. President Truman had ousted a Navy admiral for speaking against Air Force spending plans. Said Senator Nixon: "It is essential to the security of the Nation and the very lives of the people, as we look into these vital issues [conduct of the Korean War, dismissal of General MacArthur], that every witness have complete freedom from reprisal when he is given an opportunity to tell what he knows. . . . Unless protection is given to witnesses who are members of

* Who was later forced to resign because of conflict of interest charges that he was deeply implicated in a Texas financial scandal.

the armed services or employees of the Government, the scheduled hearings will amount to no more than a parade of yes-men for administration practices as they exist."

Nixon proposed a strict law that provided a five-year prison sentence
for any Government official who retaliated by dismissing or by other
action against a subordinate who testified before Congress. A demotion
was to be prima facie evidence of the superior's guilt.

The bill did not pass, though the current law is not in terms less
strict. The stern stuff of which the brash Senator was made, however,
seemed to have seeped away from him in his more mellow years as
President.

The Case of Cora T. Walker

Cora T. Walker purchased a brownstone in Manhattan. The New
York City housing code requires new owners to obtain a certificate of
occupancy, a document assuring that the dwelling is "up to code." Miss
Walker, who rented out rooms, found it difficult to get her certificate
and after a personal visit to the Department of Buildings was assured
that her papers were in order and that a certificate would be issued in
the near future. Four days later two city inspectors came to the brownstone and informed her, after inspection, that she could have the certificate if she paid them $50. Miss Walker informed the District Attorney
that she had been the victim of a bribe solicitation and the matter was
reported in the newspapers. The Housing Superintendent responded by
requiring that notices of violation of the Multiple Dwelling Law be
issued and that Miss Walker be criminally prosecuted immediately for
renting a house without a rooming house permit. The violations included
an extra room formed by a partition and the maintenance of a defec-
tive sprinkler valve.

The Manhattan criminal court judge refused to permit Miss Walker
to introduce any evidence concerning the possibility that she was being
prosecuted solely for her reporting of the inspectors' unlawful conduct.
It was her contention that the housing code was rarely enforced through
criminal prosecutions and that this was being done in her case only
because she had squealed. The judge limited testimony to the question
of whether the violations existed. The court, deciding that they did,
convicted her and imposed a small fine.

The New York State Court of Appeals remanded the case to consider the evidence that had been excluded. Miss Walker was convicted
anew. Once again she appealed her case. An appellate court this time
reversed and dismissed, saying:

> The defendant demonstrated, by a clear preponderance of evidence,
> that she was singled out for criminal prosecution by an intentional, pur-

poseful and unusual selection process. The manner of prosecution was not the same as that used in the case of other property owners similarly situated and was in sharp contrast to the then existing pattern of enforcement of housing laws in New York City. The time allowed to defendant for correction of alleged housing violations was so unreasonably short as to make correction an impossibility and criminal conviction a certainty. The evidence leads irresistibly to the conclusion that this intentional discrimination and prosecution was in retaliation for defendant's public exposure of corruption in the Department of Buildings and was in no way aimed at securing compliance with the housing laws.

THE PROSECUTOR COVERS UP

The Case of Lloyd Eldon Miller, Jr.

The people's case against Lloyd Eldon Miller, Jr., looked easy. It was an ordinary murder case, if the brutal sexual murder of an eight-year-old girl can be ordinary. For violent murder, though, the case seemed air-tight. The suspect had fled the scene, and a pair of blood-stained jockey-style underpants was found a mile from the corpse. Moreover, after he was arrested, Miller confessed to the killing, and a local waitress told police that she had gone home with him in the taxicab he drove for a living and that while they were parked in front of her home he had confessed to the crime. A dead body, physical evidence with the girl's blood on it, a confession, and corroboration. An open and shut case.

Why did appeals take more than ten years? And why, eventually, did the nine Justices of the Supreme Court of the United States claim they were stopping a crime when they unanimously reversed the conviction? How could the Government blow such a simple case?

There was the confession, of course, but this was not one of those confession cases. Unlike many cases reaching the High Court lately, the Justices expressed no qualms about the legality of the document Miller signed, confessing to an attempted rape and a panicked killing of little Janice May in Canton, Illinois, on November 26, 1955, sometime after 2:35 in the afternoon.

And yet, Miller said later, he was picked up, held incommunicado for more than fifty hours, and subjected to nearly as many hours of continuous interrogation, a round-the-clock effort by state investigators, the local police chief, and even the Superintendent of the State Bureau of Criminal Investigation himself.

The police told a somewhat different story. They said Miller was brought into jail in Springfield at 2:00 A.M. on the morning of November 29, more than two days after the death of Janice May. He slept until

6:00 A.M., when, according to jail routine, he was awakened, fed, and placed in a common room with six other prisoners. At 5:00 that afternoon he was turned over to state investigators and taken off to a laboratory to give blood, hair, and fingernail samples. From 5:30 to 8:30, the police said, their suspect was in that laboratory, being prepared for a lie-detector test he volunteered for, being asked routine questions as part of the preparation for the test. At 8:30, the investigators said, they went out to get something to eat, leaving their man with the Canton police chief and the Fulton County State's Attorney. These officials were there because Miller had done some traveling in those two days and had been tracked down to Danville, near the Indiana state line, where he was arrested in the bus depot, trying to get information about departures for Detroit.

At 9:30 the state investigators returned. They tested and questioned Miller until around 1:00 A.M., they testified later in court, and he was returned to the jail at 2:00.

Miller denied that they had gone out to eat, denied that things had been low-key. He insisted, in court, that he had been interrogated continuously from 5:30 P.M. to 3:00 A.M., that he had been shown a block of bloody concrete against which the little girl's head had been crushed, shown the underpants with the obvious, dark-red blood stains, shown a gray but bloodstained jacket, shown photographs of the scene down by some abandoned railroad cars, stacked end to end, where the crime had happened.

The next day, Wednesday, November 30, according to the official police version, Miller was again wakened at 6:00 A.M. Prison routine. He was placed in the bullpen and during the course of the day was fingerprinted and put in a lineup. At 4:30 he was given food and taken again to the state bureau where from 5:30 to 8:30 he was interrogated as he had been the evening before. At 8:30 the Superintendent of the State Bureau of Investigation came in, the other agents left, and Miller was given some dinner. At 9:30 the Superintendent and the Canton police chief talked things out with Miller and at 10:15 got him at last to admit his guilt. It took two hours, they said, to reduce his story to writing, to put it into the phraseology and sentence-form that made a connected story, and at 12:15, reading each and every line out loud while pointing with the pencil to those lines as they were read, because Miller said he would not read it, they held the document in front of Miller and he signed it and they initialed it. With that, at 1:00 A.M., he was taken off to the jail at nearby Pekin, preparatory to his trip home.

Miller disagreed. He said that he had been interrogated continuously from 5:30 to 11:00, during which time he was given a lie-detector test. That from 11:00 to 12:15 he was told he would either sign or be given the electric chair. That he was yelled at in harsh language.

That he was threatened with, among other things, lifetime tenure in a mental institution. That he was struck on the shoulder at 11:00 P.M. and slapped repeatedly over the bruise. That he denied owning the clothes he was shown; he told them, he said, that he wore "boxer"-type shorts, not the "jockey"-style underwear they were putting under his nose. That, finally, at 12:15, he could endure it no longer, so he signed a document whose contents he did not know, because he did not read it and no one read it to him; he signed it only because he had been told that if he did not do so he would die in the electric chair.

This difference of opinion was explored at an extensive pretrial hearing to determine the constitutional adequacy of the proceedings that resulted in the confession. The judge ruled the proceedings adequate; they met, he said, the standards of common decency that due process required. The testimony at the hearing showed, the judge ruled, that the confession was voluntary, uncoerced, and fully admissible. The jury did not hear these preliminary skirmishes, of course, for had they done so, and had the judge then ruled the confession inadmissible, the jurors' minds would have been hopelessly and illegally contaminated. This confession was admissible; it was admitted; and the jury convicted Lloyd Eldon Miller and he was sentenced to die in the electric chair.

Miller's attorneys contested the trial judges' rulings for more than a decade. In 1958, three years after the killing, the Illinois Supreme Court reviewed the conviction and upheld it. Of the confession, the court said:

> The testimony of the officials is not materially inconsistent or inherently improbable, and was unshaken on cross-examination. Defendant's testimony, on the other hand, particularly that relating to the use of threats and physical violence, appears strained and lacks the spontaneity and cohesiveness that would lend to its credibility.

In 1962, the United States Court of Appeals for the Seventh Circuit, the highest federal court in Chicago, reviewed a district court's refusal to let the convict out of prison. The Seventh Circuit court agreed with the lower federal court. One of Miller's contentions was that when the trial judge refused to let the defense introduce certain psychiatric testimony that would show Miller to have an emotionally inadequate personality that would crumble under the slightest pressure, they committed a highly prejudicial error. The conviction, he argued unsuccessfully, ought to be upset on this point at least. But the Seventh Circuit disagreed:

> Petitioner was not a weakling who would be expected to readily succumb to pressure. The crime which he had just committed [the Court did not bother to note that the confession was not made or signed until four days after the murder] showed a ruthlessness that belied the slightest tendency to submit to coercion, if any had been exerted.

There could be no doubt about the ruthlessness. The right side of the girl's face had been crushed. She sustained two skull fractures. There was a two-and-one-half-inch laceration on her chin. There were multiple abrasions on her neck, chest, and back. Her vagina was torn, manifesting active bleeding. And a bulging rectum was thrust into the vaginal vault through the tear.

The killer had used such force against little Janice May that when her thirteen-year-old brother first spotted her body while looking for her, because she had been missing an hour that afternoon, he thought he was seeing an injured bloody dog. He returned with his fifteen-year-old brother to the abandoned mine, where the old railroad cars were junked; and there they saw that the dog was Janice, nearly nude, seemingly thrust underneath a car, "extremely bloody," with cinders embedded in her buttocks. She died after admission to the hospital, never regaining consciousness.

One concurring judge of the federal appellate court thought the remark about ruthlessness something of a non sequitur, since the viciousness of the crime bore only on the actual killer, and who he was, at the time of the hearing, was the very question. Nevertheless, in spite of his misgivings, this judge concurred in the sustained conviction.

The Illinois Supreme Court rejected several other arguments about the confession, and the Seventh Circuit concurred in all of these rejections. The procedures used did not contravene due process. The judge and jury had rejected Miller's claim that he was threatened with violence. There had been no isolation of the suspect while he was interrogated. There was no "relay questioning." No sweatbox or third-degree methods were used. The defendant himself had asked for the lie detector. He was given "extensive time for rest and reflction between periods of questioning." He was not incarcerated illegally, since the arresting officer had a warrant issued in connection with the larceny of his taxicab; and even if it had been an unlawful arrest, a voluntary confession was nevertheless admissible. The proffered testimony of Dr. Sweazy, the psychiatrist, that Miller had a "completely inadequate emotional personality," was not considered prejudicial, since the law does not require a preliminary hearing on a confession "to extend into the background of apparently normal and mature persons."

To all of this the Seventh Circuit agreed. The court pointed out again that the psychiatric testimony would have infringed on the province of the judge and the jury and that, besides, even if the testimony did not interfere with procedure in that way, it would have had to have been rejected because it was not submitted in the form of a hypothetical question. The defense, that is, would have asked Dr. Sweazy what he had found out about his patient and what he had concluded therefrom.

But the law required defense counsel to say: "Assume these facts, Doctor. Miller, the twenty-nine-year-old defendant, with his two years of high school, changed his name to escape being apprehended by military authorities and served a seven-month sentence on a California prison farm for the taking of a bailed automobile. When he was picked up in the May case, he was apprehensive enough to inquire whether there were any warrants outstanding against him. Further background: Miller had been dishonorably discharged from the Army and enlisted in the Air Force only to be discharged again for fraudulent enlistment, and he was now married for the fourth hasty time. He knew that the police had reason to suspect him of the crime, because he had driven off in his taxicab that night at 3:45 A.M. and had gone twenty-five miles to Peoria. He sought information about a bus to Detroit, drove on ten miles to Pekin where he abandoned his cab, changed into a jacket he brought along in a suitcase, boarded the 5:55 bus for Champaign and still another for Danville, where he was so exhausted he slept for twenty-four hours in a hotel at whose desk he registered under his own name. Next evening, hearing on the radio that he was wanted in Canton in connection with a murder he had learned about with the rest of the horrified Canton townspeople the afternoon it happened, and seeing his name in a newspaper as a suspect, he panicked, realizing that his long absence and the disappearance of a cab could be interpreted as fleeing the scene. But he had left town in the dark of night only in order to escape his wife who had said she was going to sue him for nonsupport, and so he was going to Michigan. Because of his panic, he found himself in the Danville bus station where, recognized by an attendant who summoned police, he said when arrested: 'If it's about that little girl in Canton, I didn't do it.' Assume that this man, Dr. Sweazy, is then taken to a jail where he is subjected to intimidation, threats, physical violence for two days and nights without even being permitted to see a lawyer. Assuming all that, Dr. Sweazy, what is your professional opinion on the basis of these assumed hypothetical facts as to whether he would have signed a document his interrogators placed before him?"

Those hypothetical questions, the Seventh Circuit suggested, would have been all right, except that they invaded the province of the judge and the jury. In any event, some of the testimony about Miller's erratic life was later admitted into evidence—not, of course, that it could then have had much relevance to the question of voluntariness. But there was just no ground for saying the confession was unlawfully obtained and inadmissible. So these two courts said, so another federal district court judge was to say at a second habeas corpus hearing in 1963 on a different ground, so the Seventh Circuit repeated when in 1965 it reviewed the 1963 ruling, and so the Supreme Court implied in 1967. The

Supreme Court never even talked about the confession when it upset the conviction. The problem wasn't the confession.

Perhaps it was something more technical. There were many technical errors that Miller pleaded to save his life. His lawyers said that an element of proof of criminal agency was missing, that there was no independent corroboration of Miller's complicity aside from the confession. The Illinois Supreme Court said the test "is whether the whole evidence proves the facts that a crime was committed and that the accused committed it." Of course, the "whole evidence" in this case happened to be what was known by the police before the confession was signed. At any rate, according to the court, "in looking to the element of criminal agency, it is not unreasonable to consider the type, number and severity of the wounds suffered by the youthful victim." No one dissented to this easy dismissal of this critical technicality, not the two district court judges, not the various circuit court judges, not the Supreme Court justices. There was only one Seventh Circuit judge who thought that kind of talk tended to assume Miller's guilt rather than prove it, but he concurred in the majority opinion.

The trial judge admitted into evidence testimony that Miller had been seen eleven weeks before the killing, sitting in a parked taxi, waving and shouting to a blond girl in a schoolyard; he was chased away by a man in the yard. The trial judge, the upper court ruled, had discretion to admit into evidence testimony about events remote in time. Yet, the same trial judge refused to admit into evidence the dispatcher's sheet that would show the movements of the taxicab that fatal afternoon. But that refusal was an error (if it was an error) without significance, against the backdrop of all the horror of the crime, said the court.

The prosecuting attorney cross-examined Miller, when he took the stand, and skillfully elicited from him the information that when he had enlisted in the Air Force he had done so by swearing falsely—this false swearing showed Miller to be a liar, the prosecutor maintained. Defense counsel said that this line of questioning was exceeding the scope of direct examination, but the Illinois Supreme Court didn't think so. Neither did anybody else.

Miller's attorney disagreed with and objected to many of the Court's instructions. But because they weren't "error" in the technical, legal sense, the Illinois Supreme Court didn't see fit even to discuss what they were, and neither did anybody else.

Miller's attorneys thought that the prosecutor's remarks about the wounds of the little blond girl were inflammatory, prejudicial, and "constituted reversible error"; but the Illinois Supreme Court said that the prosecutor "has the right to dwell on the evil results of crime." No higher courts saw fit to question that judgment, except perhaps the lone concurring judge in the Seventh Circuit court.

The prosecuting attorney was allowed a private assistant. That was permissible, and in the court's view it hardly reflected on Miller's guilt or innocence. No one disagreed, except Miller's counsel.

Miller's counsel argued that the judge unlawfully communicated with the jury while it was deliberating. (He had responded, out of the hearing of Miller's counsel, to a juror's request, through a bailiff that no, she could not be given any more "information" about the case.) But the lack of communication could hardly be construed as communication, the Illinois Supreme Court said, and no one disagreed.

There was newspaper publicity, and that could be prejudicial. Indeed, Miller had been tried once earlier in Fulton County, where the murder happened, and that trial ended with the granting of a mistrial because of the overwhelming prejudicial publicity that surrounded the case, which was then removed to Hancock County. But there was no showing, ruled the Illinois Supreme Court, that any juror in Hancock County had read any of those newspaper accounts, nine months before; and therefore there could be no prejudice. No one disagreed.

Between the trials, Miller's original lawyer, William H. Malmgren, was cited for contempt for allegedly threatening the star witness, Betty Baldwin, the waitress to whom Miller had confessed later in the evening. The contempt citation was left pending during the second trial, and this made Malmgren nervous. Miller's other lawyers challenged the citations. But the disbelieving Illinois Supreme Court noted that there had been nine months to prepare the case and that Miller had a second lawyer, George K. Meuth, who had no contempt citation to worry about at all. No one else thought that was prejudicial, nor did any court become overly exercised because Miller was not permitted to be present when Malmgren was at *his* hearing trying to show cause why he should not be held in contempt. A defendant is entitled to be present at his own trial, but not at his lawyer's. So said the Illinois Supreme Court; no one disagreed.*

And, finally, the trial judge had denied a pretrial defense motion to have a look at the jockey-style underpants in order to make "a scientific examination." But that motion was "addressed to the sound discretion of the trial court" and there was no showing that discretion was abused. "Indeed," said the Illinois Supreme Court, "the proceeding at which the motion was denied has not been preserved in the bill of ex-

---

* The outcome of Malmgren's contempt hearing was apparently too far beneath the dignity of the Illinois Supreme Court to require comment: On the day set for the contempt hearing, Malmgren arrived at the courthouse, only to find neither the judge nor the state's attorney present. At that very time, Miller's trial judge had set a hearing in another courthouse. A telephone call to the empty courthouse in which Malmgren waited directed him back to the trial. That was the last the state ever thought about proceeding on the issue of contempt.

ceptions, thus we are afforded no basis for review of the discretionary ruling."

This looked like the end of the line. The trial judge was affirmed in every particular by the Illinois Supreme Court and the Seventh Circuit agreed, cutting down a collateral attack made in the federal courts. A second try in the Illinois court failed in 1961.

Then in 1963 there seemed to be new evidence, and Miller's lawyers went again to the federal district court in Chicago. The lawyers urged many reasons why the prisoner should be released. (To attack a state conviction after a final appeal, you can go to federal court and assert that you were deprived of your constitutional rights; the court, if it grants the writ of habeas corpus, will release you, because the judge will have decided you were unfairly tried. It is up to the state to retry you if, in light of the federal ruling, it can do so.)

The reasons being urged upon the court had been heard before. At the proceeding, however, Betty Baldwin took the stand to testify again, and now she repudiated her testimony at the earlier trial. She said that she had committed perjury, that Miller had never confessed to her that evening in front of her house. This testimony was surprising, so surprising that Miller's attorneys had not even referred to its possibility in their petition to the court. The district court ruled that Miller would have to be freed. Noting that the statute of limitations had run out, and Betty Baldwin could not be tried for perjury though she might be held in contempt of court, the district court made clear that this ruling did not reflect adversely on the prosecution, since no one had any way of knowing Betty Baldwin was a perjuror. It was not that the state had condoned perjury; whatever unfairness there was rested simply in the fact that the perjury had occurred.

The lawyers' other arguments did not impress the district court, though it did make other findings. Two years later, the Seventh Circuit reversed this 1963 judgment, saying that due process did not require retrial merely because a witness came forward eight years later to say she had lied. The stage was now set for a final appeal to the United States Supreme Court which had refused to review Miller's case four times before during the preceding ten years.

This time the Supreme Court accepted the case, but it never reached the problem of Betty Baldwin. The Justices were struck by one singular and "extraordinary" finding of the district court at the second habeas corpus proceeding in 1963. The Chicago district court had found that "some of the reddish-brown discolored spots on the shorts . . . were paint spots."

Paint?

The district court had gone on then to find that the existence of paint was "not new testimony, inasmuch as there had never been any

dispute but what the shorts did contain paint spots." There was, however, no blood on the jockey-style underpants.

No blood?

The expert witness in the 1963 hearing admitted on cross-examination that he could not say that there had never been any blood on them
eight years before since blood disintegrated in a few days. This was an
interesting piece of information in itself, since the shorts were not found
until three days after the crime. No matter. The district court found no
significance in the underpants, and, on review, neither did the Seventh
Circuit.

The Supreme Court unanimously parted company with the lower
tribunals. The fraud had been uncovered.

The device that led to the uncovering of a major crime on the part
of the state was the second habeas corpus proceeding in Chicago. Seven
hours before Miller was due to be executed, the federal District Court
for the Northern District of Illinois agreed to hear argument that Miller
had been unlawfully incarcerated because he had been denied due process of law at his trial. Earlier on that very day the Illinois Supreme Court
had turned down a separate petition for habeas corpus. (Governor Otto
Kerner had refused to issue a stay of execution.)

The basis for the unsuccessful petition was evidence uncovered by
an investigator for the Chicago radio station WAIT, whose owner, attorney Maurice Rosenfield, had become interested in the case. Miller's
landlady turned up, providing an alibi for him for the first time. Evidence also corroborated Miller's contention that the shorts were not his:
he was at last permitted to examine them and it became clear that they
were entirely too small for him to have worn comfortably. Moreover,
for the first time a druggist came forward to testify that Miller had come
to his pharmacy to fill a prescription at a time that would at least have
cast doubt on the police version of the facts.

Other facts then began tumbling out.

(1) It turned out, for instance, that a vaginal smear had been taken
within one-half hour of death and placed in a vial that was sent to the
Illinois State Bureau of Investigation at Springfield, where laboratory
analysis revealed the presence of a human hair *that did not belong to
Miller*. This fact was known to the prosecutor but never disclosed to
the judge, jury, or defense. Not only did the prosecutor keep this fact
a secret; state officials told Miller that hairs from his body had been
found. They told him this to induce his confession; Miller refused to
believe them and said so. When, at the habeas corpus proceeding, the
defense was permitted for the first time to see the physical evidence, the
state chemist's official report was deliberately withheld. (The Seventh
Circuit Court of Appeals claimed not to be impressed by any of this,
suggesting that somehow, inadvertently, some careless doctor or other

handler of the body within the half hour following death managed to put a pubic hair well inside the vagina. This was frivolous supposition by a lazy Seventh Circuit; no one else at any stage of the case had suggested it, much less explained how such a negligent act could have taken place in connection with this routine and classic rape-case procedure.)

(2) Laboratory reports showed that Miller's account in his confession of the blow to the girl's head and of the sexual act could not be reconciled with the medical evidence.

(3) Miller stated in his confession that he had thrown his bloody clothes into a passing freight train. It was established that there was no passing train at the time in question.

(4) The confession was written out in longhand during the interrogation even though stenographic services were immediately available. The confession was written entirely in the language of the police, not in Miller's own words.

(5) Five exonerating witnesses turned up. The proprietor of the rooming house in which Miller lived, her husband, and two children all testified that Miller had been asleep in his room at the time of the murder, that he was awakened by the children and then was asked to fill a prescription at a local drugstore. The pharmacist corroborated their account and Miller's that he was at the drugstore between 5:25 and 5:30 P.M. Moreover, the prosecution knew that Miller had eaten dinner at the Maid Rite Restaurant sometime after 5:00 and had then proceeded to the drugstore, even though the confession had it that Miller had gone to the cleaners, then to his room to change clothes, back to the Van Buren Flats, near the scene of the crime, to find the jockey shorts, back through town to dispose of the bundle of bloody clothes, and then back to his room (a distance of some miles) all between 5:15 and 5:45. According to the confession, Miller had walked throughout the town between 4:00 and 5:15 in a bloody jacket; yet no one was brought forward to testify that they had seen him, even though the news of the crime had been released to the townspeople at 4:32. The exonerating witnesses, it developed, had been informed that they had a "constitutional right not to talk to the defense." In a town so thoroughly enflamed as Canton, where no jury could fairly be impaneled, such a "suggestion," Miller's attorneys argued on appeal, could only be understood as a warning to keep silent.

(6) The police "had every reason to know" that their star witness, Betty Baldwin, who testified that Miller had confessed to her, "was psychologically unstable and wholly unreliable" at the time her testimony was offered. Seven months before the trial, but long after the confession, Betty Baldwin had told a long tale about narcotics to the police, a tale they found too implausible to credit. In March she threatened to leave

town and the police unlawfully jailed her for a while to cool her down; it was only later, in July, that she came forward claiming both that Miller's attorney had offered her $10,000 to help his client and that counsel had threatened her (hence her motive to leave town). Pending the trial the sheriff gave her cash on which she lived and later found a job for her (a common practice of prosecutors). A few days before the trial, the prosecutor himself lied to Betty Baldwin, claiming he thought she might be implicated with Miller, even though he knew in fact that she had spent the night of the murder with a man she had just met. Finally, at the trial in August, she testified that she had known Miller for two years prior to the time she signed a statement the previous November, even though she had actually known him only five weeks (not an insignificant fact when it was argued that Miller could be expected to confess truthfully to a close friend). The prosecution did not reveal the signed statement, which clearly showed her misstatement, to judge, jury, or defense.

None of these aspects of the case did the state of Illinois contest or deny as the appeals proceeded following the stay of execution. Attorneys for the state chose instead to make extremely artificial and technical arguments to support his conviction. They argued, for instance, that proving the hair was not Miller's was not a material finding, *since the hair was not Miller's.* That the jury might have found the lack of a relationship a material consideration was not discussed. The state was simply wrong. The fact may have been unconvincing but it was clearly material.

The state also argued that previous Supreme Court rulings had said that it was not unlawful to suppress evidence—such as that relating to the hair and the jockey shorts—unless the defendant requested the evidence. Miller's attorney's general motion to make scientific examination of the physical evidence, the state argued, was not such a request. This and other metaphysical distinctions were never finally passed on, because the Supreme Court ultimately found the nonbloody underwear a sufficient reason to reverse the conviction.

In 1963, for the first time, Miller's attorneys were able to see and examine the jockey-type undershorts. It was then discovered that the red pigment on them was paint, not blood. At the trial, the victim's mother had testified that her daughter had type "A" blood, a bit of hearsay testimony (no one bothered to take the girl's blood type at the morgue) that was itself in some dispute. Then Forrest Russel Litterly, the state's chemist, after being established as an expert who had made some one thousand such analyses, had testified as follows:

I examined and tested "People's Exhibit 3" to determine the nature of the staining material upon it. The result of the first test was that this material upon the shorts is blood. I made a second examination which disclosed that the blood is of human origin. I made a further examination which disclosed that the blood is of group "A."

In his argument to the jury, the prosecutor argued that the shorts had been found after Miller had confessed. This was a blatant lie, which the state later dismissed in its brief on appeal as "inconsequential." It was hardly that. The prosecutor also told the jury:

Those shorts were found in the Van Buren Flats with blood. What type blood? Not "O" blood as the defendant has, but "A"—type "A." . . . And if you will recall it has never been contradicted the blood type of Janice May was blood type "A" positive. Blood type "A." Blood type "A" on these shorts. It wasn't "O" type as the defendant has. It is "A" type. What the little girl had. . . .

These quoted remarks were the sum total of the discussion at the trial about the jockey shorts.

So convincing did the testimony seem that the Supreme Court of Illinois said "it was determined" the shorts "were stained with human blood from group A," and talked of Miller's "bloody shorts." Until the federal habeas corpus proceeding, no one doubted any of it.

The chemist at the 1963 federal hearing, however, said he found "no traces of human blood." There were ten reddish brown areas on the shorts and in each of them he found mineral pigments used in paints, but no blood. The attorney for Illinois argued then that "everybody" knew that the shorts were paint-stained:

Now, then, concerning the paint on the shorts the petitioner yesterday introduced scientific evidence to prove that there was paint on the shorts, a fact that they knew without scientific evidence. Everybody knew, in connection with the case, whoever looked at the shorts, and I think that the Court can look at them now and know there is paint on them. This is not anything that was not disclosed to anybody. It is very obvious by merely looking at them.

A bald-faced untruth. There had never been any discussion of paint at the trial, not even by the defendant, whose self-interest would have prompted him to raise questions about the paint had he had any reason to suspect that the key evidence was in fact nothing more than someone else's discarded paint rag. The only people who knew about the paint were the prosecutors, who had seen a Canton police report that purported to explain "how this exhibit contains all the paint on it." That report did not surface until the federal hearing.

As the Supreme Court pointed out: "A pair of paint-stained shorts, found in an abandoned building a mile away from the scene of the crime, was virtually valueless as evidence against the petitioner. The prosecution deliberately misrepresented the truth." And because the Supreme Court had consistently ruled since 1935 that "a state criminal conviction obtained by the knowing use of false evidence" was unconstitutional, Miller's conviction was at long last, after nearly ten and one-half years, thrown out.

Before the case reached the Supreme Court, more than twenty judges had heard Miller's pleas, and only one had found any merit in any of his arguments. The various officials of the state of Illinois tried, at every stage of the case, to cover up the fact that officials at an earlier stage had committed grievous errors. By the time Illinois realized how serious the issue had grown, its Attorney General and an Assistant Attorney General, rather than concede that serious problems had been raised, as attorneys general have the power to do, submitted briefs to the appellate courts so loaded with technical arguments that a few of them were simply distortions of the law.

Following the Supreme Court's decision, the Attorney General, William G. Clark (who later lost a close race to Senator Everett Dirksen) and his Assistant Attorney General, Richard Friedman (whose race against Mayor Richard Daley of Chicago in 1970 was anything but close) undertook an investigation of the case. The argument before the Supreme Court unsettled and disturbed Friedman, and he determined to look further into the facts. In later court proceedings Friedman, on behalf of the state, said that "in view of the unusual nature of this case" the state would not oppose a federal court order barring retrial. But as late as 1971 the state still refused to dismiss the charges. (In 1967, when Miller was released, his original lawyer, William Malmgren, was running for the office of Fulton County State's Attorney. His opponent's campaign underscored Malmgren's inability to prosecute Miller anew, whereas the opponent could try him. Even so, Malmgren won.)

To prevent retrial, Miller's attorneys continued appeals in his behalf following his release. Those appeals culminated nearly three and one-half years later in the ringing declaration of the Seventh Circuit, refusing to order the state to refrain from further prosecution (Friedman had left office and the state apparently reneged on his pledge), that "we have no reason to believe that petitioner would be denied due process in the courts of Illinois."

Notwithstanding the Court of Appeals, the courts and the executive branch of Illinois had flagrantly violated due process throughout the Miller case. For the Government had knowingly used fake evidence to secure a conviction. A prosecutor, in the face of his ethical obligations as a lawyer and in spite of prior Supreme Court rulings, state and federal laws against obstructing justice, and common sense, put a person on death row for ten years with manufactured evidence.*

The Cases of Thomas J. Mooney and Warren K. Billings

The case against Lloyd Eldon Miller was obviously not the first time a prosecutor ever trumped up charges to convict someone probably innocent. Manufacturing evidence found its way into our constitutional law—as an impermissible technique—in 1935, in the celebrated case against Tom Mooney and Warren Billings.

This was one of the most extraordinary examples of governmental imperviousness to the dictates of law. Through intentional disregard for legal procedures two individuals were condemned to remain unjustly in prison for more than twenty years. The affair began when California brought a prosecution against Thomas J. Mooney, a labor organizer, and Warren K. Billings, a machinist, for their alleged participation as principals in the San Francisco Preparedness Parade bombing in 1916. The case against Mooney and Billings is less well known than the Massachusetts vendetta against Sacco and Vanzetti, perhaps because when it was ultimately shown in California that both men there had been framed, the public furor ceased. That proof was acknowledged when Mooney was fully pardoned in 1939; Billings, though released from prison ten months later, was not fully pardoned until Governor Edmund G. Brown received the technically necessary consent from the California Supreme Court in 1961, forty-five years after the fatal day on Market Street.†

The illegality was well known as early as 1932 when a report prepared for President Hoover's National Commission on Law Observance and Enforcement (popularly known as the Wickersham Commission after its chairman, George Wickersham, Attorney General in President Taft's Cabinet) was officially suppressed and published privately. The principal authors were Zechariah Chafee, Jr., Professor of Law at Harvard, whose brilliant investigation and denunciation of illegal

---

* Neither the prosecutors nor the original chemist were ever indicted or tried. Indeed, the Illinois State Bar Association's Committee on Grievances, blistered by the heat of the Supreme Court's language in reversing the conviction, conducted an investigation and issued a report completely whitewashing the event and exonerating the prosecutor from any wrongdoing. Blaine Ramsey, the Fulton County State's Attorney and Chief Prosecutor, became a trust officer for a bank in Bloomington, Illinois. His assistant, Roger W. Hayes, who was primarily responsible for the presentation of the underwear phase of the case, is in private practice in DeKalb, Illinois. It was Hayes who helped keep the case alive beyond 1967 by intervening on behalf of Fulton County until the state entered an appearance. Hayes's motives were obvious: "to avoid the eye of the camera on himself."

† Billings had· a prior conviction; under California procedure, the Governor cannot pardon a two-time loser unless a majority of the Supreme Court so recommends. The memory of the Court's own complicity in the case was long; it took until 1961 for passions to cool.

acts by the Department of Justice in 1919 and 1920 during the "Red Scare" almost led to his dismissal from the Harvard faculty; Walter H. Pollak, an attorney who had defended many famous dissidents, including Anita Whitney and John T. Scopes; and Pollak's partner Carl S. Stern, who with Pollak had persuaded the Supreme Court that very year in the *Scottsboro* case that blacks accused of the capital crime of raping a white woman in Alabama were entitled to legal counsel at trial.

In brief, the *Mooney-Billings Report* laid out a damning indictment of the prosecution and police for their willingness to use perjured testimony in the trial of a case so poorly investigated that the only possible explanation for the indictments was a hatred of people with upsetting ideas.

The Preparedness Day Parade was said to be the largest gathering of people San Francisco had ever seen. As thousands of marchers joined the main parade from side streets, a bomb exploded, killing nine people and wounding at least forty others. Five days later, on July 27, the police arrested Mooney, Billings, and three others, including Mooney's wife. The trials began in September, 1916, and continued, seriatim, through the following spring. At no time during the year following the explosion did the police follow up numerous leads, including statements of witnesses that an object had been seen falling from a building very close to the center of the impact. The prosecution theorized that a time-bomb had been left in a suitcase. Moreover, the police did not restrain souvenir seekers from tearing apart the damaged sidewalks for fragments. Three men, in depositions to the police, said they had seen someone resembling neither Mooney nor Billings leave a suitcase at the corner where the explosion occurred. None of these putative witnesses was ever called to testify at trial.

Stories that did not jibe with the main theory were not checked out. The stories told by the principal witnesses were not corroborated; the police made no effort to confirm with the scores of available people events that were coming to light. So shoddy was the investigation that the defense later introduced at trial witnesses who confirmed that a man had indeed gone up to the suspected rooftop and that it was not Billings— all of this much to the surprise of the prosecutor, again because the police had not troubled to interview the people known to be watching the parade. Nor did the police bother to find or interview a large number of witnesses, known to the police as people who could provide the defendants with alibis, though they later testified at trial and confirmed the defendants' accounts that Mooney and Billings were not where the prosecution witnesses placed them; none of these witnesses was ever impeached.

The long and short of it was that once the police had arrested their "suspects," the official investigation into any leads that did not support the proposition that Mooney et al. were guilty, ceased. In fact, the captain of the Bomb Squad, organized the day after the explosion, announced to the press the day the grand jury handed down indictments that a clue leading away from the suspects would not be pursued because the police were sure they had the right "bomb gang."

Martin Swanson, an ex-Pinkerton employee, had had a long-standing feud with Mooney over his labor activities. Shortly after the Market Street explosion Swanson went to the San Francisco D.A.'s office, suggested that the police watch Mooney, and accepted employment from the D.A. himself to aid in the surveillance. Swanson, a private detective, was put in charge of the entire investigation.

One of Mooney's codefendants who was later acquitted told how Swanson tried to bribe him into implicating Mooney in an unrelated bombing. His refusal to accept $5,000 or otherwise cooperate in framing Mooney prompted Swanson to say "I'll get you yet." When the codefendant was subsequently arrested, Swanson in the company of police officers said: "Didn't I say I'd get you?" Though present at trial Swanson was not called to rebut the defense testimony concerning these facts, despite a pointed ruling from the bench that a police officer who was about to testify to them could not take the stand in lieu of Swanson. These facts went uncontested. Swanson had also talked to Billings about developing information on the other bombing, and Billings too refused to cooperate.

Not incidentally, Swanson had been working for United Railroad, whose president some years earlier had been indicted for graft. Charles M. Fickert, the same D.A. who was later to prosecute Mooney, had strenuously fought *against* prosecuting the graft case despite the continued refusals of a judge to dismiss it. Ultimately the judge was ordered by higher authority to dismiss the indictments against the railroad president. Significantly, Mooney had been attempting to organize the employees of United Railroad prior to the Market Street explosion.

Despite overwhelming evidence that Swanson had been intimately involved in the entire investigation, with private motives of his own compounded by employment in an all-too-interested corporation, the police made light of Swanson's participation. At closing argument, D.A. Fickert went so far as to say Swanson had not participated at all.

All five defendants had been unlawfully arrested without warrants; there was no evidence connecting any with the crime, not even the perjured testimony that later secured the convictions. Billings was taken from a medical clinic where he was receiving treatment for an illness. All were held three to five days without being charged—another violation of California law. The police captain even testified at trial that "in the interest of justice" he had "suspended law" in order to avoid arraigning Mooney before a magistrate.

The defendants' homes were illegally searched. They were unlawfully denied the opportunity to talk to counsel prior to their grand jury appearances. Mooney was prohibited from seeing or communicating with a lawyer for eleven days after his arrest. The prosecution admitted before the trial that the defendants had been held incommunicado. The police raided the offices of an underground newspaper called *Blast* and carried off boxloads of documents, never used in evidence, though these were quoted in statements released to the press to prove Mooney's guilt.

No identification was ever made at a lineup. One witness, identifying as "Billings" two different men at two lineups one minute apart, was courteously taken by an officer to another floor of the police station. He said, "I have got a real man up here." The "witness" quickly identified him. Other identifications were similarly prompted: The police, on taking a witness to see the suspect for the first time, referred to the suspects by name to make the identifiers' tasks easier.

The Grand Jury heard and saw all sorts of highly prejudicial and improper evidence—the jurors saw a bomb used in another, entirely unrelated explosion; they heard long series of questions trying to link the suspects with communism and radicalism.

The San Francisco newspapers gave widespread and inflammatory coverage to the whole affair. Much of the information was false and came directly from the D.A. and police officers. The connection between the defendants and "anarchy" was constantly headlined, prompted in large measure by statements emanating from the D.A.'s office almost daily that associated Mooney and the others with anarchism, radicalism, and violence. Front-page prominence was given to wild charges made against Mooney that were never substantiated (nor did anyone attempt to substantiate them), such as the charge made by the Assistant District Attorney *in court* that Mooney was a conspirator in a plot to assassinate the Governor.

At the separate trials of Mooney and Billings (the three other defendants were also tried separately, and they were acquitted), the prosecution called witnesses well known to them to be unreliable and to be motivated by hopes of obtaining part or all of a reward of $5,000 offered by the city; one witness was known to have lied in a previous court appearance. Moreover, the prosecutor called witnesses whose stories he knew would be—and were—false.

In fact, most of the witnesses responsible for the convictions were coached by the prosecution on exactly what to say. Frank C. Oxman, the key prosecution witness in the *Mooney* case, the man who the trial judge later said was responsible for Mooney's conviction, was given a crucial license plate number by the police and told to say he had in fact jotted it down as the number he saw on the getaway car the afternoon of the explosion.

To secure other testimony, the prosecution even attempted to arrange for the release from the penitentiary of one potential witness's husband, an arrangement justified on the ground that since the state could not afford to keep the destitute woman during the trial her husband should be permitted to go free and to work. (The living expenses of other prosecution witnesses were paid.) Although the woman was not called and her husband was denied parole, despite acknowledged support from the D.A.'s office, an uncle of one witness who did testify found his twelve-year prison sentence commuted to time served (four years) shortly after Mooney's conviction.

The opening and closing arguments of the prosecution at the trials were prejudicial and unlawful. They constantly harped on the evils of radicalism and on events unrelated to the case being tried. Some were outright fabrications, never supported by evidence introduced at trial.

The day after Mooney's conviction, facts began to come to light showing that the key testimony of Oxman was false. These facts included letters that Oxman had written asking a friend to come west from Illinois to testify that he had seen Oxman in the necessary place at the necessary time. The prosecution never called this witness, knowing his testimony would be false, although much had been made of the fact that a witness could back Oxman's testimony.

The entire sordid episode was summed up by Edward A. Cunha, the Assistant District Attorney, who said well after the trials: "If I knew that every single witness who testified against [Mooney] had perjured himself in his testimony, I would not lift a finger to get him a new trial." Which was literally the truth.

The trials compacted an enormous amount of factual falsehood into a very short time. The appeals expended an equal amount of legal nonsense over a very long time. The key ruling was by the California Supreme Court in September, 1917, to the effect that that court had no power to consider evidence that perjury had been committed since that evidence did not appear in the record of trial. All other courts had ruled that they could do nothing further since the case was out of their hands.

President Wilson's Mediation Commission was sent to investigate; its report recommended that the President use his "good offices" to secure a new trial. Subsequently, a special investigator went to the trouble of secretly planting a dictaphone in D.A. Fickert's office; the transcripts produced a sensation, and the week following publication of the special investigator's report the Governor commuted Mooney's sentence of death to life imprisonment.

During the period 1917–1935, repeated attempts failed to secure a pardon for both men. In 1932 a plan to gain freedom by seeking a writ of habeas corpus in the federal courts was formulated. The argument: that knowing use of perjured evidence was a violation of a person's right to due process under the Fourteenth Amendment. The state opposed the petition at every step, insisting that there could be no remedy but a pardon, which was solely in the discretion of the Governor.

In January, 1935, the Supreme Court of the United States ruled that Mooney was entitled to prove his contention that the state had violated his right to due process of law: "[I]f a State has contrived a conviction through the pretense of a trial which in truth is but used as a means of depriving a defendant of liberty through a deliberate deception of court and jury by the presentation of testimony known to be perjured," the court held, a conviction cannot stand.

It remained for Mooney's attorneys to show the "deliberate deceptions," and they failed at the hands of the California judiciary. The hearings ordered by the state supreme court lasted thirteen months and resulted in one of the most stupefying cases of whitewash in the annals of American jurisprudence. Ignoring the overwhelming weight of the evidence that the Mooney-Billings trials were concocted from beginning to end by the state, it picked out strands and pieces of testimony to weave a fragile tissue on which to rest its conclusion that no wrongdoing had been proved—just as the Illinois courts and the Seventh Circuit would do a quarter century later to vindicate the state in the *Miller* case.

The Supreme Court denied a petition for further relief, announcing its refusal in December, 1938. One month later, newly-elected Governor Culbert L. Olson gave Mooney a pardon. Mooney died in March, 1942, after two years of prolonged illness. He was fifty-eight. As noted, Billings was released in November, 1939, though he was not pardoned until 1961.

Some Cases in Brief

Mooney did not exactly dissuade prosecutors or the police from foregoing the exquisite efficiency of the manufactured evidence technique, because the *Mooney* remedy only works when the official lawlessness is detected. Detection is not always easy. Miller was spared the electric chair only because he had dedicated and persistent lawyers, and even then it took ten years. Other cases that did not withstand scrutiny show the enormous range of prosecution deviousness.

Texas has a law that minimizes the sentence if a killer is prompted by a "sudden passion" springing from an "adequate cause . . . as would commonly produce a degree of anger, rage, resentment, or terror." A sudden-passion murderer can get only five years, instead of death—a useful distinction. A Texan named Alvara Alcorta admitted stabbing his wife but claimed he had succumbed to a fit of passion when he saw her kissing one Natividad Castilleja late at night in a parked car in front of his home. Alcorta said he had suspected his wife was unfaithful. Castilleja testified, on the other hand, that his relationship with Alcorta's wife extended to driving her home from work on a few occasions. His was only a casual friendship, he said. He was parked in front of the home at 2:00 A.M., with car lights out, because of engine trouble. Castilleja denied ever having dates with the dead woman and denied talking to her of love.

After the trial, Castilleja felt pangs of remorse for having perjured himself at trial: he confessed to having had intercourse with the victim on several occasions. The prosecutor, apparently, had no such pangs, for Castilleja told these facts to the prosecutor before the trial, and the prosecutor's advice to Castilleja was to volunteer no information but to be truthful if questioned. The prosecutor corroborated Castilleja's confession, after trial: he did not think it would have made any difference to the jury. The Supreme Court was compelled, unanimously, to reverse the conviction in 1957. The following year, Hubert W. Green, Jr., the prosecutor, was named Texas' Outstanding Prosecutor.

In Pennsylvania, the prosecutorial system has been used as a bludgeon. In July, 1957, "Snooks" Jackson was told by a friend that "Teddy" Jordan, a Philadelphia detective and social acquaintance, wanted to see him. Jackson went to City Hall, where Jordan told Jackson that a robbery investigation had turned up Jackson's name. Jackson said he had loaned his car to Joseph Williams for three dollars and that he had no other connection with the suspects. Jordan assured Jackson, who had only a sixth-grade education, that if he would sign a statement admitting receipt of the three dollars, he would not be further implicated. Jackson agreed, and Jordan immediately handed over a typed statement. Without reading it, Jackson signed it. The statement in fact admitted Jackson's involvement in three robberies. There was no question that the "confession" was, in the words of the federal district court, "an obvious fabrication," since it referred to Jackson, who signed it, as someone other than himself. Thus:

> We each got $27.00 apiece, Julius Mercer, "Snooks" Jackson, Williams, and myself [i.e., "Snooks" Jackson]. . . . We went to the grocery store, we picked up Julius Mercer and "Snooks" Jackson on the way. When we got to this store, Williams and I got out of the car and I took Williams's gun, walked into the store and told the man that it was a holdup. The man gave me $75.00. "Snooks" Jackson and Julius Mercer were outside as lookouts in Mercer's car. When we got out of the store, we jumped into the car with Mercer driving and we went to South Philadelphia to a relative of Mercer's and we split the money up. We got about $18.00 apiece, Julius Mercer, "Snooks" Jackson, Williams and myself. They then drove me back to West Philadelphia and dropped me off.

In December, 1957, Jackson was arraigned, along with three other men named Jackson and ten other defendants (all of whom were represented by eight different attorneys and arraigned on forty indictments).

It was a confusing day for everyone. Jackson, charged with robbery on three counts, pleaded guilty to each. He had the advice of a bad lawyer.

On April 14, 1958, Jackson was sentenced. In the meantime, he finally realized he had pleaded guilty to robbery: a social worker told him what he had done when he returned home after the arraignment. The court denied Jackson's request to change his pleas. The D.A. had read the sworn testimony of the codefendant Joseph Williams, to the effect that Jackson participated in all three robberies. What the D.A. failed to point out was that Williams actually had named another Jackson. (In June 1963 Williams testified in a related proceeding that he had been mentally ill back in 1958 when he made the statement, and, indeed, he had spent the years 1958–1963 in mental institutions.)

Jackson did admit to one robbery. He said at his later habeas corpus hearing that he meant by that only that he had in fact received the $3.00, which, he had thought, made him guilty of the robbery.

At the sentencing, Jackson complained of an unfair trial. The judge said: "Treat you this way? How did you treat the shopkeepers? . . . You want justice from us. Why didn't you do justice to the community?" Jackson was then sentenced to twenty to forty years.

Jackson's later attempts to have the matter reheard by the Pennsylvania state courts were rebuffed without even the semblance of hearings. He finally petitioned the federal district court in Philadelphia. For two years he was conveniently held off by a little trick: the original sentences were consecutive; that is, the first chunk of time in jail related only to the first count on which he was convicted, and so on.

The petition that was submitted to the federal court in September, 1960, was denied as "premature" by an overly literal federal judge, since Jackson was not yet serving time *on that charge*. His court-appointed counsel thereupon requested the original trial judge to reduce the sentence. In April, 1963, the original order was backdated, making the sentences run concurrently, thus reducing the sentence to a maximum of twenty years. This 1963 order was, however, dated 1961. The federal court did not see all this as a metaphysical nicety, but perhaps it no longer mattered, since the original federal judge had died. The newly assigned federal judge now perceived that the charge to which Jackson had formally pleaded his guilt (through ignorance) was no longer "premature" and the way was cleared for a complete hearing. At that hearing, five years after Jackson was imprisoned, the federal district court reversed his conviction and characterized the original proceedings as "a nightmare of injustice."

In Birmingham, Alabama, in 1955, James Hatt robbed L. O. Brown, a storekeeper, and his wife as they were entering their car, taking twenty-five dollars. He held them up at gun point and told them to ride him out of town. After compelling the storekeeper to let the air out of all the tires, Hatt threatened to shoot if either of his victims left the car. They waited a long time before opening the door.

Five days later the police caught up with Hatt in the apartment of William K. Powell, in Leeds, Alabama. Hatt gave a detailed confession, saying Powell was in on the robbery. Powell protested his innocence, and neither the storekeeper nor his wife ever linked Powell with the crime.

The police and Cecil Deason, prosecutor, however, had two items of intelligence about Hatt, neither of which they revealed: (1) Hatt had been in mental institutions in three different states; throughout the trial, the state objected to every attempt of defense counsel to introduce such evidence and the judge consistently sustained the motions to keep out that evidence. (2) Hatt was permitted to testify on the stand to facts directly contrary to those contained in his written statement, which the prosecution had not bothered to show defense counsel. That statement, in the language of the Court of Appeals, "admitted that during the week preceding the robbery of L. O. Brown, Hatt had committed a burglary, an armed robbery, a kidnapping, and the theft of an automobile before meeting Powell, and had committed two other armed robberies with the claimed assistance of Powell." Moreover, one of the robberies showed the same modus as that used against the storekeeper: Hatt said he had the car driven seventy-five miles down the highway, dropped his victim off to hitchhike, and continued on for a while longer before abandoning the car.

Not only did Hatt contradict his written statement; the prosecutor led Hatt on the stand to say explicitly that he told the "same story" on the day he was arrested as he had just told on the stand. Hatt was sentenced to five years, Powell to ten.

The Alabama Supreme Court never saw the transcript of the trial. The conviction was affirmed. Five years after Powell began serving his time, the U.S. Court of Appeals for the Fifth Circuit reversed his conviction.*

It is not coincidental that state convictions unlawfully secured in these cases were reversed by federal courts. Though state courts occasionally acknowledge the force of the *Mooney* doctrine, all too often the lower courts lazily forego hearings, leaving attorneys with no alternative but to invoke federal judicial power and delaying, sometimes for years, the ultimate reversal of unjust convictions. In 1962, Chief Judge Roszel C. Thomsen of the federal district court in Maryland felt obliged to chastise the state courts for their continuing failures to hold hearings

---

* Racial prejudice was not a factor in the case: defendants and victims were white.

under the state Uniform Post Conviction Procedure Act (UPCPA), which does not mandate hearings, though it does permit them.

In the particular case, a black male defendant owed his conviction on a charge of rape primarily to racial bias; testimony the prosecution knew would cast grave doubt on the allegations was withheld, and the appointed defense counsel failed to introduce evidence that would have exonerated his client. Said Chief Judge Thomsen:

> We venture to suggest that when such a petition [under the UPCPA] is filed in a state court alleging, however clumsily, any facts tending to show a deprivation of constitutional rights, the State court might grant the prisoner one hearing at which he would be given the opportunity to present all of the facts upon which he bases his claim. This court would not then be forced, as in this case, to receive evidence about events which happened some five years ago, when most of the witnesses have lost or destroyed whatever records they may have had and remember little of what occurred, and to consider such evidence without the benefit of findings of fact by the appropriate State court. If such findings were made, this court would ordinarily be able to accept the findings and to limit its hearing to questions of constitutional law.*

HIS HONOR, THE JUDGE

Hon. Leonard P. Walsh

Under a flexible legal system where the law rarely means what it seems to say and sentences are usually prescribed within a range rather than specifically, justice depends on the quality of judges administering it. Just as there are prosecutors who have an obvious contempt for law, so too there are judges to whom the impartiality of law is a relatively meaningless concept.

Trial judges get their law not merely from the codebooks; they are also supposed to abide by the rulings of appellate courts, which oversee the administration of justice at the trial level. But trial judges have shown themselves adept at avoiding both statutes and rulings, thus oppressing individual defendants trapped in the courtroom of a lawless oligarch.

Here is an example typical of the thousands of instances of judicial malfeasance that occur annually. The Honorable Leonard P. Walsh, United States District Judge in Washington, D.C., on March 10, 1970, unlawfully forced a defendant prior to trial to trade one right for

---

* The suggestion is fraught with some peril: a perfunctory state hearing could rob the federal court on review of the only basis on which justice could be premised. Implicit in this doubt is the disbelief that state judges are more concerned with equity than technicality, but there are ample grounds to support the doubt.

another. Criminal defendants are entitled to notice at least three days before trial of the list of people from which the jury will be chosen, and also to bail. Bail can be revoked, legally, only where there is reason to believe that an accused will not appear at trial. The following partial transcript makes the judge's abuse clear:

THE DEFENSE COUNSEL: The defendant advises me he has not seen a copy of the jury list or the names of the witnesses.

THE PROSECUTOR: Your Honor, our secretary gave it to the marshal. The address that it was to be served on was an address that is listed on the Bail Reform Act form, that the defendant had to sign.

If the defendant did not receive one, of course, he is entitled to a three-day continuance which the Government would not oppose at this time. I think the record should be clear as to whether he wants it or whether he is ready to proceed at this time.

THE DEFENSE COUNSEL: Your Honor, I advised the defendant under the law, and he claims that he was never served with a capital list, list of the witnesses, or a list of the prospective jurors.

I have advised him that under the law he is entitled to be served with those documents three days in advance of trial. He wants to insist on his right in this matter.

THE PROSECUTOR: May the defendant be asked, your Honor, whether in fact he has been living with [a named person and address].

THE COURT: All right.

THE PROSECUTOR: That is where the marshals were to have served him.

THE DEFENSE COUNSEL: That is where he lives, your Honor.

THE COURT: Let's get the marshal up here. Is the defendant on bond?

THE DEFENSE COUNSEL: Yes, your Honor.

THE COURT: Let's cancel the bond then and make certain that he will have the information.

THE DEFENSE COUNSEL: Your Honor, may we approach the bench?

THE COURT: Yes.

(At the bench.)

THE COURT: This doesn't have to be on the record.

(Discussion off the record.)

(A short recess was taken.)

(The defendant and his counsel were present.)

THE DEFENSE COUNSEL: Your honor, we have endeavored to try to get in touch with the marshal that had the capital list. He is on the street.

I have talked to the defendant's sister who is home all the time, where he lives, at the address. She advises me that the only thing that the defendant got pertaining to this case was the notice from the Bail Agency to be present here this morning, and no marshal had been around.

However, I realize what the purpose of the capital list is. I picked up a copy of it last week. I have gone over it with the defendant. We have gone over the names of the witnesses who are listed. They are primarily names of police officers who had some connection with this case one way or another and a minor number of them would be actual witnesses.

I am satisfied after going over the list, and going over it with the defendant during your Honor's absence that we can proceed with this matter.

THE COURT: Does the defendant understand his rights?

THE DEFENSE COUNSEL: Yes, I have advised him of it.

THE COURT: Do you understand?

THE DEFENDANT: Yes.

THE COURT: You are entitled to personal service.

THE DEFENDANT: Yes, sir.

THE COURT: Now, Mr. —— has been representing you?

THE DEFENDANT: Yes, sir.

THE COURT: And you know that Mr. —— has a copy.

THE DEFENDANT: Yes, sir.

THE COURT: If you had received a copy—

THE DEFENDANT: No, sir.

THE COURT: I say if you had received a copy, you would have given it to Mr. —— anyhow, wouldn't you?

THE DEFENDANT: Yes, sir.

THE COURT: All right. So, is it clear that you are waiving the filing of the capital list?

THE DEFENDANT: Yes, sir.

THE COURT: What?

THE DEFENDANT: Yes, sir.

THE COURT: And, the jury list, is that correct?

THE DEFENDANT: Yes, sir.

THE DEFENSE COUNSEL: Your Honor, I would like to say this. The defendant is employed. He works long hours during the day. Apparently if there was any attempt made at all, it may have been made during the day time when he was at work at his job. The time when I talk to him primarily is during the day when he is at work. So, knowing that the Marshals have a lot of work down there—

THE COURT: The Court is going to take the defendant's word; however, if the deputy marshal has the return of personal service, and identifies the defendant in this case as the person that he served, obviously the Court takes an entirely different position.

THE DEFENSE COUNSEL: Yes.

THE COURT: But, at this time the defendant will remain on the bond he formerly was on.

The incident is minor. The judge's threatened ruling was not appealed following the defendant's conviction; it was not even further commented on. It simply illustrates one of the countless ways judges can get around inconvenient and awkward laws.

Minor Derelictions

The Walsh incident is typical in its mundane disregard of the law. Judge Thomas C. Scalley, formerly of the D.C. Court of General Sessions, has been known to turn cases over to his clerk. Scalley has been reported to have left the small claims court bench for thirty minutes one morning while his clerk "disposed of more than fifty cases."

Another General Sessions Court judge, Edward A. Beard, once discovered one of two codefendants asleep. He found each guilty of contempt and rapped out thirty-day sentences. "But I'm all right," the wide-awake defendant was reported as saying. "Why me?" "You are guilty by association. Get them out of here," Judge Beard yelled.

Occasionally Beard has even been called to task, as for instance in a trial during which he asked the courtroom audience to show by raising their hands whether they believed the defendant was lying or not.

Then there is—or was—the redoubtable Milton S. Kronheim, Jr., also a judge of the General Sessions Court. Kronheim was appointed by President Truman in 1949. His father is a liquor distributor and generous campaign contributor. Kronheim knew very little law, and his decisions were frequently reversed by appellate courts. He was reappointed in 1959 after heavy pressure was brought to bear on the White House in his behalf. He managed to extend his tenure on the General Sessions Court beyond 1969 when his father's friend, Congressman Emanuel Celler, made threats about not enacting legislation if Kronheim were removed.

In 1971 the District of Columbia courts were reorganized and the General Sessions Court was abolished, its former jurisdiction transferred to a new Superior Court, and Kronheim was not reappointed. That has not prevented Chief Judge Harold Greene from calling Kronheim back from obscurity to serve anyway because of the backlogged docket. Two cases give the flavor of Kronheim's lawlessness:

In the first, the defendant wanted to appeal the conviction:

THE COURT: The imposition of sentence is suspended. You are placed on probation for a period of one year. All right.

MR. ROSEN: Your Honor, I would also like to appeal the Court's findings. I would ask that the papers—even though the defendant got a suspended sentence—I would ask that the papers reflect that a motion was made to note an appeal.

THE COURT: In this case?

MR. ROSEN: In this case, yes.

THE COURT: All right. There will be a two-thousand-dollar bond.

MR. ROSEN: Well, you are going to suspend his sentence so I believe he will be out free today, but I would still like to appeal the finding.

THE COURT: No, they don't go on probation until after the finding of the Court of Appeals. Step back.

MR. ROSEN: Then I won't—let me make this representation. In light of that, Your Honor, I would not want to see this defendant locked up any longer so I will not appeal the case.

THE COURT: No, we can't bargain about a substantive right like that. Now step back, sir.

(The defendant withdrew from the courtroom.)

THE COURT: Get him back again, will you please?

(The defendant was brought back.)

THE COURT: I put him on probation only because they recommended it. It was against my better judgment. I am going to revoke that and give him three hundred and sixty days concurrently.

In the second case, Judge Kronheim shows how he reaches a judgment:

THE COURT: Well, I am going to give him credit for his complaint. There is a finding for the landlord in the amount of fifty dollars for possession for nonpayment of rent. No cost.

COUNSEL FOR LANDLORD: Your Honor, this is for both months, sir?

THE COURT: This is for this month. This is for the complaint I have before me, sir.

COUNSEL: Your Honor, I would like to make one statement.

THE COURT: You better not because I can change my mind. That's the way I am going to handle this case.

COUNSEL: Very well—I can only say this: There was no request to plaintiff's counsel to make any remark for the record.

THE COURT: All right. Change that. There is a finding for the tenant. Finding for the tenant. Go from there.

The list of examples of lawless judges could be extended endlessly. Thus Arlington County (Virginia) Court Judge L. Jackson Embrey, who received brief notoriety in 1969 when he coerced a mother to beat her eighteen-year-old daughter in open court with a strap provided by the local sheriff. Judge Embrey was suspended briefly from the bench but soon regained it. In late 1971, however, he was removed from criminal court and permitted to hear civil cases only.

Chief Judge Edward M. Curran

Judicial lawbreaking is not restricted to the making of rulings that have no rational basis; judges also willfully refuse to follow nonambiguous rules because they dislike them.

Judges are supposed to be guided in their decisions by law. One time-honored rule is that the decisions of the higher, or appellate, courts must be followed by the lower, or trial, judges. This simple rule of precedence is known to most judges, but apparently not to then-Chief Judge Edward M. Curran of the U.S. District Court for the District of Columbia. In a 1962 case, *Jenkins* v. *United States,* Judge Curran told the jury:

> A psychologist is not competent to give a medical opinion as to a mental disease or defect. Therefore, you will not consider any evidence to the effect that the defendant was suffering from a mental disease or a mental defect on June 10, 1959, according to the testimony given by the psychologists.

The Court of Appeals reversed the resulting conviction, holding that Judge Curran erred in refusing to let the jury consider the testimony of the psychologist. "The critical factor in respect to admissibility is the actual experience of the witness and the probable probative value of his opinion," said the court. In a concurring opinion, then-Circuit Judge Warren Burger said,

> The issue is not now and never was whether a psychologist's testimony is admissible in litigation where "sanity" is in issue. Such testimony has long been admissible in the form of psychological tests and the analysis and explanation of such tests by a psychologist. No one doubts that such matter is admissible.

Eight years later, Judge Curran was presented with a petition from an inmate of St. Elizabeth's Hospital in Washington, D.C. The patient had been confined to the mental institution following a trial on charges of taking indecent liberties with a minor child, a trial that ended with a verdict of not guilty by reason of insanity. After two years at the hospital, the patient sought release on the ground that he was and had been an alcoholic, that he had committed the alleged acts while intoxicated, and that he would not be a danger to the community if he were to visit a clinic daily for antabuse treatment (antabuse is a drug that causes illness in anyone consuming alcohol).

Two hearings were held before Judge Curran, who denied the requested release each time. Although required by the rules of court to file findings of fact and conclusions of law, he did not do so. A transcript of the second proceeding, only thirty minutes long, was made, however, and on the basis of that transcript, the patient appealed to the U.S. Court of Appeals.

A clinical psychologist and a psychiatrist had been called to testify on behalf of the patient. The gist of the testimony was that on the basis of Rorschach tests the patient did not appear to present a further danger to the community if he could be given antabuse therapy on the outside. The petitioner had been a "model patient," his behavior "exemplary," except for "intermittent episodes of drinking." The United States Attorney did not oppose the patient's release.

When the clinical psychologist took the stand he was grilled by Judge Curran as follows:

THE COURT: What are his responses to the Rorschach test?

THE WITNESS: In 1969—no, in 1968, there were four—as I recall, four— responses which were explicitly related to female genitalia.

THE COURT: What are they? I don't know what they are. What were the responses from the Rorschach test? What were the four?

* * * *

THE COURT: Are you telling me from the cards you showed him in the Rorschach test he said that it was a woman's genitalia?

THE WITNESS: Yes, sir. That was in 1968 and again in 1969.

THE COURT: Don't you think he is a little mentally sick, then, if he picks out something from a Rorschach test like that? Do you think that is normal? Can you pick out a woman's genitalia in the Rorschach test?

* * * *

THE WITNESS: . . . .

I did not finish in regard to the Rorschach test in which I in- dicated that both in the original testing and again in the testing late last summer these female genitalia responses were there and he was making no effort to hide them.

Also, as well as these, there were also—

THE COURT: When you looked at the Rorschach test, did you get any idea it represented female genitalia?

* * * *

THE COURT: Is there anything in the Rorschach test that will lead a nor- mal person to determine that there was a female organ involved?

THE WITNESS: Yes, Your Honor.

THE COURT: There is?

THE WITNESS: Yes. Female breast is a good, plus response.

THE COURT: There is nothing about a female breast in the Rorschach test. You are a Clinical Psychologist and you are telling me that as a result of looking at these ink spots there is a female breast in there?

THE WITNESS: I didn't say there was a female breast there. I said it is not abnormal to see a female breast.

THE COURT: There isn't?

THE WITNESS: Female breast by standard, statistical analysis has been shown to be a frequent response of normal people and it is a good, plus response.

THE COURT: A normal person looks at a Rorschach test and sees a female breast, right?

THE WITNESS: Not every normal person, but it is not abnormal to do it. Many normal people do it.

THE COURT: That's all. Step down.

The psychologist was immediately followed by a staff psychiatrist:

THE COURT: Are you familiar with the Rorschach test?

THE WITNESS: Yes, sir.

THE COURT: As I am.

Are you going to tell me that a normal person looking at that Rorschach test is going to find anything resembling a female organ?

THE WITNESS: Your Honor, the only way I can answer is to say that some normal people will and some won't.

THE COURT: You don't know then. You are the psychiatrist and you don't know. Right?

THE WITNESS: I can't answer your question.

THE COURT: That is pretty good. You can't answer the question.

The judge then rejected the rule announced by the Court of Appeals in the *Jenkins* case, which expressly permitted psychologists to testify:

THE COURT: I take it that you agree as a psychiatrist that a Clinical Psychologist is competent to give medical testimony as to a man's insanity?

THE WITNESS: I would agree.

THE COURT: Then you don't agree with any of the else [*sic*] of your brothers.

[APPELLANT'S COUNSEL]: The Court of Appeals agrees with that, Your Honor.

THE COURT: That doesn't make any difference, what the Court of Appeals says. That doesn't convince me.

[APPELLANT'S COUNSEL]: Well, Your Honor, does the Jenkins opinion convince you in its proposing a man—

THE COURT: I don't think a Clinical Psychologist has any competency to tell me what a man's mental condition is. The Court of Appeals says he does.

Judge Curran denied the motion to release, suggesting that justice, if any, would have to emanate from the Court of Appeals (meaning more time and money to be spent on a matter that would obviously be sent back for further proceedings):

THE COURT: How do you know he won't drink, if I release him?

THE WITNESS: Well, because, Your Honor, we have a plan devised to assure that he takes antabuse.

THE COURT: How?

THE WITNESS: We plan to watch him.

THE COURT: How?

THE WITNESS: Well, we watch him while he is in the hospital. We give it to him and watch him swallow it. Our plan would be to arrange, when and if he gets to the community, to have a community based clinic [or] physician administer it to him and watch him take it.

THE COURT: You can't convince me that you have a man charged with this type of crime—

I am not going to release him.

[APPELLANT's COUNSEL]: Judge—

THE COURT: That is all.

[APPELLANT's COUNSEL]: Let me just ask the doctor one more question.

THE COURT: I am not going to release him.

[APPELLANT's COUNSEL]: Judge, when are you going to release him, may I ask?

THE COURT: I may never release him.

[APPELLANT's COUNSEL]: Doctor, what is the prognosis for this man's total recovery?

THE COURT: Prognosis?

[APPELLANT's COUNSEL]: Yes.

THE WITNESS: I would say the prognosis—

THE COURT:—is bad.

THE WITNESS: The prognosis for him ever being rid of his diagnosis [unspecified sexual deviation] is poor. The prognosis for not acting antisocially is very good, if he doesn't ingest alcohol.

[APPELLANT's COUNSEL]: Very well, Your Honor. The statutory standards are a dual one—

THE COURT: Take it up to the Court of Appeals. I am not going to release him.

[APPELLANT's COUNSEL]: Very well, Your Honor. I would like to emphasize one other thing: This man is 61 years old. He has already served more than the minimum, if he had been convicted.

THE COURT: He is not serving time. He is at St. Elizabeth's.

[APPELLANT's COUNSEL]: Your Honor, I am not sure he would make that distinction so clearly.

THE COURT: That could be. If I am wrong, the Court of Appeals can turn him loose. If they turn him loose, there is nothing I can do about it.

But I am not going to turn these people loose that are convicted of this type of a crime.

[APPELLANT's COUNSEL]: Your Honor, it is not just turning him loose. He would be closely supervised and take this antabuse every day.

THE COURT: All right. Motion denied.

[APPELLANT's COUNSEL]: Very well, Your Honor.

The Court of Appeals vacated Judge Curran's decision and remanded the case for the development of evidence at a hearing based on a proper regard for the law.

In all, Judge Curran's handling of the case is a model of how to break the law:

Judge Curran "was more interested in providing answers than eliciting them." He was more a participant than a judge. He "even sought to block answers that appeared contrary to [his] own evident views." He cut off cross-examination. He rejected a rule of law he knew was binding on him since the rule had been established on appeal in a case over which he had presided. He misapplied the statute dealing with commitment of the insane by asserting that he would not turn loose people "that are convicted of this type of crime," despite the fact that the law requires a judgment relating to the prognosis for recovery of each patient. In short, his actions were patently unlawful.*

HOW TO GET A TAX EVADER

The Case of Reuben G. Lenske

In May, 1959, a Special Agent of the Bureau of Internal Revenue was assigned to investigate Reuben G. Lenske, a lawyer in Portland, Oregon. Special Agents are only called into federal income tax cases when there is reason to suspect, on the basis of evidence already developed by a revenue agent, that the tax laws have been willfully violated. For two and one-half years after the Special Agent was first called into the case, both he and the revenue agent investigated the files and acquaintances of Reuben Lenske on a full-time basis.

The Special Agent reported to the District Director in Portland, recommending criminal prosecution, in June, 1961. The report was not coy: it stated at the outset that there was reason to believe Lenske was a communist. So, at least, the FBI in Portland and the Intelligence Division of the Portland Police Department believed; according to the Special Agent, "they each maintain an extensive file on Mr. Lenske." In those files were some of the exhibits the Special Agent attached to his report: Exhibit 3A was a short news story about Lenske's having called a meeting with another lawyer to form a local chapter of the Lawyers' Guild; Exhibit 3B, characterized by the Agent as "Mr. Lenske's thinking on the subject of Cuba, Laos, China, etc.," was a letter to the editor of a newspaper, stating Lenske's belief that in the named countries the United States was guilty of violating national and international law.

Though never introduced into evidence, the Government managed to show the Agent's report to the trial judge (two trial judges, in fact, since the first died during the trial and a second had to be assigned to

* Following the Court of Appeals' decision, Judge Curran disqualified himself on a motion of defense counsel. After more testimony persuaded another judge that the antabuse program was medically and legally sound, the inmate was conditionally released.

retry the case) and to the defendant himself. The report also came before the Court of Appeals (though apparently not formally, since two of the three judges thought it could not properly be referred to as a ground for reversing Lenske's conviction). This was a measure of the Government's strategy, for all parties thus had access to a highly prejudicial document not legally a part of the case. That is a little like everyone's agreeing that certain testimony is hearsay, which cannot be told to the jury, and then telling it to the jury anyway, just sort of informally.

In this case, however, it is rather obvious that the Government tripped up, since it was the opinion of two of the three judges of the Court of Appeals, which ultimately upset the conviction, that the "motivation of the Government's investigation of this case" was burdened with "gross impropriety." Indeed, one judge went so far as to conclude that the investigation was "a scandal of the first magnitude in the administration of the tax laws of the United States. It discloses nothing less than a witch-hunt, a crusade by the key agent of the United States in this prosecution, to rid our society of unorthodox thinkers and actors by using federal courts to put them in the penitentiary. No court should become an accessory to such a project."

The Government alleged that Lenske had attempted to "evade and defeat" his 1955, 1957, and 1958 taxes and that he had filed a false return in 1956. To prove its case, the Government relied on the "net worth" method: in the absence of direct proof that Lenske made more money than he declared or that he took deductions to which he was not entitled, the prosecution sought to introduce circumstantial evidence that Lenske managed to spend money he could not have possessed on the basis of the income declared in the returns.

Lenske was a lawyer in private practice who owned "some 90 pieces of property of varying types, ages, and conditions." In view of the complexity of the tax laws governing depreciation on real estate, the outcome of the prosecution hinged on estimations of the value of buildings and their life expectancies. No one can make these estimations with any certainty. Indeed, during the course of the trial, the judge himself said that the depreciation figures were based on speculation. "All [the Government's appraiser] can do is speculate," said the judge. "You are dealing, as I said, in probabilities—these intangibles." Government counsel agreed.

It is said that those who are guilty of crime can scarcely be heard to complain about the Government's motivations in prosecuting them. In light of the Government's motivation in the *Lenske* case, however, the alleged crime and the Government's method of proving it takes on a significance that lifts this prosecution from the humdrum record of citizens caught in the act of craving more money than they are entitled to.

To begin with, the indictment *charged* that Lenske owed, for the years 1955 through 1958, the following sums in back taxes not paid: $11,465, $5,225, $19,412, and $7,746, or a total of nearly $39,000. In fact, however, the Government managed to *prove* that Lenske owed for these same years: in 1955 $414, in 1956 nothing owed but instead a tax loss of more than $9,000, in 1957 $1,000, and in 1958 $4,683, or a total tax loss of some $3,000.

The net result was that the Government said Lenske owed $39,000 in back taxes; it managed to prove that Lenske actually paid $3,000 too much. These figures all hinged on the amount of depreciation allowed for each of the years in question; the judge found that he was entitled to deduct more than $85,000 for that purpose. Thus, "a relatively small variation in the amount of depreciation might have erased any tax liability for one or more or all of the years."

The Government's method of investigation was as interesting as what it ultimately proved. The Special Agent testified that he had interviewed at least five hundred witnesses and perhaps as many as fifteen hundred. He had, he said, "thousands, thousands" of documents. Most of these were supplied willingly by Lenske, who furnished the investigating agents all his financial papers and cancelled checks, and permitted the agents to work in the library of his law firm.

The trial judge who ultimately convicted Lenske discovered that the agents had secretly carried papers out of Lenske's office each evening to photostat them. "It is irregular to have taken them from the building without advising Mr. Lenske, and the proof is clear that that is what they did," the judge said. He found, moreover, that Lenske was not aware that the agents had seen at least one document. (This course of conduct takes its significance from the Government's steadfast refusal to permit Lenske to know specifically what transactions would become pertinent in the case.)

Despite the intensive, thirty-month investigation, the agent was found to have made a string of errors. He overlooked $2,000 in estimated taxes actually paid by Lenske toward his 1958 return. The agent added to his estimate of income an insurance company check which said "in full settlement of wind policy." He claimed to have simply "overlooked" a $500 item in Lenske's favor. Fees that might have been attributable to the law partnership rather than to Lenske personally were attributed to Lenske without further investigation, though it was never suggested that information sought from Lenske or the partnership had been withheld.

An expert witness for the defense, a former IRS supervisor with seventeen years' experience in more than five hundred "net worth" cases, found in the agent's treatment of various transactions scores of errors obvious enough that the Government incorporated many of his corrections when it revised its charts. The expert witness also pointed out that the Special Agent failed to follow several leads that would have yielded accurate answers. In particular, he spoke of

> the Special Agent's failure to use the microfilms, which banks made and retain and which identify the bank on which a deposited check is drawn, to determine whether the deposit represented taxable income, or the repayment of a debt, or a deposit for investment, or the payment of an insurance loss, or whatever else it might represent. [The expert witness] testified that in seventeen years of tax practice he had not once been unable to so trace a deposit to its source. The Special Agent appears not to have made use of this important, practicable and reliable follow-up method.

Having thus conducted a sloppy investigation, premised on a suspicion of the defendant's political beliefs, the Government then refused, as a practical matter, to let Lenske defend himself. The indictment charged in only a general way an attempted evasion of the taxes. It did not particularize the alleged unlawful acts, and the Government successfully opposed Lenske's motion to the first trial judge for some notice as to what he would have to defend against. At the second trial (the first judge having died), the Government opposed Lenske's request to see documents that might aid him: the prosecutor claimed to have provided Lenske with documents "the night before" their use but said that he would not permit Lenske to see statements of witnesses who would not testify.

There were, to reiterate, at least five hundred witnesses, some of whom might conceivably have exonerated the defendant. The Government (and the trial court) ignored a Supreme Court case that explicitly requires the prosecution to follow up leads advantageous to the defendant. (Private noncorporate defendants, obviously, would find it prohibitively expensive to attempt to interview between five hundred and fifteen hundred witnesses, a task that took two full-time investigators thirty months.)

Finally, the Government very carefully undertook to transcribe testimony of only certain witnesses before the Grand Jury. When these witnesses testified at trial, the prosecutor had copies of the transcript in his hand in order to impeach them or to rebut the testimony should they change their stories. The Government did not transcribe any Grand Jury testimony of the Special Agent, the key Government witness. As the Court of Appeals later noted: "[I]t is evident that the Government so arranged matters that there would be available transcripts by which neutral witnesses could be held to Grand Jury testimony and checked if they varied from it, while as to government partisan witnesses, who presented no danger of their being swayed from their recitals, there would be no writing which the taxpayer might use for cross examination. It was a clever scheme, but one-sided and unfair."

The case against Lenske was, of course, a criminal prosecution, which had to be proved to the satisfaction of the judge (there was no jury) beyond a reasonable doubt. But it was inherent in the nature of the case that the fundamental set of figures—depreciation on the buildings and land—was premised on speculation and probabilities. "A relatively small variation in the amount of depreciation might have erased any tax liability for one or more or all of the years," the Court of Appeals had pointed out. The errors the Government sought to prove were willful errors, which could have sent Lenske to jail for years. But the Government's expert witnesses, called to establish the value of ninety pieces of property and the duration of their economic lives, admitted that there was nothing precise about his figures. They were estimates, educated guesses. The expert himself admitted that the figures might be high and they might be low (though he guessed that his guesses balanced out). So theoretical were the calculations that, as indicated, the Special Agent overestimated the taxes due for 1955 by twenty-seven times; for 1957, by nineteen times; for 1958, by three times; and for 1956, when there turned out to be a large tax loss, by an infinite amount, at least.

Such is not the stuff of criminal convictions that will stand appellate scrutiny. The Special Agent admitted on cross-examination that this was the first time he had ever recommended prosecution where depreciation was alleged to have been fraudulently determined. The Court of Appeals, in August, 1967, more than eight years after the official harassment of a man for his political beliefs, threw out the conviction.

SOME PARAGRAPHS ON SENTENCES

The Case of Vincent Scott

Sentencing procedures in the United States are almost never subject to the scrutiny of appellate courts. "For more than 70 years," according to Chief Judge David L. Bazelon of the United States Court of Appeals in Washington, D.C., "federal appellate courts have declared themselves impotent to modify sentences imposed within statutory limits." The theory, if there is a theory, is that the discretion to fix sentences for convicted criminals is within the exclusive province of the trial judge—without threat of reversal. This peculiar rule leads to wildly inconsistent types of sentences and a patchwork system of sanctions throughout the country.

Just how unregulated is the trial judge's power to sentence unlawfully can be illustrated by a rare case in which the judge was held by a higher court to have exceeded his authority. Vincent Scott, eighteen years old, was convicted of robbing a bus driver with a toy pistol in the District of Columbia. His codefendant pleaded guilty and was spared a trial. Following the trial, Scott was brought before federal District Judge John J. Sirica (now Chief Judge of the District Court for the District of Columbia) for a hearing, as required by law. At that hearing, Judge Sirica repeatedly stated he did not believe Scott's testimony at trial. He also obviously did not believe Scott's continued protestations of innocence. Nor, for that matter, was Judge Sirica pleased that Scott had made the Government resort to a trial in the first place:

"Now the Court didn't believe your story on the stand," Judge Sirica said; "the Court believes you deliberately lied in this case. If you had pleaded guilty to this offense, I might have been more lenient with you." The judge went on to say that Scott's sentence would be compatible with others in like cases: "I have to think of those other men I imposed sentences of five to fifteen years, four to twelve, etc. What would they think if I gave him a light sentence?"

When Scott heard these remarks, he gave the judge a letter his attorney had written, relating the story of the attorney's visit to Judge Sirica's law clerk. According to the attorney, the law clerk thought "there was only one way to get a light sentence from Judge Sirica and that was to confess that you did the robbery, to apologize four or five times and to say that you were willing to turn over a new leaf."

This statement was corroborated by the clerk himself, when Judge Sirica called him to the hearing. Said the clerk: "I told [defense] counsel that I had heard you mention in court . . . that you are waiting for the day when someone would come into this court and say they were guilty at sentence, that when a jury finds a man guilty and it is clear a man is guilty they only do themselves a disservice by maintaining they are innocent, and consequently it has always been my opinion you view sentencing differently when someone admits guilt rather than maintaining innocence. . . . This has nothing to do with private conversations we have had in chambers. It is from things I have heard while sitting in that seat during sentencing hearings."

Judge Sirica did not deny the thrust of any of these comments; he confirmed them: "I have said more than one time, I have said it in open court, it is a strange thing to me that a defendant who comes up after getting the benefit of good representation, trial before jury, the evidence being overwhelming as it is in this case, I hope sometime I hear some defendant say, 'Judge, I am sorry, I am sorry for what I did.' That is what I have in mind . . . I didn't tell [the clerk] or anyone else I would throw the book at [defendant] or anyone else if he didn't come up to confess. . . . He has a perfect right to maintain his innocence from now to eternity if he wants to. I am doing what I think is right." Whereupon Scott was given the maximum sentence: prison for five to fifteen years.

The Court of Appeals reversed and remanded the case to Judge Sirica for a rehearing on the sentence only. To pressure a convicted defendant into admitting guilt by threatening a heavier sentence if no confession is made is equivalent to forcing the defendant to forego his right against self-incrimination. Confession of guilt would moot any appeal following trial. Moreover, having spoken to the contrary during trial, defendant's admission thereafter would be tantamount to confessing perjury. To impose a heavier sentence because the judge believes perjury has been committed is tantamount to the imposition of a criminal penalty without trial. Finally, awarding a heavier sentence because the defendant forced the Government to try the case ("If you had pleaded guilty to this offense, I might have been more lenient with you") is to impose a price tag on the exercise of fundamental constitutional rights, a price the appellate court thought illegitimate in this case.

On remand, Judge Sirica announced the same sentence that he had given originally, but he neglected to specify that the sentence was under the Youth Correction Act, which in practical terms meant he was giving a longer sentence than before. When it was hurriedly pointed out by embarrassed Government counsel that the judge could not do that, Judge Sirica simply awarded the original sentence, without giving his reasons.* The case was noted for appeal once more. Judge Sirica was saved from further difficulty by the unfortunate fact of Scott's subsequent and untimely murder; his death rendered the appeal moot.

What underlay the Scott case was the policy of "plea bargaining," currently a hot problem in criminal jurisprudence: whether and under what circumstances it is permissible for prosecutors to negotiate with suspects for guilty pleas to lesser offenses (often never committed) in return for "promises" of leniency. This is not the place to explore the difficulties of the problem: on the one hand it permits prosecutors to bring heavy pressure against possibly innocent defendants; on the other, it allows the judicial system to breathe, free from the staggering load that would descend on it if every case had to be tried. Suffice it to say that the process stylizes and ritualizes the act of forced perjury, which is committed every day in state and federal criminal courts across the country.

---

* As the law permits him to do. Indeed, if Judge Sirica had kept quiet during the first sentencing, it is unlikely that it would have been upset on appeal.

Yankee Independence

Judicial contempt for the law is not confined to Washington, D.C., of course; it's just that judges there have such obvious models to pattern themselves after. A 1970 study of the lower criminal courts of metropolitan Boston, by the Lawyers Committee for Civil Rights Under Law, turned up much the same kind of disregard by judges for legal procedures. Boston, is, after all, the home of Yankee independence. Thus, despite the universal rule concerning the burden of proof, one judge resolved a difficult case by saying: "Well, I don't know who to believe. Just to be safe I'll find you guilty."

The district courts of Boston are regarded by the law as so inferior that any defendant is entitled to have his case retried before a higher court. The right to retry the case is clear and absolute. Judges normally manage to forestall the retrial by proceeding as follows: "The court sentences you to six months in the house of correction. The sentence is suspended. If you appeal, the sentence will be imposed." Or: "The court sentences you to six months in the house of correction. You have the right to appeal. Not appealing, the sentence will be suspended."

Not merely will sentence be imposed if the defendant exercises his right to ask for a new trial, but some judges will even increase the sentence, as the following indicates: "You ask him if he wants to pay the money back. If not I'll sentence him to six months on the island. If he wants to appeal, I'll make it a year." The law in Boston is summed up best by the judge who declared: "We don't follow those Supreme Court decisions here."

3
Crimes Affecting Groups

CIVILIAN DISSIDENTS

THE UNITED STATES has a long history of welcoming dissent in the abstract and punishing it in the concrete. Local vigilantes—private citizens and public officials alike—have tarred and feathered nonconformists from the beginning of the Republic. Lynching was a publicly accepted form of official murder of blacks and other minorities in the South and many other states. In 1933, California Governor James Rolph, Jr., stated for the record his approval of the lynching of two people suspected of kidnapping and murder. Said Governor Rolph: "I believe that it was a fine lesson to the whole Nation. If anyone is arrested for the good job, I'll pardon them all." Only relatively recently brought to a halt, lynching was revived in the late 1960's in a new and equally deadly form by policemen in Chicago and elsewhere.

More than 320 vigilante movements have been catalogued in the United States since the first outburst in Piedmont, South Carolina, in 1767. These movements have perpetrated violent episodes, from attacks against ethnic and racial minorities to massacres in the name of political principle. Every minority group in the United States has been subjected to criticism that at some time and place has erupted into violence against it.

A long history of violence does not, of itself, prove that the Government will not tolerate dissent. Vigilantes are extralegal; they are not usually organs of the Government, though local law enforcement officials have often been members of vigilante groups. Quite simply, vigilante action is citizen anarchy, often aimed against supposed radicals who, it is thought, would destroy the lawful organs of government themselves. To save a principle, you must destroy it—that is the essence of the vigilante philosophy. So fearful and violent have vigilante movements been, including the renascent Ku Klux Klan, that the Government has often been unable to bring these anarchists to account.

Often, however, police and local law enforcement officials have been willing accomplices. The 1964 slayings of the three civil rights workers, James E. Chaney, Andrew Goodman, and Michael H. Schwerner, were carried out largely through the cooperation and planning of Mississippi officials. In recent years, as a result of violence in Chicago, at Kent State in Ohio, and at Jackson State in Mississippi, there has been a growing realization that brutal assaults, the killing of unarmed students, and bullet holes in the backs of blacks without weapons, were not pristine and lawful acts of a benevolent Government. Still, they were acts perpetrated in the heat of the moment, by groups that, if they were not asking for death, were nevertheless itching for action. That does not excuse wanton murder, but if twelve honest bishops were to sit in judgment on the police and troops who did the shooting, convictions of second-degree murder would be a distinct possibility.

But mass violence may not be the best example of the Government's illegal intolerance of dissenters. When mobs are formed and shots are fired the ensuing rhetoric becomes as hot as the death and carnage that induced it, and it becomes difficult to prove clearly and dispassionately that the blame was one-sided and that the destruction and killing were direct results of the Government's inability to abide by the law.

More telling are examples of premeditated unlawful governmental repression of legitimate dissent. In times of crisis, people tend to think that order is more necessary than law; often crisis is defined simply by the audible amount of dissent in society. At the very time respect for law is most necessary, it is all too often least respected.

Congress, for example, has passed wartime laws restricting the freedom to speak and to dissent, making it possible for prosecutors and courts to equate doubts about the wisdom of the course the Government was pursuing with overt acts of sedition, disloyalty, and overthrow. Although some of these laws were later declared unconstitutional by the Supreme Court, they were very effective in snuffing out freedom during crisis.

The Sedition Act passed during World War I lingered on for years, but it did its most extensive damage shortly after the war when the incumbent Attorney General, A. Mitchell Palmer, converted the law of the United States into a tool of frenzy fed by public hysteria over a supposed Communist threat. The same pattern occurred after World War II, culminating in the Internal Security Act of 1950, which contained, according to one commentator, "more provisions held unconstitutional and unworkable than any other statute in our history." Even so, laws do not become unconstitutional until the Supreme Court so declares them: everyone knows in retrospect that slavery was brutal; what counts is what we acknowledge of contemporary events to be unlawful.

The Blunt End of the Law

On December 4, 1969, at 2237 West Monroe Street in Chicago, shortly after 4:30 A.M., police broke into an apartment and killed two members of the Black Panther Party. The State's Attorney, Edward Hanrahan, protégé of Mayor Richard Daley, described the police as brave, restrained, and disciplined. Police claimed that they were searching for illegal weapons, that they were fired upon as soon as they entered the apartment, and that they retaliated with submachine gun fire. According to Hanrahan: "As soon as Sgt. Daniel Groth and Officer James Davis, leading our men, announced their office, occupants of the apartment attacked them with shotgun fire. The officers immediately took cover. The occupants continued firing at our policemen from several rooms within the apartment. Thereafter, three times Sgt. Groth ordered all his men to cease fire and told the occupants to come out with their hands up. Each time, one of the occupants replied 'shoot it out,' and they continued firing at the police officers. Finally, the occupants threw down their guns and were arrested." In order to subdue the nine people within the apartment, police fired dozens of shots.

It might have been simply another shoot-out in Chicago's colorful criminal history. But this was a planned predawn raid against members of a self-styled revolutionary party, and the contradictions that arose between the police story and that of the survivors lent an ominous credence to charges of police criminality. So riddled was the apartment with bullet holes at so many angles that the police version of the slaying of Fred Hampton and Mark Clark reads something like the Ptolemaic theory: enough epicycles will account for any degree of complex movement. But the far greater likelihood is that the simpler the explanation, the greater the truth. An independent commission, whose co-chairmen were Roy Wilkins, president of the National Association for the Advancement of Colored People, and Ramsey Clark, former Attorney General, concluded in a 1971 report that the events could be characterized as "slaughter and summary execution."

Among the contradictions between the police and Panther versions were these:

¶ *Front door bullet holes.* The living room door had two bullet holes. One was four feet from the ground and came from a bullet fired from the outside into the living room. The other, only 30 inches from the ground, came from a shotgun blast that appeared, from the angle of the shot, to have been fired by someone lying on the floor. The police said nothing about the first hole. They said that two officers broke down the door after the shotgun was fired through it, but they did not explain why, if shots were being fired, they entered the room in so foolhardy a manner. The other explanation fits the facts more closely: Mark Clark was found dead behind the door, a bullet wound in the chest at about the height where the first bullet entered the door, had he been standing. The shotgun hole could then have been caused by a wild shot from inside before the police broke in.

¶ *The living room wall.* The south wall was riddled with 42 bullet holes from a machine gun and a .45 calibre weapon. The shots could only have been fired from the doorway and the middle of the room. Some of the bullets went through two rooms. The police say that after two more shotgun blasts were fired a policeman wounded a girl in the bed from which the shotgun was fired and turned and killed Clark. In a second police version, given to the *Chicago Tribune,* the police said the machine gun was used for covering fire. In a third police version, which Hanrahan staged for television, the machine gun was fired manually, one bullet at a time, to answer fire coming from the adjoining bedroom. Unfortunately for the police accounts, there was not a single trace of any gun's having been fired from the bed, nor was there evidence of any shooting from the inside bedroom, except for one bullet hole of uncertain origin. The actual explanation may simply be that the police fired into the wall, heedless of who was behind it, to forestall anyone who might have thought of shooting.

¶ *The back door.* The back door, a kitchen window, and a window and door leading to Hampton's room were broken from the outside. The police claimed they had been fired on, and showed photographs of the kitchen doorframe and a bathroom door with bullet holes. Upon inspection, however, it turned out that the police had willfully given the press fraudulent evidence: the holes in the kitchen doorframe were nail holes, and the purported bathroom door was actually a bedroom door that police had punctured with machine gun fire.

¶ *An early autopsy.* The police claimed that Hampton was found dead in bed. His death was caused by two bullets, both of which entered the skull in a downward direction, one entering above an eye and another below an ear. An independent autopsy conducted shortly after the killing showed that Hampton had been shot from above.

The word of authority is usually more believable than the word of dissenters and disrupters. But the American public had been treated to televised acts of police lawlessness too frequently in the past years to believe that Hanrahan's story was the whole truth. The following year, after more contradictions arose, indictments against the remaining Panthers were dropped. In 1971, Hanrahan himself and some of the police involved in the shoot-out were indicted for obstruction of justice.*

Shortly after the violence attending the National Democratic Convention in Chicago in 1968, a group of off-duty New York policemen assaulted a small number of Black Panthers and their sympathizers as they were making their way to a courtroom on the sixth floor of the Brooklyn Criminal Court. Some one hundred and fifty white men, many of whom were policemen out of uniform, were proceeding to a hearing for Panthers arrested for assaulting a policeman. As the Panthers and their unarmed escorts approached the hearing room, the mob surged forward and began to attack. Many of the policemen carried weapons under their coats; two of the victims were struck by blackjacks that caused blood to flow freely from their heads.

No arrests were made, though on-duty policemen quickly restored order. The next day, New York City Police Commissioner Howard R. Leary issued a formal statement, which read in part as follows: "This department will not tolerate any unlawful actions on the part of the individual police officers on or off duty, and when the situation warrants, violators will be arrested." Elliot L. Golden, Chief Assistant District Attorney for Brooklyn, conducted an investigation and impaneled 'a grand jury to hear evidence. Aaron E. Koota, the District Atorney, did not associate himself with the investigation, having just been nominated to state judicial office by the Democratic, Republican, and Liberal Parties. No indictments were ever returned, and the investigation concluded quietly.

The *Walker Report* to the National Commission on the Causes and Prevention of Violence has amply documented the capacity of some policemen to use unlawful and excessive force in putting down riots. Pedestrians, journalists, photographers, and dissidents alike were indiscriminately attacked and beaten into submission in Chicago at the 1968 Democratic Convention. Not all policemen went out of control, of course, but then neither were all those attacked implicated in the behavior that was being quashed.

According to the *Walker Report,* for example, a priest in the crowd told of a "boy, about 14 or 15, white, standing on top of an automobile yelling something which was unidentifiable. Suddenly a policeman pulled him down from the car and beat him to the ground by striking him 3 or 4 times with a night stick. Other police joined in . . . and they eventually shoved him to a police van. A well-dressed woman saw this incident and spoke angrily to a nearby police captain. As she spoke

---

* At the time this book went to press, Hanrahan had not yet stood trial.

another policeman came up from behind her and sprayed something in her face with an aerosol can. He then clubbed her to the ground. He and two other policemen then dragged her along the ground to the same paddy wagon and threw her in."

The *Walker Report* took the testimony of an Assistant United States Attorney who related of the same Chicago disturbances that "the demonstrators were running as fast as they could but were unable to get out of the way because of the crowds in front of them. I observed the police striking numerous individuals, perhaps 20 to 30. I saw three fall down and then overrun by the police. I observed two demonstrators who had multiple cuts on their heads. We assisted one who was in shock into a passerby's car."

The Disorderly House of Effete Intellectuals

Police misbehavior is not confined to the outdoors in the midst of emotional demonstrations nor to attacks against self-styled revolutionaries. In their attempts to deter people from meeting together to discuss their grievances with governmental policy, Minneapolis police (with the active cooperation of their superiors in the District Attorney's office) have raided a private home on the pretext that it was a "disorderly house."

In May, 1970, Dr. David T. Lykken, a clinical psychologist and professor at the University of Minnesota, held a meeting in his home to raise funds for a group that wanted to halt construction of a missile base in Nakoma, North Dakota. An announcement of the meeting had been posted on the University Bulletin Board; the flyer indicated a "donation and cash bar."

The day before the Saturday-night meeting police officers who had obtained a copy of the flyer consulted with Edward Vavreck, an Assistant City Attorney of Minneapolis. He told them that the evidence was insufficient to permit a search warrant to be issued. Police decided, therefore, to catch Dr. Lykken in the act.

At 10:00 on Saturday night, two police officers in plain clothes came to the Lykken home, engaged in conversation with one of the guests, and "purchased or acquired several bottles of beer." After observing baskets for donations, three women drinking beer or liquor, and most of the guests watching the late news on television, the two officers regrouped outside, where they met other policemen who were waiting to participate in the planned raid. At 11:30, with seventeen guests left in the house (at its peak, the party consisted of no more than thirty people), nineteen policemen entered the house without a search warrant and proceeded to look through every cranny (and toilet bowl) of its three stories. Outside a number of squad cars and two paddy wagons waited. Along with some bottles of beer and liquor, the police seized, in the words of a county judge who presided over a subsequent trial:

> Soft drinks, moneys in the form of currency and checks, two boxes containing numerous articles including, among others: 1. A study belonging to the National Institute of Mental Health apparently the property of the federal government. 2. Files and records including names and addresses of volunteers working for the American Civil Liberties Union, who had been observing (as any citizen is invited to do) the proceedings of the Hennepin County Municipal Court. 3. Buttons with the words, "Stop A.B.M." 4. A Minneapolis public school study of integration. 5. About 5 forms entitled, "For Peace. Earl Craig" [Craig was Senator Hubert H. Humphrey's opponent in the Minnesota primary that spring]. 7. A floor plan of the building located at a church camp at Cass Lake. 8. An envelope addressed to defendant David T. Lykken from the Journal of Nervous and Mental Diseases. 9. A copy of a work published by Berkeley Unified School District. 10. Four issues of the "Progressive" dated January, 1969, June, 1969, July, 1969, and October, 1968. 11. A sealed envelope to Mrs. David Lykken from "Clergy and Laymen Concerned about Viet Nam." 12. One copy, "Nation's Business Magazine," edition of March, 1970. 12. A manila envelope containing material relating to the University of Minnesota strike. 14. One manila envelope containing correspondence with one Mr. Chesterton. 15. A brown folder containing conservation materials and magazines of various conservation groups. 16. An envelope from "First Universalist Church of Minneapolis," addressed to Mrs. Lykken. 17. Posters, minutes of school meetings, various professional papers relating to the field of psychiatry and psychology. 18. Pamphlets, materials and cards relating to the war in Viet Nam. 19. Twenty-two copies of printed cards entitled, "Know Your Rights" published by "Minnesota Civil Liberties Union Foundation."

Dr. Lykken (but not his wife) and the remaining seventeen guests were taken off to police headquarters, where Dr. Lykken was charged with "operating a disorderly house" and with "selling liquor without a license." Mrs. Lykken and the seventeen guests were charged with "participating in a disorderly house." Eleven days later the various books, papers, letters, and other items unrelated to the charges were placed in a sealed box.* Vavreck, the Assistant City Attorney, told Hennepin County Municipal Court Judge David R. Leslie that the defendants' complaint about the seizure was meaningless because the materials were to be returned within a week to ten days. (Dr. Lykken privately asked Vavreck whether he could burglarize the City Attorney's home so long as the stolen items were later returned. Vavreck thought the analogy neither amusing nor relevant.)

---

* The box is to remain sealed pending a civil suit filed against the police by the unhappy citizens.

Jon Prentiss, Chief of the Minneapolis Police Morals Squad, said the raid was "a normal, common, every-day arrest." Prentiss said that neither Mayor Charles Stenvig (a former police chief and a tough law-and-order candidate in 1968) or Police Chief Basil Lutz had been briefed prior to the raid, which was conducted without a search warrant because, according to Prentiss, the notice on the University board made the party a "public gathering." The director of the raid, Officer Kenneth Tidgwell, called Dr. Lykken a communist in front of several guests, when Dr. Lykken sought to restrain the police from opening his mail by asking Tidgwell whether he realized he was "behaving like a Nazi storm trooper."

In September, 1970, Judge Leslie ordered two of the charges dismissed. Minnesota law is unequivocally clear that to sustain a charge of violating the ordinance entitled "participating in a disorderly house," there must be a showing that the unlawful acts are "habitually permitted on the premises." The Minnesota Supreme Court, earlier interpreting the Minneapolis disorderly ordinance, had said that "the commission of single or isolated disorderly or immoral acts on the premises does not constitute the place a disorderly house within the meaning of the penal laws."

In dismissing two of the charges Judge Leslie said:

It is sheer nonsense to equate this meeting with the ordinary tippling house raid. . . . Moreover the flyer which openly announced the meeting to be held is quite similar to the kind of invitation most of us observe or receive from candidates for political office from both political parties and for those running without political party designation, or from fund raisers, for various causes. The only difference being the politically sophisticated avoid such words as "cash bar" and substitute such words as refreshments and donations. It is difficult not to speculate as to whether there would have been such a raid and warrantless search had this been a fund raising party for an alderman, mayor, legislator, congressman, etc., of any political persuasion. . . . It is sufficient to emphasize this was obviously a very peaceful meeting and that no neighbors complained. The officer speaks of a serious discussion with one of the defendants on conservation of our natural resources, and there are no charges of profanity, resisting arrest, assault or breach of peace. Defendants, from all the facts before this court as to the two charges, were clearly exercising their constitutional right to gather together and ask their friends to join with them in protesting a government policy with which they honestly disagreed. This right is the very essence of democratic government.

The third charge (unlawful selling of liquor) was dismissed by another municipal judge in November.*

* For a further discussion of the police and other official responses to the Minneapolis raid, see Chapter 7, page 225.

Raids and searches without warrants against dissident groups are not uncommon. In tiny Telluride, Colorado, population 521, town Marshal Everett Morrow conducted a raid on a house suspected of harboring local hippies. Although there had been undercover investigative work carried out in 1971 by the county deputy sheriff, the raid, which apparently netted some marijuana, was conducted first and a search warrant was procured later. Marshal Morrow drives his car around the old silver camp town with a bumper sticker reading: "If you don't like cops, the next time you're in trouble call a hippie."

Fomenting Unrest and the Frame-up

The response of law-enforcement officials to behavior that they personally detest is not limited to summary corporal punishment and raids without basis. Another popular form of police lawbreaking is the "roust." To keep people off the streets, to deter them from activity which is lawful, and to subdue dissent, the police in many cities at different times have been known to sweep the streets and make arrests without basis. This dragnet type of operation is clearly unlawful because the police cannot legally arrest without having a reasonable belief that a crime has been committed; the courts universally recognize this law when they release those arrested several hours or days later. But during the interim the innocent as well as the guilty are deprived of their liberty.*

The use of informants by police and other law-enforcement agencies can lead to an even more devastating form of official lawlessness: entrapment and the frame-up. The courts have long held it unlawful for the police to induce a person to commit a crime that he otherwise would not be disposed to commit.

To be sure, the line between helping an illegal scheme along and actually creating it is a thin one. While it is permissible for agents to purchase narcotics from pushers in order to have evidence on hand to convict them, it is not lawful for agents and informants to foment crime themselves. It would be unlawful, for instance, for agents themselves to walk down the streets selling dope and arresting those who made the purchases. Yet with the increasing use of agents and informants by police and the FBI it has become increasingly clear that the tempo of demonstrations and violence has been increased by Government agents themselves.

In a New York case, for instance, a jury acquitted a number of black militants because the facts showed that the police agent who infiltrated the group had actually committed the illegal acts charged to the mili-

---

* National attention was focused on this tactic following the 1971 Mayday arrests in Washington, D.C. See pp. 115 ff.

tants. A police informer in Alabama committed arson, and the fire was then used as the pretext for the arrest of dissident university students.

A case that gained some notoriety was that against a former New York City prosecutor, Michael H. Metzger, who went to California to become a criminal defense lawyer. Having played the game himself for several years, Metzger knew every conceivable defense for accusations and charges made against his clients; he was successful in destroying many a prosecutor's case.

In 1970, pursuant to a search warrant, police found four and one-half ounces of marijuana, one-quarter ounce of cocaine, and more than one hundred tablets of suspected drugs in his home. Metzger was charged with illegal possession; he claimed the drugs were those seized in connection with his clients' cases and that they were awaiting laboratory tests. The search warrant was based on testimony of one Jerold N. MacDonald, who said he saw Metzger smoke marijuana while he was in Metzger's home as a client to discuss a stolen gun charge on which he had been arrested some months before. MacDonald turned out to be a paid Government informer, who had been brought to the office of Alfred Teixeira, the leader of the agents searching Metzger's home. State narcotics agent Gerritt Van Raam promised MacDonald that charges against him would be dismissed if he could produce any information which would lead to Metzger's arrest. Van Raam took MacDonald to Teixeira three days before Metzger's arrest. Van Raam's motive was simple: Metzger had charged him with perjury in an unrelated narcotics case and Van Raam had been ordered to take a liedetector test the very day he arranged for MacDonald to talk to Teixeira and contact Metzger. Three days after Metzger's arrest, charges against MacDonald were dropped and the inquiry into Van Raam's alleged perjury was suspended.

At a preliminary hearing on the charges against Metzger, Teixeira said he had discussed the perjury charges with Van Raam and had paid MacDonald $50 to pose as Metzger's client. Van Raam, it developed, was intimately involved in shepherding MacDonald to Metzger's house and in returning him to the District Attorney's office and to a judge's house to secure a search warrant. The charges against Metzger were dismissed. The stated grounds were the fraudulent representation by MacDonald that he wished to be Metzger's client but the real reason for the dismissal is obvious: a police frame-up.

Guilty Because You Disagree

If the Government cannot always frame its defendants, it can attempt to prejudice their rights by the simple expedient of publicizing the case. Thus, in the federal case against the Rev. Phillip F. Berrigan and others on charges of conspiring to kidnap Henry A. Kissinger, National Security Advisor to President Nixon, FBI Director J. Edgar Hoover first accused Berrigan in public before an indictment had been handed down.

Several weeks later, when a federal grand jury saw fit to issue an indictment, the Government attempted to buttress its case by releasing the text of letters, which were to be evidenced in the case. Indictments handed down later contained the text of the letters. Defense attorneys have occasionally been held in contempt for trying their cases in the newspapers, but the Justice Department said merely that it was "not an uncommon practice" to disclose evidence in advance of the trial.

Despite its self-serving declaration, the Department was hard pressed to name a case in which the common practice had been used; John Wilson, a Justice Department spokesman, could name no case in which the Government had ever released in advance of trial the text of a threatening letter that would be a central part of the evidence in the case, nor could he name a case in which any other evidence was released. The reason he could not was because the practice is illegal.

Police and prosecutors are not the only violators of the rights of citizens. Judges have played a large role in shaping the legal reaction to dissent. Federal District Judge George H. Boldt * of Tacoma, Washington, for one, simply refused to go along with an order of the Court of Appeals directing him to set bail for the so-called Seattle Seven, defendants in a conspiracy trial pending before his court. In the face of a clear mandate by the Ninth Circuit Court of Appeals, Judge Boldt decided to take the law into his own hands and keep the defendants locked up.

Incidents such as this are numerous. An all-too-typical case of judicial contempt for the law occurred in the courtroom of Judge James E. Rea of the People's Court of Prince Georges County, Maryland, in May, 1971. A husky, six-foot University of Maryland student and his classmate, a petite girl, were on trial for assault.

The case developed one afternoon over an altercation near a Marine recruiting booth on campus. The young lady was manning her own nonmilitary booth and seeking contributions to a charity. Sitting immediately behind her was a bearded, slightly built student holding a sign bearing the legend "Join the Marines, Kill for Peace." The male defendant, a veteran, chanced to walk past the recruiting booth and saw the picketer sitting on a railing. Enraged, he lunged behind the girl and grabbed for the sign and its holder, pulling both toward the ground. After ripping up the sign he proceeded to beat up the picketer.

---

* Named by President Nixon as chairman of the Phase II Pay Board.

Horrified at the wanton mayhem, the girl picked up the nearest object at hand, a four-page issue of the University of Maryland student newspaper, and twisting it into a bat proceeded to swat the assailant on his shoulder. He brushed her aside and continued to beat the student underfoot until he was pulled off by a crowd that gathered.

The picketer brought charges of assault against the veteran; the veteran in turn brought charges of assault against the girl. Both wound up in Judge Rea's court.

A Maryland statute permits a person to go to the aid of one who for any reason is the subject of an assault. But despite that statute and the testimony of the veteran himself (who said that he had laughed at her feeble physical attempt to dissuade him from his attack), Judge Rea found her guilty of assault, after delivering a lengthy tirade against students, motorists, and other evil-doers. In the course of his discussion he remarked that he could not understand why it was that the Supreme Court had ever let students have constitutional rights. When his soliloquy was over and he had announced his finding of guilt, Judge Rea was reminded that the veteran too was before him on the same charge, with slightly weightier evidence against him. The Judge had no alternative but to find him guilty as well. Fortunately, People's Court is so insignificant in Maryland that anyone may choose to have his case retried merely by asking. Unfortunately, the cost of retrial was prohibitive and the girl's conviction stands. It should not cost money to vindicate rights that should be obvious.

Domestic Subversives, We're Listening to You

In 1928, the Supreme Court ruled in *Olmstead* v. *United States* that governmental wiretapping is not barred by the Fourth Amendment's prohibition against unreasonable searches and seizures. Writing for the bare five-man majority, Chief Justice Taft distinguished the search of a room or home and the seizure of particular papers or things from the eavesdropping brought about by telephone wiretaps.

The case itself was a contradiction in terms since the evidence leading to a conviction under the Volstead Act was obtained through wiretaps unlawful in the state of Washington, where the tapping occurred. Because the Supreme Court read the Fourth Amendment restrictively, the fruits of the unlawful wiretap were not excluded from the trial; at stake was a mere rule of evidence.

In a noted dissent Justice Brandeis thought the Court majority unwarranted in its narrow reading of the constitutional prohibition against unreasonable searches and seizures. He went on to say that "independently of the constitutional question, I am of opinion that the judgment should be reversed. By the laws of Washington, wire-tapping is a crime.

To prove its case, the Government was obliged to lay bare the crimes committed by its officers on its behalf. A federal court should not permit such a prosecution to continue. . . . Decency, security, and liberty alike demand that government officials shall be subjected to the same rules of conduct that are commands to the citizens."

Six years later Congress enacted the Federal Communications Act of 1934, absolutely prohibiting wiretapping. Section 605 contained the following provision:

> No person not being authorized by the sender shall intercept any communication and divulge or publish the existence, contents, substance, purport, effect, or meaning of such intercepted communication to any person.

In 1937 the Supreme Court ruled that prohibitions in §605 of the Communications Act applied to Government officials as well as to private persons.

Notwithstanding the strict wording of the law, which remained unmodified until 1968, the Justice Department has followed a continuous course of violating the strictures of the statute. In 1940, President Roosevelt authorized his Attorney General, Frank Murphy, "to secure information by listening devices directed to the conversation or other communications of persons suspected of subversive activities against the Government of the United States, including suspected spies. You are requested to limit these investigations so conducted to a minimum and to limit them insofar as possible to aliens."

In 1946, Attorney General Tom C. Clark received President Truman's approval of recommendations Clark had presented to him. Clark's memorandum read in part as follows:

> It seems to me that in the present troubled period in international affairs, accompanied as it is by an increase in subversive activity here at home, it is as necessary as it was in 1940 to take the investigative measures referred to in President Roosevelt's memorandum. At the same time, the country is threatened by a very substantial increase in crime. While I am reluctant to suggest any use whatever of these special investigative measures in domestic cases, it seems to me imperative to use them in cases vitally affecting the domestic security, or where human life is in jeopardy.

For twenty-five years, until 1965, when President Johnson narrowed the permissible scope of wiretapping, the Department of Justice carried on a program that flagrantly violated the law of the United States. (Even the 1965 order did not do away with wiretapping altogether; it continued the so-called "national security" exception to §605 of the Communications Act.) As austere a civil libertarian as Ramsey Clark, an Attorney General who prided himself on successful investigations and prosecutions of federal criminal cases without the use of wiretaps or bugs, continues to insist on the distinction between wiretapping for foreign security purposes and for domestic purposes, while recognizing somewhat paradoxically the ease by which the words "national security" can be used as a cover to legitimize wiretapping for any purpose, no matter how unlawful.

More than occasionally, however, the Department of Justice has been caught in the act. In 1940, the new Attorney General Robert Jackson distinguished the act of tapping itself from the act of tapping-and-divulging. Thus, according to Jackson, it would be lawful for the Government to wiretap, but the Government could not divulge information so obtained. Divulgence to officials within the Government was not construed to be within the Act's terms because the Government was considered to be one solitary person. Unlawful wiretapping was therefore permitted to continue.

Just what kind of wiretapping was encompassed with the scope of the Attorney General's policy was revealed in the Judith Coplon case. Miss Coplon was an employee of the Justice Department, beginning her time there in 1943. In 1948, she was assigned to its Internal Security Section. Her mission: to examine FBI reports concerning the activities of foreign agents. In 1949, it became apparent to her superiors that she was transmitting or attempting to transmit information to Soviet agents.

The Department arranged for certain information to be made available to her on a confidential basis and she was followed to New York, where in the course of an afternoon, after several "furtive" and "remarkable" meetings with Valentin A. Gubitchev, a Russian agent, she was arrested on charges of espionage. She was tried separately in New York and the District of Columbia and convicted in both places. Her New York conviction was upset because the Court of Appeals agreed with Miss Coplon's contention that the FBI agents unlawfully arrested and searched her without the requisite warrants. Her Washington conviction was not thrown out on that ground, though it was premised on the same arrest.

Shortly after the court decision reversing the New York conviction, Congress noted the result and passed a law making it unequivocally clear that FBI agents were to have the power Congress presumed they always had to arrest under the circumstances then present. The appellate court ruled that Congress's action "made unmistakable what we think was true before revision" and construed the law at the time of the arrest, contrary to the New York interpretation, as permitting the agents to make the arrest.

The Court of Appeals for the District of Columbia Circuit did, however, upset the conviction. After her trial in Washington, Miss Coplon discovered evidence that led her to believe the FBI had tapped her home and office telephones in Washington and New York and that the

Bureau had been listening to her conversations before, during, and after trial. Among those overheard, Miss Coplon alleged, were conversations she had with her lawyer in preparation for the trials.

The FBI denied the charges, but the court ruled that such allegations, if proved, would establish the Government's violation of her constitutional right "to have the effective and substantial aid of counsel." The court remanded the case for a hearing on the question whether the Government had in fact carried on the eavesdropping. The rehearing was never held, nor did the Government ever attempt to retry Miss Coplon, who in the words of the federal court in New York was "clearly guilty."

The case was discussed sporadically in the newspapers and in Congress for some six years after the trial, and at one point Attorney General Herbert Brownell indicated that retrial depended upon the outcome of an effort in Congress to enact legislation permitting wiretapping in certain instances. The legislation did not pass, and the case was quietly dropped. The Government thus implicitly admitted breaking the law.

Though the *Coplon* case never went to the Supreme Court, many other instances of wiretapping did come under its scrutiny. In 1952 the Court refused to rule that evidence gathered in violation of the Communications Act by state officials must be excluded from state trials. Five years later the Court ruled that evidence gathered from state wiretaps could not be introduced in federal trials. In 1967 the Supreme Court overruled the old *Olmstead* case, holding at last that wiretaps are searches subject to the Fourth Amendment's requirement that searches and seizures be reasonable and that warrants authorizing them be premised on probable cause to believe that a crime has been committed.

One year later, the Court overruled its 1952 decision, now requiring that any evidence unlawfully gathered by wiretapping be excluded from any trial, state or federal.

In another 1967 case, a New York District Attorney, pursuant to a state statute permitting electronic eavesdropping upon the issuance of a warrant by a magistrate, sought and obtained an order permitting the installation of a "bug" for sixty days in the office of a person suspected of conspiring to bribe the Chairman of the State Liquor Authority. The Supreme Court ruled that the warrant was overly broad. Dissenting, Justice Byron R. White noted in passing that "the Court should draw no support from the Solicitor General's confession of error in recent cases, for they involved surreptitious eavesdropping by federal officers without judicial authorization. Such searches are clearly invalid because they violate the Fourth Amendment warrant requirements." The Justice Department's disregard for the law had become so cavalier that the

Solicitor General did not even care to make a perfunctory defense of the practice.

In 1968 Congress for the first time authorized wiretapping and eavesdropping pursuant to judicially sanctioned orders. The authority is contained in Title III of the Omnibus Crime Control and Safe Streets Act of 1968. Section 2511(3) gratuitously added that

> nothing contained in this chapter or Section 605 of the Communications Act of 1934 . . . shall limit the constitutional power of the President to take such measures as he deems necessary to protect the Nation against actual or potential attack or other hostile acts of a foreign power, to obtain foreign intelligence information deemed essential to the security of the United States, or to protect national security information against foreign intelligence activities. Nor shall anything contained in this chapter be deemed to limit the constitutional power of the President to take such measures as he deems necessary to protect the United States against the overthrow of the Government by force or other unlawful means, or against any other clear and present danger to the structure or existence of the Government. The contents of any wire or oral communication intercepted by authority of the President in the exercise of the foregoing powers may be received in evidence in any trial, hearing, or other proceeding only where such interception was reasonable, and shall not be otherwise used or disclosed except as is necessary to implement that power.

It is hardly likely that Congress could ever limit the constitutional power of the President or for that matter could ever create a power where none previously existed.

In 1969, the Supreme Court ruled that convictions obtained in a number of prosecutions had to be upset when evidence was uncovered that the Department of Justice had unlawfully eavesdropped on various defendants. The Court did not rule that the particular wiretaps were unconstitutional; but it did rule that since the Government had not disclosed at trial that the defendants had been subjected to eavesdropping, the cases would have to go back to the trial courts for a determination whether the particular eavesdropping was unlawful.

The Government conceded that it was required to turn over to the defendants "any surveillance records which are relevant" to the ultimate question of guilt and that "this disclosure must be made even though attended by potential danger to the reputation or safety of third parties or to the national security—unless the United States would prefer dismissal of the case to disclosure of the information." (This concession was necessitated by the recognized rule that the "fruits" of unlawfully gathered evidence cannot be used at trial.)

Though admitting the legal requirement to disclose information, the Government by its actions showed that it was willing to comply with the law only when caught in the act of breaking it. For the trials had gone to completion and conviction with nary a word from the Department of Justice that it had listened to the defendants' conversations.

It was also argued in these 1969 cases that the Justice Department could make the determination whether the records of conversations were "arguably relevant" to the prosecutions' cases. If the conversations were "arguably relevant," said the Department, it would turn the records over to defendants and their counsel. If in its judgment the records were not, the Department would hold them back.

The Court refused to permit the Government to make this determination. Since the object of disclosure is to permit the defendants to determine whether leads from any of the evidence unlawfully obtained were used to secure convictions, the purpose of the constitutional rule could obviously be thwarted by a Government that, by its very actions, was already guilty of violating the law and that might well do what it could to minimize its wrongdoing.* The Court held that the defendants were entitled to "the records of those overheard conversations which the Government was not entitled to use in building its case against them."

Since two of the 1969 cases involved conspiracy to transmit national defense information to Russia, Justice Department officials were obviously not pleased with the Court's decision. Fred R. Graham of the *New York Times* reported that Government attorneys were "stunned": "Officials had assumed [Graham wrote] that at least two of the Justices— Byron R. White [who wrote the majority opinion] and Thurgood Marshall [who did not participate in the cases]—would have known from their recent service in the Justice Department that the lines of a substantial number of embassies . . . have been illegally tapped for years, and that some are still being tapped. . . . It is understood that unless the Supreme Court agrees to change its ruling, the Justice Department could be forced to dismiss the convictions of Cassius Clay . . . [for] draft evasion, and the case of some or all of the group of four men, including Dr. Benjamin J. Spock and the Yale chaplain, William Sloane Coffin, who were convicted in Boston last year of conspiring to obstruct the Selective Service System." †

---

* Indeed, in a petition filed for rehearing, Solicitor General Erwin N. Griswold argued to the Court that unless the ruling was overturned, the Department of Justice might decide for itself which transcripts were relevant and simply refuse to tell the Justices of the existence of any other transcripts in future cases. Griswold implied that the only reason the Government was cooperating in disclosing the existence of such transcripts was the belief that the Court would be reasonable in permitting the Department to conduct unauthorized snooping.

† The convictions of Muhammed Ali (Cassius Clay) and Spock and Coffin were later reversed on other grounds.

A Court decision shortly thereafter qualified the apparent blanket requirement that the defendant be entitled in every case to examine every item of surveillance. Though a defendant is entitled to see transcripts of conversations in which he participated, he is not entitled to such records when he did not participate and the surveillance was not conducted on his property.

Two weeks after the first series of decisions, the Court ruled that a defendant was not entitled to question the trial judge's determination that certain disputed records of electronic surveillance did not in fact pertain to him. But it is important to note that, despite the welter of seemingly technical issues, behind the entire debate lay the Government's conceded habit of snooping on people without benefit of lawful authority.

Whether because of the 1968 language or despite it, Attorney General John N. Mitchell has asserted the inherent constitutional power of the President to order wiretaps and surveillance without prior court approval of domestic groups suspected of threatening the national security. No one doubts that this is an elastic concept; under an antecedent version of this theory, the FBI monitored private conversations of Martin Luther King for years. At any one time, according to annual testimony of J. Edgar Hoover before various Congressional appropriations committees, the Federal Government was conducting between fifty and one hundred wiretaps—and these in the days before any were legal.*

The Attorney General's argument has not fared well before the courts and in his brief to the Supreme Court, Solicitor General Griswold dropped the argument that the inherent constitutional power of the President permits the FBI to wiretap without prior court order. Instead, Griswold shifted the argument to the proposition that national-security wiretapping is an exception to the Fourth Amendment.

Either argument permits the President to break the law, but Solicitor General Griswold's proposition can only be characterized as disingenuous, since the only conceivable reason for national-security wiretapping to be an exception to the Fourth Amendment would be because the President has inherent power to safeguard the nation under these particular circumstances. If the Supreme Court fails to legitimize Attorney General Mitchell's position, it cannot be said that he did not at least try to supply a rationale for making lawful conduct that will surely be carried

---

* The statistics are themselves subject to disbelief. In 1971, the Justice Department said that in 1969, there had been forty-nine national security wiretaps (and related electronic surveillance) and in 1970, only thirty-six. The Department cited these figures as proof of the decline in such surveillance. Some months later, however, the actual figures were disclosed as ninety-four in 1969 and 113 for 1970. The Department accounted for the discrepancy by claiming the original figures were for surveillance at any one time—a qualification the Department did not bother to make when it released the lower set of figures.

on in any event, regardless of the language of federal statutes or Supreme Court decisions.*

Lest anyone come away with the idea that the Justice Department alone is responsible for unlawful monitoring of the conversations of private citizens, the Post Office Department deserves brief mention. The Department has had a curious policy called "the mail watch"—monitoring by postal inspectors of first class mail sent to persons listed by authorities on a so-called "mail cover."

This technique came to light in 1964 when an attorney for Roy Cohn (who had been indicted for perjury) discovered his mail was being watched. The attorney, Thomas A. Bolan, requested a hearing in federal district court on the issue. The United States Attorney compounded the lawbreaking by committing contempt of court, though it went unpunished: an official affidavit denied the prosecution's implication in the request to place the watch on Bolan's mail; an Assistant U.S. Attorney backed down at the hearing in response to a question from Judge Archie O. Dawson and admitted that his office had indeed instigated the mail cover on Bolan. Although the custom is old, dating back to 1893, there is no statutory sanction for the practice.

In 1965 a Senate Post Office Subcommittee held hearings on Post Office procedures. In another instance of perjury, this time before a Congressional committee, Chief Postal Inspector H. B. Montague said: "The seal on a first class piece of mail is sacred. A person puts first class postage on a piece of mail and seals it, he can be sure that the contents of that piece of mail are secure against illegal search and seizure."

The Senate subcommittee subsequently discovered that the Post Office Department had been delivering mail addressed to people with delinquent tax accounts to the Internal Revenue Service, whose agents proceeded to break the sacred seals of first class mail. The Post Office finally owned up to the practice, and in response Congress enacted specific legislation prohibiting seizure and opening of first class mail by anyone.

The habit of federal officials lying, either to Congress or to the American public, appears to be a common one in the area of Government surveillance of citizens. When the story first broke that since 1968 the Army had been spying on civilians, including candidates for federal office and members of Congress, Secretary of the Army Stanley Resor issued a blanket denial; some months later, presented with overwhelm-

---

* In 1972, the Department faced extreme embarrassment when it was revealed that more than three hundred wiretaps had been unlawfully authorized by persons within the department other than the Attorney General or a specially designated assistant, as required by the 1968 crime control act. A federal court of appeals reversed six convictions based on improperly authorized wiretaps.

ing evidence that the Army's spying program had been conducted on a vast scale, Mr. Resor grudgingly admitted that "some reports . . . could have contained the names" of various federal and state office holders.

Given the history of the Government to date, the luminous statement of then U.S. Assistant Attorney General William H. Rehnquist in 1971 that "self-discipline on the part of the executive branch will provide an answer to virtually all of the legitimate complaints against excesses of information gathering" is not merely ludicrous but indicative of the very mentality Rehnquist was supposed to be countering.

If self-discipline would do it, we would not only not need law but we would not need a government to administer it—nor would any complaints be "legitimate." Mr. Rehnquist neglected to point out that unlike private citizens, agents of the Government need rarely fear that the law will be enforced against them.

MILITARY DISSIDENTS

From the Navy's Arlington Annex in Virginia you can look across the Pentagon roof and see the Potomac River and much of Washington. The main entrance of the Annex fronts on the flank of Arlington National Cemetery where of an afternoon in the late '60's and early '70's gravediggers, flags, flowers, and bugles were not uncommon sights, until the massed colonnades of pure white tombstones threatened to encroach on the Henderson Hall Marine Corps Exchange parking lot.

The Annex is a series of eight long, drab buildings, or "wings," built on a sloping hill during World War II, when the naval establishment grew and spilled out of its "temporary" headquarters in Washington. The Annex serves mainly as home for the Commandant of the Marine Corps and his staff, for the Bureau of Naval Personnel (BuPers), and for the Office of the Judge Advocate General of the Navy (JAG). In 1970, when the federal Government grew jittery about walking bombers, guards were posted at the gates of the compound, but cars passed freely. Security was not tight.

In the middle of the long perpendicular wing in front that connects the eight other buildings is a conference room where, on a breezy day in May of 1970, Rear Admiral Donald D. Chapman, then the Deputy Judge Advocate General of the Navy, called a meeting of all junior officers and Division Directors attached to the Office of JAG. (The JAG himself was in Europe.) The subject: the mounting official worry about the newly discovered and growing Concerned Officers Movement (COM).

Admiral Chapman is a tall, gaunt Texan, a graduate of the Texas Technological College and the University of Texas Law School; he served as a line officer during World War II, becoming Commanding Officer of the U.S.S. PC 792 (Personnel Carrier), Staff Judge Advocate to the Commander Atlantic Fleet, and Legal Officer of the Fourteenth Naval District (Pearl Harbor) before getting his stars in the spring of 1968. He is a man of few words, and he speaks in a dry, blunt, nasal twang. Though outwardly calm, on this day he spoke nervously.

He opened the meeting by holding up a copy of a newsletter that had been distributed by COM; ridiculing it, he denied that there was any right within the military to dissent in this fashion. He said that COM's existence had come to the Navy's attention and that any among the group who had thoughts about joining it—or what might be worse, giving legal advice to members—had better disabuse themselves of any such notions. He added that he had no reason to believe that any of the officers at the meeting had any relation to the group at the present time. He wanted to forestall possibilities. Then he opened the floor for questions and discussion.

He got both. For more than one hour a controversy raged between the senior officers and the young lieutenants. One captain expressed his amazement that there could be any officer within the Navy who could or did disagree with Nixon's conduct of the war. He was severely rebuked by a number of juniors who suggested that such a position would not be entirely unreasonable. Feeling was particularly intense, in fact, because the very evening before the President had gone on national television to explain the invasion of Cambodia.

The political discussion was purely incidental to the legal issue. Not long after the discussion was underway, a soft-spoken lieutenant from Massachusetts rose to say that he had been to COM meetings. He explained that they were meetings only in the sense that young men met to discuss common feelings. The discussions were conducted in the evening during off-duty hours in the private homes of concerned officers. There was no denial that the newsletter had been published, but the lieutenant did categorically deny, somewhat paradoxically, that it was an attempt to influence Congressional action in contravention of Article 1247 of Navy Regulations, which reads as follows:

> Combinations of persons in the naval service for the purpose of influencing legislation, remonstrating against orders of details to duty, complaining of particulars of duty, or procuring preferences, are forbidden.

This Article was Admiral Chapman's rationale for concluding that the Concerned Officers Movement was unlawful, for it was obviously a combination, he said, whose aim was to influence legislation.

Thus, in COM's third newsletter of July, 1970, the following policy statement appeared:

> The concerned officers movement (COM) is made up of active duty officers in the Armed Forces who want to express responsible dissent on

the Indo-China war . . . all of us have served honorably in the Armed Forces. Many of us have served in Vietnam. We are only challenging encrusted traditions which have worked to make servicemen afraid to form and express their views on national problems.

To this end, we propose the following program:

1. To support the right of all servicemen to publicly express their views on matters of national concern.

2. To give speeches and join in debates in the community in which active duty officers express their opposition to the war.

3. To encourage all officers to join us in expressing their views on the war to the community and to the Department of Defense.

4. To seek support from civil leaders, retired officers, senators and congressmen.

For Admiral Chapman, the alternative was clear: one could "work within the system." That meant, he said, that naval officers could talk with the Secretary of the Navy, John Chafee, and they could write articles individually, expressing their views. Someone suggested that they might write something like the Naval Institute's 1970 Prize Essay entitled "Against All Enemies" by Captain Robert J. Hanks, U.S.N., but the sarcasm in the suggestion went unnoticed. Certainly, but Admiral Chapman would deny, for public consumption, that the implicit argument of the Hanks article was that Senators Fulbright, Case, Mondale, Mansfield, Symington, and Goodell were domestic enemies of the United States. This implication, if made—and many believed it was being made—would be a possible violation of Article 88 of the Uniform Code of Military Justice, proscribing the use of contemptuous words against Congress. Second Lieutenant Henry H. Howe of the Army suggested on a sign he had carried while picketing in 1965 that President Johnson was a fascist; for that Howe got two years under Article 88 (though he ultimately served only three months). Captain Hanks got a prize for his essay.

At any rate, the message of the morning meeting was unmistakable. As Admiral Chapman put it, membership of any sort, no matter how loose the affiliation, in or with COM, "is clearly illegal." Judge advocates of the Navy were not to give any legal advice to members of the Naval service, except to "give it to 'em straight"—meaning, of course, tell them that "it's clearly illegal." (After all, as one captain put it, "our client is the Navy.")

For judge advocates in the Washington area, the order not to give legal advice was not as surprising as it might seem, since there is an office of legal assistance in the Pentagon, staffed by Naval judge advocates, whose official duty is to render legal advice on a confidential basis to any personnel seeking legal help. What was surprising, and what did not come out at the meeting, was the order—clearly illegal itself— privately communicated to the lawyers in the legal assistance office that even they were not to provide legal counsel concerning COM to Naval personnel, except to suggest that they disaffiliate.

That afternoon, Lieutenant S., who had admitted attending some of COM's meetings, sought a discussion of the matter privately with Admiral Chapman. He was turned away with the words, "Go see Captain Rood."

Captain George H. Rood, U.S.N., was Assistant Chief for Performance of the Bureau of Naval Personnel, more popularly known as Pers.-F. Pers-F is the Smersh of BuPers. It carries on intelligence work. It maintains dossiers. It spies.

The next morning, Friday, Admiral Chapman sent for Lieutenant S. with an ultimatum: if he did not withdraw from COM, his name would be put on the Pers-F "list." That morning, CBS-TV news had broadcast video tapes of a COM news conference held the previous Wednesday evening. The officers at the meeting were dressed in civilian clothes, but their faces were clearly visible and they did not try to hide; they would have had no reason to do so, since they had invited the cameras into the home of one of their members.

Pers-F watched the broadcast, made tapes, pulled officer records, made dossiers, and put the names of all who were visible on a list. Lieutenant S. asked whether failure to withdraw meant court-martial. Admiral Chapman said he did not know; he read Article 1247 and remarked that at a later meeting on the same topic to another group of Navy lawyers the day before, he had been given an even harder time: some of the judge advocates had suggested that Article 1247 was unconstitutional.

Admiral Chapman told Lieutenant S. that he could not pass on whether the regulation was unconstitutional, but he did want, he said, "your answer now." Lieutenant S. asked for some time to think; Admiral Chapman allowed the weekend. On Monday, Lieutenant S. said he would continue with COM, and Admiral Chapman dismissed him from his office without another word.

Meanwhile, Pers-F had been busy. A week before, the Pers-F action officer, Lieutenant G., had obtained a copy of the newsletter and begun discussion with the signers. To one he made clear he had no personal relation with the Naval Investigative Service (NIS) but he did not disavow NIS activity. At a COM meeting shortly thereafter, to which he was invited, Lieutenant G. hinted that one of the members' apartments had been unlawfully searched, by commenting, "I notice you've changed shaving lotion."

This was to be the general tack. Lieutenant G. would come almost daily to Lieutenant S.'s office and attempt to "persuade" him to quit COM. "Of all these guys," he said more than once, "you're the one who can still be saved. . . . The Navy can go back into your childhood, dig out facts, ruin you for life. . . . Captain Rood wanted me to tell you one lawyer to another, a court-martial means disbarment for life."

Lieutenant G. once came up to the judge advocate's office and inspected a bamboo stick he found lying on a desk, remarking that he was checking it to make sure it was not bugged. Lieutenant G. monitored the friends of Lieutenant S.: he once went so far as to take a picture of another lawyer-lieutenant who sported a bushy mustache and who was seen talking to Lieutenant S. (because they worked in adjacent offices) and to ask around to see whether he could uncover any unlawful activity by the mustached officer. None was found.

Lieutenant G. played his badgering game three weeks. He came up one day to say that he had learned that the judge advocate had told Admiral Chapman at the Friday morning meeting that he was "COM's lawyer." The lieutenant responded that not only had there been no such discussion, but he did not know enough about this aspect of military law to advise.

Lieutenant G. came up another day to report that a couple of COM members had gone to a National Lawyers' Guild meeting. Did Lieutenant S. know that that group was on the Attorney General's list as a subversive organization? (It is not.)

Still another day Lieutenant G. came calling to say that the politically active wife of a well-known Navy officer was on the brink of getting a divorce from her husband. The woman had participated in picketing and protests and was known to some of the COM membership. One of the members called her up to confirm the rumor, and she hotly denied it.

On another occasion, Lieutenant G. said he had absolute authority to arrange any meetings between the concerned officers and Secretary Chafee. Such a possibility was favorably viewed; preparations were being made, Lieutenant G. said. A few days later the meeting was "imminent." The concerned officers who were to attend put their gripes in order, but in the end, there was never any meeting scheduled, nor any explanation, at least for this group.

Those being watched began, in their words, to "get psyched up about it." They told themselves they should not feel nervous, but no one who knows he is being watched can avoid developing the feeling of paranoia over time. Lieutenant S.'s wife began to develop daily fears that she would return home in the afternoon to find her apartment ransacked.

The contents of a message from BuPers to JAG were leaked to

Lieutenant S.: his name had been placed on a "don't promote or decorate" list along with the names of many other concerned officers and those deviant in other ways. The presence of his name on the list was immaterial since Navy judge advocates are not promoted during their initial period of obligated service. For the line officers, many of whom were ensigns and j.g.'s, the promotions, which should have been assured, were in serious doubt.

Vice-Admiral Charles Duncan, then the Chief of Naval Personnel, had agreed previously to keep on the promotion list those junior officers who had already been selected, though that would not prevent the Navy from simply releasing those men it did not want to keep, action the Navy ultimately took against several junior officers. When the policy of retaining the concerned officers on the promotion list came to the attention of James D. Hittle, Assistant Secretary of the Navy for Manpower and Reserve Affairs, Admiral Duncan's position was reversed (in the absence of Secretary Chafee, who was out of town). A later opinion, standing up to Hittle, stating that it would in fact be unlawful to take the action he wanted, was signed by the Judge Advocate General, who had returned from his month-long inspection tour of Europe. The names were restored to the list.

Finally, however, Lieutenant S. gave in. Three weeks after the initial meeting, he went to Admiral Chapman's office and said he was withdrawing from COM. His original purpose in meeting with other concerned officers, he said, was to go on record that he and others did not just do nothing in a time of turmoil, that they had done something about the war. But after much thought, he said, he realized that it was not wise to have officers on either side of the issue discussing national policy. If he could do it, so could admirals and generals who supported even more vigorous war.

He also began to realize, he said, that he did not know and could not know all the members of the burgeoning Movement; he did not want, for the sake of the right to discuss matters with his close friends, to be damned later on by associations over which he had no control. He did not want to throw away for all time his ability to be independent. The decision to sever his ties from the movement had been communicated, he assured the Admiral, to his friends still in.

Admiral Chapman smiled at last: "I don't know whether it's too late and I don't promise anything," he said, "but I'll go to bat for you." A few days after the JAG had returned from Europe, he offhandedly remarked when the lieutenant was in his office on an unrelated matter that he was glad to hear of the decision. And that was all, except for a call some months later from Lieutenant G. who said casually: "Someone just left a note on my desk that you're working with COM again. I wanted to check it out with you."

"Not that I know of," was the reply.

"O.K." said Lieutenant G., "I just wanted to check it out," and he disappeared, at least from the visible surface, of his judge advocate's life.

A minor incident in the busy flow of events in the United States Navy, and even more minor against the backdrop of more significant problems in the other services. No doubt. Except for the fact that Admiral Chapman himself belonged to an organization that violates Article 1247 as a matter of course.

The Judge Advocates Association, to which the Navy, Army, and Air Force Judge Advocates General, their deputies, and many other officers belong, is, in the words of a president, "the only association devoted primarily to the legal problems of the armed services and to the interests of the uniformed lawyer. It comprises over 1,500 dues-paying members and is thus larger than the bar associations of some 18 states. Its members comprise primarily active duty judge advocates and legal specialists, lawyer Reserve officers and retired military lawyers."

At joint hearings in 1966 before the Senate Subcommittee on Constitutional Rights and a Special Subcommittee of the Committee of Armed Services, Cmdr. Penrose L. Albright, USNR (Ret.), took a position on behalf of the association on seventeen pending Senate bills concerning military justice and military administrative and legal procedures. The express purpose of Cmdr. Albright's appearance before the subcommittees was to influence legislation; he made numerous suggestions for changes and revisions in the bills under discussion. None of the members of the Judge Advocates Association has even been court-martialed or released from the service for membership.

Other examples of military officers combining to influence legislation are not rare; such combinations may not be daily occurrences, but they do occur. For instance, in the spring of 1969, Rear Admiral Henry L. Miller, Commander of the Naval Air Test Center at Patuxent River, Maryland, called a meeting of all officers attached to his command to discuss various matters that had been brought up at a briefing in Washington a few days previously.

One of the topics was the fate of the ABM system, then in some doubt in the Senate. Admiral Miller pointed out to the several hundred officers assembled in the base movie theater that a tide of sentiment was running against the military in the nation and that it was up to the military to see that decisions adverse to the nation's interests were not made. He noted that the Patuxent River Naval Air Station was close to Washington (about seventy miles) and that many of the officers had occasion to travel to Washington frequently. He also noted the presence of Congress in Washington, remarked that many officers knew their Congressmen, and then suggested that the officers stop in to visit "to let them know what we think of the ABM."

The military views any kind of abnormal behavior as evidence of psychiatric disorder, malingering, or subversion. Because so often the objectionable behavior is none of these, the military response inevitably entails violation of the law. Except for drunkenness, a disease which seems to strike a certain stratum of enlisted men and officers' wives, physical illness, especially during training, is viewed simply as an excuse to avoid onerous assignments. Anyone who has ever been through Army or Marine Corps basic training can tell stories of sergeants physically assaulting soldiers who were in fact ill. This occasionally leads to murder.

In 1961 at Fort Dix, New Jersey, during a twelve-week session of advanced infantry training, a soldier showed the captain in charge of his training unit a document from the Army hospital stating that he was to be given only light work because of a heart murmur. The captain disregarded the medical excuse. A few days later, because the soldier failed properly to run up a sand dune in full battle dress with more than thirty-five pounds of equipment, the captain ordered the soldier to run up the hill again and again. It was a sultry September day and the temperature was in the eighties. That night the soldier's heart gave out, and he died in his sleep. When a corpse was discovered the next morning in the barracks, the ambulances came to tote it away and a discreet investigation was made. It is doubtful that lawyers were ever even involved; the captain was not charged with murder or anything else, and who knew the name of the medical officer who permitted an unfit boy to join and train with the United States Army?

Sometimes behavior of an educated soldier simply affronts the esthetic sensibilities of senior officers. The armed services prefer soldiers and sailors with closely cut hair; page after page of military regulations describe precisely in what manner and to what length hair may be cut. As the pressure to conform to the changes in civilian hair styles swept across the military in 1969 and 1970, the severity of the former regulations gave way to a certain flexibility. When the Navy's newly appointed Chief of Naval Operations, Admiral Elmo R. Zumwalt, became visible in Washington sporting sideburns that seemed to violate the existing Navy hair regulations, a "new interpretation" was put on those regulations to lower the length of sideburns.

Even before the appearance of this official visage, a sufficient number of problems had cropped up in the Navy concerning the wearing of mustaches and beards that the outgoing Chief of Naval Operations, Admiral Thomas H. Moorer (who became Chairman of the Joint Chiefs of Staff) felt compelled to issue a personal letter to all flag officers, unit commanders, and commanding officers. It had become clear that a significant number of commanding officers were refusing to permit beards and mustaches at sea, and there were even shore commanders who were balking at allowing these hirsute effulgences. The fact was, however, as Admiral Moorer reminded his leaders of men, that Navy regulations explicitly permitted beards and mustaches. In his May, 1970, letter he asked the various commanders to stick by the regulations.

He also noted that "we should not attempt to regulate the fashions of the civilian members of the military community. Commanding officers are requested to review their base and station regulations to insure that no limitations, based on the arbitrary application of purely military standards, have been promulgated which would preclude civilian dependents and other authorized personnel from access to base/station facilities to which they are entitled by statute."

This was an oblique reference to the fact that a score of documented and unpleasant incidents had arisen during the past year from Hawaii to Washington involving refusal of commanding officers to permit long-haired teenaged dependent sons to enter post exchanges, commissaries, and in one case, the base itself—thus, since his parents lived aboard the base, effectively barring the boy from his home. In each situation, the commanding officers claimed that the sight of long hair might undermine the morale of their men; in no case did commanding officers ever introduce evidence to show that morale was in fact affected.

But even Admiral Moorer weaseled in his attempt to get his commanding officers to abide by the law: the rights to live with one's parents, use base hopsitals, and shop in the commissaries and exchanges are not controlled by "statute." They are rights accorded military personnel and their dependents, if accorded formally at all, by Department of Defense regulations. So the degree to which Admiral Moorer requested a willingness to abide by the law was rather slight.

Moreover, he provided an escape clause that would be all but conclusive in the vast majority of situations to arise in the future: he exempted from his admonition regulations barring entrance to military facilities "where there is a demonstrated case of demoralizing active duty military personnel attached to a particular command." After all, doesn't a commanding officer have the right to guard and protect the morale and well-being of his men? Of course; it says so right in Navy Regulations. And it was quite obviously the case, since a number of commanding officers were saying so, that long-haired children were causing acute anxiety attacks in virile sailors who, being true Americans, felt like committing mutiny upon sighting the foul specter. A man has a right in America to be protected from indecency. Especially sailors.

The Army is less subtle. When faced with an undesirable situation, it simply makes up its own law. Existing federal law gives the United States Government no authority to seize first-class mail without explicit court approval. In 1971, annoyed because antiwar literature was being addressed personally to soldiers in Vietnam and mailed first class, the

Army prepared a secret directive to intercept such mail. A general regulation issued by the Secretary of the Army in 1970 prohibited seizure of any literature unless the Secretary himself rules that it "presents a clear danger to the loyalty, discipline, or morale of troops." The letters being mailed to Vietnam asked the soldiers for contributions for the peace movement; the Secretary of the Army never placed such a mailing on his list of proscribed literature. Army headquarters in Washington were never able to justify the legality of the Army directive, written by senior personnel in Long Binh. It just seemed like something that had to be done.

Partly as a result of the military's concentrated attacks on those whose actions were within the law, many dissident groups began what promises to be extensive litigation to secure their rights to perform activities that at present might well not be legally protected. Dissidents aboard military bases throughout the country are seeking to establish that it is their right, under the First Amendment, to hold meetings, to discuss war policies, and to distribute antiwar literature of all descriptions throughout their local commands.

Whether or not courts ultimately recognize a constitutional right to dissent within the military, it is quite clear that had the armed services been more quickly willing to stand by the law than to break it the response of those who feel aggrieved would not have been so broad or vociferous.

DRAFTEES

The United States Armed Forces are usually considered to serve the purpose of defending the nation from armed attack, direct (Pearl Harbor) or indirect (Vietnam). No matter the extent of disagreement on the latter proposition, there is virtual unanimity that the Army is not intended to serve as a penal repository for disaffected but able-bodied males. The purpose of the Selective Service System is implied by its name; its director is not supposed to be a jailor.

Its long-time Director, Lieutenant General Lewis B. Hershey, once thought differently. In November, 1967, at the height of draft resistance, General Hershey announced a policy of inducting men of draft age, including those with college deferments, who were interfering with the draft process. Since deferments were only to be given in the national interest, he reasoned, they would be revoked when interference was shown, since "illegal activity which interferes with recruiting or causes refusal of duty in the military or naval forces could not by any stretch of the imagination be construed as being in the National interest." General Hershey had in mind such popular activities as the draft board doorway sit-in.

The Selective Service Act does not permit binding national directives to be sent to local boards. In the words of a Selective Service System pamphlet: "Instructions to local boards are distinguished from the regulations and are advisory only. Neither such instructions nor the opinions of the Director of Selective Service have the force of law." It was uncontroverted that General Hershey did not have the power to change the regulations to permit the selective call-up of militant protesters. These prohibitions notwithstanding, preventing him from ordering the local boards to follow his new policy, and in spite of his having been rebuffed earlier in federal court when he had attempted to revoke deferments for such activity at the University of Michigan in Ann Arbor, he now purported to be making a national policy "suggestion" to thousands of local board members.

The Selective Service regulations permitted giving priority to the induction of delinquents, defined as anyone who "has failed to perform any duty or duties required of him under the Selective Service law"—for example, failure to carry a draft card or to report for a physical examination. But General Hershey had in mind broadening the definition of delinquency to include other violations of the Selective Service law itself, not merely failures to perform duties specifically imposed by the Act. Sit-ins, of themselves, were not violations of any law. Militant interference with the rights of others to volunteer and with the duty to register might be punishable through criminal prosecutions, but even the rankest dissidence (except, again, the personal refusal to carry a card or to register) could not be controlled by speeded-up induction.

The Justice Department recognized this awkward fact. General Hershey said he had spoken with "someone at the White House" before he issued his personal "suggestion." Indeed he had, but in the wake of the public outcry—which Hershey described as "hocus pocus"—that "someone" never stepped forward. One month after the fuss began, the Justice Department issued a face-saving joint memorandum with the Director of Selective Service upholding the right to dissent but promising prompt criminal prosecution of those who willfully violate the law.

Shortly thereafter, the trial of Dr. Spock and his four remote confreres, for conspiring to interfere with the draft, got under way.*

Draft boards during this period were so lawless that federal courts began upsetting classifications on a variety of grounds—for instance, that it was unconstitutional for a board to deny a claim without stating any reasons for the denial, or, as happened in Minnesota, that a board proc-

---

* This case represented the criminal counterpart of the abortive Hershey memorandum. On appeal, the case against three of the defendants was dismissed outright and that against the other two was dismissed for failure of proof. Though the Government could have retried the two defendants, the new Attorney General had his own schemes in mind and the case was quietly dropped.

essed 122 appeals in two hours, for an average consideration of 59 seconds per case. Congress finally responded to this willful lawlessness by passing legislation in 1971, requiring the boards to hear witnesses in person, to have a quorum at each hearing, and to give reasons for decisions.

SUSPECTS AND DEFENDANTS

By no means the only way, but a frequent and galling way, by which the government holds the law in contempt is in the process of "law enforcement" itself—by which is usually meant the system of "criminal justice." Here, the harm is direct and ironic, because the Government— chiefly prosecutors and police—by investigating, interrogating, searching, seizing, arresting, and prosecuting, is asserting the necessity of holding unlawful behavior to account.

Examples of lawlessness in law enforcement have been presented earlier in these pages, and other examples will follow. Thomas J. Mooney and Lloyd Eldon Miller were victims of Governmental lawbreaking. But political, local, and racial passions are not the sole explanations of lawlessness in law enforcement; it has its own peculiar logic, directed against that class of unfortunate citizens we call suspects and defendants.

So pervasive has been the lawless behavior of officers of the law that it may fairly be said that the development of American constitutional law in the field of criminal justice is chiefly the history of Governmental lawbreaking.

For the most part, it is a history of hindsight, since the Supreme Court has a habit of announcing constitutional decisions that take lawyers and politicians by surprise, or so they say. The rule announced usually sets aside a long-practiced custom (such as not advising those arrested of their constitutional right to remain silent). Although failure to abide by the Supreme Court decision is unconstitutional, it does not automatically follow that the same practices were unconstitutional prior to the decision. Thus, the Supreme Court has occasionally ruled that its new rules will not be used retroactively to upset past convictions.

This method of constitutional decision-making is nearly as old as the country, and it would not be strange or puzzling except for the fact that almost every school in the nation from the first grade through the senior year of college completely omits from the curriculum any discussion of the American legal process. And while the police and prosecutors let out a plaintive wail after every new Supreme Court decision because, they say, they were unprepared, this merely attests to the relatively low state of legal intelligence that exists within the local community.

It may well be that Supreme Court decisions always come at the last possible moment; they are never new and should never be surprising, for the Court acts only in desperation. Thus, a bolder Court might have spared the nation a generation of civil rights litigation over schools alone. Another example: in 1914, the Supreme Court ruled that evidence seized by federal officers in violation of the Fourth Amendment's prohibition against unreasonable searches and seizures could not be admitted in federal courts. Not until 1961 did the Court decide that the same result should be reached in state trials, even though a 1949 case established the rule that the "core" of the Fourth Amendment applied to state as well as federal procedures. Despite the fact that police in the 1961 case had acted in violation of the 1949 rule, local communities, at least many of them, found themselves unprepared.

Be that as it may, it is not the contention here that practices occurring before the Supreme Court announces a constitutional decision are always lawful. Nevertheless, the search and seizure cases do provide a clear example of unlawful police behavior.

Search and Seizure

In 1914, the Supreme Court was presented with a case concerning a man named Weeks who had been convicted of the federal crime of mailing lottery tickets. His conviction was based in part on papers seized by a United States marshal without a search warrant. The marshal had conveyed them in turn to the prosecutor. The Supreme Court overturned Weeks's conviction on the ground that a warrantless search violates the Fourth Amendment. Said the Court:

> If letters and private documents can thus be seized and held and used in evidence against the citizen accused of an offense, the protection of the Fourth Amendment, declaring his right to be secure against such searches and seizures, is of no value, and, so far as those thus placed are concerned, might as well be stricken from the Constitution. The efforts of the courts and their officials to bring the guilty to punishment, praiseworthy as they are, are not to be aided by the sacrifice of those great principles established by years of endeavor and suffering which have resulted in their embodiment in the fundamental law of the land. The United States marshal could only have invaded the house of the accused when armed with a warrant issued as required by the Constitution, upon sworn information, and describing with reasonable particularity the thing for which the search was to be made. Instead, he acted without sanction of law, doubtless prompted by the desire to bring further proof to the aid of the government, and under color of his office undertook to make a seizure of private papers in direct violation of the Constitutional prohibition against such action. Under such circumstances, without sworn information and particular description, not even an order of court would

have justified such procedure; much less was it within the authority of the United States marshal to thus invade the house and privacy of the accused.

But this rule that warrantless searches are unconstitutional and that evidence so seized cannot be admitted into the record of a trial applied only to federal prosecutions. In the *Weeks* case, the Court expressly declined to give any relief for earlier similar seizures of Weeks's papers by state officers.

In 1949, thirty-five years after the *Weeks* case, the Court was presented with the appeal of a Dr. Wolf, who had been convicted in Colorado for conspiracy to commit abortions. The conviction was obtained primarily on the basis of an appointment book seized from his office without a search warrant. The state conceded that had the search and seizure been undertaken in the same manner by federal officials and had the case been tried in federal court, the evidence would have to have been excluded because the search would have been unconstitutional.

The Supreme Court decided that, notwithstanding the federal rule, evidence unconstitutionally seized by state officials need not automatically be excluded from state trials. Nevertheless, the Supreme Court did rule that the "core of the Fourth Amendment"—"the security of one's privacy against arbitrary intrusion by the police"—is as applicable to the states as it is to the federal government. By this decision against Dr. Wolf in 1949, therefore, the Supreme Court said that searches without warrants were unconstitutional, whether conducted by state or federal officials. But the Court declined to rule that the unlawfully seized evidence must be excluded from state trials.

Thus, from 1949 until the Court's decision in *Mapp* v. *Ohio* twelve years later, no one could doubt that it was unconstitutional for governmental officials, no matter who they were, to search without warrants. The only question was whether the "fruits" of the unlawful search could be used at trial. So poorly did the states police the police, however, that the Supreme Court ultimately felt compelled to reverse the *Wolf* decision in 1961.

The reversal came about in the following way. Three policemen knocked on the door of Miss Dollree Mapp's Cleveland home on May 23, 1957. Information in their possession led them to believe that "a person [was] hiding out in the home who was wanted for questioning in connection with a recent bombing, and that there was a large amount of policy paraphernalia being hidden in the home." They sought entry to Miss Mapp's second floor apartment. After a hurried phone call to her lawyer convinced her that she need not admit police without a search warrant, Miss Mapp kept the door closed.

Three hours later seven policemen were at the door, and when it was not immediately opened they broke into the house. As the police were searching throughout the house Miss Mapp's attorney arrived; his way was barred by the police who permitted him neither to speak to his client nor to enter the house and watch the goings-on. Miss Mapp asked to see a search warrant; a piece of paper was produced and she yanked it from the policeman's hand, placing it, in the delicate words of the Supreme Court, "in her bosom." She was thereupon attacked by the police, who managed to recover the "warrant." For her "belligerence" in hindering the police search and rescue operation, she was handcuffed.

The police then carried her up the stairs to her bedroom where, still searching for a fugitive, they proceeded to look in a dresser, a chest of drawers, a closet, and some suitcases; the rest of the apartment was also searched and a check of the basement produced a trunk which was opened and searched. From these diverse sources the police could find no fugitive, but they did manage to extract several allegedly lewd and lascivious books, pictures, and photographs (which later turned out to belong to a former boarder). It was for possession of these books and pictures that she was convicted.*

The search warrant was never produced at the trial, nor did the prosecution explain or attempt to explain its absence. Even the Ohio Supreme Court, which upheld the conviction, doubted the existence of any warrant.

Before the Supreme Court the State of Ohio vigorously argued that the rule of *Wolf* v. *Colorado* required the conviction to be left standing. The Supreme Court noted that in 1949 nearly two-thirds of the states had no rule requiring unlawful evidence to be excluded from trials. By 1961, on the other hand, "more than half of those [states] since passing upon it, by their legislative or judicial decision, have wholly or partly adopted or adhered to the *Weeks* rule." The California Supreme Court had been "compelled to reach that conclusion because other remedies have completely failed to secure compliance with the constitutional provisions."

Moreover, in 1954 the Supreme Court had specifically rejected an opportunity to overrule the *Wolf* case, saying then that until the state had "adequate opportunity to adopt or reject the [*Weeks*] rule" the Court would adhere to its position. Whatever the relevance of trends of state decisions, by 1961 the Court had had enough:

Today we once again examine *Wolf's* constitutional documentation of the right to privacy free from unreasonable state intrusion, and, after a dozen years on our books, are led by it to close the only courtroom door remaining open to evidence as secured by official lawlessness and fla-

* Laws prohibiting the mere possession of obscene material were declared unconstitutional by the Supreme Court in 1969.

grant abuse of that basic right, reserved to all persons as a specific guarantee against that very same unlawful conduct.

Wolf was overruled, and the exclusionary rule was made to apply to the states. As Mr. Justice Clark said: "We no longer permit [the Fourth Amendment] to be revocable at the whim of any police officer who, in the name of law enforcement itself, chooses to suspend its enjoyment."

Mapp was not a unanimous decision. The dissent of Mr. Justice Harlan was eloquent and tough, but his objections applied simply to the notion that the Supreme Court ought to be in the business of policing state police. The dissenters, like the majority, were far more concerned with the technical underpinnings of the old rule and the new rule then announced than they were with the particular facts and abuses in Miss Mapp's case. Both failed to come to grips with the essence of the problem: police have their needs as well as citizens. For the police, it is imperative to find evidence and make arrests. If hypertechnical rules are announced, it is no more difficult for the police to find ways around them than it has been for white racists to foil the courts year after year.

One of the latest techniques—latest in the sense that it is still being successfully employed—is the so-called "dropsy" testimony. This occurs typically in narcotics cases in which the police unlawfully and routinely pick the pockets of the suspected addicts, pushers, and possessors. At the hearing on the constitutionality of the search, the police change the facts a bit; they testify that as they approached, the suspect hurriedly took the drugs from his pocket and dropped them on the ground in an effort to rid himself of the incriminating evidence before apprehension. Similarly, where the search warrant does not exist or where it does not cover the search of certain rooms or drawers, the police testify that drawers were open and the drugs were in "plain sight."

In a given case, standing by itself, a policeman's word is not to be doubted by the presiding judge, at least not unless there are eyewitness accounts other than the self-interested story of the defendant or overwhelming contradictions in the stories of the police, as not infrequently happens. But, as New York City Criminal Court Judge Irving Younger put it in 1970,

> [t]he difficulty arises when one stands back from the particular case and looks at a series of cases. It then becomes apparent that policemen are committing perjury at least in some of them, and perhaps in nearly all of them. . . . Spend a few hours in New York City Criminal Court nowadays, and you will hear case after case in which a policeman testifies that the defendant dropped the narcotics on the ground, whereupon the policeman arrested him. Usually the very language of the testimony is identical from one case to another. . . . The judge has no reason to disbelieve it in any particular case, and of course the judge must decide each case on its own evidence, without regard to the testimony in other

cases. Surely, though, not in *every* case was the defendant unlucky enough to drop his narcotics at the feet of a policeman. It follows that in at least some of these cases the police are lying.

An equally effective technique is the "furtive gesture" testimony. In these cases, police will flag down cars bearing "suspicious" individuals. Without grounds to search, the police nevertheless ransack the cars and occasionally come up with contraband—e.g., dope or liquor unlawfully carried across state lines.

To justify the search, and get around the awkward rule that would otherwise exclude the evidence from the case, the story is that the passengers in the car made a "furtive gesture." Justice Stanley Mosk of the California Supreme Court has written that "the furtive gesture has on occasion been little short of subterfuge in order to conduct a search on a basis of mere suspicion or intuition."

The practice of stopping to search those who look a little funny has been so prevalent that a New Jersey court felt compelled to suppress evidence found in one such incident along the New Jersey Turnpike. The arresting state trooper testified that three long-haired youths were driving their truck "at an apparent high rate of speed." Flagging them down, he noticed a small aspirin bottle on the floor and arrested them for unlawful possession of a prescription drug and possession of a narcotic drug. The grand jury refused to indict, but the case was sent to a municipal court for prosecution.

Before the case came to trial, the youths succeeded in persuading the Appellate Division to call off the proceeding. From the arresting officer's testimony, the court concluded "that it was a combination of the appearance of the defendants and the otherwise unobtrusive bottle that led him to believe a violation of the law might be occurring under his very nose." It was the appearance—"long hair and beards"—that apparently upset the officer.

The court ruled that "there is nothing under the law of this state, as far as we know, which makes the wearing of long hair and/or a beard a criminal activity. State Police officers are commissioned to uphold the law. . . . They do not enforce their own personal likes and dislikes." A state police lieutenant noted that such conduct reflected the desire of troopers to act out their own "personal feelings"; he said that the troopers' actions did not constitute official policy.

Still another example of unlawful search techniques is in the execution of search warrants. The police are required to announce the purpose of the warrant before entering the premises to be searched. Often, they testify they knocked, announced their presence, heard running steps, and barged in—rather than tell the truth, which is that they kicked the door in at the outset.

The irony of this conduct—that hard-pressed police must find awkward and perjurious methods of getting around inconvenient laws in the drug enforcement area—lies in the responsibility of other policemen for much of the flourishing drug trade. Research done for President Johnson's Crime Commission in 1966, but not published until late in 1971, established that of 5360 police-citizen contacts in Boston, Chicago, and Washington, D.C., one of five policemen "was observed in criminal violation of the law." Two of every five policemen were observed to have violated such departmental regulations as drinking and sleeping on duty and falsification of reports. These statistics did not include involvement with organized crime, excessive use of force, or the acceptance of free food. The contacts did include theft, extortion, and bribe-taking in connection with narcotics traffic and other offenses. These observations were made by trained sociologists *with the understanding and cooperation of the police themselves,* whom the observers accompanied on their rounds. So ingrained are police mores that this significant number of police crimes was not even hidden from federal observers.

That policemen take bribes, kickbacks, and blackmail money in return for an official disposition to ignore the existence of the flourishing business and to look the other way when arrests might be made, has not yet been proved to be activity directed by the highest officials (though the Knapp Commission's investigation in New York City has shown that the undertaking has not been confined to the cop on the beat). Inasmuch as the unlawful cooperation of a small minority of policemen in the narcotic business cannot be classified as state or local policy, the law-breaking remains rather as an example of the corruption of public officers.*

Bail

The right to bail in the United States is not absolute; it may be denied in any case where there is reasonable ground to believe that the defendant will not appear for trial. Otherwise, bail, a sum of money the defendant must post to insure his appearance at trial, must be set to permit the defendant his freedom before trial.

Under the Constitution if bail is granted it may not be "excessive." What "excessive" is no one knows, but it seems reasonably clear that the constitutional provision is widely ignored by judges throughout the United States. They ignore it especially in times of tension, during riots and other periods of disorder. In those cases bail is deliberately set in amounts higher than defendants could reasonably be expected to pay. The result is that they are kept behind bars before any determination of

* See page 213.

guilt is made, merely because judges think that they are dangerous, that they will go back on the streets to perpetrate further riots, or that for other reasons they should be locked up.

Widespread unlawful denial of bail by judges and the practice of requiring excessive bail have been widely documented. In Chicago in early 1967, for example, acts of looting and vandalism occurred during a severe snowstorm that paralyzed the city and the police. The judicial response was high bail. Bond hearings preceded by at least three weeks the preliminary hearings on the question whether there was probable cause to hold the suspects. This meant that though a particular suspect was entirely innocent and could easily show he had been mistakenly rounded up by the police, he would because of high bail have to spend at least three weeks in jail before he could even engage the state in a colloquy about his innocence. In setting bail, judges routinely made their determinations as in the following examples:

THE CLERK: Sam B.

THE COURT: Branch 46. 1–31.

THE CLERK: Bond, Mr. State's Attorney?

THE COURT: Bond for B. . . . ?

STATE'S ATTORNEY: On Sam B. . . . , your Honor, the State will recommend a bond of $20,000.

THE COURT: $20,000.

THE COURT: What do you do for a living, son?

DEFENDANT: Sir, I work for the post office and for . . . two jobs.

THE COURT: Can you afford to hire a lawyer?

DEFENDANT: Yes, I could, your Honor.

THE COURT: All right. You hire yourself a good lawyer, sir. We will continue this case.

DEFENDANT: Your Honor, I have a wife and three kids and I only left them with twelve dollars in the house. Could I possibly get. . . .

THE COURT: Twelve dollars.

DEFENDANT: But I get paid from the post office this coming Thursday and I get my check at the other job, your Honor.

THE COURT: You should have been on the job instead of out on the corner that night.

DEFENDANT: I had to get milk for my baby. I avoided this crowd as far as I could and then I was afraid they would rob me, your Honor; and my baby was crying. He is only 9 months old and I was going to—I was two blocks from my house avoiding these crowds because I am afraid they would rob me, but, your Honor, I got there and the police I saw—I could only see the top of the police car. Then I wasn't afraid any more because I thought the police wouldn't bother me. Then when the police got close the people went out of the store and dropped goods all over the ground.

THE COURT: Someday you'll learn how order is in Chicago.
DEFENDANT: Sir, may I please have a personal bond?
THE COURT: No, sir.
STATE'S ATTORNEY: Motion State, February 20, 1967.
THE COURT: I will not interfere with the bond. February 20, Bailiff.

Despite the possibility that some of these suspects were in fact innocent Circuit Court Chief Judge John Boyle justified his unconstitutional actions as follows: "What do you want me to do—cry crocodile tears for people who take advantage of their city? Didn't I read . . . all about President Johnson's 'War on Crime'?" And Magistrate Maurice Lee unburdened himself of the opinion that "this type of crime during a city-wide emergency is comparable to grave robbing." Even the Public Defender, sworn to make arguments from the defendant's point of view, said he was "not going to start fighting with judges because they set some bond some people think is too high."

Somewhere the other side of the rioter in the degree of criminality is the prostitute. In New York prostitution is a misdemeanor, and the maximum sentence is ninety days in jail and a fine of $500. The New York criminal code provides for bail in all misdemeanor cases without exception. In July, 1971, coincident with the arrival of several thousand members of the American Bar Association for their annual convention, two streetwalkers were arrested and held without bail by Judge Morris L. Schwalb of Manhattan Criminal Court. The number of prostitutes in midtown Manhattan was rapidly increasing—the judge complained of "inundation" in the midtown area. Police estimated that prostitutes in all of Manhattan numbered two thousand. Judge Schwalb said: "While we do not have preventive detention, nevertheless, there is authority for police action when the welfare of the public is in serious jeopardy. Disease is spreading rapidly. We are facing a plague."

The judge said his decision to deny bail to the two prostitutes was based on a 1970 New York case in which a suspected bomber was denied bail in the interests of the "safety of the community." But unlike prostitution, bombing is a felony. Whatever legal merit is to be found in the preventive detention aspect of the bombing case, it simply isn't present in the misdemeanor called prostitution. Judge Schwalb handily ignored the law. When Mayor Lindsay appointed Schwalb in 1968, the august Association of the Bar of the City of New York refused to endorse him because, it said, he had little experience in criminal law. Subsequently, Judge Schwalb's three years of experience on the bench prove how irrelevant the Bar Association's criterion was.

The Third Degree

With the publication of the Wickersham Commission's *Report on Lawlessness in Law Enforcement* in 1931, it was shown beyond any doubt that the "third degree" was a prevalent police practice: whippings, beatings, relay questioning under conditions of prolonged sleeplessness, near drownings, starvation, and protracted unlawful detention were documented in a collection of hundreds of cases from cities throughout the country. For years police chiefs had been denying that these practices existed and for years investigators and judges were presented with concrete cases in which confessions had been extracted through these methods.

The conservative American Bar Association, in the 1930 report of its Committee on Lawless Enforcement of Law, concluded in a decidedly modern vein:

> The use of the third degree is obnoxious because it is secret; because the prisoner is wholly unrepresented; because there is present no neutral, impartial authority to determine questions between the police and the prisoner; because there is no limit to the range of the inquisition, nor to the pressure that may be put upon the prisoner. . . . Probably the third degree has been a chief factor in bringing about the present attitude of hostility on the part of a considerable portion of the population toward the police and the very general failure of a large element of the people to aid or cooperate with the police in maintaining law and order.

A follow-up study by the President's Commission on Civil Rights in 1947 found that things had not changed much in sixteen years. In 1951, policemen in a midwestern city responded to the question: "When do you think a policeman is justified in roughing a man up?" as follows:

Reason	*Percentage*
Disrespect for police	37
To obtain information	19
For the hardened criminal	7
When you know the man is guilty	3
For sex criminals	3
When impossible to avoid	23
To make an arrest	8

The U.S. Civil Rights Commission in 1961 considered that "police brutality is still a serious problem through the United States."

The 1967 Report of the Task Force on Police to the President's Commission on Law Enforcement and Administration of Justice concluded somewhat more optimistically that "physical abuse is not as serious a problem as it was in the past." The Task Force cited FBI statistics for fiscal 1965 showing only nine convictions resulting from 1,787 investigations into charges of excessive force; comparable figures for fiscal 1966 showed three convictions of 1,671 investigations. Of course, the conviction rate for such police crimes is hardly indicative of the size of the problem; the difficulty of proving charges of police brutality is monumental

Despite ample documentation, including visual demonstration on television in the years following the 1967 Report, a vast number of Americans refused to credit charges of brutality as anything more than a calumny on the police and an excuse to keep people from focusing on excesses of citizen lawlessness. Indeed, in the wake of the shootings at Kent State University in the spring of 1970, a grand jury indicted students but not the untrained National Guardsmen who, a widely discussed FBI report hinted, employed their deadly fusillade without legitimate cause.

The 1967 Task Force Report did not deny the existence of some brutality. Aside from the well-documented attacks by police on civil rights demonstrators in the South, the 1967 Report made a series of independent findings. Commission observers undertook to accompany police patrols on a systematic basis in many major cities. These "observers witnessed, during 850 eight-hour patrols, 5,339 police-citizen encounters—encounters which included police contacts with suspects, witnesses, victims, and bystanders." Out of these contacts, twenty cases of excessive force were plainly observed. Though the number seems miniscule, it must be remembered that these contacts occurred while the police were being watched. A description of one of the incidents follows:

> White officers responded to a man with a gun . . . and heard three shots fired. Then the white man with the gun got a drop on the officer— somehow they got the gun away and handcuffed him (gun was a 12 gauge 1905 musket). When they got him to the station garage, they kicked him all over, but the principal one was the officer who had been in danger when the man had the drop on him. He beat him as the others held him up. I got to the scene and the lockup man whistled for them to stop but they didn't. The Lieutenant arrived with everyone else and said there's going to be a beef on this one so cover it up and go find the empty shells. Someone call an ambulance (he needed it badly). Then the Lieutenant took complete control. They got the shells, got a complainant who said the three shots were an attempt to kill the officer, and he would sign a complaint, say he called an ambulance, etc. They wrote a cover for the incident. The officer who beat the man most was shaken by then but the others gave him support, telling him how brave he was and how wise he had been not to kill the guy at the scene, etc. They then set about to put all the stories in order and I was carefully notified of it in detail so I would have it straight. I had enough rapport with these officers that they talked about it even after. The man was in pretty bad shape when he got to the hospital.

How often police indulge in the third degree at the stationhouse to obtain information and confessions is impossible to say. With the constitutional requirements imposed by the Supreme Court on police to provide legal counsel to indigent defendants and to warn suspects fully of their rights, it is probably safe to hazard the guess that the third degree is not nearly as rampant as it once was, unless there are special circumstances, such as a violent (or potentially violent) civil disturbance, or unless the suspects are black or young and not dressed like the sons and daughters of policemen.

Nevertheless, the police have depended for years on a modified version of the third degree: verbal harassment and abuse. Nonstop, continuous interrogation techniques have long been thought necessary to secure confessions. Lloyd Eldon Miller was subjected to it. So was George Whitmore, Jr., a young black drifter who "confessed" to killing Janice Wylie and Emily Hoffert, two Manhattan "society" girls whose unsolved murders had been a source of some embarrassment to the police for many months. A high level assistant to Manhattan District Attorney Frank Hogan said in 1965 after the confession:

> Let me give you the perfect example of the importance of confessions in law enforcement. This, more than anything else, will prove how unrealistic and naive the [Supreme] Court is. Whitmore! The Whitmore case. Do you know that we had every top detective on the Wylie-Hoffert murders and they couldn't find a clue. Not a clue. I tell you, if that kid hadn't confessed, we never would have caught the killer.

Six months later the case against Whitmore was dropped. A confession solved the murder, all right, but it was the confession of another man. Whitmore, it seems, had simply been browbeaten during an extended interrogation into confessing whatever the police desired. In no small part because of the publicity that followed the Whitmore trials the Supreme Court issued its famous *Miranda* confession guidelines in 1966.

The Unlawful Arrest

In an era of citizen demonstrations (and riots), confrontation with police is inevitable. Violence and arrests are not merely by-products of these occasions but pretty nearly the central purpose; and it is as inaccurate as it is biased to assert that most such arrests are unlawful. But that most arrests are lawful, whether because the police caught the lawbreaker in the act or because the police were honestly mistaken, does not mean that all arrests are to be so excused. A roll call of American cities —Los Angeles, Chicago, Detroit, New York, Washington—will catalogue bloody scenes earnestly dissected in more than a score of staff reports to half a dozen Presidential commissions; these reports all amply document that sweeping the streets of human debris leads to passionate as well as cold-blooded acts of unlawful arrest.

What may in time be considered the classic example of such behavior—much as Chicago's finest in the dark hours of 1968 will serve for a long time to illustrate the awful fury of the "police riot"—was the puerile attempt of the "May-Day Tribe" to force the federal Government to close down its operations by preventing federal employees from reaching their jobs in Washington during the first week in May, 1971. As the District of Columbia Human Relations Commission later described the events in a special report:

> The [Tribe's] plans appeared in a "tactical manual" of the militants. Like a winter snowstorm, the plan threatened massive traffic snarls in the city. It is clear that the criminal actions threatened by some people could not be tolerated and that the authorities responsible for the security of Washington faced a great challenge. By every credible report the city was kept open and traffic moved so well on May 3rd that many employees found it easier than usual to get to work.

The events of the week began in a zany enough manner. Several thousand members of a loosely organized group called "Vietnam Veterans Against the War" had begun camping out on the Mall grounds two weeks earlier, in connection with a massive peaceful demonstration on the west front of the Capitol. In the face of explicit refusal from some military units and municipal police to clear the area, the Justice Department sought a court injunction and took their case to the Supreme Court, which approved an order evicting the veterans.

Upon the refusal of the veterans to decamp, the Justice Department went back to court to seek dissolution of the ban, to which a district judge, angry at the Department's vacillation, acceded. A compromise was arranged; the veterans and others who were coming to Washington could use the West Potomac Park grounds, between the Washington Monument and the Potomac River. Six days before the agreed-upon removal date, one day before the planned traffic tie-up, the police swooped into the camp grounds early in the morning and dispersed 50,000 sleepy youths.

The next day, May 3rd, at 5:00 A.M., the planned disruptions began. Reports began to spread that cars were burning, that nails and trash had been strewn on major highway arteries, that traffic was already being blocked across the bridges leading into the city from Virginia suburbs. At 6:25 A.M., Police Chief Jerry V. Wilson was reported to have suspended the use of "field arrest cards." A simple form prepared for use in the event of widespread civil disturbances, the field arrest card was devised after the Washington riots attending the assassination of

Martin Luther King, Jr., in 1968. The police abandoned also the practice of photographing persons arrested.

By 8:00 A.M., the police had arrested 2,000 persons. Buses were coming downtown in increasing numbers to transport those arrested to municipal jails, the courthouse cellblock, a playing field across from the court, and the fields adjacent to the Robert F. Kennedy Memorial Stadium. By 10:00 P.M. on the evening of May 3rd, 6,892 people had been arrested. Late that night, many thousands of prisoners were taken for housing to the D.C. Coliseum and were not processed out until the following day or later in some cases. Between May 4th and 7th, nearly 6,000 additional people were arrested and similarly detained, many for periods well in excess of twenty-four hours before being charged, and many without the opportunity to call friends or relatives to inform them of their plight.

Undoubtedly, some people caught in the police "sweep" were guilty of a variety of misdemeanors. As the Human Relations Commission noted:

> It is unlawful within the confines of the District of Columbia to kindle bonfires within certain hours, to make or commit lewd, indecent or obscene acts to annoy, disturb, interfere with, obstruct and be offensive to others or wander abroad and lodge in any vacant building, parking lot or open air and wander about the street at late or unusual hours of the night without any visible or lawful business and not give a good account of oneself.

> It is also unlawful to obstruct public roads by removing milestones or placing any rubbish upon such or to obstruct public highways to the free use of the public or to deposit, cast, throw, drop or scatter upon the streets, avenues, highway, sidewalk or any public space in the District of Columbia, any paper, refuse, garbage, gravel, straw, refuse of any kind upon any paved sidewalk or roadway. Nor may persons set up, maintain or establish any temporary place of abode in any tent, wagon, van, auto, truck, [or] house trailer on public or private property without consent.

Many of these code provisions were violated in plain sight of the arresting officers. But, though the number is disputed, a large proportion of those arrested did not commit any infraction at all, in or out of sight of the arresting officers. The Human Relations Commission estimated that of the 12,000 people arrested at least half had not violated any provision of the penal code.

The observations of many neutral observers are underscored by the failure of a "substantial number" of policemen to wear their badges or name tags while on duty, by the charge of "disorderly conduct" ultimately entered on a large proportion of arrest forms, regardless of what the arrested person had been told he was being arrested for, and by the falsification of the actual arresting officers' names on the arrest forms. (At one point Justice Department attorneys were given instructions to use the names of one of seven policemen on all arrest forms.)

It was also charged that a common criterion for arrest was appearance: "evidence of youthfulness in dress and hairstyle, rather than evidence of crime, was generally acted upon by arresting officers," the Human Relations Commission report noted. It continued:

Commission observers reported that on the morning of May 3, they witnessed an incident involving a large group of people which included men with short hair dressed in business clothes, women wearing cosmetics and office attire, and young men and women groomed and costumed in the manner characteristic of American college campuses today. All were crossing the street en masse at 14th and Pennsylvania Avenue, N.W. Without the occurrence of any actions among people in the group that appeared to disrupt traffic or otherwise violate laws, police officers waiting at the corner picked individuals out of the crowd and steered them to a waiting truck where they were arrested. It was noted that only people youthful in appearance and attire were selected for arrest.

Two letters, from among hundreds collected, illustrate what happened to some of the unwitting spectators and passersby.

Dear Judge Green:

Your Court will be overloaded today with persons arrested during the course of the morning in connection with the disruptions of traffic. Perhaps my personal observations at DuPont Circle will be useful to you and the other Judges.

I stood at the south end of the Circle at the foot of the Guardian Federal Savings and Loan Building from 7:30 A.M. to 8:30 A.M. During this period of time I saw no violence, but a number of arrests that were completely arbitrary and, in my judgment, without any basis whatsoever.

At one point, a chap was talking with me and a policeman seized him by the arm and when I asked whether he was under arrest, the policeman said, "Yes." I asked why. The policeman said, "Failure to move on." I pointed out that the man was talking with me and that I was as involved as he was, and asked why he did not arrest me. He replied, "Personal judgment, sir," . . . .

People with long hair were pushed away from DuPont Circle, people with short hair, like myself, were permitted to move freely.

Unfortunately, I lost one page of my notes, however I can provide you with this. A policeman, with Badge Number 2741, arrested a youngster at 7:50 A.M., who was talking with me and had committed absolutely no violation of law that I could ascertain. At 8:10 A.M. police officers, with Badge Numbers 82 and 3940, observed about ten youngsters walking along the curb with about four or five walking in the street right next to the curb because the sidewalk was crowded. One officer said, "All right, let's take these two," and they each took a young girl by the arm to the center of the Circle under arrest. I asked the basis for the arrest and again received the reply, "Personal judgment, sir," . ...

And from a student:

On Monday May 3, 1971 at approximately 11:00 A.M. I was walking to class along 20th Street between F and G Streets, N.W., when I was approached by a member of the Civil Disturbance Unit and was told to come with him. I offered no resistance and was led to a green bus, frisked, and told to get on the bus. I told him that I was a student and that I was on my way to class. He said that he couldn't believe me and that it didn't matter if I was a student anyway. I asked him what I was charged with and got no answer. I was then led to the door of the bus and was pushed aboard. On the bus I saw three friends of mine, who were also on their way to classes. They were indignant, as I was, for being grabbed off of the streets for no reason. We were then driven to the training field of the Washington Redskins, an area about the size of a football field but with high fences all around it.

When we arrived we saw many other people, mostly young, who looked like P.O.W.'s. I was terrified at what appeared to be a Nazi concentration camp, but tried not to show it. My stay there was filled with feelings of hate and frustration for being thrust into the middle of what I had decided to avoid. What further aggravated my state of mind was the fact that there were no sanitation facilities, no water, and no food. Food was finally brought into the camp at about 6:00 P.M., but there was not enough to go around. Seeing this, some of the pedestrians who had been watching this whole scene went and bought food to give to us. When the police wouldn't give this food to us they began to throw it over the fence. They were arrested, on what charges I don't know, and were led away. By this time it was getting cold, I had no coat on, so we went to one of the tents which had been set up by some of the people in the camp. It was warmer in the tents, I guess because so many people were crammed in to them, but in any case I was still cold.

At approximately 9:00 P.M. the police began moving the two or three thousand people who were in the camp to the Coliseum. I arrived there at about 10:00 P.M. On entering I saw a line of about 200 or 300 people waiting to process [put up bail and be released], so I didn't bother to stand on line until about 12:00 midnight. I waited for about an hour and after not moving more than five feet I sat down. The conditions there were somewhat better than in the camp, but they were still grotesque. The major problem was crowding for all of the people who were in the training camp were crowded into an area about one half the size. Sleeping was almost impossible because there was no room to lie down and because the floor was cold hard cement. Later on in the morning we were provided with army blankets so that if you could find room to lie down you could sleep. One major improvement over the training field was that there were real toilets, instead of the ground. It was worth the hour wait to use them because it beat going in your pants and because they were the only source of water.

At approximately 2:00 A.M. we were informed of Judge Green's order that if by 8:00 P.M. Tuesday the police couldn't show just cause why we should be held we would be released, so I decided to wait until then to leave. We were told at about 9:00 A.M. by some lawyers that the police might try to force us to process; this both angered and frightened me, but I was determined to wait until 8:00 P.M. so that this wouldn't be on my record.

At approximately 12:00 noon we were told by the same people that if we didn't process we would be charged with resisting arrest along with disorderly conduct. It was then that I decided to get on line to process because I didn't want a felony added to the misdemeanor that I already would get.

At approximately 1:00 P.M. Tuesday I was processed, which included giving them my name and address. I was printed, photographed, and then free to leave, once I had paid a non-refundable ten dollars. I was lucky enough to have a friend who was willing to put up this sum, but many did not have any money or friends in the District area. It turns out that none of the people who refused to process were charged with resisting arrest, but it was enough to make me process.

At no time during this 26 hour period was I given my rights and was only told formally that I was being charged with disorderly conduct at 1:00 P.M. when I processed. When I got outside I found out that a friend, ———— ————, had posted my bond and that it was his congressman, Mr. Robert Tiernan, who had procured the blankets for us.

Unfortunately, arbitrary arrest is not limited to the arena of politics. There is extensive evidence that many New York City policemen routinely make up charges and lie in court to secure convictions. In most cases, the arrest is premised on a threat, communicated directly or implicitly, to police authority.

In one case, two patrolmen arrested a black man in a bar, charging him with "robbery, assault, and possession of a dangerous weapon, as well as felonious assault on the policemen," after a struggle in which it was claimed that the defendant had fired at the police and one of the patrolmen had returned warning shots. It later developed that the patrolmen had concocted the story about the shooting and that one of the patrolmen had shot into the Harlem River.

The facts came into the open only with the admission of one of the patrolmen (prompted by a confession to his priest) that he had invented much of the story to win a departmental medal. The other policeman was compelled to admit his culpability and at a subsequent departmental trial both lost thirty days' pay (and their departmental medals).

The defendant was the victim of circumstances: he had managed to escape from jail during the 1965 Northeast power blackout, and the charge of escape was added to the list. Because he had a prior criminal record, the defendant agreed to plead guilty to the escape charge in return for the prosecutor's agreement to drop all other charges. He received a suspended sentence.

Since prostitution is usually immune to the normal methods of law enforcement, many states reach for bizarre devices to control it. In 1965, in Atlanta, the city officials unearthed a clearly unconstitutional 1910 ordinance that made it unlawful for "a woman of notorious character" to go about on "public thoroughfares." One woman with a conviction record was arrested for the act of dining in a public restaurant.

But examples need not be multiplied here. The reader wishing to gorge himself on a diet of police lawlessness is referred to citations at the back of this book. The unfortunate fact is that though they rarely admit it, the police do commit acts that are not merely mistakes or momentary lapses, but crimes.

PRISONERS

Perhaps because of an ancient prejudice that anyone convicted of a felony is no longer entitled to civil rights, prisons are by far the most lawless places in American life today. So degrading are the facilities, so starved are correction officials for cash, so undertrained are prison guards, that the brutality common to any major jail and most minor ones has been accepted as an inevitable fact of prison life.

Because law rarely penetrates behind the jail walls acts of prison guards are seldom viewed as unlawful acts of government; the official tolerance of the brutal acts of prisoners toward each other is equally condoned. But much of what goes on behind bars is unlawful and it has an incalculable effect on the nation's crime rate, since fully eighty percent of all reported crime is committed by previously convicted felons who have served time in jail.

There is no sanction in law for murder, torture, or punitive segregation as a punishment for a prisoner's assertion of his legal rights. But these acts are daily occurrences. Gordon Carr, Superintendent of the Caddo Correctional Institute in Louisiana, his assistant, and five guards were indicted by a federal grand jury for the beatings of prisoners during the period 1968 to 1970. Governor Reubin Askew of Florida in May, 1971, suspended ten officials and guards of the Raiford State Prison for "serious errors of judgment" and "excessive force" during disorders. In Arkansas, the evidence is all but conclusive that sprawling Cummins Prison Farm, whose grounds cover ten thousand acres, for years was the scene of systematic murder by officers and employees of the prison.

Fatal shootings and beatings at Cummins were common and were often provoked by a prisoner's refusal to submit to punitive whipping. One former inmate recalled how in 1940 an aged Negro was choked to death by barbed wire strung around his neck by a horse-mounted guard who pulled him across a field until he died.

The Superintendent of Arkansas's Tucker State Prison Farm was convicted in 1970 of employing the "Tucker Telephone" on inmates: wires from antique telephones were attached to prisoners' genitals and electrical shocks were administered by a hand crank. Superintendent James L. Bruton did not contest the charge and was sentenced to a $1,000 fine and a one-year prison sentence, which federal district Judge J. Smith Henley suspended for fear that Bruton would be murdered if sent to jail: "I don't believe you could live 60 days in a federal penitentiary or jail," the judge said. "I think that long before that time, someone or more of these persons or their friends with whom you have dealt with in the past as inmates of the Arkansas Penitentiary will kill you. The Court doesn't want to give you a death sentence."

The death of a fifteen-year-old black prisoner in Arkansas's Mississippi County Penal Farm shed a much-needed light on another unlawful aspect of the penal system of the state. By state law, prisoners must be adequately cared for. By decision of the U.S. Supreme Court, no one may be sent to prison to work off a fine he is too poor to pay. Arkansas violated both. The facts came to light when a youth was forced at gunpoint to wade into a swollen stream and was drowned by the heavy current. The level of diet, sanitary conditions, housing, and medical care at the Penal Farm were far below legal standards. Moreover, the Farm accepted prisoners sentenced only to pay off fines (for such misdemeanors as driving without a license) and worked the men and boys at a rate of five dollars a day.

The situation in military prisons is comparable. The Presidio mutiny case was touched off when a guard at the stockade in San Francisco's Army Post killed a private who walked away from a work detail by shooting him in the back. Much of the pent-up hostility of the prisoners at the Presidio, like prisoners everywhere, was due to the Army's abysmal failure (like the failure of supervising authorities elsewhere) to abide by its own regulations.

No one wants to spend money to improve prison conditions and enlarge prison spaces; when the Presidio "mutiny" broke out, one hundred forty prisoners were confined to spaces that by regulation could hold no more than eighty-nine. Segregation cells, to which prisoners were often sent, by regulation are to be eight feet long by six feet wide; but the Army's own generous claim was that the cells were only six feet by five feet in area. Toilets were stopped up and overflowing. Very little in any prison, civilian or military, would pass the test of conforming to applicable laws and regulations.

A *New York Times* survey in 1971, finding a relaxation of brutal discipline in prisons throughout the United States, cited a number "of the more brutal measures employed in some of the prisons in the past":

¶ In North Carolina a decade or so ago, men were thrown naked into solitary confinement cells where guards used high pressure water hoses from time to time to "knock them up against a wall";

¶ In Maryland inmates were disciplined until recently by receiving a meal only once every 72 hours;

¶ In Pennsylvania, before a reform movement in 1953, prisoners were placed for days in dark, damp, underground holes;

¶ In Arkansas five years ago, men were whipped on the bare buttocks with rawhide straps (flogging was practiced in 26 prisons as recently as 1963) and had needles pushed under their finger nails.

Civil rights demonstrators arrested in Mississippi in 1965, pursuant to an ordinance (later held unconstitutional) requiring marchers to secure a parade permit, sued prison officials for the hideous treatment they received. In a decision holding state officials liable for injuries to the demonstrators, Judge Irving L. Goldberg of the U.S. Court of Appeals described the treatment as "subhuman" and said it "beggars justification and taxes credulity":

On October 2, 3, and 4, 1965, plaintiffs and many others paraded in Natchez to publicize their grievances, particularly discrimination on account of race. At the time a Natchez ordinance prohibited parades without the written permission of the Chief of Police. . . . The ordinance was later found unconstitutional, but at that time it had not been so declared.

Shortly after the march commenced on Saturday morning, October 2, defendant Robinson, Natchez Chief of Police, and defendants Rickard, Cowart and Beach, Natchez police officers, arrested approximately 700 persons for parading without a permit in violation of the Natchez ordinance. Following the arrests, plaintiffs and others were transported to the Natchez city auditorium. There defendant Flowers, a Natchez police officer, defendant Cameron, Natchez Fire Chief, and firemen acting pursuant to Cameron's directions assisted Chief Robinson and officers Rickard, Cowart, and Beach in detaining plaintiffs. There is some evidence that many of those arrested, particularly minors, were permitted either to post bond or to obtain release on personal recognizance. The evidence, however, also reveals that many of those arrested were either not permitted to make bond or were unable to do so during the time they were incarcerated in Natchez. Furthermore, no effort was made to secure a magistrate, and as a result none of the plaintiffs or other arrestees were brought before a judicial officer for examination. No youth court order was obtained with respect to any of those arrested who were minors.

Late that Saturday night approximately 150 of those held at the auditorium were transported by bus over 200 miles to the Mississippi State Penitentiary at Parchman. Mississippi Highway Safety Patrolmen provided the escort. This initial group of prisoners arrived at the penitentiary early Sunday morning, October 3, and were taken to its maximum security unit upon order of defendant Breazeale, the penitentiary superintendent. Thirty-nine cells had been vacated in the unit, and, following the arrest and transfer of additional protesters on Sunday and Monday, more than 250 prisoners were ultimately housed there.

On arrival all male prisoners were required to strip naked and all women prisoners were ordered to remove their shoes, stockings, sweaters, coats, jewelry, and wigs. All were compelled to consume a laxative and were deprived of all personal belongings, including sanitary napkins and medicines. The prisoners were then led to the cells. Up to eight persons were placed in each cell, which contained two steel bunks without mattresses or other bedding, a toilet without a seat, and a washbasin. There were no towels or soap and there was inadequate toilet paper. The temperature ranged from 60 to 70 degrees, the chill being aggravated by exhaust fans which blew intermittently on the occupants. Some of the men eventually were permitted to get their underwear, but others were nude for a period of 36 hours. Many were subjected to blood tests. Moreover, while standing in the prison courtyard awaiting processing several plaintiffs were kicked, pushed, cursed, and abused by the highway patrolmen and others guards.

On Sunday morning, October 3, and Monday evening, October 4, more protest marchers were arrested and detained in Natchez. Nearly 100 were subsequently transported to Parchman and given similar treatment to that accorded the first group of prisoners. Plaintiffs, after individually posting $200 property bonds, were released on Monday, October 4, Tuesday, October 5, and on Wednesday, October 6.

Prisoners are often abused for their desire to make known conditions prevailing in their cells and for their attempts to seek relief through proper judicial channels. One extreme instance of prison officials' unlawful intolerance of the legal maneuvering of their wards is the series of acts committed against Martin Sostre, a long time black inhabitant of New York jails.

Imprisoned during the period 1952–1964, Sostre spent four years in solitary confinement at Utica State Prison because of activity on behalf of the Black Muslim movement. In 1968 he was convicted of narcotics violations and sentenced in Erie County Court to a term of thirty to forty years. The warden of Green Haven prison, to which Sostre had been removed, decided that the preparation of legal papers, including a motion for change of venue in the trial of his codefendant, was unlawful because Sostre did not have a license to practice law. The papers had come into the warden's possession because all outgoing prisoner mail must be screened through the prison staff.

In an earlier letter to his attorney Sostre had mentioned an organization called the Republic of New Africa. Sostre refused to answer the warden's questions about it. In a letter to his sister, Sostre said "there is no doubt in my mind whatsoever that I will be out soon, either by having my appeal reversed in the courts or by being liberated by the universal forces of liberation." For these acts of letter writing the warden placed Sostre in what prison officials called "punitive segregation" and left him there for more than a year, until Sostre's release was ordered by a federal district court in New York in July 1969.

On the day he was sent into solitary confinement, prison authorities searched his cell and found, according to an affidavit filed by the warden one year later when Sostre was released from solitary, three items of contraband—a letter belonging to another inmate and two pieces of emory paper. Prison officials also discovered on that same day that Sostre had taken to distributing copies of the *Harvard Law Review* to fellow inmates.

The letter, the emory paper, and the distribution of legal material were alleged by the warden to have been among the reasons why Sostre was ordered to solitary confinement. Before trial on the issue, the warden apparently realized that the first and third points would not support punitive segregation for more than a year (would not, indeed, support punitive segregation for a day). The alleged finding of the emory paper was only a little less shaky. The court dropped all three issues as inadequate to support the confinement.

The day following his release under the court order, Sostre was confined to his cell for having dust on his cell bars. Federal district Judge Constance Baker Motley found from the foregoing facts that "Sostre was sent to punitive segregation and kept there until released by court order not because of any serious infraction of the rules of prison discipline, or even for any minor information, but because Sostre was being punished specially by the warden because of his legal and Black Muslim activities during his 1952–1964 incarceration, because of his threat to file a law suit against the warden to secure his right to unrestricted correspondence with his attorney and to aid his co-defendant . . . and because he is, unquestionably, a black militant who persisted in writing and expressing his militant and radical ideas in prison."

Uprisings at the Attica Correctional Facility in New York and at other prisons across the country in 1971 demonstrated that prison reform had not really begun. The federal Court of Appeals for the Second Circuit ordered a preliminary injunction against "physical abuse, torture, beatings, or other forms of brutality" at Attica. Following the insurrection at that prison, the evidence showed, guards subjected the inmates to an "orgy of brutality," including beating of injured prisoners lying on stretchers, burning with matches, and forcing some to "run naked through gauntlets of guards armed with clubs."

Prisoners can be treated in far more subtly unlawful ways. The Administrative Procedure Act (APA) requires all "decisions" of federal agencies to include a statement of the reasons supporting the findings and conclusions, and denials of applications must be "accompanied by a brief statement of the grounds for denial." In the quarter century since the enactment of the APA, the U.S. Parole Board, an agency within the Department of Justice, has consistently violated those provisions. The Board has, of late, been granting or denying parole at the rate of 15,000 cases per year. Since that works out to some 50 cases every business day, the consequences of decisions announced without reason can be serious.* As Kenneth Culp Davis, one of the nation's most eminent administrative law scholars, suggests:

> If a board member is in such a hurry to get to his golf game that he votes in sixteen cases without looking inside the files, no one under the board's system can ever know the difference, even though the personal liberty of sixteen men may be at stake. How could a board member have less incentive to avoid prejudice or undue haste than by a system in which his decision can never be reviewed and in which no one, not even his colleagues, can ever know why he voted as he did? Even complete irrationality of a vote can never be discovered. Should any men, even good men, be unnecessarily trusted with such uncontrolled discretionary power?

The answer to this rhetorical question is that by law board members are *not* entrusted with the kind of uncontrolled discretionary power they exercise. Board members have unlawfully assumed it, an unseemly affair for members of a parole board and hardly conducive to the rehabilitation of prisoners.†

BLACKS

Murder and Other Harassments

That the black minority—and other racial and ethnic minorities as well—have been persecuted and oppressed throughout the history of the United States is as obvious as it is embarrassing to state the fact. Not

---

* No reasons are given at the original sentencing in court. The judiciary is not bound by the APA, but the failure of judges to announce their reasons in sentencing is just as serious as the failure of the Parole Board, if not more so.

† In early 1972, the Parole Board made an oblique announcement in a parole case that it would, henceforth, give its reasons.

quite so obvious, though always just below the surface, is Governmental complicity in that oppression. Though the beginnings of official oppression were not unlawful, the growing sense of moral outrage led to an erosion of legally imposed discrimination. The closer we journey to the present time, therefore, as the old legal props of slavery and segregation have withered away, the Government's continuing complicity in fostering conditions of second- and third-class citizenship has become increasingly unlawful.

Slavery, of course, was not unlawful in the beginning. The Constitution explicitly recognized it and even prohibited legislative attempts to end the slave trade until 1808. After the Civil War, the moral indefensibility of slavery was translated into legal prohibitions. The unwillingness of whites to accord their fellow human beings the decencies of what was loosely called civilization, however, led to a complex of thousands of state laws, local ordinances, and customs sanctioned by courts, all of which trapped the new black citizens in a matrix of poverty, ignorance, and political inferiority.

The legitimation of American apartheid was wrought by the Supreme Court itself in the famous 1896 case of *Plessy* v. *Ferguson.* Though the Fourteenth Amendment to the Constitution prohibited any state from denying to any person the "equal protection of the laws," the Court was not long in deciding that in reality that phrase and its sister phrase "due process of law" had little or nothing to do with racial discrimination.

True, an 1874 West Virginia law prohibiting blacks from sitting on grand juries or trial juries was struck down by the Supreme Court in 1880. But in 1883 in the *Civil Rights Cases* the Supreme Court declared unconstitutional a federal law requiring "the full and equal enjoyment of accommodations in inns, theatres . . . and public conveyances on land and water" for peoples of all races.

The Constitution—meaning the Fourteenth Amendment and federal law enacted pursuant to it—could not reach the purely private acts of the citizens of the several states, the Court announced. If railroads prohibited blacks from sitting in white cars, this was an act of the private railroad, not the state. (Never mind that the railroad was chartered by the state, endowed with tax advantages by the state, and usually subsidized by the state to support its operation.)

A stinging dissent by the first Justice John Marshall Harlan recalled the Fugitive Slave Laws of 1793 and 1850, federal laws providing criminal penalties for private persons who aided runaway slaves. Said Harlan: "I insist that the National Legislature may . . . do for human liberty . . . what it did . . . for the protection of slavery and the rights of the masters of fugitive slaves."

Emboldened by the logical thrust that the *Civil Rights Cases* implied, Southern states began to pass laws of segregation. By 1890, Alabama,

Arkansas, Florida, Georgia, Louisiana, and Tennessee had enacted legislation prohibiting the mixing of races in railroad cars. A Louisiana law was titled "An Act to Promote the Comfort of Passengers"; it required railroads to "provide equal but separate accommodations for the white and colored races."

L. A. Martinet, editor of the *New Orleans Crusader,* founded the Citizens Committee to Test the Constitutionality of the Separate Car Law, and he and his lawyer Albion W. Tourgee decided on a test case. In 1892, they induced Homer Adolph Plessy to step aboard a white car on the East Louisiana Railroad in New Orleans. Plessy had the misfortune of being one-eighth black; his family had suffered the indignity of having included among his eight great-grandparents an African immigrant. Plessy was arrested.

Four years later the test case wound its way to the Supreme Court, which went on to ignore two salient considerations: first, unlike the facts presented in the *Civil Rights Cases,* the separation of the races here was not enforced by private persons but by the coercive power of state law. Second, Louisiana law contained a curious provision: "[Colored] nurses attending the children of the other race" were exempted from the segregation provision. A black nurse could sit in a white car. These odd regulations were swept aside in a majority opinion denying that "the enforced separation of the races stamps the colored race with the badge of inferiority. If this be so, it is not by reason of anything found in the Act, but solely because the colored race chooses to put that construction upon it." (If a person of one-eighth black blood could not sit in a white car it would seem only logical that a person of one-eighth white blood could not sit in a black car, but this fanciful conception of equal justice was obviously not a deciding factor in the case.) The only value of *Plessy* v. *Ferguson* was Justice Harlan's eloquent dissent, which by virtue of its ultimate vindication has become one of the most famous dissents in the history of American constitutional law.

Such dissents are expressions of concern, disgust, or outrage; they are never law, and they don't keep you out of jail. Henceforth, therefore, it was legal to discriminate on the basis of race.

The period following the turn of the Twentieth Century was open to all forms of discrimination. Discrimination did not have to be masked; it could flourish openly. It was therefore direct and effective. Not until the Supreme Court began to take a close look at the methods by which Southern states prohibited blacks from voting, in violation of their unambiguous Fifteenth Amendment right, did the states and their lawyers begin to be devious and underhanded. When what you are doing is confessedly unconstitutional, it behooves you to be shrewd; before the Court began to take an active role in civil rights, public officeholders had no reason to be sly.

Nevertheless, even during the heyday of lawful oppression, governments in the United States found it necessary to violate the law. Between 1882 and 1930, somewhat more than forty-five hundred people were lynched in the United States. Most of the victims were black; most of them were murdered by vigilante groups known to law-enforcement officers throughout the states. One or two lynchings—or twenty or one hundred—may be unavoidable; forty-five hundred are a direct result of government complicity.

From the start to an end that has unfortunately not yet come, public officials have been implicated, grossly at some times and in minor ways at others, in the activities of the Ku Klux Klan. During the Reconstruction period following the Civil War the Klan was virtually synonymous in many communities with the official establishment. During a three-month period in Georgia in 1878, the Klan's activities included "143 major outrages including 31 killings, 43 shootings, 5 stabbings, 55 beatings and 8 whippings of 300 to 500 lashes apiece." The Klan's activities have been known to sheriffs and prosecutors alike because, at least in the early years, sheriffs and prosecutors were members of the Klan.

Though the number of reported incidents of terror has declined, the total unsolved bombings, assassinations, and arson attempts against civil rights activists during the 1960's is by no means small. The three civil rights workers, James Earl Chaney, Andrew Goodman, and Michael H. Schwerner, who were murdered in Neshoba County, Mississippi, in 1964, were killed by a posse of armed men, including members of the local police. Mississippi brought no prosecutions, but after a complicated and drawn-out legal battle the Supreme Court cleared the way for a federal prosecution. The Justice Department prosecuted a number of individuals, including a local sheriff and his deputy, for activities—i.e., murder—that deprived Chaney, Goodman, and Schwerner of their civil rights. For the first time in a modern racial killing, a Southern jury brought back convictions in 1967. (Although some of the defendants were acquitted, those who were found guilty included Deputy Sheriff Cecil Price.) *

There are more subtle but equally unlawful methods of murder or attempted murder. One of thousands of such cases amply illustrates the point. On November 15, 1923, the aptly named Mamie Snow, an unmarried white woman, claimed that she had been raped in Waukegan, Illinois. The police arrested James Montgomery, a Negro. He was subsequently convicted of the crime and sentenced to life imprisonment at the Illinois State Penitentiary. One quarter of a century later, in 1948, he sought release from prison on a writ of habeas corpus. He submitted

---

* In May, 1971, Joetha Collier, an eighteen-year-old black girl, was killed as she was walking into a store an hour after she graduated from an integrated high school in Drew, Mississippi. Police arrested and charged three white suspects the next day.

to the court a document obtained from the Victory Memorial Hospital in Waukegan, indicating that Miss Snow had been examined on November 15, 1923, by Dr. John E. Walter and that he had found her to be a virgin. The state courts of Illinois denied Montgomery all relief. Turning to the federal district court in Chicago he sought and obtained a hearing in which the following facts came to light.

On the day Miss Snow claimed to have been raped, Dr. Walter examined her and discovered that the only indications of injury were some contusions around the head. At the 1948 hearing Dr. Walter testified that Miss Snow's clothing was not disarrayed when she was brought to the hospital for examination and that his findings that she could not have been raped were communicated to the police that day. He testified, moreover, that Miss Snow had been a casual acquaintance of his because she had been a door-to-door peddler of needles and thread; from conversations she initiated of a "highly irrelevant nature" and "peculiarities about her speech and manner" Dr. Walter concluded that she was "mentally irresponsible." Dr. Walter said further that he had told the police he would be available to testify at the trial but that he had never been called.

Following Montgomery's arrest (and a beating that left scars on his face visible twenty-four years later) he was brought into a room with Miss Snow, who said "I never saw this fellow before in my life." At a preliminary hearing to set bail, the Illinois State's Attorney told Montgomery: "If you were down in Georgia or Mississippi where you come from, we would turn you over to the Ku Klux Klan and we are liable to do it up here now. You know I am a member of that organization."

Montgomery dropped his request for bail but did insist to his attorney that twelve witnesses, all of whom were willing to testify that Montgomery was far from the place where Miss Snow claimed to have been raped, be called in his behalf. The attorney refused. The State's Attorney went one better: he told Montgomery that if he were to take the stand in his own behalf, the Klan would be called in. The entire trial lasted twenty minutes.

The court reporter for the trial, still living twenty-four years later, submitted an affidavit in the federal habeas corpus proceeding stating "that he has made diligent search among his official files for the stenographic report of the proceedings [in the Montgomery case] but has not been able to locate [them]; that his stenographic report of the evidence, either oral or documentary, that was introduced upon the trial are missing from his custody and cannot be found."

The state could not—or did not—contradict any of the testimony at the 1948 hearing. The Governor had refused Montgomery's request for a pardon the preceding year. Finally in 1949, after twenty-five years in jail for a crime that was never committed, Montgomery was released by order of the federal court in Chicago.

To harass and intimidate organizers pressing for black registration in Selma, Alabama, Dallas County Sheriff James G. Clark and his deputies brought a series of baseless prosecutions during the period of civil rights activism in the 1960's. In 1963, the Dallas County Voters League was formed for the express purpose of registering black voters. To the League came volunteers from the Student Nonviolent Coordinating Committee (SNCC). The League planned voter clinics, and to publicize them it sponsored a series of mass meetings at local black churches.

Sheriff Clark's first move against the workers occurred on June 17th when he arrested a young local volunteer who was interviewing people in the registration line at the Dallas County Courthouse. Clark said the man was "molesting" those in line and arrested him a short time later in the courthouse for failing to obey the sheriff's order to leave. The charge was later changed to disturbing the peace and resisting arrest. Conviction followed.

On the next day, Clark arrested Bernard Lafayette, Field Secretary for SNCC and head of the Dallas County effort, charging him with vagrancy. Clark said at the trial he had had reports that Lafayette was seen begging, though Clark admitted he never investigated the matter and that he persisted with the arrest despite the discovery that Lafayette had thirty dollars in his pocket when booked. Clark said he was unaware that Lafayette had any visible means of support, though he did know, he said, that "Lafayette was a representative from an organization in Atlanta, which was 'trying to organize the niggers.'" Lafayette was acquitted.

Some days later, Clark stopped one Alexander Brown for allegedly driving a car with only one headlight. The driver's license Brown carried showed his name to be Alexander Love. Though born with the name shown on the license, Brown had been reared by his grandmother, whose name he took; by Alabama law, however, he was required to use the name appearing on his birth certificate to secure a license. Clark arrested him on a charge of concealing his identity. Brown was later acquitted.

On July 29, a fleet of Clark's deputies arrested twenty-nine blacks attending a registration meeting. In each case the charge was operation of a motor vehicle with improper license plate lights. Clark also maintained a constant surveillance of the meeting houses, arresting large numbers of juvenile and adult demonstrators who were doing nothing more than quietly carrying signs in a picket line.

He even attempted to subpoena several federal attorneys who worked for the Civil Rights Division of the Justice Department to testify before a grand jury in connection with the charge that the Justice Department had rented an automobile to transport Dr. Martin Luther King to make a speech in Selma. (When the U.S. Court of Appeals for the Fifth Circuit restrained the grand jury investigation on the publicly stated ground, it was then announced [and later claimed to have been the intent all along] that the grand jury would investigate charges that the Government attorneys "consorted with, concealed and harbored known criminals and dope addicts . . . consorted and associated with admitted sex perverts" and committed other assorted crimes.)

In the midst of the turmoil, the Justice Department filed suit in 1963 against Dallas County to restrain its officials from further intimidating the registration effort. Because of numerous procedural delays the United States did not succeed in preventing the acts perpetrated by Sheriff Clark outlined above. Nevertheless the United States proceeded with its suit under a provision of the Civil Rights Act of 1957, which states:

> No person, whether acting under color of law or otherwise, shall intimidate, threaten, coerce, or attempt to intimidate, threaten, or coerce any other person for the purpose of interfering with the right of such other person to vote or to vote as he may choose.

Ignoring the evidence before his eyes, as well as the troubled history of Selma and Dallas County, federal District Judge Daniel H. Thomas densely found no violation of that section.

In 1959, of eighteen thousand blacks living in Dallas County, only 163 were registered. Of twelve thousand whites, nearly nine thousand were registered. In 1961 the United States brought suit against Dallas County to enjoin it from violating the Civil Rights Act. In 1965, one commentator described the situation: "four years, two suits, and a great deal of intimidation later, Negro registration in Dallas County has risen all the way to 385."

Despite this repeated history of malevolent interference with the right to vote, despite the widely known disturbances in Selma, and despite the plain fact that following Sheriff Clark's actions the registration clinics, which had been drawing forty persons a month, were suspended for lack of attendance, Judge Thomas showed his ignorance of the law, if not his contempt for it, by ignoring the Civil Rights Act and holding that the "constitutional" rights of those arrested in 1963 were not violated.

The U.S. Court of Appeals for the Fifth Circuit in 1967, one year after Clark lost his bid for reelection as sheriff, reversed Judge Thomas and ordered all fines returned to the victims of Alabama's crimes. Further, all arrest and conviction records were expunged, and the County was ordered to reimburse all the defendants for their costs, including reasonable attorneys' fees.

In 1954, with the Supreme Court's reversal of *Plessy* v. *Ferguson,* governmental lawbreaking in the civil rights field picked up tempo because segregation and repression could no longer be carried on under cover of law. To intimidate those willing to brave the inevitable rebuffs, states throughout the country (but especially Southern states) deliberately kept Negroes from serving on all types of juries. The Supreme Court had made it unequivocally clear in 1880 that the failure to permit Negroes to serve would invalidate convictions. Due, nevertheless, to the active apathy of federal officials since 1880, discrimination against blacks eligible to serve on juries has been widespread and still exists today, despite recent Court decisions reaffirming the basic right.

The response of Southern officials to each new decision of the Supreme Court is well known. It would serve no useful purpose to catalogue the Southern political response to the fitful march of the United States Supreme Court in the area of race relations; in no other area of American law have the constitutional decisions of the Supreme Court been so blatantly ignored.

The trouble is just this: an open legal system has an almost infinite capacity for translating legal proclamations into political evasions. A compassionate and fair mind would admit that the tedious and disingenuous distinctions raised at every stage of the tortured path to civil rights for minorities since 1954 have been unlawful. But the official rejoinder is sure to be that it is not unlawful to plead a defense to the next encroachment of the federal Government by pointing to distinctions between the last case and this. Never mind that the distinctions are without a difference, nor that the distinctions are merely subtle subterfuges to evade the plain law—American law, it should be clear enough by now, is never plain enough.

Voting

It happens to be the law in the United States that black citizens are entitled to vote. Until recently in the South, and in certain other places as well, no one really believed it. Because Southern officials refused to own up to this, it became necessary for federal voting rights laws to make the fact inescapably plain and to create a program for enforcing those rights.

A common technique for denying the right to vote is the requirement that the would-be registrant read and explain provisions from various state constitutions. Since the provisions are usually unintelligible, it is not surprising that very few black registrants subjected to these schemes pass, proving only that many blacks are no smarter than many white officials, who still don't understand the federal Constitution.

There are—or were—other techniques. These were described in the President's Special Message to the Congress in 1965 urging passage of the Voting Rights Act:

1. *The technique of technical "error."*

Negro applicants for registration are disqualified on grounds of technical "errors" in their registration forms. Instances of record show Negroes disqualified for "errors" such as failure to write out middle names, abbreviating the words "street" and "avenue" in addresses, or failing to compute age exactly to the day. Where this technique is employed, "errors" are found in substantially all applications filed by Negroes, but few or none in applications filed by whites.

2. *The technique of non-cooperation.*

A technique commonly used in conjunction with the "error" technique involves simple non-cooperation by the registrar. Thus, he may be "out" for most of the day during registration periods. Registration may be possible only on certain days each month. Limits may be imposed upon the number of applicants processed each registration day. The variety of circumventions possible by this device is endless.

3. *The technique of subjective tests.*

By far the most common technique by which Negro citizens are prevented from exercising their right to register and to vote is the use of subjective tests, unfairly administered literacy tests, tests of "understanding" and tests of "character." The only standard used is the whim of the registrar. Such devices are used as vehicles for the rejection of untold thousands of voters solely on the basis of race and color.

Once, in a moment of extraordinary candor, Senator Allen J. Ellender, Democrat of Louisiana, explained in a colloquy with Hubert H. Humphrey on the Senate floor exactly why these techniques were used:

> SEN. ELLENDER: It is true that in some states there are counties where the ratio of Negroes to whites is 2 to 1 and there is little or no registration. But why? For the reason that the few whites in those counties would be scared to death to have Negroes in charge of public office without qualification.
>
> SEN. HUMPHREY: Then what the Senator from Louisiana is saying, in other words, is that while the whites are in the minority they do prevent the colored majority from registering to vote?
>
> SEN. ELLENDER: I do.
>
> SEN. HUMPHREY: How does the Senator justify that under the Constitution? The Constitution is rather explicit, Senator, on those terms.
>
> SEN. ELLENDER: I understand that, but [the registrars] do not apply it. I am not saying [the Negroes] should not be registered, but I am giving the Senator the reason why. If this happened in the State of Minnesota, the Senator from Minnesota would do the same thing.
>
> SEN. HUMPHREY: No. . . .

SEN. ELLENDER: The Senator from Minnesota has not lived among them. I am frank to say that in many instances the reason why the voting rights were not—I will not say denied, but not made possible—is that the white people in those counties who are in the minority are afraid they would be outvoted. Let us be frank about it.

In their desperate struggle to prevent their being outvoted, the townspeople of Tuskegee, Alabama, carved up the city into an irregularly shaped twenty-eight-sided figure in the late 1950's, neatly keeping the whites inside and making the blacks former residents of Tuskegee. The Supreme Court voided the districting in 1960.

The Voting Rights Act of 1965 began to end the rankest discrimination. But there is another side to voting: as important as the right to cast the ballot is the right to run for office as a candidate.

J. Dennis Herndon, Green County (Alabama) probate judge, thought that blacks really had no right to run for seats on the Green County Commission and the Board of Education in 1968, so he ordered the names of six blacks off the ballot. He did not appear overly concerned that a federal court in Alabama had ordered him to include on the general election ballot the candidate of the National Democratic Party of Alabama. The removal was kept something of a secret; four days before the 1968 elections, a Justice Department attorney was shown a sample absentee ballot with the black candidates' names on it. The attorney did not trouble to ask whether the regular ballot was the same—almost anywhere else he would not have needed to ask. The candidates themselves did not know about the omission of their names until Election Day, when they went to vote. Green County, seventy miles west of Montgomery, happens to be more than 80 percent black. The Supreme Court ordered the candidates restored to the ballot, and in a special election in 1969, all six candidates whose names were previously omitted now won.

Judge Herndon went on trial in federal court for civil and criminal contempt and was found guilty of both in January, 1971. He drew a year's probation and was fined $5,700 to reimburse the candidates their out-of-pocket expenses.

Schools: Modern Techniques

Judge Herndon's difficulties lay in his making a minor and highly visible error that could be easily and predictably corrected by the Supreme Court. Others, who commit larger crimes, have so far managed to escape with only verbal abuse as their reward.

The U.S. Department of Health, Education, and Welfare, for example, was anxious in 1970 to dole out massive sums of money to Southern school districts pursuant to a federal law authorizing appropriations to smooth the way for desegregation. But certain conditions on the grant-

ing of the desegregation funds were ignored. The law prohibited granting of funds to school districts that continued on a course of segregation. The law also required written applications from the various school
districts stating how the funds would be used, and districts entering the
final phases of desegregation were ineligible for such funds.

So anxious was the Administration to spend the money that only days
after Congress appropriated the funds Jackson, Mississippi, received $1.3
million without even applying for a grant, and the Jefferson County
(Kentucky) school district received $32,000, though it was ineligible for
the money because the school system was already entering the final phase
of desegregation. Talladega County (Alabama) received $168,000 on
a promise that the district was not discriminating against teachers, but
the Department of Justice only two months later was compelled to bring
suit for the reinstatement of teachers fired because of their race.

The Administration agreed, when questioned, that many of the
grants were awarded "hastily"; the first $75 million, ready in August,
had to be spent in six hundred school districts opening white doors to
black children for the first time, and since Congress had not appropriated the money until August 18th, there was little time, the Administration said, to spend it before the opening of the schools. The Administration neglected to note that federal and state elections were less than
three months away. After the November elections were over, Acting
Commissioner of Education Terrel H. Bell announced the Department's intention to "monitor and follow up and to crack down on school
districts that are not meeting the assurances they gave us." He pointed
out that HEW had already denied grants to more than four hundred
school systems in the South.

Meantime, the Internal Revenue Service announced a policy of re-
voking tax exemptions for private schools that remained segregated. The
IRS method of detection was simple: affidavits stating that the schools
were not practicing discrimination were sufficient to preserve the tax
exemption.

In June 1970, a federal court in Washington, D.C., ordered IRS to
suspend the tax exemption of forty-one school districts in Mississippi
until a determination could be made whether they were in fact segregated. In July the Service had discovered an ingenious way to avoid
provoking the wrath of deep-South districts: to comply with the civil
rights laws, IRS said, the schools needed only to announce an open-
admission policy.

By the time the schools opened in the fall, only eleven school districts
refused to give IRS the requisite assurances. The exemptions for these
eleven districts were suspended. The other thirty schools, however,
though they did not have a single black student enrolled, maintained
their exemptions on the strength of their pious promises. In March, 1971,

well after the preceding November elections, IRS announced the revocation of exemptions for twenty-three of those schools and said it was continuing an investigation.

Discrimination in Federal and State Contracting

One keystone of federal civil rights enforcement is Title VI of the Civil Rights Act of 1964, forbidding discrimination in any federally assisted program. It says:

> No person in the United States shall, on the ground of race, color or national origin, be excluded from participation in, be denied the benefits of, or be subjected to discrimination under any program or activity receiving federal financial assistance.

Under this law, federal funds must be withheld from any program or activity violating the antidiscrimination provision.

This powerful provision of Title VI has been used most sparingly. Although the language of the provision is mandatory and has no exceptions, the provision has almost never been used, despite the President's constitutional obligation to execute the laws faithfully. During the late 1960's, the Johnson Administration invoked it to prod integration of some school districts and hospitals. If the law were invoked, a major portion of the federal budget would immediately cease to be spent. Some laws, obviously, just cannot be enforced.

This conclusion is firmly supported by the example of the Office of Federal Contract Compliance, which for years (until 1971) never saw fit to terminate federal contracts, pursuant to authority explicitly delegated to it by Congress, in cases in which federal money was being paid to contractors or others who discriminated in hiring. The Office has the power also to prohibit further federal contracting with employers or others who have been shown to have discriminated in the past; despite clear examples of discrimination, the Office has been equally sluggish in using its power to serve notice to others that discrimination is not to be tolerated.

Racial discrimination is hardly confined to the South, and official lawbreaking by state agencies to avoid legal requirements is hardly unknown. Take the liberal state of New York. One-quarter of all construction in New York state is carried out by the state government and its subordinate agencies. Unlike the Southern states, New York has a number of statutes—the Human Rights Law, the Labor Law, and the Executive Law—prohibiting discrimination in employment, both by the state and by labor organizations, and giving the state vast powers to investigate suspected cases of discrimination and to correct abuses when found. As for its own construction projects, the state has the absolute authority to cancel contracts where discrimination is discovered. Moreover, citizens of New York state must be given preference in hiring (and failure to abide by this provision requires automatic cancellation of the contract).

Nevertheless, despite overwhelming evidence of discrimination by all construction crafts, the state has never taken affirmative action. So loath have the state agencies been, in fact, that, according to one student of the problem, the State Division of Human Rights has refused even to hold hearings into 92 percent of the industrial cases actually brought before it. The state labor law requires all contractors to maintain lists of their employees' state citizenship; contractors as a matter of course do not maintain such records, and the Industrial Commissioner has never seen fit to challenge any of them, despite the law's absolute requirement that the contractors maintain such lists when working on state projects.

Contrary to the law, the state permits Canadian workers to come across the border in the face of widespread black unemployment in the Buffalo area. The result of all this violation can even be measured in dollars: because thirty thousand jobs go to out-of-state workers, in clear violation of the law, it has been estimated that the state loses some $125 million a year, or the money that is paid out in welfare payments to men who might otherwise be employed on just the state projects alone.

If New York's Attorney General Louis Lefkowitz would consider enforcing a few more laws like those which make it unlawful to discriminate in apprenticeship programs and in union membership, the state might save even more money. There are no signs of any activity yet, and Attorney General Lefkowitz is aware that there are more headlines to be made in the consumer field than in breaking the white barrier in the Empire State.

Miscegenation

In 1967 the Supreme Court declared unconstitutional the so-called miscegenation statutes, which prohibited intermarriage between whites and nonwhites. At that time sixteen states still had such laws on the books. In the 1967 case, an interracial couple named Loving moved from Virginia to Washington, D.C., to be married; they were arrested and convicted upon their return to Virginia. A prison sentence was suspended for twenty-five years on condition that they leave Virginia. In language broad enough to make it unequivocally clear that miscegenation statutes would not be countenanced, the Supreme Court unanimously reversed that decision. There was "patently no legitimate overriding purpose independent of invidious racial discrimination which justifies this classification. . . . We have consistently denied the constitutionality of measures which restrict the rights of citizens on account of race," said Chief Justice Warren for the Court.

Nevertheless, it has taken court orders in many states, for years after 1967, to permit blacks and whites to intermarry. In 1970, Calhoun County (Alabama) Probate Judge C. Clyde Brittain refused a marriage license to Army Sergeant Louis Voyer (white) and Phyllis Bett (black). Judge Brittain's refusal to abide by his obligation to uphold the federal Constitution prompted the Justice Department to file suit to enforce the couple's right to wed.

In 1971 in Georgia, the federal Government was required to go to court before an interracial couple could be issued a marriage license. The Georgia law prohibited state officials from issuing licenses and ministers or other officials from performing the marriage ceremony. Despite the clear import of the Virginia case four years before, the Clayton County official would not issue the license until a federal court order restrained anyone in Georgia from enforcing the state law.

INDIANS

It was against the Indians that President Andrew Jackson is reputed to have uttered his celebrated retort against the rule of law: "John Marshall has made his decision; now let him enforce it."

Whether or not Jackson made the statement, the sentiment was real. By a 1791 treaty with the Cherokees, the United States "solemnly guaranteed the Cherokee Nation all their lands not therein ceded." These retained lands included millions of acres in Alabama, Georgia, North Carolina, South Carolina, and Tennessee. In 1823, the Supreme Court, speaking with forked tongue, ruled that Indians did not have title to lands made the subject of treaties but had instead the right to occupancy only. The Court reasoned that since the British discovered the land, title had passed to the British Crown and thence to the United States following the Revolution. (Vacationers might want to try out that method of acquiring a second home. But the techniques will probably only work if the land-hungry urbanite is willing to assume title to Indian reservations.)

As a result of the Court's decision, the long-standing desire of the citizens of Georgia to assume control of Indian land (reinforced by the discovery of gold within the Cherokee Nation) led to a series of laws in 1829 invalidating Cherokee laws. These Georgia laws were clearly unconstitutional, since they were inconsistent with the federal treaty.

Resisting the efforts of Georgia to remove them from their land, the Cherokees asked the recently inaugurated Andrew Jackson for federal protection. He replied "that the President of the United States has no power to protect them against the laws of Georgia." Instead, he proposed that Congress pass a removal law. The Cherokees, suing as a foreign nation, brought a test case to the Supreme Court.

In the meantime, in defiance of the Cherokees' right to operate their own political society, Georgia arrested an Indian named Corn Tassel on a charge of murdering one of his fellows within the boundaries of the Cherokee Nation. He was sentenced to be hanged, and an appeal was made to the Supreme Court, which commanded the state to appear before it to answer the appeal. Governor Gilmer and the state legislature refused to submit to the Court's jurisdiction; the day before Christmas, 1830, Corn Tassel was executed. President Jackson was silent. It was against a backdrop of public hysteria over Georgia's practical nullification of the Constitution that the suit brought by the Cherokee Nation against the state was filed in the Supreme Court. Georgia never deigned to answer.

Shortly before the *Cherokee Nation Case* was argued in March, 1831 (and decided against the Cherokees for lack of jurisdiction), Georgia enacted a statute requiring any white person who desired to go upon the Cherokee lands to obtain permission from the Governor. Two Vermont missionaries, failing to secure the proper licenses, were tried and sentenced to four years in prison. The Supreme Court took jurisdiction to hear the appeal, and again Georgia did not enter an appearance. One year later, in March, 1832, the Court decided in favor of the missionaries; Chief Justice Marshall ruled that the state had no constitutional powers to prohibit entry into Cherokee land. The convictions were reversed. It was at this point that Jackson is supposed to have made his famous statement.

In the months following, it was widely reported that Jackson would refuse to enforce the Court's order when it was served on the state. Thus, Henry Clay wrote: "It is rumored that the President has repeatedly said that he will not enforce it, and that he went so far as to express his hope, to a Georgia member of Congress, that Georgia would support her rights." *

As of the summer of 1832, the Supreme Court had not issued an order to Georgia to release the convicted missionaries. Nevertheless, Georgia's receipt of the Supreme Court's decision of that year was greeted with contempt and open disobedience. The missionaries remained in jail.

---

* It has been argued that much of the virulent criticism of Jackson's anticipated failure to enforce the Court's order may have sprung from a willful misinterpretation of Jackson's stand on the National Bank issue. Though the Supreme Court had said a national bank was constitutional, Jackson believed that his responsibility as President of the United States empowered and obliged him to veto the bank bill notwithstanding, if he believed it to be unconstitutional, which he did. But unlike the anticipated action in the Georgia missionaries case, the Supreme Court had never issued a mandate in connection with the Bank dispute; it had merely given the National Bank judicial sanction.

The political climate was especially hot because Jackson was running for reelection.

Shortly after his victory, however, an action by the South Carolina legislature suddenly changed the course of events. Around Thanksgiving the South Carolina legislature enacted the "Nullification Ordinance" (held unconstitutional by the South Carolina legislature the following year). This law prohibited appeals from any South Carolina court to the Supreme Court of the United States.

Jackson now seemed to change his position. He issued a proclamation against the Southern rebellion and pressed vigorously for the "force bill" that was greatly to increase the power of federal courts and federal officials to enforce their orders. The strong stand in South Carolina required an equal degree of willingness on Jackson's part to back the Court's expected mandate to release the imprisoned missionaries; anticipating the course of things to come, the Georgia Governor pardoned and released the missionaries in January, 1833.

All of this was of little use to the Cherokee Nation, for Jackson still perceived the national interest to lie in the forced removal and relocation of the Cherokee Nation in Oklahoma and other interior states.

The Cherokees were, by white standards, the most "civilized" of Indian nations. In 1827, a Cherokee Tribal Council promulgated a written constitution patterned after the federal Constitution. The following year the first Indian newspaper, *The Cherokee Phoenix,* was established. But Andrew Jackson was not impressed. He suggested to Congress that a law be enacted requiring the Indians' removal. Following the Court's decision in the Georgia missionary case, John Ridge, son of a Cherokee leader, visited the White House to argue the Cherokees' case. Jackson was adamant. A split in the Cherokee government developed, and a minority faction negotiated a highly questionable removal treaty with the Administration on December 29, 1835. The forced march westward resulted in deaths of some four thousand Cherokees.

A history of the federal Government's dealings with all the Indian tribes would reveal the longest consistent course of lawbreaking in the nation's history. The very first treaty between the new American nation and an Indian tribe—the Pickering Treaty of 1794, with the Seneca Tribe of the Iroquois Nation—was broken in the 1960's. One provision in the Pickering Treaty read as follows: "The United States will never claim [all the land within the aforementioned boundaries], nor disturb the Seneca nation, or any of the Six Nations, or their Indian friends residing thereon and united with them, in the free use and enjoyment thereof; but it shall remain theirs, til they choose to sell the same to the people of the United States, who have the right to purchase." But a dam constructed in the early '60's flooded much of this same land, even though the Senecas hired an engineer who showed how the dam could have been built at less cost and been made to operate more efficiently elsewhere.

The gross and continued violation by the United States Government of Indian rights has been amply demonstrated; crimes committed against them have ranged from murder to fraud. The fraud continues to this day. A 1971 report of the N.A.A.C.P. Legal Defense and Educational Fund charged the federal Government with defrauding Indian children of millions of federal dollars appropriated to benefit their education. The 162-page report, prepared in conjunction with the Center for Law and Education at Harvard University, listed more than two hundred fifty ways by which state and local officials, with the full cooperation of federal officials, diverted the funds from the Indians—from purchasing "fancy equipment" for white schools to the reduction of local white property taxes. The report was drawn on data from school districts in Arizona, Montana, New Mexico, New York, North and South Dakota, Oklahoma, and Oregon. Assistant Secretary of the Interior Harrison Loesch was silent on demands that two Bureau of Indian Affairs officials be dismissed, but he did state that "on the whole, the report is a balanced one."

The demonstration of how the Government has been permitted to break the law is fairly simple: the way was opened up for it by the Supreme Court of the United States, which in this instance provides us with a classic model of the failure of international law. The Constitution provides in Article VI that "this Constitution, and the Laws of the United States which shall be made in pursuance thereof; and all Treaties made, or which shall be made, under the Authority of the United States, shall be the supreme Law of the Land." But the Constitution does not give any clues as to the relative importance of laws and treaties.

In 1871, the Supreme Court held that an act of Congress contradicting a previous Indian treaty (once again a treaty with the Cherokee Nation) must prevail over the treaty. Said the Court:

> The effect of treaties and acts of Congress, when in conflict, is not settled by the Constitution but the question is not involved in any doubt as to its proper solution. A treaty may supersede a prior act of Congress. . . . And an act of Congress may supersede a prior treaty. . . . Treaties with Indian nations within the jurisdiction of the United States, whatever consideration of humanity and good faith may be involved and require their faithful observance, cannot be more obligatory. They have no higher sanctities; and no greater inviolability or immunity from legislative invasion can be claimed from them. The consequences in all such cases give rise to questions which must be met by the political department of the government. They are beyond the sphere of judicial cognizance. In the case under consideration the act of Congress must prevail as if the treaty were not an element to be considered. If a wrong has been done, the power of redress is with Congress, not with the judiciary,

and that body, upon being applied to, it is to be presumed, will promptly give the proper relief.

But since by the very Act Congress had breached the treaty, there can be only puzzlement over why the Court chose to utter the pious hope that Congress would remedy its own wrong. That, it is to be supposed, is what courts are for.

In 1884, the Supreme Court reaffirmed that decision in a case involving treaty obligations with foreign nations:

> A treaty is primarily a compact between independent nations. It depends for the enforcement of its provisions on the interest and the honor of the governments which are parties to it. If these fail, its infraction becomes the subject of international negotiation and reclamations, so far as the injured party chooses, to seek redress, which may in the end be enforced by actual war.

If it is understandable that the Supreme Court should be reluctant to hold the United States to treaties with foreign nations, it is not at all clear that the same reasoning must apply to treaties with domestic Indians. For to the degree that the Indian tribes are viewed, as the Court has said, as alien nations,* the Court in reality sits as a quasi-international tribunal to uphold contractual obligations between the Indian Nations and the United States.

To suggest that Congress by law can unilaterally breach solemn treaty obligations on the specious reasoning that the Court cannot control the political department of Government is to abdicate completely its role as arbiter. The Supreme Court does not lightly permit the federal Government to break its civil contracts, and the Constitution itself forbids any state from "impairing the obligation of contracts" (though the practical effect of this clause has been much watered down). The pernicious doctrine that treaties may lightly be disregarded at the whim of Congress, a doctrine with firm roots now in American jurisprudence, is neither necessary nor logical.† The Supreme Court had struck down laws of Congress before and it could have struck them down again. But the occasional fortitude of John Marshall's Court was replaced by the excessive timidity of later generations, to the utter devastation of Indian rights.

---

* In 1884 the Supreme Court ruled that an Indian who had severed himself from his tribe was nevertheless not a United States citizen, though he was born in the United States. The Court characterized members of the Indian tribes as "alien and dependent."

† Modern American generals still advocate winking at treaties. See p. 158.

JUVENILES

It is exceedingly difficult for the Government to break the law when it comes to juveniles because the law provides youths with so few rights. When they get into trouble, juveniles are tried apart from adults in different courts, often before very different kinds of judges, almost always without juries. When they are sentenced, they are sent to detention centers that violate the very premise that keeps them from being called jails. If, in a moral sense, the United States has a lawless policy against juveniles, it is one that is nevertheless sanctioned by the formal laws of the states.

Notwithstanding the permissive laws—laws that give judges and other officials wide latitude in their handling of youngsters—ingenious officers of the Government have found ways to violate the law. Juvenile Judge Edwin F. Berliner of El Paso, Texas, is a lawbreaker. There happens to be no way, under law, by which someone can be committed to any institution in the United States without some kind of hearing. According to Steven L. Bercu, an El Paso Legal Assistance Society lawyer, between 1966 and 1971 Judge Berliner sent 375 children to juvenile homes without even troubling to hold a hearing.

Judge Berliner's ally, Chief Probation Officer Morris W. Raley, has protected the rights of degenerate children by hiring as chief guard at the El Paso detention home a man whose own children had to be taken into protective custody while charges that he handcuffed them to their beds and beat them were being investigated.

In 1967, the Supreme Court ruled that a fifteen-year-old boy sentenced to a detention home in Arizona until he was twenty-one for an offense (making a lewd telephone call) that was punishable by a maximum adult sentence of *two months,* was unlawfully convicted because, among other things, he was not represented by a lawyer at his trial.* Despite this decision and a Texas law reflecting the constitutional rule, juveniles in El Paso were regularly denied counsel until February, 1971. Change came then only because of an enormous amount of unfavorable publicity given to local practices by the legal aid society and by Bill Payne, a reporter for the *El Paso Times.*

The following table, taken from the juvenile minute books of El Paso County from May 9, 1969 (when the Texas law requiring counsel became

* Other reasons: the boy's parents were not notified of the charges. A verbal complaint was made by a neighbor, but she never came to court to testify. None of the witnesses was sworn in, no transcript of the hearing was ever made, and the boy was sentenced to the juvenile home after making admissions in answer to questions from the judge.

effective), until October 6, 1970, shows the extent to which the El Paso juvenile authorities ignored the law:

Total Cases	164
With Counsel	23
Without Counsel	141

Punishments	*With Counsel*	*Without Counsel*
Probation	22	54
Commitment	1	78
Probation Revoked	0	9

Commitments Without Counsel and Also Without Parent or Guardian by Age

Age	*No. of Cases*
16	2
15	2
14	1
13	1
11	1
	—
	7

Without Counsel Committed by Age

Age	*No. of Cases*
17	3
16	15
15	26
14	12
13	10
12	3
11	8
10	1
	—
	78

Of the seventy-eight juveniles sentenced without benefit of counsel, at least thirty-four were never even given a hearing.

The flavor of the appallingly corrupt El Paso system was dissected in testimony before the Senate Subcommittee to Investigate Juvenile Delinquency in 1971:

The week of April 17 [1970], for instance, two juveniles were arrested with warrants issued by a justice of the peace. The warrants were issued and the arrests made, over the protests of El Paso City policemen, I might add, who knew better, on orders of Asst. County Atty. Jesus Hernandez, the juvenile prosecutor, despite the fact that Texas law forbids issuance of arrest warrants on juveniles by anyone except the judge of the juvenile court.

And despite the fact that the practice of "baby-sitting" juveniles in the County Juvenile Detention Home at parental request without formally charging them was exposed as illegal in THE [El Paso] TIMES as far back as Oct. 29, 1970, in February and March of this year [1971] a 16-year-old girl was locked up for more than a month in the Detention Home at her mother's request. The mother simply said the girl was "incorrigible," and during the girl's confinement by obliging juvenile authorities, the mother actually went on a two-week vacation with her paramour.

When the mother returned to town, the little girl was released, never having seen a lawyer, never having been formally charged, never having been produced "forthwith" before the judge as required by Texas law and certainly never having been convicted of anything.

And these are only the milder cases, mentioned here to show that what is wrong is not wrong simply because of ignorance or lack of resources, though both these factors play a part.

On the contrary: what is wrong with "juvenile justice" in El Paso County and the state of Texas is wilfully and purposefully wrong, and it is wrong from front to back and from side to side.

* * *

It is probably safe to say that since construction of the County Juvenile Detention Home in the early 1950's, in El Paso County there has probably never been a legal arrest of a child, there has probably never been a legal commitment of a child from that County to a state reformatory. . . .

The "agreed judgments," wherein parents affix their signatures to delinquency judgments pleading their children guilty to charges of "uncontrollability" lodged by the parents, and during which no court hearing has ever taken place, were at first thought to be strictly a local aberration in El Paso County. However, reaction of officials of the Texas Youth Council, which operates the reformatories, to my articles, as well as statements of children who had been in the reformatories, very quickly aroused suspicions that El Paso was not the only county where this has taken place. . . .

Even this, however, only scratches the surface of the crime which has been committed against Texas children for many years, since one of the more interesting discoveries in El Paso County was the fact that many, if not most, of the children illegally committed to state reformatories are mentally retarded.

It should be noted here that the Texas Youth Council Act specifically prohibits commitment of mentally retarded children to reformatories, and yet a survey of the "state schools" (reformatories) by the Youth Affairs Committee of the Texas Senate last year showed that of 1,477 children in Gatesville, more than 500 had IQ's below 80, generally considered the threshold of mental retardation. One child even shows in that report as having an IQ of 36. . . .

Reformatories and detention homes, in other words, are dumping grounds for unwanted, retarded children, and the fact that their parents have been, quite literally, pandered to by juvenile authorities, is reflected in other, even more disgusting, ways.

A case history here, just to give an idea. In 1969 a girl was committed to the TYC on her father's signature as "uncontrollable." The girl, then 16, admittedly was into drugs, and having met her I can say that she is obviously mentally sick.

Her father's signature was sufficient to incarcerate her in what is effectively a prison for nearly 18 months; she never saw a lawyer or the charges against her; the commitment was consummated with a telephone call between Chief El Paso County Probation Officer Morris W. Raley and Judge Berliner, after which the papers were sent to Berliner for his signature.

What makes this case especially interesting is the fact that while the little girl was in prison, the state Child Welfare Agency stepped in and took custody of the girl's younger sister on dependency-neglect proceedings because of statements by the younger sister and the mother that the father had been having incestuous sexual relations with both daughters since they were little tykes.

Even after the Child Welfare action, however, Raley, who does "courtesy supervision" for the TYC on girl parolees from state schools in El Paso County, approved parole of this little girl back to the same parents that Child Welfare and a court had found unfit.

Later, when the girl jumped parole last December, Raley attempted to revoke her parole and send her back, but here the El Paso Municipal Police must be given high marks.

When Raley asked them to pick up the girl, the police, who knew the story, said they could do nothing without a valid arrest warrant, knowing full well that the juvenile court judge has always refused to trouble himself with such trivial technicalities.

The little girl, fortunately, got away, and, having turned 18, was discharged as a matter of course from custody of the TYC. Nevertheless, it seems a strange sort of justice when the police have to gently conspire to help a little girl escape the clutches of another so-called "law enforcement agency" that has, on more than one occasion, knowingly allowed a father who has committed the capital felony offense of incest with a minor female to consign his victim to prison.

* * *

Though I have no specific knowledge of hiring practices of the TYC, it should be obvious from my earlier comments that the caliber of employees at the El Paso Detention Home is unbelievably low. While college degrees are not necessarily the be-all and end-all nor a solution to the problems of juvenile justice, I find it amazing that even a high school degree is a rarity in juvenile probation in El Paso. . . .

One matron at the Detention Home has been repeatedly accused by little girls held there of lasciviously fondling their sexual organs during strip-search procedures. This same woman was actually proceeded against by Child Welfare for child neglect after the principal of the school attended by the woman's children turned her name in because the kids always looked so ratty. . . .

The superintendent of the Detention Home, a retired truck driver who literally cannot spell his own title, is known for his rough and brutal treatment of the kids. In one case not too long ago, a 16-year-old girl, booked in the home on drunk charges, fought when employees of the home attempted to strip-search her.

Pinned to the floor, she asked that the two men in the room, one of them the superintendent of the home, please leave the room, and then she would allow one of the women to strip her. At that point, the ex-truck driver picked the little girl off the floor and threw her against the wall, ripping off her blouse and brassiere. He then left the room cracking jokes about the size and shape of the little girl's breasts.

In another incident several years ago, a "caseworker" at the home who is a retired Air Force CWO, prescribed and administered tranquilizers to a little girl on probation to him, in violation of both state and federal statutes. Further, since Jan. 1, 1969, the El Paso County Probation Department has purchased and presumably administered 1,800 Coricidin cold tablets, despite the fact that the El Paso Public Schools will not even allow their registered nurses to administer these pills to children under their care. All medicines at the Detention Home are administered by the ex-truckdriver superintendent.

The El Paso legal aid lawyer collected a number of affidavits from incarcerated juveniles. One follows:

My name is Javier Salas and I live at 263 Limonite, El Paso, El Paso County, Texas. I am seventeen years old. On the 19th of November, 1970, I made a statement to Steven Bercu which was as follows: In June, 1967, when I was fourteen years old I was picked up at my house by the police. The police asked my mother, "is this him?" My mother answered yes, that's him. I was taken to the city jail and then fingerprinted and then taken to the detention home.

At the detention home I asked if I could make a phone call after I had been strip-searched. I was told that no phone calls could be made unless Mr. Raley approved. I was put in a small room where I waited four hours and then I was taken up to the front. The guard asked me, "we want to know where you were last night and what you did and if you stole anything," and other things of that nature. I asked him what I was there for and he told me incorrigible and runaway. I asked him how I could be a runaway when I was at home and I asked him how I was an incorrigible. He answered that my mother had said so.

I made no statements because I had nothing to say. I was put into a cell and left there for two weeks when I was finally released to my mother.

In May, 1969, I was picked up at my house again by the police and again taken to the city jail and fingerprinted, then taken to the detention home where I was again strip-searched, and I again asked for a phone call, but again I was told that no phone calls could be made unless Mr. Raley approved. I asked what charges were against me. They told me incorrigible, and then they locked me up.

I spent two weeks in my cell and then my mother came to talk to Mr. Raley. Mr. Raley talked my mother into sending me to Gatesville. She told me that she was confused and that she didn't know what to do and she thought that she could get me out of jail any time she wanted to get me out.

One week later I was sent to Gatesville.

I was never in any court at any time for any of this.

The day I was sent to Gatesville, I asked the guards what was going on; they evaded the question and would give me no answer. I asked them where I was going but they told me that they wouldn't be able to tell me. I found out when I arrived at Gatesville.

I spent five months in Gatesville and was finally released in November of 1969. While at Gatesville I was given psychiatric testing. The case workers told me they were amazed that I was there on just the kind of charge that I had been charged with.

While I was at the dentention home I found many windows to be broken, I saw no screens on the window and there were bugs everywhere.

The second time I was in the detention home prior to being sent to Gatesville, I cut my wrists. A guard saw me about an hour later and came into my cell. There was blood all over the cell and all over the clothing. The guard said to me, "you stupid son of a bitch! What did you do that for? Next time borrow my knife and split your neck so you'll get it for sure." Then he told me that "Mr. Raley told me to tell you that if you pull another stunt like that we are going to put handcuffs on you and lock you up in solitary confinement." The guard then went out to get me medical aid. I then washed my cuts on my arms in water and then put on the bandaids that he had brought back to me. The blood in my cell and on my clothing was left and not touched. The next morning I saw that the wounds were still open and I was afraid that there might be an infection so I asked for a doctor but I was completely ignored.

Finally, the following day, a guard named Walley came walking by and I asked him for a doctor. He went to talk to Mr. Raley and then came back and said that it was o.k. finally, and I was taken to Thomason General Hospital. I was given a tetanus shot and the doctor told me that my cuts had needed stitches but that now it was too late.

While at the detention home it was quite common to see in the mornings at 7:00 when we had lineup the guards banging boys into the wall anytime that they thought the boys were not "acting right."

So complete has been their hold over juveniles that the Texas authorities have managed to violate the Thirteenth Amendment to the Constitution, thereby committing the rarest of crimes—slavery. Again, from the Senate testimony:

> In El Paso County, the exploitation is far more direct and reprehensible. I have attached to this statement a work permit and application to drop out of school on one boy whose address is given as the Detention Home. On one sheet is the statement, "Work for therapy at KGH Riding Stables c/o Mr. Raley."
>
> This boy was later taken back to the Detention Home by the owners of the stable because he had stolen some jewelry from them. The boy said he was not getting paid for his work, and that was why he stole. The stable owner claims he had "temporary custody" of the boy—and the evidence is a sheet signed by the boy's father and notarized by Morris W. Raley, surrendering "temporary custody" of the boy to the stable owner. . . .
>
> At this same stable in January of this year, a 13-year-old boy was working while in "protective custody" at the Detention Home. The boy had originally been placed in the home of his stepmother as an "incorrigible," but during his stay there, police found the little boy's sister out in the desert in a half-dug grave, badly beaten and hysterical. She said her stepmother had tried to kill her, and Child Welfare stepped in and took custody of the two children.
>
> Overnight, the little boy went from "incorrigible" to "dependent-neglected"—and still he worked at the stable. Undoubtedly, he was not paid, and even if he had been, he is still too young to work in the state of Texas legally.
>
> My investigation has also uncovered bits and pieces of evidence that some young girls have been steered into prostitution by local "juvenile authorities"—and this matter, too, is under investigation by the District Attorney's office.
>
> And finally, there is the question of the "little wetbacks." As mentioned earlier, they are kept totally separated from the other children in the home, and the U.S. Immigration Service admits it has no way of determining how many are held there or what disposition is made of them.
>
> Obviously, a variation on the custody transfer theme would be easy to work here—and people who need cheap labor, along with those who supplied that labor force, could turn an excellent profit.
>
> I have also supplied this subcommittee with an El Paso Probation Department phone bill with a phone number in a particular Oklahoma town. The phone number is that of the town's high school principal, who "refers" errant children to any one of a number of farmers in that town.

Following public revelations of the extent of the El Paso juvenile justice system, unusual things began to happen. A lawyer filed a writ of habeas corpus on behalf of a juvenile client. Morris Raley unlawfully removed the youth from the County. Judge Berliner, aware of the removal, did not interfere. The writ was granted, and the granting judge wrote the members of the Juvenile Board, asking for Raley's resignation. Raley became "ill," and no meeting was held. Two weeks after the writ was filed, the records of the County Detention Home were seized by a County grand jury. Raley was subsequently convicted of grand larceny and embezzlement. Judge Berliner has escaped criminal charges, although several private suits are pending against him. He was transferred from the juvenile bench to the city's domestic court.

Folks in Madison Heights, Michigan, have a different solution to juvenile crime. In response to the felt need to control wayward children in the Detroit suburb, an ordinance was passed making it a criminal offense on the part of the parents if their children below the age of seventeen violated city or state laws, including traffic regulations. The penalties for the parents are a $500 fine and ninety days in jail. After ten months in operation, the city fathers claimed the law was working: no parent had been prosecuted; but thirty-five warnings had been sent out, and the children thus far had not gotten into trouble again.

The only trouble with this "effective" ordinance is that it is patently unconstitutional. It is a basic premise of American jurisprudence that a person cannot be held criminally liable for the criminal acts of another (with the significant exception of the acts of co-conspirators). Municipal Judge Edward Lawrence of Madison Heights agrees: "It will remain a good weapon against juvenile offenders as long as it stays out of the courtroom," he commented about the ordinance, "but if someone is convicted and challenges it, I'm afraid it won't hold up."

Perhaps because this was merely an extrajudicial comment, elders in the other suburbs of East Detroit, Roseville, Pontiac, West Bloomfield Township, and Troy, Michigan have all seen fit to adopt the unlawful law.

THE POOR

Without money to enforce them, the rights of the poor are often lost. In Nevada, believing that a sizable number of welfare recipients were "cheating," George E. Miller, State Welfare Administrator, eliminated many families from the welfare roles in the fall of 1970. Because the law requires that any persons terminated from the welfare program must be given notice and a right to a hearing, the Las Vegas Legal Aid Society secured a federal temporary restraining order against the State Welfare Administration.

Notwithstanding the order of the federal court, however, Miller continued to terminate welfare benefits of those who he suspected were violating welfare regulations. By December, more than one thousand welfare recipients were cut off altogether and another one thousand or more found their benefits reduced. The terminations and reductions affected more than 50 percent of all those on the Nevada welfare roles. Notice and hearing were not provided—a clear violation of the federal directive.

It remained for Judge George P. Foley of the federal District Court of the District of Nevada to order reinstatement and back allowances. The court ruled that the state "ran roughshod over the constitutional rights" of those affected. The court did not declare the state in error in asserting that welfare recipients were cheating (by understating their incomes); it merely ruled, twice, that the state should be compelled to prove its case. This Nevada proved unwilling to do.

Although it had ample opportunity to prove its case before a three-judge federal court convened for the purpose, in April, 1971, the state reached a compromise with the litigious welfare recipients and agreed to restore to the rolls all those previously cut off and to increase benefits of those whose benefits had been reduced. Nevertheless, the reductions that had been in effect from October 1, 1970, through April 30, 1971, were not to be restored retroactively.

Officials in Sacramento, California, have shown an equal contempt for the law. Despite a provision of the state constitution that prohibits the executive department from making selective cuts in welfare payments, the California Welfare Department in November, 1970, coupled an increase in the maximum benefits payable (the raise was required by federal law) with a declaration that only 69 percent of the assessed needs of the individual recipients would be paid. A suit was filed, and the California Supreme Court rejected the asserted power that would have affected more than four hundred thousand families in California.

A more ingenious device to purge a state's participation in welfare was dismantled by the New Jersey Supreme Court when it held that laws against fornication could not be prosecuted selectively against welfare recipients. Fornication laws are almost universally disregarded in the United States, except when some other purposes are to be served by enforcing them.

In 1967, for example, a twenty-eight-year-old woman admitted to Secaucus County welfare officials that a man to whom she was not married was the father of her three children.

In New Jersey law failure to state the name of the father would have rendered the woman ineligible to receive welfare benefits. Magistrate Steven Kushner of Paterson brought charges against the couple for criminal fornication, an act made unlawful by a 1796 statute. Kushner stated that he was "fed up" with the results of poor people's fornication. Because the couple had already admitted the act, the convictions were speedily secured. In 1971 the New Jersey Supreme Court reversed the convictions.

Another way to forestall increases in the welfare budget is the one-year residency requirement. In the mid-1960's, Connecticut, the District of Columbia, and Pennsylvania enacted laws that barred various welfare payments, such as those under programs like Aid to Families with Dependent Children, to people who had lived in the states for less than one year. A number of people who had moved to these states to be near family members were denied support.

In Washington, a woman who had been mentally ill and hospitalized for twenty-four years was denied funds required to help support her in a foster home because the period of treatment in the Washington hospital did not count under the residency requirement, even though the hospital was public and the question was one of transferring public funds from one institution to another.

Suits were brought in each of the states and in the District, and in every case a three-judge federal court ruled the residency requirement an unconstitutional burden on the right to travel.

In April, 1969, the Supreme Court affirmed the lower courts' decisions, striking down the various laws on the ground that the distinctions between needy families in a state for one year and those there for a shorter period was unconstitutional in the absence of a compelling governmental interest. Though many reasons were asserted to justify the residency laws, the primary purpose of each law was to deter an influx of needy newcomers and thus to put a damper on soaring welfare budgets.

The states also argued that they had a rational interest in limiting benefits to those who contributed to government by way of taxes and that "the requirement (1) facilitates the planning of the welfare budget; (2) provides an objective test of residency; (3) minimizes the opportunity for recipients fraudulently to receive payments from more than one jurisdiction; and (4) encourages early entry of new residents into the labor force." The Supreme Court ruled that none of these contentions would bear scrutiny, and the one-year residency requirement was overturned.

A year later the Supreme Court affirmed the decision of a fourth federal court, which had struck down a New York law refusing payment to dependent children whose mothers had lived in the state less than one year and who could not prove they had come to the state for any other reason than to receive welfare. Undaunted, the New York state legislature in 1971 enacted another law requiring a one-year residency before welfare money would be paid to these domestic "immigrants" to the state. The state claimed the law was passed in response to an "emergency," that the residency requirement would lapse in five years, and that the requirement was "an essential step in protecting the State's economic and social viability." Another glorious monument to New York's official contempt for law, the new residency requirement was struck down by the Supreme Court in early 1972.

ALIENS

The United States is a jealous gatekeeper. The Statue of Liberty symbolizes the ideal of free immigration, but she is hardly an appropriate symbol for the actual practice; the official United States attitude toward aliens has been and is a hard one. For nearly fifty years the great "melting pot" frankly discriminated on a racial and religious basis in admitting immigrants to the United States. The immigration laws have been construed in a draconian manner, and high government officials have ordered the indefinite imprisonment of aliens seeking admission to the United States on Ellis Island in New York harbor. Repeated constitutional tests have borne no fruit.

In 1950, the Supreme Court rejected a contention that a German war bride was constitutionally entitled to know the charges against her that had landed her on Ellis Island and kept her imprisoned there for twenty-eight months. Justice Sherman Minton, for a five to four majority, said that "whatever the procedure authorized by Congress is, it is due process as far as an alien denied entry." (The woman was ultimately admitted into the United States when a hearing before an immigration appeal board showed that the Government had absolutely no evidence to prove that she was a security risk.)

Three years later the Supreme Court ruled that it was constitutional for an alien to be kept imprisoned on Ellis Island for life. The man in the case had lived in the United States for twenty-five years. In 1948, he went to visit his dying mother in Rumania, and upon his return to his wife and family, immigration authorities declined to let him enter. Other nations, afraid of him if the United States was afraid of him, rejected him also. He was thus condemned to live on Ellis Island, stateless. Shortly after the Court's decision, the Department of Justice relented and paroled him to his American family. But the principle still stands as it has been recognized for nearly two hundred years—ordinary aliens seeking entry to the United States have no rights.

A rare example of lawbreaking in this area does exist, however, and that was the Coast Guard's return to Soviet control of the defecting Lithuanian sailor Simas Kudirka. In November, 1970, the U.S. Coast

Guard Cutter *Vigilant* was tied up to a Russian ship off Martha's Vineyard during fishing talks. Kudirka signaled to American seamen his intentions to defect, and he ultimately jumped aboard the cutter. After hours of deliberation and delay the commanding officer of the *Vigilant*, on orders from his Coast Guard superiors in Boston, returned the reluctant sailor to the Russians by permitting Soviet seamen to come aboard the United States vessel and drag him away.

Article 33 of the 1951 Convention Relating to Status of Refugees, to which the United States subscribes, states that "no contracting state shall expel or return a refugee in any manner whatsoever to the frontiers of territories where his life or freedom would be threatened." The United States has not always been unwavering in its belief that the lives of refugees escaping from Communist nations would be jeopardized were they required to return. In this instance, Kudirka was severely beaten by Russian sailors in clear view of many Americans as he was being returned to his ship.

President Nixon denounced the entire affair as "outrageous." Following an expedited investigation, Secretary of Transportation John Volpe announced that he was permitting the Coast Guard Admiral and Captain whose decisions resulted in Kudirka's repatriation to retire and that they were being issued "punitive letters of reprimand." The skipper of the *Vigilant* was issued an "administrative letter of reprimand (nonpunitive)" and immediately dismissed from the ship for permitting "foreign nations to exercise authority on board a Coast Guard vessel." The White House announced new guidelines requiring all defector cases to be called to its attention immediately. How effective the cure is remains to be seen since the cause of the Coast Guard's bungling was its ignorance of the regulations and a breakdown in communications with the State Department.

Inside the United States, aliens have some shadowy rights. They are entitled to hearings before deportation, for instance. But the hearings need merely show that the alien committed the act for which deportation is being sought, and anything—or nearly anything—may be made the grounds for deportation.

The Supreme Court has even sanctioned the deportation of aliens who committed lawful acts later made illegal. During the 1920's and '30's, mere membership in the Communist Party was not a crime (nor, after an interlude of some years, is it a crime today). Many people, aliens and citizens alike, joined the Party in the midst of the Depression. In 1939, the Supreme Court ruled that an alien who had resigned from the Party could not, under the existing law, thereafter be deported for the prior membership. This decision prompted a mass of expulsions from the Party. In 1940, the Smith Act made membership in the Communist Party a deportable offense no matter when the alien was a member.

In 1946, the Department of Justice moved to deport three aliens who had been long-time residents of the United States. Peter Harisiades had lived in the United States since 1916, when at the age of thirteen he emigrated with his father from Greece. Harisiades had been an active Party member since 1925, and an order for his deportation issued in 1930 was finally served in 1946, the delay ostensibly occurring because of his extensive use of aliases. Luigi Mascitti emigrated from Italy in 1920 at the age of sixteen. He was a member of the Party between 1923 and 1929, when he resigned. A deportation order was not issued for seventeen years. The third alien, Dora Coleman, came to the United States from Russia in 1914 at the age of thirteen. She was a member of the Party from 1919 to 1920, from 1928 to 1930, and again from 1936 to 1938. All three admitted knowledge of the Party's belief in the necessity for force or violence.

In 1952, the Supreme Court upheld the deportation of these three aliens, against contentions that the law authorizing deportations under these circumstances was ex post facto and therefore unconstitutional. The Court went on to say:

> However, even if the Act were found to be retroactive, to strike it down would require us to overrule the construction of the ex post facto provision which has been followed by this Court from earliest times. It always has been considered that that which it forbids is penal legislation which imposes or increases criminal punishment for conduct lawful previous to its enactment. Deportation, however severe its consequences, has been consistently classified as civil rather than a criminal procedure.

The Court also stated that this interpretation of the ex post facto clause was settled and that the Court would not reopen the question.

The conclusion that deportation is a civil penalty, though it meant in each of the cases separation from wives and children with whom the three aliens had lived for decades, was all the more remarkable in view of one of the earliest decisions in American history, a 1798 case on which the Court relied in 1952. In that early case, Justice Samuel Chase, discussing the ex post facto clause in connection with illegal acts of the British government committed under the claim of lawful authority, said:

> Sometimes [Acts of Parliament] respected the crime, by declaring acts to be treason, which were not treason, when committed; at other times, they violated the rules of evidence (to supply a deficiency of legal proof) by admitting one witness, when the existing law required two; by receiving evidence without oath; or the oath of the wife against the husband; or other testimony, which the court of justice would not admit; at other times they inflicted punishments, where the party was not, by law, liable to any punishment; and in other cases, they inflicted greater punishment, than the law annexed to the office. The ground for the exercise of such legislative power was this, that the safety of the Kingdom

depended on the death, or other punishment, of the offenders; as if traitors when discovered, could be so formidable, or the government so insecure!

The "punishments" cited by the Supreme Court in 1798 in support of the proposition that inflicting punishments "where the party was not, by law, liable to any punishment" were the banishments by Parliament of Lord Clarendon in 1669 and of the Bishop of Atterbury in 1723. So much for the Court's historical prowess.

But these cases are not cited for the proposition that the Government has acted illegally toward the alien; they are mentioned only in passing to suggest just how far the Government may go in dealing with aliens even inside the United States.*

If the United States can treat resident aliens within its borders with a casuistry befitting kings, its bad treatment of aliens outside its borders —that is, everybody else in the world—need hardly be cause for surprise. In 1966, Bertrand Russell, Jean-Paul Sartre, and other world-famous philosophers accused the United States of committing war crimes against the Vietnamese. Their announced intention to hold mock trials in Europe was looked upon in the United States as an act akin to madness. Since then, of course, fantasy became reality.

By the spring of 1971, the collection of thirty-three books reveiwed by Neil Sheehan in the *New York Times* was indicative of the evidence of war crimes being amassed. As Sheehan reported:

> The Army Field Manual says that it is illegal to attack hospitals. We routinely bombed them. The destruction of Vietcong and North Vietnamese Army hospitals in the South Vietnamese countryside was announced at the daily press briefings, The Five O'Clock Follies, by American military spokesmen in Saigon.
>
> *   *   *
>
> Since 1965, a minimum of 150,000 Vietnamese civilians, an average of 68 men, women, and children every day for the past six years, have been

---

* The distinction between a criminal "punishment" and a civil "penalty" has a curious ramification in the Armed Forces. In order to sentence a soldier to a "bad-conduct" or a "dishonorable" discharge, he must be tried by a court martial and found guilty of the offense charged. Constitutional procedures must be followed, including the right to counsel. If he is sentenced to one of these types of discharge, it is beyond doubt that he has been subjected to a criminal punishment. However, if the military services do not wish to go through the trouble of constitutional legal proceedings, they often avail themselves of the curious "administrative discharge proceeding," in which no procedures need be followed and the unlucky soldier can be "awarded" an "undesirable" discharge *for the very same* offense that should have been tried by a court martial. Except that the undesirable discharge is not tantamount to a criminal conviction, the soldier suffers the same disabilities as he does under the other two types of discharge. The military explains away its embarrassing failure to abide by constitutional procedure by unashamedly claiming that the "undesirable discharge" is a civil matter and not a punishment.

killed in the South by American military action or by weapons supplied to the Saigon forces by the United States. Another 350,000 Vietnamese civilians have been wounded or permanently maimed. This is a very conservative estimate. I remember asking one of the most senior American Generals in the late summer of 1966 if he was not worried by all the civilian casualties that the bombing and shelling were causing. "Yes, it is a problem," he said, "but it does deprive the enemy of the population, doesn't it?" *

In his exceedingly cautious book *Nuremburg and Vietnam: An American Tragedy,* Telford Taylor takes the layman through the legal maze and concludes that it is indisputable that some war crimes were indeed committed.

The trials of Lieutenant William Calley and others are testament to the tragedy. Calley was following orders, he said, but he neglected to buttress his case by introducing evidence of the Army's widespread failure to instruct the troops and officers in the laws of land warfare. The teaching of these rules was observed mainly in the breach; though they were the law, it is fair to say that something less than meticulous attention was paid to the books in class. This is not to minimize the difficulty of following the rules in particular situations. But the Army's failure, as the more than one year long cover-up of Mylai suggests, was not one of occasional mistake.

Some military officers have come right out in favor of lawbreaking. General J. H. Rothschild (U.S. Army, retired), a "leading chemical warfare specialist," argued in a guest column in the *New York Times* against ratification of the Geneva Gas Protocol (first presented to the Senate in 1925) prohibiting the use of "asphyxiating, poisonous, or other gases" in war. "Chemical weapons are powerful," he said, "and the U.S. may need them to reduce the enemy manpower superiority" (meaning, may need them to kill with). Moreover, the General continued:

> We must be prepared to fight with chemicals even if the Protocol is ratified, as our retaliatory strength will be a much surer deterrent than the Protocol. We can't depend on myths that treaties are sacred to all nations, e.g., Italy used gas against Ethiopia in 1936 even though both had ratified the Geneva Protocol.

Treaties become myths because people like General Rothschild make statements notifying nations in advance that we have no intention to abide by them. The argument is not merely theoretical: one week after General Rothschild wrote, the Army conceded that officers of the Americal Division in South Vietnam used a defoliant called Orange Herbicide,

---

* General Tomoyuki Yamashita was executed by the United States after World War II for his failure to prevent his troops from killing 25,000 noncombatants, though it was proved he personally knew nothing about the massacre and was in no position to stop it.

which, fully known to them, had been banned pending an investigation of its potential for causing stillbirths or birth defects. The Army indicated it would not prosecute the offenders. The affair came to light when Ronald L. Ridenhour, the journalist who as a Vietnam veteran prompted the Department of Defense to begin the Mylai investigation, received permission from a commanding officer (unaware of his troops' use of the defoliant) to talk to the crews who had released more than ten thousand gallons of the noxious chemical.

No purpose would be served here to reiterate the many other facts and arguments attempting to convince us that war crimes have been consciously committed and condoned, and the passing reference to them at the end of a section entitled "Aliens" is only slightly facetious. Vietnam and Mylai are staggering problems, but it is not surprising that they have occurred in places beyond the reach of our laws and our courts.

The point is simply that war crimes should not be viewed as isolated phenomena. They are the inevitable by-products—perhaps end-products—of a Government contemptuous of its own laws.

4
Crimes Affecting Everyone

CIVILIAN CONTROL OF THE MILITARY

A PROVISION OF THE federal code prohibits any regular (as opposed to reserve) officer of the armed forces from holding a civil office. The penalty for violating this provision is automatic forfeiture of the commission. The ostensible purpose of the law is to prevent the encroachment of the military on the normal civilian operation of the Government.

The original law in 1870 imposed forfeiture even for retired officers who accepted governmental office. During debate on the original bill, Representative Jones of Kentucky said in support of his amendment to exempt retired officers: "If it be inconsistent with our system of government to appoint military officers to civil positions, all I have to say is, that these [retired] men are not connected with the Army of the United States . . . and their holding civil offices will not conflict with any such theory of the Government." His amendment failed, though his position ultimately prevailed. Today only the regular officer on active duty is prohibited by this law from accepting a civil office.

Despite this law, the 1971 Government Organization Manual listed eight regular officers of the armed forces as holding positions as Deputy Assistant Secretaries of Defense. The names and positions follow:

Deputy Assistant Secretary (Inspection Services): Lieutenant General Hugh M. Exton, USA

Deputy Assistant Secretary (Intelligence): Vice Admiral Harold G. Bowen, Jr., USN

Prin. Deputy Assistant Secretary (Health & Environment): Brigadier General George J. Hayes, USA

Deputy Assistant Secretary (Materiel): Vice Admiral Eli T. Reich, USN

Deputy Assistant Secretary (Military Assistance & Sales): Lieutenant General Robert H. Warren, USAF

Deputy Assistant Secretary (Manpower & Reserve Affairs): Vice Admiral W. P. Mack, USN

Deputy Assistant Secretary (Military Personnel Policy): Major General Leo E. Benade, USA

Deputy Assistant Secretary (Public Affairs): Brigadier General Daniel James, Jr., USAF

The manual further indicates that Vice Admiral John M. Lee, USN, is Assistant Director (Weapons Evaluation and Control Bureau) of the U.S. Arms Control and Disarmament Agency.

The meaning of "civil office" has never been statutorily defined. Department of Defense (DOD) regulations do not deal directly with this law, but one DOD regulation does refer to the term for the related purpose of defining the permissible scope of political activities by members of the Armed Forces. That directive states:

> *Civil office* is an office, not military in nature, that involves the exercise of powers of or authority of civil government. It may be either an elective or appointed office under the United States, a territory or possession, or a state, county, or municipality, or official subdivision thereof. The term "civil office" shall not include offices to which military personnel may be assigned in a military status.

Since this directive by its terms includes enlisted as well as officer personnel and regular officers as well as reserves, and since DOD cannot add to or subtract from the content of a law by issuing a regulation, the directive cannot be claimed to contain an authoritative definition of the meaning of "civil office." It does, however, suggest a principle: a public office of the United States, such as the Office of a Deputy Assistant Secretary, responsible for the administration of a major part of an executive department, ought to fall within the definition. That the Deputy Assistant Secretary is within the Defense Department should not serve to convert the civil office into one "military in nature" because that phrase relates to those offices created by federal law, such as the Army Chief of Staff or the Chief of Naval Operations; and by law those posts call for the appointment of military officers.

The law prohibiting military officers from holding civil office, Section 973(b) of Title 10 of the *United States Code*, contains an explicit exception for those positions that Congress by law chooses to exempt. A handful of these positions, such as the Director of Selective Service, the Director of the Central Intelligence Agency, various foreign-affairs positions and positions in the Environmental Sciences Service Administration, have been expressly denoted by federal law as offices that the President may fill with military officers. The offices of Deputy Assistant Secretary have not been so exempted.

Since military officers are frequently called upon by executive officials to provide advice and assistance, it is clear that a staff assistant or a director of a departmental bureau need not be considered to hold a "civil office." The hundreds of military officers serving at various levels within DOD need not be considered to hold "civil office."

The office of Deputy Assistant Secretary, however, is not an insignificant office; it unquestionably involves "the exercise of the powers of or authority of civil government." The various generals and admirals serving in these positions are not merely assigned to those offices. They do not sign directives or letters *"for* the Deputy Assistant Secretary"; they sign *as* "Deputy Assistant Secretary."

Yet high-ranking officers holding these jobs are not likely to be dispossessed of their military emoluments. The operation of Section 973(b) will serve, therefore, as a concise example of how federal law is ignored by the Government.

The officers will claim that notwithstanding the looks of things they have not and are not violating the law. First, they will point to the fact that Congress has not provided by law for the positions of any Deputy Assistant Secretaries of Defense except one—that of Deputy Assistant Secretary of Defense for Reserve Affairs. The law establishing that office specifies that the incumbent must be a civilian.

Therefore, our admirals and generals will argue, other Deputy Assistant Secretaries may be military officers. Appealing as the argument may seem, the legal fallacy is evident: Section 973(b) does not preclude *reserve* officers holding civil office; it prohibits only regular officers. The law establishing the one office of Deputy Assistant Secretary prohibits *any* officer from holding it.

Moreover, Congress does not permit by silence what it has elsewhere condemned. Congressional redundancy does not create exceptions to other laws, and Section 973(b) permits only those exceptions explicitly made by law. The explicit requirement that a particular Deputy Assistant Secretary of Defense be a civilian hardly amounts to statutory language exempting other positions from the same requirement.

Our admirals and generals will then retreat to a second line of defense, premising their argument on a curious line of interpretative rulings by the Comptroller General, the Comptroller of the Treasury, and the Attorney General of the United States. According to these various rulings "civil office" means "public office," which in turn is defined to require the following elements: "the specific position must be created by law; there must be certain definite duties imposed by law on the incumbent, and they must involve exercise of some portion of the sovereign power."

This line of cases began with an opinion of the Attorney General in 1871 that if Major General George Meade accepted the position of Parks Commissioner of Philadelphia, as he was about to do, his commission would terminate. In 1950, the Comptroller General of the United States (an officer not part of the Executive Branch but responsible solely to Congress) concluded that the position of Commissioner of Roads for Alaska was not a civil office, since it was not created by statute but by an administrative decision of the Secretary of the Interior. Our generals and admirals advance a step.

In that same decision the Comptroller General said that the level of importance of the office does not alone determine the status of the office. Support for that position was drawn from the Wisconsin Supreme Court, which had ruled in 1941 that the President of the University of Wisconsin did not hold a civil office (his difficulties arose under a similar law when he became head of the Selective Service System), "while a justice of peace or notary public is a public officer." Better and better, say our admirals and generals; obviously Section 973(b) was intended as nothing more than a joke.

Indeed, here is how Section 973(b) was employed in an actual case. In 1964, an officer was appointed in the regular Army. Subsequently, he was permitted to go on extended excess leave (without pay) to attend law school in preparation for his transfer to the Army's Judge Advocate General's Corps. While attending law school he obtained a part-time job as guard at the Library of Congress. In that capacity he worked four hours five evenings a week.

To his surprise, the officer found himself holding a "civil office." Under federal law, the Librarian of Congress is empowered to designate employees of the library as special guards to police the building and grounds. The law specifically directs that the guards can be used to maintain "suitable order and decorum" and that they can make arrests if necessary. The Comptroller General of the United States held that the law thus created the position and defined its duties, some of which included the necessity of exercising the sovereign power of the United States.

Though he no doubt intended the job as one which would permit him to earn some money while studying in the evening, the officer found his commission revoked. Moreover, said the Comptroller General, "the fact that an appointment to perform the statutory duties of an office may be temporary provides no basis for determining that a position is not a 'civil office.' "

We seem to be left with a conclusion so anomalous that some fault must surely lie within the logic: a temporary guard at the Library of Congress holds a civil office; a Deputy Assistant Secretary of Defense does not. Innocence or subterfuge?

The answer must be that the Comptroller General is simply wrong.* No matter how unnecessary or absurd occasional official acts of Congress are, we are not to suppose that the supreme legislature of the nation would be so frightened at the prospect of a regular military officer's going uncontrollably beserk as a notary public that they should declare an acceptance of such a position as reason to terminate a commission. It is comforting to realize, of course, that should a Library of Congress guard suddenly begin to shoot down stray passersby he would at least be doing it in a civilian capacity.

It may also be that Section 973(b) is totally devoid of meaning and that like many statutes it is a sop to reassure the public that even if the undesirable conduct is engaged in, it is at least against the law.

The Comptroller General's rulings on the notary public issue have been flatly contradicted by a 1971 opinion of the Attorney General, who sensibly interpreted a line of his predecessors' opinions as establishing that where the governmental position was one in which the duties were "extensive, engrossing, and responsible" (unlike the sporadic duties of a notary public), it should be regarded as a public office. Noting that a notary public may refrain from performing any duties, yet still retain his "office," the Attorney General in a letter to the Judge Advocate General of the Air Force concluded that the contrary Air Force doctrine should be overruled. Curiously, the Attorney General did not mention the Comptroller General's past discussion of the subject. This could lead to the anomalous result that an officer becoming a notary public will retain his military commission and be required to remain on duty (courtesy the Attorney General) but will not be paid (courtesy the Comptroller General).

The Attorney General's opinion points to a far more logical position than that of the Comptroller General's, for it would require the realities of the duties of the office to outweigh archaic technicalities from a by-gone age. The duties of a Deputy Assistant Secretary being "extensive, engrossing, and responsible," the position should be regarded as a "civil office," requiring immediate termination of the present incumbents' military status.

The Army has recently come up with a potent weapon to emasculate Section 973(b). A regular Army officer was appointed to the Board of

* The line of opinions usually relied upon ignores an old Supreme Court case, predating the 1870 Act, that defined "office" as follows: "a public station, or employment, conferred by the appointment of Government. The term embraces the ideas of tenure, duration, emoluments, and duties."

Directors of a State Water and Sanitation District created by statute. In serving on the Board, he performed duties defined by law and exercised various sovereign powers, such as the use of public property, condemnation, and the power to set rates for services.

All the tests were met, and accordingly the Judge Advocate General of the Army was compelled to recognize that the officer did hold a civil office in violation of Section 973(b). Having no other choice, he was compelled to terminate the officer's commission in the United States Army. But, said the Judge Advocate General, the officer's status as a member of the Army of the United States ("AUS") was not affected; the officer was, therefore, permitted to continue as before on extended active duty in the Army while holding on to his job as board member of the Sanitation District.

Since except in the rarest circumstances (not present here) it is impossible under law for a military officer to hold two different commissions, the Judge Advocate General's opinion must have been divinely inspired. No one but a military officer who was also a lawyer could ever have hit upon such an ideal solution to a complex problem. The solution, in fact, is more elegant in its power and beauty than the most precise mathematical equation: in mathematics plus one and minus one equal zero, but in military law you can have your cake and eat it too.

The Air Force has a more efficient method of forestalling operation of the law. They ignore it. Thus, when an Air Force captain was appointed to the Virginia Polytechnic Institute Board of Visitors, the president of the Institute asked his superiors to issue him orders to permit his attendance at a meeting of the Board. The Air Force responded instead (probably erroneously) by notifying the officer that he had lost his commission. The Air Force permitted him to remain on the payroll in a "de facto" status, however, until he was provided with a reserve commission. Secure with that appointment, he then reapplied for a regular commission. Presumably he resigned from the Board.

A few Air Force officers have apparently found a use for the law: they automatically terminated their military obligations by having themselves appointed notaries public.* Unfortunately for most officers disenchanted with military life, the law, as already noted, does not apply to reservists.

---

* A similar factual situation lay behind the Army's original opinion setting forth the "two commissions" theory: a regular officer, having served his obligatory three years, submitted his resignation. The Army refused to accept it and issued him procedurally dubious orders for a second tour in Vietnam. Successive requests for compassionate reassignment and a hardship discharge were denied.

Faced with being sent to Asia, the officer went instead to Pennsylvania, became a notary public, and notified the Army that he was entitled to an honorable discharge because his commission had terminated. To plug the gaping escape valve, the Army ruled that his permanent commission as a second lieutenant was indeed terminated but his temporary "AUS" commission as a captain was not.

The Comptroller General may still not be convinced by the foregoing discussion that most of our admirals and generals are unlawfully
holding the offices of Deputy Assistant Secretaries of Defense. Vice
Admiral John Lee, however, is in somewhat more danger. As indicated
above, he has served as an Assistant Director of the U.S. Disarmament
and Arms Control Agency. That office and its duties are defined by federal law, and those duties encompass the exercise of part of the sovereign
power of the United States. Moreover, the office is not elsewhere exempted in the federal code from the prohibition imposed by Section
973(b). It follows that Vice Admiral Lee is in violation of that statute
and that the Navy ought forthwith to declare Admiral Lee's commission
terminated.

This the Navy will not do, however, because it has a vested interest
in having one of its flag officers on the agency. That this is what Section
973(b) was intended to prevent will hardly persuade the Navy. Vice
Admiral Lee, it will be argued, was not fully warned of the consequences
of his accepting the office of Assistant Director (the Navy was not subjected to Section 973(b) until 1968, ninety-eight years after the law was
first applied to the Army). Moreover, in the past the commissions only
of low-ranking officers have been revoked. Finally, Vice Admiral Lee is
a military man and he must accept his orders: how was he to know they
were illegal? * Military men don't ask questions. Neither does the
American public.†

Civilian control of the military is threatened not only by military
officers holding executive office. Civil officials holding military office can
be equally threatening, and perhaps more so if they happen to be
members of Congress.

Members of Congress are forbidden by Article I of the Constitution
from holding "any office under the United States." ‡ Since it has been
good politics for candidates to have military affiliations, it is not surprising that many successful candidates hold reserve commissions. In
1970, in fact, 122 members of the Senate and House of Representatives
held such commissions. They compose more than twenty percent of
the entire Congress.

Of these, thirty-five were officers in Reserve or National Guard components in "ready" status; an additional twenty-four were on inactive
status and more than sixty others were on retired lists. These reservists

---

* The very question regarding illegality was asked of the Navy JAG in 1969. When
it appeared that the answer would be that the appointment would be unlawful, the
question was withdrawn by the Secretary and the JAG was not permitted to render
an opinion. Vice-Admiral Lee was appointed shortly thereafter.

† The Comptroller General has officially responded to a draft of the foregoing
discussion. His response and a critique set out in the Appendix, pp. 274 ff.

‡ "[N]o person holding any office under the United States, shall be a Member of
either House during his continuance in office."

were not distributed randomly throughout the Congressional committees but, as might be expected, were heavily concentrated in the committees with jurisdiction over the military. More than one-third of the House Armed Services Committee was composed of these reservists and two-thirds of the members of one of its subcommittees dealing with compensation and pensions of veterans were reservists. In the Senate, more than a majority of the members of the Armed Services Committee were reservists.

This incestuous relationship had never been challenged in any court until 1970, or 181 years after the law went into effect.* When the case was finally heard, a federal district judge ruled that members of Congress could not constitutionally hold reserve commissions.

FUND IMPOUNDING: PARSIMONIOUS SPENDING OF THE PUBLIC MONIES

The Constitution of the United States gives to Congress the power to authorize and appropriate funds for the development and implementation of federal programs. Appropriation and authorization bills, once passed by Congress, must be signed by the President to become law. (If a President refuses to sign an "enrolled bill" it becomes law anyway after the expiration of ten days, unless Congress has adjourned.) Of course, a President may veto a bill, but Congress then has the opportunity to reenact it by a two-thirds majority vote in each house. The Constitution gives the President no authority to exercise the so-called "item veto," whereby a President would strike from a given bill particular items or provisions which he finds undesirable. A President must take or leave the entire bill.

Since 1941, Presidents of both parties have created and maintained a dubious doctrine that permits them to violate the rather tightly drawn strictures of the Constitution. That is the doctrine of the impounded fund. According to this doctrine, whenever the President decides that a particular program or policy is undesirable, even though it is already authorized by law with accompanying appropriations, he may simply refuse to spend the money. In so refusing the President violates his constitutional obligation to see that the laws of the land are faithfully executed.

Franklin D. Roosevelt took the first step toward the modern doctrine of impounding when he refused to go ahead with a public works program that sprang forth from Congress unrequested; he noted the necessity for economizing in areas unrelated to the national defense, given the clear emergency which had befallen the nation. Funds have been

* See pp. 261 ff.

impounded, if not regularly at least from time to time, by every President since.

President Truman impounded the funds for a fifty-eight-group Air Force. Secretary of Defense Louis A. Johnson defended the impounding before the Defense Subcommittee of the House Appropriations Committee in the following manner:

SEC. JOHNSON: When there is a finding by the Commander-in-Chief that there is sufficiency of defense . . . I think we are charged with the obligation, and I must so interpret it, of not spending the excess money. . . .

MR. ENGLE: He overruled the Act of Congress.

SEC. JOHNSON: He may have overruled the Act of Congress, but not without consideration. . . .

MR. MAHON: Where in the law or Constitution would you take away from Congress the authority of raising and equipping and maintaining armies and navies and delegate that authority elsewhere?

SEC. JOHNSON: I think the power was vested in the President of the United States to impound. . . .

MR. MAHON: In what way is this power vested in the President of the United States? Where does the Constitution say it?

SEC. JOHNSON: In the power of the Commander-in-Chief. I think he has the power. . . . I think it is an inherent authority vested in the Commander-in-Chief and the President.

President Eisenhower fared better than his predecessor in escaping a strong denunciation by members of Congress; but impound he did.

The heat of debate rose sharply with decisions by Presidents Kennedy and Johnson to impound funds for certain weapons-systems programs. In the controversy surrounding the manned bomber in 1962 the House Armed Services Committee amended the military procurement authorization bill by explicitly stating that the Secretary of the Air Force is "directed, ordered, mandated, and required" to spend the entire amount of $491,000,000 authorized for the RS–70 weapon system (a modification of the B–70 bomber). To avoid a constitutional showdown President Kennedy agreed with House Armed Services Committee Chairman Carl Vinson to state in writing to Congress that Secretary of Defense Robert McNamara would "study" anew the RS–70 system if Congress would delete the mandating language. Compromise was agreed upon.

In 1965, stunned by the refusal of the Department of Defense to accept funds for the construction of a nuclear-powered guided-missile frigate in the 1966 procurement budget, the House Armed Services Committee succeeded in pushing through Congress a $150,000,000 authorization for the construction of such a ship, the funds to be included in the 1966 fiscal budget. The Defense Department simply refused to permit

the Navy to proceed to construction, and the Department further refused to consider a request for more funds for the 1967 budget.

In response, the House, in 1966, passed a strongly worded bill mandating the expenditure of the funds; the Senate version of the bill, although it included provisions for the funds, was not as strongly worded.
The bill finally adopted and signed by President Johnson provided that
a "contract for the construction of the nuclear power guided missile
frigate . . . shall be entered into as soon as practicable unless the President fully advises the Congress that its construction is not in the national
interest."

The Defense Department acceded to the release of the 1966 and 1967
funds but requested no further sums for completion of the ship even
though the necessary funds were already included within the military
procurement bills in 1967. Congress again authorized and appropriated
funds for the construction, this time of two nuclear-powered frigates.
Again, the 1968 authorization signed by President Johnson required the
letting of contracts unless the President advised Congress that construction was not in the national interest.

Though the only justification for not proceeding was that the project
was not "cost effective," the Department refused to release the funds.
Faced with imminent reprisals by the Joint Atomic Energy Committee
and the House Armed Services Committee, President Johnson gave in
and ordered the ships built.

Throughout the Johnson Administration the justification for impounding was sought in the Presidential war power. Even the Bureau of
the Budget, which concocted President Roosevelt's original impounding
plan, found the justification somewhat tortuous to make out. The staff
of the Bureau in 1941–1942 was "unanimous" in its opinion that "no
statutory authority existed for impounding funds under continuing appropriations for specified projects as distinguished from annual appropriations for maintenance and operation of government agencies."
Though the President could "not violate the specific intent of Congress,"
according to the Bureau, "there can be little question of the President's
power to defer or suspend construction under his authority to prosecute
the war."

In the face of doubts, the Bureau proposed legislation to permit the
President to control programs funded by Congress. In 1950 the Bureau
was given authority to effect savings in programs as a result of "changes
and requirements, greater efficiency of operations, [and] other develop-
ments subsequent to the date on which such appropriations are made
available." But the law did not permit impounding.

Moreover, there are limits even to the President's war powers, which,
after all, are based entirely on the constitutional text that makes the

President Commander-in-Chief of the Armed Forces. When President Truman seized the nation's steel mills in 1952, citing the danger to national security if steel production were curtailed as a result of what threatened to be a protracted strike, the Supreme Court denied that the President's inherent power as Commander-in-Chief and as Chief Executive extended to the seizure of the steel properties. The Court intimated that the President would have been on much stronger ground had Congress enacted legislation permitting him to take appropriate action.

But if legislation can cure the lack of inherent power, it does not follow that the President may *disregard* Congressional action in the name of the war power. Furthermore, as one astute commentator has pointed out, "the power to act quickly to save the nation from disaster and the power to overturn a public law intended to strengthen the nation's defense, are not comparable. Only the former can in any sense be justified by necessity."

Another attempt to justify impounding is the theory that appropriation and authorization of funds does not necessitate spending the entire amount. Thus, President Kennedy responded to a question concerning impounding by claiming that an appropriation is "only a ceiling, not a mandate to spend." Acting Attorney General Ramsey Clark in 1967 wrote the Secretary of Transportation that "the Courts have recognized that appropriation acts are of a fiscal and permissive nature and do not in themselves impose upon the Executive Branch an affirmative duty to expend funds."

But the Courts are extremely reluctant to enter intermural debates between Congress and the President, and the essence of Clark's letter is the proposition that the President need not spend *all* the funds of a particular program. This obviously is a very different assertion than that the President need not spend any money whenever he wishes to kill a program or seriously weaken it. The argument for not spending every penny appropriated makes sense only when it can be shown that the program can be carried out as efficiently at lower cost.

However tenuous the argument may be for impounding funds relating to military appropriations, the argument must surely fall apart altogether when the President decides to withhold funds for domestic programs. By March of 1971, the Nixon Administration had impounded more than $12 billion of federal funds already authorized and appropriated for a variety of domestic programs, including farm programs ($757,000,000); urban renewal ($200,000,000); water and sewage facility grants ($200,000,000); Appalachian regional development ($191,000,000), as well as some $5 billion for programs concerning mass transit, pollution control, education, development of regional medical programs, air safety, and others; and $6 billion in highway-construction funds.

Responding to allegations that the impounding was unlawful, Caspar

W. Weinberger, Deputy Director of the Office of Management and Budget (formerly the Bureau of the Budget), made a familiar argument with new words: the amount of impounding was "normal," he said, and "approximately the same percentage of total budget as for every year since at least 1959." Moreover, he said, the withheld funds represent "technical" decisions; thus, according to Mr. Weinberger, the $6 billion in highway-construction funds represented an excess of trust funds accumulated over the years as a result of prior Presidential decisions to keep the spending down.

Weinberger appeared to be arguing that President Nixon believed he was under no more obligation to execute the laws faithfully than were any of his predecessors. Apparently embarrassed by the precedents which Democratic Presidents had set, House Speaker Carl Albert managed to point out that President Nixon's impounding was on an "unprecedented" scale, and not merely in terms of the amount of money, for President Nixon held back funds from a greater variety of programs than prior Chief Executives had done.

Weinberger dissembled. He agreed that an appropriation was "a direction to be followed whenever it's possible to do so," but, he added, in the classic manner of bureaucrats who cannot be caught characterizing what they are doing as unlawful, that impounding was "not a means by which the President attempts to thwart the will of Congress." It was, he said, a means of fighting inflation and keeping the federal budget within borrowing and spending limits. Weinberger omitted to note that President Nixon had successfully sought from Congress an increase in the debt ceiling.

The Senate Separation of Powers Subcommittee of the Senate Judiciary Committee, commissioned to investigate the constitutionality of impounding, was told by Weinberger that in order to fulfill his constitutional obligations to execute the laws faithfully, the President might even have to disobey those laws; these actions, he assured the Subcommittee, would only be taken pursuant to the President's inherent authority as, for instance, Commander-in-Chief. Weinberger added that "any action to prevent or defer the expenditure of funds which have been appropriated by law is obviously not one to be taken lightly, nor do we take it lightly."

Some days after making these remarks, Weinberger held a briefing for House and Senate Republicans to mute a swelling chorus of Democratic indignation. He told the Congressmen that, on the one hand, only a small amount of the money in controversy was being withheld to curb inflation, and, on the other hand, it was "demagogic" of the Democrats to talk about releasing funds to spur the economy since the money could not be released and spent fast enough to have a sizable impact on the economy. It is clear, at least, why Weinberger was chosen as the Government's spokesman in this recondite area: he is an adroit reconciler of the unreconcilable.

When the President impounds funds, he is not merely exercising an item veto (a power he does not have in any event); he is retroactively vetoing legislation. A retroactive veto is the suspension of law. The President has no such power.

When President Nixon froze prices and wages in August 1971, he was faced with a dilemma: what to do about potentially inflationary wage increases for military personnel then being debated in Congress. The pay increases were part of a major military bill intended to make feasible the President's proposal for an all-volunteer Army. The pay provision doubled the salaries of some categories of enlisted personnel and substantially increased the pay of all personnel, enlisted and officers. When passed in September, the bill contained a clause specifying that the new pay table would take effect on October 1. Politically unable to veto it, the President signed the bill into law on September 28.

The provision mandating payment of the increased allowances and salaries was ignored. The military services were ordered not to pay out the extra amounts. The President claimed that the Economic Stabilization Act of 1970, under which his initial August freeze order was issued, also gave him the authority to freeze increases in federal pay mandated by a later law. The President argued that the old law superseded the explicit language of the new law.

This argument was a sham. Congress debated the pay increase not merely during the existence of the law that gave the President authority to act; Congress debated during a period after which the President had in fact acted by freezing wages. Notwithstanding the freeze, and as part of a compromise that went into making the general military bill, Congress chose to increase the pay and used specific language stating that the pay increase was to take effect during the freeze. It is an elementary principle that later legislation repeals earlier conflicting legislation.

In reality, the President simply refused to abide by the law. Although the new pay table was permitted to take effect in November when Phase II controls were instituted, service personnel were unlawfully docked six weeks' of increased pay, amounting to some $500 million in gross. The use of the item veto may be understandable, but it is no more constitutional because used as a deflationary device.

Around the time of King Charles I, it was assumed that the King did have the power to suspend law. In 1637 a court held that "the King *pro bono publico* may charge his subjects for the safety and defense of the Kingdom, notwithstanding any act of Parliament, and a statute derogatory of the prerogative doth not bind the King, and the King may dispense with any laws in cases of necessity." Charles I was executed twelve years later. As Edward S. Corwin, a leading scholar of the U.S.

Constitution, has concluded, the doctrine of executive suspension of law is "one against which most of the framers unquestionably thought they had provided by the 'faithfully executed' clause."

ABUSING THE TAXPAYER: PROFLIGATE SPENDING OF THE PUBLIC MONIES

Perhaps the most regularly abused citizens of the United States are the taxpayers. Though the abuse is rarely deliberately cruel or brutal, it is constant. The greatest source of abuse is the income-tax code itself. The tax laws are full of so many preposterous rules that the only skein of consistency to be found in them is the fundamental axiom that the very rich need not pay taxes. But the Internal Revenue Code, as a set of established laws, is beyond the scope of this book.

As members of the loyal opposition will willingly testify, the amount of governmental waste and questionable use of public monies is monumental. They are less eager to point out that much of the waste is an outright violation of laws and regulations intended to minimize the fraudulent expenditure of funds, since it is a violation they are pleased to countenance when the budget is under their control.

But the public treasury is always subject to systematic attack; so immense are the possibilities of private gain that the pressure to corrupt is relentless. Aside from the petty corruption of those in public office— by bribe, blackmail, extortion, or graft—there remains a costly residue of official lawbreaking that is very much a daily affair.

The largest and most open violator of laws governing expenditures of public funds is the Department of Defense. Since its creation after World War II, the Department has been notorious in violating literally scores of rules governing the methods of granting and regulating public contracts—with a resulting increase in expenditures. Laws requiring bidding have been widely ignored; contractual provisions permitting the Department to cancel contracts for hosts of violations and irregularities, including racial discrimination and cost overruns, have rarely been invoked.

A typical example is the practice of the Air Force in underwriting expenses of the Communication Satellite Corporation (COMSAT). According to a General Accounting Office (GAO) study conducted in 1970 and 1971, commercial carriers such as telephone and telegraph companies lease satellite circuits from COMSAT and in turn re-lease them to the Air Force; COMSAT's charge to the commercial carriers was discovered by the GAO study to be $4,875,000, and the charge to the Air Force for leasing the same facility from the commercial carriers was $8,250,000. For this modest bonus, the commercial carriers performed no useful work; nothing was manufactured, sold, or transferred except legal rights.

The Department is also required to recover the cost of launching COMSAT's satellites from the company, but the Government's rate of recovery has been small. The first Early Bird shot cost the Air Force $922,110. It recovered $23,557. The next four satellites cost nearly $3,000,000; the Air Force asked COMSAT for only $933,000.

The Defense Department is not the only profligate spender. In early 1971, it was revealed that Robert W. Eidson, a U.S. Postal Service officer, had awarded a job-evaluation contract to the Westinghouse Electric Corporation but had omitted to request competitive bids from any other companies. When, under pressure, bids finally did go out, only five days were allowed for responses, despite the fact that Eidson had engaged in lengthy discussions with Westinghouse prior to the bid request. Bids from other companies were apparently solicited only because Postal Service lawyers said that the Westinghouse contract could not be awarded without them. Westinghouse, which got the contract, was the highest bidder and had less experience in the job-evaluation field than the other responding companies. A member of the House Post Office and Civil Service Investigations Subcommittee asked Eidson whether he thought he ought to resign "in view of all the testimony this subcommittee has received." Eidson didn't think so.

The states are no less loose with the public monies. Take, for instance, Alabama. Federal anticrime funds delivered to that state under the Omnibus Crime Control and Safe Streets Act of 1968 amounted to $4,200,000 in the 1971 fiscal year. By January, 1971, the following misuse of funds was uncovered by state and federal grand juries investigating the widespread scandal:

> $200,000 allocated for an officer-education program was spent for scholarships of up to $6,000 a year for the sons of state Public Safety Department officials, presumably to help out beleaguered parents and permit these youths to receive a higher education;
> $91,570 was paid as an advance to Criminal Justice Systems, Inc., a corporation formed by three persons who had no legal experience. Money was paid out, despite the absence of any competitive bidding, for the preparation of the Alabama Law Enforcement Planning Agency's 1971 report, which under the law had to be read in Washington. Two of the three members of Criminal Justice Systems continued to work at other jobs during the writing of the report;
> $16,500 was paid to an advertising firm under a contract arranged by a regional attorney for the Law Enforcement Planning Agency (or LEPA); the firm, in which the attorney held stock, was to write another guidebook for law officers on legal procedure. Of the total sum, $13,268 was paid over to the attorney's former law firm to do the work. Former Governor Albert P. Brewer joined the firm in January, 1971;

$111,000 allocated for a scholarship program for state highway patrol cadets went instead to the sons of a former Public Safety Director, a board member of LEPA, the State Prison Commissioner, six officers of the Highway Patrol and a security guard for Governor Wallace. When these facts were made known, the scholarship program was hurriedly cancelled on the grounds that funds had unlawfully been allocated from planning rather than from action grants.

Unlawful noncompetitive bidding is a commonplace in every political jurisdiction. Money is the taproot of politics, and it is unlikely that there has ever been a city, state, or federal administration able to escape pressures that compel them to award certain contracts illegally.

In New York City, Mayor John V. Lindsay charged in 1970 that Comptroller Abraham D. Beame had awarded more than $100,000 in two contracts without having first submitted them, as required by law, to the City Board of Estimate. Beame did not deny the charges. Indeed, he had already stopped payment on contracts that Mayor Lindsay himself had awarded to certain city consultants without first submitting them to the Board of Estimate and without competitive bidding. Mayor Lindsay's consulting contracts were a good deal larger than Comptroller Beame's: however the money is counted, it is certain that consultant fees ran well over $60 million in 1970.

The facts in the dispute are confusing, inasmuch as Mayor Lindsay approved both contracts and later charged that the approval was an unlawful action by Beame. The Deputy Budget Director, David A. Grossman, supported Mayor Lindsay in an affidavit stating "that the comptroller himself had acted in accordance with the corporation counsel's interpretation of law on consultant contracts—which is that they can be approved by the Mayor without going to the Board of Estimate."

Not to be outdone by Grossman, Beame countered that the contracts could not legally be approved by the Mayor without going to the Board of Estimate; thus, he undercut his own position as well. New Yorkers have a flair for comedy, perhaps an inevitable result of the unspeakable maze of local regulations under which the city operates. The scandal, if it can be called that, was a technical one, since no one could charge that either Mayor Lindsay or Comptroller Beame was personally profiting from any of the contracts.

One curious way in which the Government abuses the taxpayer is through its administration of the federal copyright laws. Section 8 of the Copyright Act states: "No copyright shall subsist . . . in any publication of the United States Government, or any reprint, in whole or in part."

The prohibition against Government copyright originated as a reaction to the activities of Tennessee Congressman James D. Richardson at the turn of the century. Richardson collected the speeches of the

Presidents, including Washington's Farewell Address and Lincoln's Gettysburg Address, and had the collection printed at Government expense. He took out copyright in his own name and collected $11,320 in royalties.

In 1962, M. B. Schnapper, editor and publisher of Public Affairs Press, blew the whistle on the United States Army; in an "open letter" published as an advertisement in the *Washington Post,* Schnapper wrote that a "careful check will reveal that literally scores of works commissioned by the Army have been placed under restrictions by or with the sanction of civilian and military personnel of your department."

The Army's Chief of Military History had been in the habit of copyrighting most works written by his office. The histories were written by men on the public payroll in the course of their official duties. Without any signs of embarrassment, Major General C. G. Dodge, Army Chief of Information, replied that "the [Army historical] works were copyrighted . . . to prevent quoting of material out of context." Another officer thoughtfully added that the copyright policy prevented "sensationalizing." It was a flimsy excuse, as General Dodge himself implicitly admitted when he announced that "it is the Army's policy that, in the future, work from the Office of the Chief of Military History will not be copyrighted."

But this dubious practice is commonplace throughout the Government. The first editions of *To Turn the Tide,* a collection of President John F. Kennedy's public statements between November, 1960, and December, 1961, contained the notice "Copyright 1962 by John F. Kennedy" and the accompanying statement: "no part of this book may be used or reproduced in any manner whatsoever without written permission except in the case of brief quotations embodied in critical articles and reviews." Another of Schnapper's "open letters"—this time to the President—resulted in the admission that the copyright notice "was a mistake that is being corrected in future editions."

A more ambiguous way of circumventing the copyright prohibition is the widespread policy of permitting the private contractors who have been commissioned to undertake governmental studies at public expense to copyright their final reports. For example, a report entitled *Scientific Study of Unidentified Flying Objects* was copyrighted in the name of the Board of Regents of the University of Colorado. The Air Force originally commissioned the study for more than half a million dollars. The University of Colorado, in turn, licensed the paperback rights to Bantam Books. All the royalties go to the University of Colorado, by way of Dr. Edward U. Condon, head of the University team that undertook the study.

Proponents of selling Government-sponsored studies commercially have several contradictory justifications. Some publishers, and the Association of American Publishers, argue that the market for most Government publications is too small for more than one publisher to share; unless a publisher is guaranteed the copyright monopoly he will not be willing to undertake the risks of publication. The response, of course, is to ask why a publisher of a work of narrow appeal should fear a second publisher's competition or need a copyright monopoly. Moreover, many Government reports sell remarkably well without any copyright protection at all. The Warren Commission Report was distributed by five publishers, all of whom made money on it.

It is also argued that publication by the Government Printing Office (GPO) would cost taxpayers still more money than they have already paid to finance the original study. But the GPO generally runs a profit on its book-publishing operations. And if it costs more for the GPO than for private publishers to produce the same book, the remedy is to increase the efficiency of the GPO (or amend the Copyright Act), not to violate the laws of the United States.

CAMPAIGN PRACTICES

Among the boldest, most notorious, and most flagrant occasions of contempt for the law are American political campaigns. The spirit of the law—if not its literal content—is violated by incumbent Presidents, Congressman, Senators, and candidates alike; and the lawbreaking has been ratified by a forty-five year refusal of Attorneys General to prosecute obvious violations. This is an area transcending partisanship: from Eugene McCarthy to Gerald Ford the law is regularly ignored.

In 1925, in a fit of overzealousness, Congress passed the Federal Corrupt Practices Act. That Act makes it "unlawful for any corporation whatever . . . to make a contribution or expenditure in connection with any election" to any federal office. Moreover, an amendment to the Act sets a $5,000 ceiling on donations to any candidate or national election committee by individual contributors. A committee contributing to campaigns in more than one state is required to report all contributions to Congress.

Like other aspects of the law these provisions are ignored. In the 1970 elections, for instance, funds sponsored by executives of Ling-Temco-Vought, Olin Corporation, McDonnell Douglas, Northrop Corporation and Union Oil, among others, went unreported. Ling-Temco-Vought gave $100,000 to candidates in various political contests; one of them, Congressmen Gerald Ford of Michigan, the House Minority Leader, received $2,000. The Olin fund, which paid out more than $25,000, went to fifty-four congressional races in thirty-one states.

The American Medical Association donated some $700,000 to groups throughout the United States. Most contributors actually abide by the law and file reports with Congress revealing the candidates to whom the money is given. Not the AMA. The Association has set up an intermediary organization called the American Medical Political Action Committee (AMPAC), which has established state affiliates to which it gives the money. The AMA then simply reported to Congress that it gave so much to each AMPAC affiliate—for instance, $42,500 to the California affiliate. AMPAC itself claimed not to be connected with the American Medical Association; it must be by coincidence, then, that all members of AMPAC's board belonged to the AMA. In 1970, only the Indiana affiliate of AMPAC filed a contribution report with Congress. The other affiliates, since they made contributions in only one state, ignored the filing requirements.

The American Bankers Association plays the game a little differently. Through its efforts the Bankers Political Action Committee (BANKPAC) was formed to distribute thousands of dollars to candidates who sit on congressional banking committees. In order to minimize discussion of how much the Committee was spending, BANKPAC reported only half of its money on the last preelection filing date, October 29, 1970. The next day $46,000 was distributed, none of which was reported until two months after the election. BANKPAC claimed that the law was not violated because the late expenditures did not occur until the checks were actually cashed. Some members of Congress were so embarrassed by reports of this clear evasion that they actually returned money to the organization. Expenditures are usually considered to be made when the checks are written; otherwise checks could simply be held uncashed beyond the required filing dates, as apparently happened in 1970.

The Corrupt Practices Act does not single out only corporations as violaters. Candidates themselves are required to file reports before and after an election. In 1970, more than fifty successful candidates failed to file, along with scores of unsuccessful contenders for office. Moreover, many of those who did file disclosed that they had in fact spent nothing.

Senator Lloyd M. Bentsen, for instance, reported in Austin, Texas, that he had spent close to $460,000 in his successful race against Republican Congressman George Bush. In a report filed with the Secretary of the Senate, however, Senator Bentsen claimed he had spent nothing. The contradiction is explained roughly as follows: Texas requires a report of all money spent, and to meet this requirement Senator Bentsen said that the $460,000 was spent "with my knowledge and consent." To the United States Senate, however, Senator Bentsen disclaimed any connection with the campaign committee spending the $460,000: "Since the statutory provisions apply only to the candidate and not the campaign committees which support his candidacy this report does not encompass money received or expended on behalf of my candidacy by campaign committees for Lloyd Bentsen, Jr.," the Senator explained.

But the Federal Corrupt Practices Act, contrary to Senator Bentsen's statement, expressly says that candidates for the Senate must file with the Secretary "a correct and itemized account of each contribution received by him or by any person for him *with his knowledge or consent*, from any source, in aid or support of his candidacy for election, or for the purpose of influencing the result of the election, together with the name of the person who has made such contribution." In light of the law, Senator Bentsen's statement is pathetic.

Senator Bentsen should be in jail. So, of course, should scores of Congressmen and thousands of corporate executives throughout the United States.

But for forty years, no Attorney General has ever prosecuted any person, successful or unsuccessful, rich or poor, for violating the campaign-disclosure laws. Before 1969, corporations were prosecuted only on two occasions for violating provisions of the federal campaign laws. Since that time a handful of violators have been prosecuted, and the Justice Department has managed to obtain guilty pleas in some of these cases, which date back to investigations made in 1966 at the behest of the Commissioner of Internal Revenue, Sheldon S. Cohen. President Nixon and Attorney General John Mitchell, his campaign manager, have shown little inclination to initiate new investigations or prosecutions for violations after 1968, the year in which their own campaign committees violated the laws and were cited as delinquent by the Clerk of the House. The Justice Department did manage in 1972 to get a conviction of W. A. (Tony) Boyle, president of the United Mine Workers, on thirteen counts of unlawful campaign contributions, the majority of which went to Hubert H. Humphrey in his 1968 campaign against President Nixon.

The ostensible purpose of the Corrupt Practices Act is to prevent elected federal officials from being purchased by special interests. Instead, the Act serves merely to underscore the possibility that private enterprise can purchase elected representatives, not excluding the President of the United States. The Corrupt Practices Act, and the violations of it, exemplify the American genius for feeling secure with laws that leave the people utterly unprotected. That the Attorney General of the United States has conspired with Congress to prevent any enforcement of the Act is overlooked or ignored.

Many Congressmen are anxious to be shielded from publicity about their patrons. One, Congressman Thomas P. (Tip) O'Neill, Jr., a Democrat from Boston, became in 1970 Chairman of the House Special Committee to Investigate Campaign Expenditures. Some time after this committee began its work, enterprising newsmen discovered that Representative O'Neill had formed his own secret committee in Washington, D.C., to hide the fact that though unopposed for reelection he had received $12,000 in campaign donations.

Funds from Boston were sent to the "D.C. O'Neill Committee" and then routed back to Boston to the "O'Neill for Congress Committee." The Massachusetts committee then reported only that it had received its funds from the Washington committee, without disclosing any other names. Mr. O'Neill explained that he did not want the names of donors made public because other candidates might find out who was the soft touch in Massachusetts.

Said the Congressman (who became House Majority Whip in 1971), "in fairness to the friends who contributed to our campaign, we do them a service by sending it to the Washington committee and then transferring it to the Boston account." He added: "You know the law—you don't have to report it down there [Washington]." Mr. O'Neill was mistaken, however, for the loophole he had in mind permits individuals to contribute beyond the $5,000 limit to committees in the District of Columbia (and to state committees, a loophole that eviscerates the law)—but it does not permit escape quite as easily as the learned Congressman imagines.

Congressman O'Neill is not the only suspicious Congressman. A great exemplar of virtue, Representative Gerald Ford, plays the same trick with the American public. Mr. Ford, who wanted to impeach Justice William O. Douglas for acts that the Republican Congressman believed included shady financial dealings, neglected to report in his 1970 campaign $11,500 in contributions from stock, oil, banking, medical, and labor interests. Mr. Ford collected the money, sent it to Republican headquarters in Washington, D.C., and then had the money returned to various Ford-for-Congress committees to pay off campaign debts. The law requires Mr. Ford to disclose all monies received with his knowledge; certainly he knew all about these contributions. His limp excuse is that he did not know that the Republican headquarters returned the money to various committees supporting his reelection. It is a common tactic of elected politicians to claim they do not know about various committees supporting their campaign bids; if Mr. Ford had asserted this proposition in a court of law, he could have been indicted for and convicted of perjury—especially in view of the odd fact that he was his own treasurer. Congressmen usually pick trusted lieutenants to serve as treasurers of their various campaign committees so that they can be insulated from any charges that they knew what was happening to the money. Ford's self-serving justification of his actions was a simple denial that the law had been broken: "I would say, under the interpretation of the law as it has been interpretated over the years, that my action was within the law," he said after the election. He meant, of course, simply that he, like so many other Congressmen, had in fact violated the law but he knew he was in little danger of ever being prosecuted.

So lightly has the law been regarded that until 1968, neither the Clerk of the House nor the Secretary of the Senate ever made certification to the Attorney General—a necessary step if the Justice Department were to prosecute a violation by any candidate. In 1968, W. Pat Jennings, Clerk of the House, reported certain violations for the first time. The Department declined to prosecute, noting that doing so would be unfair inasmuch as no one had ever been prosecuted before.

In May, 1970, Will Wilson, an Assistant Attorney General for the Criminal Division of the Justice Department, warned candidates that failure to file reports was illegal, but that, given the forty-five-year history of nonenforcement, fair play required him to give notice. Thereafter, he said, prosecutions would be in order. Under the Nixon administration, though, the excessive fear of irritating criminals who seek votes as well as dollars makes any major enforcement program an unlikely prospect.

In February, 1971, the Department of Justice was already denying that it had given candidates adequate warning the preceding May. A departmental spokesman said that the warning applied only to committees and not to candidates; since the Clerk of the House had referred a case concerning a candidate only—that of Dennis J. Morrisseau, a defeated candidate of the Liberty Union Party for the Vermont House seat, who said he had refused to file a report to test the law—the Department, the spokesman intimated, would drop the case.

The excuse is novel, and lawyers should bear it in mind: the next time the local police announce their intention to enforce the Sunday Blue Laws and then go after a shopkeeper client of yours, you should act surprised and indignant and retort quite hotly that the District Attorney was supposed to arrest kosher butchers only.

If Congressmen don't know that they break the law, it is only because they don't want to know. If you ask a Congressman's lawyer, however, you will get an explanation of why it is perfectly legal for candidates to do what they do. For instance, our hypothetical lawyer will say, the law prohibits contributions of more than $5,000 to a single (national) committee, but the law puts no limits on the number of committees that may be formed, even by the same individuals. The law prohibits corporate contributions, but it does not prohibit individual contributions. Therefore, our lawyer will say, it is perfectly permissible for a corporation to pay cash bonuses to its officers and employees; the understanding that the bonus or part of it will go to a candidate hardly adds up to an illegal contribution.

Likewise, says our lawyer, extra-large salaries that become campaign contributions at the direction of employers can scarcely be held to violate the Corrupt Practices Act. If a corporation makes its employees available to work for candidates for free, where has the law been violated? Or suppose a corporation pays a very large fee to an attorney for a minimal amount of work—really not an unknown phenomenon even outside the campaign fields—and the lawyer pays over some of that fee; is the nation the loser and should the lawyer be in jail? Or suppose corporations purchase large quantities of books for the benefit of candidates or committees—the Corrupt Practices Act says nothing about that. If a corporation has a billboard or two and does not use them during October in an election year, is there any reason why the corporation cannot give them to deserving candidates to advertise themselves?

Surely a corporation is permitted to request its employees to pay over a percentage of salary to a political action committee formed by corporate officers—after all, it is merely a patriotic appeal, and obviously no one's job would be in jeopardy over a refusal to contribute. Finally, when an election is over and a corporation writes off a large debt for services or supplies, could anyone, the lawyer would ask, seriously call that a campaign contribution?

All these are the techniques used by corporations and committees in every election year to buy seats in Congress. Our Congressman's lawyer would report that his clients were merely taking every fair advantage of loopholes in the law. But it is not very difficult to prove that far from being loopholes the devices used are in fact blatant violations of the Corrupt Practices Act.

Courts have become very adept over the years at "piercing the corporate veil," and there is no reason to believe that prosecutions under the Act based on a similar piercing in this area would not be sustained. Corporations that forgive the debts of campaign committees—such as AT&T in writing off $230,000 and American Airlines in forgiving $140,000 owed by Senator Eugene McCarthy's committees after the 1968 campaign—have obviously made campaign contributions for which they could be prosecuted.

Corporations are not the only masters of illegal contribution. Numerous federal laws prohibit the solicitation of civil servants or military personnel for political contributions. Is it merely a coincidence that Representative John J. Rooney, Democrat of New York and Chairman of a House Appropriations Subcommittee that funds the State Department and the U.S. Arms Control and Disarmament Agency, received from fourteen officers of both agencies in 1968 contributions ranging in amount from $25 to $1,000? Some of the officers thoughtfully put their contributions in their wives' names. Nobody was prosecuted; presumably they were happy to give.

Not so in Alabama during the 1970 elections. There the Commander of the Alabama Air National Guard required of all his career officers a modest $100 contribution for the campaign funds of both Governor George Wallace and the man he beat, former Governor Albert Brewer. Major General George Reid Doster knew what he was doing; when he asked for the contribution he said, "Gents, it's illegal as hell, but I've got to do it anyway. I've got to have $100 political contribution from each of you." The affair came to light when a major in the General's unit became angry at being harassed for failure to contribute. The major brought suit for an injunction, and the ensuing publicity led directly to the dismissals from the Guard of Major General Doster, five colonels, a lieutenant colonel, a major, and a lieutenant. Neither Brewer nor Wallace was asked to return the money.

The payment of larger salaries and bonuses to employees, a method of circumventing the Act that may at first blush seem at least technically legal, actually violates two laws. The corporation violates the Corrupt Practices Act, because a criminal cannot avoid the law by asserting that his agent did the foul deed. The man who arranges the murder, no less than the gunman, is guilty. Moreover, the salaries and bonuses paid to employees are accounted for as expense items to be deducted from the corporate income taxes. But since the payments are in fact contributions to political causes, they cannot legally be deducted. That is why the employee must have extra cash in order to pay personal income taxes on the amount received. Thus, the American public is unlawfully required to bear the burden of half the corporate campaign contributions that are in any case unlawful. Bribes, it seems, are tax deductible.

This is all the more ironic in view of the serious attempt made by President Nixon's first Commissioner of Internal Revenue, Randolph W. Thrower, to prohibit tax deductions for contributions to public-interest law firms. The Justice Department claimed that violators of the Corrupt Practices Act did not have fair warning; but the Internal Revenue Service in the fall of 1970 announced that contributors to organizations that filed environmental and other public-oriented law suits might lose a tax deduction. The IRS said that it was conducting a sixty-day delibera- tion as to whether the tax-exempt status of such organizations should be revoked; if the status were changed, the Service would retroactively tax the contributions made during that same period.

Under intense political pressure Commissioner Thrower backed down, ruling that in any event contributions made during the sixty days of deliberations would be deductible. Shortly after the 1970 elec- tions but shortly before an antagonistic Senate subcommittee was to open hearings, Commissioner Thrower announced that the general pol- icy of permitting deductions for contributions to the public-interest organizations would be continued.

Unfortunately, it is not at all clear that the guidelines themselves conform to the law, since they depend on an extremely loose definition of "charitable." The law now bends too far the other way, exempting from taxes the money that organizations use to promote causes through litigation, when they could not claim exemptions on money spent placing ads in newspapers requesting that Congress change the law. If you sue, it's legal; if you advertise, it's not. This appears to be inconsistent until you remember that the people who write the rules are lawyers, not advertising executives, and lawyers get fees for lawsuits and not for advertising. With that in mind, you have the satisfaction of knowing that it is an understandable inconsistency.

It is unfair, of course, to charge the Government with the pecadilloes of industries or even of candidates. The Government's lawbreaking is not the Congressman's failure to report or his complicity in the lawbreaking of others (although under statutes making the aiding and abetting of criminal acts a crime those who know about and aid private illegal contributions are equally guilty). Rather, the Government's infractions lie in its *failure to prosecute.* The Government's attitude toward violations of the Federal Corrupt Practices Act seems to be the same as its attitude toward fornication: both are illegal but neither is worth worrying about.*

LEGISLATIVE DISTRICTING: HOW LEGISLATURES BREAK THE LAW

During the 1960's, the Supreme Court ruled that the Constitution requires all legislative districts to consist of roughly equal populations. Although the Court's decisions were premised on a reading of the federal Constitution, the facts underlying the original 1962 case as well as several subsequent ones showed a blatant disregard on the part of state legislatures and courts for their own constitutions.

The original case came from Tennessee. The Tennessee Constitution provided that the "standard for allocating legislative representation among [the] counties is the total number of qualified voters resident in the respective counties." The constitution provided that an enumeration and reapportionment should occur in 1871 and every ten years thereafter. Enumerations and apportionments were carried out in 1871, 1881, and 1891. But in 1901, no new apportionment was made and for sixty years thereafter the legislative districts for the general assembly remained static.

---

* In February, 1972, the Corrupt Practices Act was amended by the Campaign Financing Act, which changes some of the previous rules—but not, apparently, the Government's attitude. The new law was written to take effect April 7, giving contributors five weeks to make hefty contributions the source of which will not have to be revealed.

Between 1901 and 1961, the state's population grew from 2,000,000 to more than 3,500,000 people; the voting rolls swelled from 487,000 to more than 2,000,000. The internal movement and growth of Tennessee's population by 1961 resulted in the power of 37 percent of the voters to elect more than 75 percent of the state senators and 40 percent of the voters to elect more than 60 percent of the representatives. Moore County, with a population of 2,300, elected two representatives. So did Rutherford County, with a population of more than 25,000. Likewise, Decatur County, with 5,500 population had the same representation as Carter County with 23,300 people; Loudon County with 13,000 people had the same representation as Houston County with 3,000 and Anderson County with almost 34,000.

The Supreme Court's order that the state legislatures be reapportioned invoked a storm. Forgotten in the fury of criticism was the plain fact that the states themselves had violated their own constitutions. An investigation by the Advisory Commission on Intergovernmental Relations, a federal body created by Congress in 1959, revealed that in mid-1962, thirteen states required by their own constitutions to apportion both houses of their legislatures on a population-only basis had failed to comply. The failure was not only that of the legislatures; state courts generally refused even to hear cases brought to them, and when occasionally they did so, the decisions never required the legislatures to reapportion their districts. A colloquy between Senator Joseph D. Tydings of Maryland and Justice Millard F. Caldwell of the Florida Supreme Court at the 1965 Senate hearings concerning proposed constitutional amendments sums up the problem:

> SENATOR TYDINGS: In your Florida constitution, do you have a provision which requires automatic, regular, periodic reapportionment of either house?
>
> JUSTICE CALDWELL: On a 10-year basis. The constitution requires review of the situation once each 10 years.
>
> SENATOR TYDINGS: In both houses?
>
> JUSTICE CALDWELL: Both houses.
>
> SENATOR TYDINGS: Does it actually direct the legislature to reapportion or not? What does it do?
>
> JUSTICE CALDWELL: Yes; but there is some division of opinion about how compulsory that requirement is and it has been observed in the breach as well as in the observance.
>
> SENATOR TYDINGS: The reason I ask you that, Governor, is we have the same provision in the Maryland constitution and the legislature has even gone so far as to put the matter on referendum in the State of Maryland to determine whether or not the people wanted the State reapportioned and when they said yes, the legislature still—and I was a member of the body—disregarded it. I was wondering whether Florida had that same history, too.

> Governor, one problem which bothers me, assuming that the
> constitutional amendment is passed and ratified, before a State such
> as my own, Maryland, or another State which is badly malappor-
> tioned, could reasonably be expected, once this amendment is
> adopted, a legislature which is already badly apportioned, could
> they reasonably be expected to make any effort to reapportion one
> house?
>
> JUSTICE CALDWELL: Yes; I think you can expect them to make a good-
> faith effort. But of course, you always have the human factor of vot-
> ing oneself out of office. It is a compulsive sort of condition.
>
> SENATOR TYDINGS: It is almost too much to ask.
>
> JUSTICE CALDWELL: It makes it very difficult.

The reapportionment cases illustrate an extreme of institutional lawbreaking. Power once granted is rarely ceded. For decades every political
institution in the United States declared or assumed itself powerless to
put the matter to right. The state courts refused to act. The governors
saw no reason to change the political bases of their states. Congress itself
was malapportioned. And the Supreme Court consistently ruled, until
1962, that the issue raised before it from time to time by disaffected
voters was a "political question" beyond its competence to answer.
When the situation grew desperate, a majority of the Court at last found
a way to invoke the federal Constitution.

GATHERING NUMBERS: HOW THE CENSUS BUREAU BREAKS THE LAW

Section 2 of Title 2 of the *United States Code* provides that congressional districts must contain approximately the same number of people.
A 1911 version of the law read simply that "the representatives to Congress shall be elected by districts composed of contiguous and compact
territory, and containing as nearly as practicable an equal number of
inhabitants." In 1929, the language was changed to require congressional
districts to be apportioned "by the method known as method of equal
proportions." Though the matter is not entirely free from doubt, it was
apparently the intention of Congress that, except for those few states
that are constitutionally required to have one member of Congress
despite their small populations, each Congressman throughout the land
is to represent the same number of people.

Consequently, two determinations are required: first, the number
of congressional districts in each state must be determined, based on the
population within each state. Second, the size of the districts within

the states must be ascertained. Different states may therefore have different sized districts. Fractional districts are not allowed, and a state whose population is slightly to one side of the line will require a different congressional distribution than another state whose population falls just the other side of the line. But within each state each district is to be equal.

Since apportionment of legislatures became subject to federal judicial approval on a large scale, it has become all the more obvious that the desideratum in fashioning legislative districts is equality of population. This is true not only for Congress but for state legislatures as well.

The reapportionment cases began with one critical assumption—that the census figures from which apportionments are to be made counted the people correctly. That is, for example, visiting aliens who happen to be in a given congressional district on the date of census are not to be enumerated, and counting them would unlawfully swell the size of the district. But the reapportionment cases did not themselves consider how the Census Bureau should count people within the districts; just who is to be regarded as an inhabitant of the district for purposes of the census and apportionment?

Title 13 of the *United States Code,* which deals with the census, is uninformative. The only section directing the taking of the census reads entirely as follows:

> (a) The Secretary shall, in the year 1960 and every 10 years thereafter, take a census of population, unemployment, and housing (including utilities and equipment) as of the first day of April, which shall be known as the census date.
> (b) The tabulation of total population by States as required for the apportionment of Representatives shall be completed within 8 months of the census date and repored by the Secretary to the President of the United States.

Yet it is difficult to believe that "population" is to be defined so broadly as to include all persons physically residing within the state. If it were, significant congregations of people having no legal ties to the state might well be permitted to expand the numbers of the state sufficiently to add a Representative or at least to alter the district lines. Foreign aliens would never be in sufficient numbers to produce this effect, but there is a class of domestic aliens that might: members of the armed forces.

Since the time of the first census in 1790, military personnel have been counted in those states in which they physically resided at the time of the census. According to George H. Brown, Director of the Bureau of the Census in 1970:

[This] definition of residence is consistent with the Bureau's definition of usual residence since the areas in question are those in which the members of the armed forces usually work and sleep. Moreover, their presence in these areas increases the volume of demand for public services, water supply, sewage disposal, highways, schools, and other county and municipal services. Without entering into an extended legal debate as to the correct method of congressional apportionment, it would seem, if justice is our goal, that the state from which an individual derives the greatest benefit should be entitled to include that person as a resident for purposes of congressional representation. Further, in many states, grants-in-aid made by the state governments are determined on the basis of population. In these states, it is equitable to assign such funds to the communities which are involved in furnishing services to members of the armed forces, rather than to governmental units which the member may visit infrequently.

The difficulty with this position is that in states with large military bases significant concentrations of military personnel are being counted as part of the state and district populations though they cannot legally vote there. The Soldiers' and Sailors' Civil Relief Act explicitly preserves the serviceman's legal residence. Thus, no matter in which state he may be stationed, the serviceman is taxable only by his home state, and he may continue to vote in that state by absentee ballot.

The Census Bureau's method of counting thus leads to an anomalous result: the serviceman stationed out of state is counted in a district of a representative for whom he cannot vote, but he may vote for a congressman in a district in which he is not counted. While the meaning of "population" is surely not limited to eligible voters (children, for instance, are counted) the term should as a minimum include those people who may by law vote there.

Anyone who stumbled onto these figures in the late 1960's and who remembered, or thought he remembered, that disproportionate numbers of military personnel are stationed in Southern states, might attribute this method of taking the census to a "Southern strategy." In fact, he would be wrong, at least in terms of practical effect, since relative to the population, a greater number of people from Southern states wind up in the military and are stationed outside their geographic region than the reverse.

On July 1, 1969, of ten Southern states (Alabama, Arkansas, Florida, Georgia, Louisiana, Mississippi, North Carolina, South Carolina, Texas, and Virginia) only four had a net population gain as a result of indigenous military bases. These are Georgia, North Carolina, South Carolina, and Virginia, as the following table shows:

Military Population by Station and by Home of Record on July 1, 1969 (In thousands)

States	Military Population by Station	Military Personnel by Home of Record	Net Population Gain or Loss
United States and AFO Total	3,531	3,531	
Alabama	35	74	−39
Alaska	33	5	+28
Arizona	27	30	−3
Arkansas	8	42	−24
California	387	287	+100
Colorado	55	42	+13
Connecticut	12	43	−31
Delaware	7	9	−2
District of Columbia	14	11	+3
Florida	98	118	−20
Georgia	109	89	+20
Hawaii	57	16	+41
Idaho	5	15	−10
Illinois	61	162	−101
Indiana	9	85	−76
Iowa	1	54	−53
Kansas	43	40	+3
Kentucky	52	66	−14
Louisiana	40	63	−23
Maine	12	25	−13
Maryland	64	64	0
Massachusetts	36	93	−57
Michigan	17	148	−131
Minnesota	5	68	−63
Mississippi	30	38	−8
Missouri	39	94	−55
Montana	6	16	−10
Nebraska	11	29	−18
Nevada	10	6	+4
New Hampshire	4	18	−14
New Jersey	65	89	−24
New Mexico	17	22	−5
New York	37	236	−199
North Carolina	128	102	+26
North Dakota	11	14	−3
Ohio	20	186	−166
Oklahoma	38	58	−20
Oregon	4	44	−40
Pennsylvania	21	213	−192
Rhode Island	26	18	+8
South Carolina	75	59	+16
South Dakota	5	16	−11
Tennessee	34	82	−48
Texas	199	200	−1

States (cont'd)	Military Population by Station	Military Personnel by Home of Record	Net Population Gain or Loss
Utah	4	17	—13
Vermont	—	8	—8
Virginia	184	86	+98
Washington	73	65	+8
West Virginia	—	46	—46
Wisconsin	2	71	—69
Wyoming	3	7	—4
Overseas	1,296	43	+1,253

With ninety-eight thousand more military personnel in the state than have left it, Virginia has the largest surplus population of the southern states. Nevertheless this total is only 2 percent of the 1970 population of the state, which means that the surplus has no effect on producing an extra congressman for Virginia.

On the other hand, since the average congressional district has half a million persons in it, a net addition of one hundred thousand servicemen might well have an effect on the geographical boundaries of a particular district. Thus, in South Carolina, which had a military population within the state of 75,000, for a net surplus of 16,000 troops, the impact within a district might be substantial. The population of Charleston according to the 1970 census was 230,000 people. If 50,000 troops and their families (for families are also counted as residents of the states in which they physically reside) were stationed in and around Charleston, the military population would account for 20 percent of the entire metropolitan area, or 10 percent of a congressional district.

A far more pronounced effect of the surplus military population is seen at the local level. For there, within cities and counties, a military population on the order of 50,000 constitutes a considerable percentage of state legislative districts. Both federal and state courts have taken judicial notice of federal census statistics for the purpose of determining the legality of apportionments.

California, with a military population of 387,000 troops (these figures do not include accompanying families) and a military surplus population of 100,000 on July 1, 1969, has the largest potential for distorted districts. If families are added, in fact, the impact of allocating military personnel and their families to states in which they physically but not legally reside may affect even federal congressional districts in the two largest states (California and New York). Assuming two accompanying family members per serviceman, the excess population of California would be 300,000 or 60 percent of the average congressional district.

In New York, a state that has a net deficit of 200,000 military personnel, the same assumption would mean 600,000 fewer people are counted in the state than are eligible to vote or are the families of the people who vote there—a number greater than the size of the average congressional district.

To justify its unlawful method of counting * the Bureau cites a number of legal precedents and facts. A 1950 opinion of the Attorney General is cited as permitting the current method of counting. But that opinion concerned the counting of college students away from home on the census date, and the Acting Attorney General said nothing more than that the director of the Bureau has wide latitude and that the Department of Justice would acquiesce in the Bureau's position that it was inconsistent to enumerate everyone but students at their physical residences on the census day. The opinion assumes the legality of so counting military personnel without analyzing it.

Moreover, regardless of the merits of the college student situation it is a very inexact analogy: large numbers of people in uniform are serving under compulsion, direct or indirect, and have been ordered away from their homes. In recognition of this military need, Congress has enacted the Soldiers' and Sailors' Civil Relief Act, specifically preserving for tax purposes the legal residence of those in uniform.

It would be strange indeed if a person could not vote in a state that by law can tax his federal pay. If a person cannot be counted in the apportionment of a district in which he is legally entitled to vote, the traditional theory of representation, as embodied in the Fourteenth Amendment, is abandoned.

The Bureau also suggests that since Congressmen respond to pressures from those living within their districts it makes sense to count all the people living there. Alas, if it were only true—unfortunately, in the daily practice of politics, Congressmen are not overly concerned about those who cannot vote them out of office. Electoral pressure, not noise, determines congressional activity.

The Bureau ultimately buttresses its case on a highly practical judgment. As Director Brown has written:

> The position that members of the armed forces should be allocated back to their parental homes, where presumably they have legal and voting residence, reflects a considerable oversimplification of the problem. It assumes that all members of the armed forces are inducted from their parental home and when discharged will return there. There is considerable evidence that service in the armed forces leads many persons to settle in a different state on discharge. Many men at the time of induction had already left their parental home and were living in apartments

* The Census Bureau keeps figures of military personnel by station as well as by home of record, so it would not be difficult for the Census Bureau to report two sets of statistics to Congress.

or rooming houses. To assign them back to these living quarters—now occupied by someone else—raises the disturbing question as to who are the real residents of the living quarters.

Persons making a professional career of service in the armed forces may not have any real residence other than in the area in which they are serving. Take for example, an officer in the Air Force, now assigned to the Pentagon, whose parental home is located in Minneapolis, who married in Denver an Army nurse whose parental home was San Francisco, and their infant son who was born in Arlington where the couple now lives. Clearly this officer and his family are not residents of Minneapolis.

These difficulties, of course, could be taken care of by the simple expedient of asking one or two more questions on the census form. Thus:

(a) Are you on active duty in the armed forces?

(b) Do you vote in a state other than that in which you are currently residing?

(c) If so, where?

The possibility remains that the recipient of the census questionnaire might lie (but so might he, of course, about the efficiency of his kitchen). Surely there are many members of the armed forces who do not vote at all, and there may even be some who change their voting residences every time they are reassigned by the military. But these objections, if they are that, do not vitiate the fact that voting residence is more relevant to apportionment than the accident of stationing. No one said that census-taking is easy; every American should sympathize with the Bureau's problem of tracking us all down. But sympathy is not a substitute for constitutionality.

Since the Census Bureau has not been told precisely what or how to count, some might object that the fault lies with Congress. That may be, but no matter who should be held responsible the effect is no less real. The net effect of legal policy concerning the census, as it is now implemented, is to deprive states of lawful voters for apportionment purposes and to add to specific geographic areas (determined in the main by the power of Congressmen building military bases) large congregations of military personnel and their families who cannot legally vote where they reside.*

---

* Since this discussion was written, the U.S. Court of Appeals for the Third Circuit has decided the issue squarely to the contrary. But following the Census Bureau's reasoning, the court ruled first that the method of counting physical presence was correct as to college students. The court immediately concluded, without enumerating reasons and without taking note of the compulsion under which military personnel are forced to act, that the military population was equivalent to the college student population.

BUREAUCRATIC INACTIVITY

Buried within the vast bureaucracies of the federal, state, and local governments is a vast network of lawbreaking. Bureaucrats blithely ignore the laws and regulations under which they are supposed to operate. This lawbreaking is usually invisible, since the activity or inactivity of an administrative agency springs from loosely and vaguely worded guidelines that give the agency "discretion." The legislative "standard" for many military programs dictates that the armed forces are to take actions consistent with their "needs." Whatever else it is, this is not a "standard." Other offices, including the federal regulatory agencies, are commanded to take actions consonant with "the public interest." What that interest is or how it is to be ascertained is rarely made clear.

It is difficult to find a consistent pattern in administrative lawbreaking, but it tends to fall into two categories: widespread failure of administrative agencies to follow their own regulations and widespread disinclination to enforce policies they have been created by law to implement. Often these are only different ways of describing the same thing.

When John McGee, a civilian engineer for the Navy, discovered gross corruption in the Bangkok operation of the Navy Fuel Supply Office (NFSO) delivery of petroleum, oil, and lubricants to Thailand and South Vietnam, he uncovered both the failure of the agency to follow its own regulations in accounting for invoices and its complete unwillingness to monitor and control the supply system it had been established to watch over. NFSO neglected to keep required records; and preliminary estimates made by the General Accounting Office when McGee finally "blew the whistle" on the agency to Senator William Proxmire disclosed that more than half of all petroleum sent to Thailand in a ten-month period in 1967 had been stolen out of the NFSO delivery system. The GAO study was made after the NFSO Commanding Officer refused McGee's request for an investigation. In fact, McGee's private communications with the Commanding Officer resulted not in expressions of thanks but a demand that he resign or be fired.

It was only at this point that McGee felt compelled, in self-defense, to make his discoveries public. John Chafee, formerly the Governor of Rhode Island and in 1969 the incoming Secretary of the Navy, showed his lack of political courage by keeping McGee in a nonexistent Washington job for five months before severe senatorial pressure forced him to reassign the engineer, if only to a low priority project in Pensacola, Florida. The point is not to score Secretary Chafee but to underscore the strength of the bureaucratic mentality: showing clearly that an agency's regulations have been violated requires covering up rather than reform. Chafee could have given McGee a medal, but the Secretary preferred to show that he supported the criminals in uniform.

The bigger an agency's budget, the more widespread the lawbreaking is likely to be. Thus, in 1970, the Department of Health, Education, and Welfare, second only to the Defense Department in its share of the federal budget, disclosed a nationwide disregard for regulations in federal welfare and social programs. Federal regulations specify the manner and means by which federal welfare funds will be doled out. For years, HEW knew that the states were blatantly violating these regulations; yet funds were never cut off and no effort was made by the Federal Government to bring the states into line, as required by the regulations.

In its 1970 report, HEW finally admitted publicly that thirty-nine states and the District of Columbia were in open contempt of the regulations. More than a handful of states refused to comply with a 1967 federal law requiring states to adjust their welfare levels to take account of the rising cost of living, and three years later HEW was only beginning to look into the possibility of holding hearings to investigate the states' failure to implement the law.

Other federal agencies are also guilty of failing to insure that federal standards are implemented and obeyed. Many regulatory agencies are directly concerned with the great mass of American consumers in one way or another: prosecuting restraints of trade, regulating stock exchanges, passing on the quality of foods and drugs, insuring the safety of vast numbers of workers, checking deception and misrepresentation in the market place, regulating the rates of transportation and communication companies across the country, and containing pollution. Yet the Interstate Commerce Commission, the Federal Trade Commission, the Food and Drug Administration, and other agencies have ignored in gross the needs of consumers. It has been estimated that the failure to enforce the antitrust and other trade laws adequately costs the American consumer some $100 billion every year.

The Food and Drug Administration is responsible for allowing scores of drugs to get on the market in spite of memoranda circulated within the agency that strongly suggested their possible dangers. Once the FDA went so far as to suggest that a company might remove its own health warning from a product label. Benjamin S. Rosenthal, Congressman from New York, told a House Government Operations subcommittee how the FDA had suggested to the Lederle Laboratories Division of the American Cyanamid Company that its label on methotrexate (MTX) could be omitted but that "we would not insist upon its deletion." The label said that MTX should be dispensed "only to physicians, never to patients. Dispense only with full statement of warning. Physicians should give the drug personally to patients and should not dispense more than six or seven days' supply at one time." Long before the FDA told the company it could remove the warning, MTX, a skin preparation, was known to have caused the deaths of fifteen people. Rosenthal also charged that in permitting eight years of experimentation on psoriasis with MTX the FDA had violated its own regulations, which prohibit experimentation that "is unduly prolonged."

In like manner, the United States Bureau of Mines has a long history of omissions, neglect, and malfeasance, some of which resulted in the deaths and injuries of thousands of coal miners. In November, 1968, an explosion at Farmington, West Virginia, claimed the lives of seventy-eight miners; the federal Coal Mine Health and Safety Act was enacted thirteen months later. A year and a half after the Act was passed, the General Accounting Office released an eighty-page report fully documenting the Bureau of Mines' failure to enforce the new law.

In 1970, there were 260 fatalities (an increase of nearly one-third over the preceding year) and more than ten thousand work-related injuries in the coal mines. The GAO investigated in two areas in the Appalachian coal region and found that fewer than one-third of the 1969 requirements for safety inspections were observed and that only one percent of the required health inspections were conducted by the Bureau of Mines in 1970.

The United States Department of Labor is required to enforce the Walsh-Healy Act, which applies safety requirements to all manufacturing plants with federal contracts; but the Department ignores the safety codes almost entirely. Inspectors have found violations in more than ninety percent of the plants they visit, but they visit only two or three percent of the factories covered by law. And although the factories violating the safety standards number in the thousands, between 1963 and 1968 the Department of Labor proceeded against only 154 companies and fined only 15 of them.

The Federal Housing Administration was shown in 1971 to have permitted real estate speculators to abuse the Omnibus Housing Act of 1968 so badly, at the expense of the poor, that a Congressional study described the FHA procedures as "sheer fraud." Under the "235 Program," the Government is to pick up the tab on part of the interest for refinancing home loans, permitting poor families to purchase homes at low cost. But instead of monitoring the program, a House Banking and Currency Committee report stated that "FHA has allowed real estate speculation of the worst type to go on in the 235 program and has virtually turned its back to these practices." The report continued: "It is common practice in the inner city to pick up houses for minimal amounts, perform a so-called 'paste-up' or 'cosmetic rehabilitation' which, in many cases, amounts to a few hundred dollars and then resell the property under FHA Section 235 for a profit of thousands of dollars."

A speculator purchased one house, for example, in Paterson, New

Jersey, for eighteen hundred dollars. After making repairs totalling four hundred fifty dollars, he managed to sell it under the §235 program for twenty thousand dollars. The FHA has responsibility to insure that houses are of sufficient quality that they will maintain their value for the life of the loan; "FHA views itself solely as a mortgage insurer whose interest is in the adequacy of the security for the loan rather than decent, safe and sanitary housing for people," the House report said. Even so, "FHA is insuring existing homes that are of such poor quality that there is little or no possibility they can survive the life of the mortgage."

When the Penn Central Railroad filed for bankruptcy on June 21, 1970, it was revealed that large institutional investors had disposed of more than $1,860,000 in shares of the railroad company's stock since the previous April 1st. So large a sale so soon before a major bankruptcy petition indicated rather clearly the possibility that inside information was being leaked out illegally. Wright Patman, Chairman of the House Banking and Currency Committee, saw a "massive shell game carried on by financial entities in a position to know the innermost financial secrets" of Penn Central; Patman charged both the Securities and Exchange Commission and the Interstate Commerce Commission with failure to disclose information to the public that might have indicated the impending disaster.

There are many more cases, at all levels of government, of failure to enforce even long-established laws. The Refuse Act of 1899 was not used as the basis for a prosecution until 1970. Similarly, municipal codes have remained unenforced; in 1971, the city of Philadelphia was itself discovered to be fourth-worst polluter. Congressman William J. Green of Philadelphia discovered during his unsuccessful primary campaign for the mayoralty that city incinerators "pour out three times as much pollution as the Code allows." Thousands of local governments are equally prone to violate their own ordinances.

But they are not alone: the federal Government is likewise an unlawful polluter. The Mayport (Florida) Naval Station recently collected its waste oil, totalling some 637,000 gallons, and dumped it fifty-five miles off the Florida coast; only ocean currents prevented the massive oil slick from becoming a disaster for Florida beaches. Navy Secretary John Chafee admitted that the dumping was a violation of the "spirit" of federal antipollution laws; it was also a direct violation of the National Environmental Policy Act of 1969 requiring an "environmental impact statement" before "major federal actions significantly affecting the quality of the human environment" can be undertaken. No impact statement had been issued prior to the dumping. Chafee's excuse was simple: "If we had known this was going on it wouldn't have been going on."

But no one can hope to exhaust the Government's capacity for inactivity. It is enough simply to observe that much of the Government's inactivity is not only regrettable but illegal. Professor Kenneth Culp Davis has concluded that "a startlingly high proportion of all official discretionary action pertaining to administration of justice is illegal or of doubtful legality. This is true in all units of American government— federal, state, and local."

Davis's definition of "administration of justice" is not narrow; he means acts affecting the rights of "individual parties," which in turn he defines to include people, corporations, governmental units such as school boards and districts, and other legal entities. That does not leave very much out: bureaucratic inactivity reaches everywhere because the Government reaches everywhere; and a day does not go by during which it has not broken the law and done injustice to individuals, groups, and society in general.

5
Crimes Affecting No One

THE UNLAWFUL APPOINTMENT
OF MR. JUSTICE BLACK

WHEN WILLIS VAN DEVANTER announced his retirement as an Associate Justice of the Supreme Court after the 1936 term, Franklin D. Roosevelt found himself in something of a dilemma: how to appoint 'a liberal to the vacancy, placate the South, and get the nomination through the Senate, which was still ruffled from the effects of the court-packing plan. The answer was a typical and happily conceived Roosevelt solution. The Senate Democrats themselves had already made a revolutionary break with the past practice of letting the President have the sole voice in choosing the nominee in recommending their Majority Leader, Joseph T. Robinson. Robinson's unexpected death shortly thereafter removed any necessity of considering him. Roosevelt saw that the obvious way to secure the Senate's consent to his nomination was to choose a Senator. And there was one Senator who met the other criteria as well: Hugo Lafayette Black of Alabama, ten years a member of the Senate and a staunch liberal and New Deal supporter.

With no prior warning, President Roosevelt personally wrote Senator Black's name on a blank nomination form and had it delivered to the Senate chamber by messenger. The nomination was quickly confirmed, amid sensational publicity concerning rumors that the Senator had once been a member of the Ku Klux Klan. (Just before the opening term of Court, the new Justice admitted on a nationwide radio broadcast that he had indeed once joined the white-robed marauders. But, he said, that time was in his earliest political career long before; he had never carried their card, never renewed his membership, and did not adhere to any of their ideals.)

In August, some six weeks before the October term began, a former federal judge from the Virgin Islands named Albert Levitt, who had recently resigned as a special assistant to Attorney General Homer Cummings, filed a petition in the Supreme Court, asking that the new Justice be required to show his eligibility for the seat to which he had been appointed. According to Levitt, there were two constitutional infirmities in the new appointment. First, by law there can only be nine Justices. The retirement of Justice Van Devanter did not really create a vacancy on the Court, Levitt asserted, because under the terms of a new retirement act, retired Justices would continue to draw full pay—in effect, since Van Devanter was still salaried, there were ten Justices. Second, since the emoluments of the office of Associate Justice had been increased during a term in which Black was a Senator, he could not, according to Levitt, constitutionally assume his place on the bench. Attorney General Cummings termed the petition "a typical Levitt escapade." The Attorney General continued: "It is an entirely futile action which contains many elements of comedy. It is not taken seriously by the Department of Justice."

The first argument was weak. To be sure, Senate Republican leader William E. Borah had sent to the Judiciary Committee the draft of a bill declaring that new members could be added to the Court whenever a sitting Justice retired. When the Black appointment was announced, Senator Borah withdrew his bill, since a Senator cannot constitutionally accept appointment to an office created while he was serving in the Senate. The prevailing view was that Borah's bill was unnecessary, since the Sumners Act, which created the new plan to induce elderly conservative Justices to retire by permitting them to become "retired Justices" at full pay, obviously contemplated the appointment of a new Justice to take the place of the retiree. That being so, there was nothing to the argument that the retired Justice was still one of the nine Jusices called for by statute. What the Sumners Act did, proponents of the Black nomination said, was to create a new office of retired Justice.

The second argument had merit. Article I, Section 6, Clause 2 of the Constitution says that

> No Senator or Representative shall, during the Time for which he was elected, be appointed to any civil office under the Authority of the United States, which shall have been created, or the Emoluments whereof shall have been encreased during such time.

The Sumners Act, it can cogently be argued, increased the emoluments of the Supreme Court bench by greatly liberalizing the retirement benefits. The Act was passed in 1937 when Black was serving a senatorial term that would not end for two years. No one doubts that an Associate Justice of the Supreme Court is serving in a civil office under the authority of the United States. It follows that the appointment of Hugo Black to the Supreme Court was unconstitutional.

On October 4, 1937, at the opening day of the Court's new session, the somber Black was seated in a packed courtroom. The audience had come to watch the threatened attempts to have him barred from taking his place on the bench. But the bewhiskered Chief Justice, Charles Evans Hughes, would have none of it.

The first order of business was a long, dull process of granting motions for the admission of candidates to the Supreme Court bar, a dull and perfunctory matter. Shortly after the assembled members of the bar began presenting their motions on behalf of their sons, associates, or clerks, a dapper gentleman in a gray flannel suit and bright red tie jumped up and presented himself to the Court. "Mr. Chief Justice," he said, "I wish to introduce myself. My name is Patrick Henry Kelly of Boston." Hughes asked whether he was going to present a candidate for admission. Kelly intimated he was going after Black, and he was ruled out of order. Impatiently waiting for the roll of lawyers to finish, Kelly was out of his seat when the last motion was done, pleading "a question of personal privilege." Hughes refused to permit him to present his request to the Court since it was not in writing, though he had, Kelly said, made the same request earlier in letters to each of the Justices.

Then Albert Levitt rose to submit his brief as a member "of long standing" of the bar of the Supreme Court. His brief was in writing, and the Chief Justice directed that he submit it to the Clerk for submission to the Court. During this brief procedure, Kelly was furiously scribbling his plea on a single sheet of paper. When Levitt finished, Kelly was on his feet again: "I have the motion in writing now, Your Honor," he said. The Chief Justice agreed that it could be submitted to the Clerk for consideration. "At this session?" Kelly asked. "At this session," the Chief Justice assented.

Five days later, on October 9, the Court denied the petitions in a brief per curiam opinion, Justice Black not sitting. As knowledgeable lawyers had expected, the Levitt petition was dismissed for "lack of standing," an established rule of law that requires the Court to refuse to decide a case in which the litigant has no other interest than the desire to learn the answer to an abstract question.* The Kelly petition was dismissed even more perfunctorily and on the basis of precedent— the *Levitt* case.

These dismissals were purely procedural, of course; they did not go to the merits of the controversy at all. On October 12, it was announced that a new challenge might be forthcoming in the case of some Florida oil men whose private telegrams had earlier been seized by the Secu-

---

* The requirement of "standing" has been considerably weakened, as noted at pp. 261 ff.

rities and Exchange Commission and passed along to Congress with Senator Black's support. The seizure prompted a suit by the oil men; a federal district court quashed a subpoena for the telegrams, but this decision was reversed.

On October 18, the Court denied the Floridians' request for review. Two weeks later it denied, also, a motion for rehearing that had been filed with the claim that the original denial was void because Justice Black had failed to disqualify himself. The final attempts at disqualification came from two more interested citizens, Elizabeth L. Seymour of Salamanca, New York, and Robert Gray Taylor of Media, Pennsylvania; their petitions were denied in November.

That same month the *Columbia Law Review* said that Black should be reappointed after the expiration of his Senate term in January, 1939, to stave off the possibility that proceedings might be brought by a future administration. The only clear-cut method for challenging an unconstitutional appointment is for the Government itself to bring a suit against the incumbent. Franklin Roosevelt would not bring the case, of course, and neither would Harry Truman, and by the time Dwight D. Eisenhower took his oath of office everyone had forgotten the issue.

All of which merely proves that moral injunctions in the Constitution will not restrain Presidents who wish to avoid its silly provisions.

DESECRATING THE FLAG

Federal laws, and laws in every state as well, provide varying degrees of criminal punishment for acts concerning the American flag that can loosely be lumped under the term "flag desecration." These laws lay down a host of rules regulating the use of and proper bearing toward Old Glory. Many state laws make criminal any acts tending to mutilate, deface, defile, defy, trample, or cast contempt upon the flag. These laws have been interpreted to cover the wearing of flags sewn into the seat of pants, making flags into shirts, or the use of flags as decals along with other symbols.

A North Carolina statute prohibited "contemptuous" acts against the flag, defined as any combination of stars and stripes in red, white, and blue. The police arrested one person for wearing on his jacket a flag with the superimposed legend "give peace a chance" and a hand with two fingers making a "V," and they got another man for having made a hole in the flag by pinning it to his car ceiling. A federal court felt compelled to strike the law down as unconstitutional. "It seems to us," the court said, "that red, white and blue trousers with or without stars are trousers and not a flag and that it is beyond the state's competence to dictate color and design of clothing, even bad taste clothing.

. . . The definition of a flag in the North Carolina statute is simply un-believable. Read literally, it may be dangerous in North Carolina to possess anything red, white and blue. Such a definition is a manifest absurdity. Since it is not suggested that the State has the slightest inter-est in singling out from the spectrum certain colors for unique protec-tion, this definition alone is sufficient to void the statute."

A federal court in New York was likewise compelled to strike down that state's flag-desecration law, which prohibited the placing of any "word, figure, mark, picture, design, drawing, or any advertisement" on any "flag, standard, color, shield, or ensign of the United States of America." Defendants in the case were arrested for their use of a peace symbol that contained seven white stars on a blue background in the upper left portion of the circular emblem and red and white stripes in the rest.

Although the police have managed to arrest quite a number of scat-tered violators of the various flag provisions, the number of instances in which the police politely ignore the laws is at least as large. The Ameri-can Legion in Hauppauge, New York, flew its flag upside down follow-ing the capture of the U.S.S. *Pueblo* by the North Koreans in 1968. No one was arrested, although a Long Island neighbor of the Legionnaires, a young housewife unhappy about the war in Vietnam, was arrested when she also flew her flag upside down in protest.

In July, 1970, the cover photograph on the current issue of the *American Bar Association Journal* brought the controversy to a high point; it showed the Alabama State Capitol flying the Confederate flag atop its dome: the United States flag was not to be seen. A correspond-ent from Columbia, South Carolina, was outraged: "When I was last in Montgomery," he said, "the flag of the United States flew from an in-significant halyard in a side yard of the capitol building." The cor-respondent contended that the (apparent) solitary flight of the Confed-erate flag was a violation of Section 175 of Title 36 of the *United States Code,* which prescribes the manner by which the United States Flag is to be displayed.

The matter is not free from doubt since that statute does not pre-scribe criminal penalties for its violation, nor does it require the Ameri-can flag to be flown at all. It simply describes the proper placing of the American flag when it is flown. But if the Alabama instance was not an offense, it clearly bordered on the offensive in this murky area of ran-dom enforcement. In defense of the people of Alabama, a lawyer re-sponded in a later issue of the *Journal:* "The flying of the Confederate flag over the Alabama State Capitol is not disrespectful to our national flag. . . . [Alabamians] are proud of their beautiful land, proud of their communities, proud of their freedom and proud of their heritage. The confederate flag represents all of these things. To some it may represent racism, but to many it represents home and family and friends. It represents unpolluted lakes and flowering forests. It represents a spirit of independence and individuality which flourishes in the South. . . . [T]o love and honor the South is not disrespectful to the United States of America . . . [and] to honor a part of the United States is to honor all of the United States." He neglected to add that the practice represents —indeed, symbolizes—the American penchant for lawbreaking.

OTHER FOIBLES

When the Zambian Government purchased a mansion in Washington in 1970, and converted it into a chancery, it was in violation of a 1964 federal law prohibiting the operation of offices other than embassies of foreign governments in that part of town. The response to this illegality wasn't exactly striking; everyone in America was immobilized into inaction. Foreign governments are immune from suit in federal courts. Hampton Davis, the State Department's Assistant Chief of Protocol, showed penetrating insight in commenting on the situation: "Exactly where we go from here, I'm not able to say." And Marion H. Smoak, Deputy Chief of Protocol, said: "The problem is, here we are; it's happened. I'm sure these people were not aware of this restriction. You cannot take legal action." Senator J. William Fulbright, sponsor of the law being violated, said he would write the Secretary of State to urge diplomatic action. Two years later the chancery was being illegally operated in the same quarters.

The police in New York City park their cars illegally but never get ticketed. An enterprising newsman counted sixty-three illegally parked cars one April day on the blocks surrounding the Seventeenth Precinct station on East 51st Street between Third and Lexington Avenues. The policemen, some of whom were parked in front of fire hydrants, fire lanes, and crosswalks, marked their cars for the benefit of the men on duty with the equivalent of a "soul brother" label on the windows: Patrolmen's Benevolent Association membership cards for the would-be ticketer to see. The police claim they must park unlawfully because the city has failed to live up to its "contractual" obligation to provide parking spaces for on-duty policemen.

Lyndon Johnson, in one of his lesser acts of lawbreaking, ordered Secret Service agents to stay clear of House Speaker John McCormack when he became next in line for the Presidency in 1963—McCormack said he didn't want protection. But the law is adamant that potential successors be guarded.

Investigating the Nixon Administration's signing of an "executive agreement" extending the use of military bases in Spain (thus subverting the Senate's constitutional power to consent to treaties), Senator Stuart Symington, chairman of a Senate Foreign Relations subcommittee, discovered that the Defense Department "doctored" information given to the investigators. Copies of messages were altered by senior State and Defense Department officials. When the alteration was detected, the subcommittee demanded the originals and they were produced. If you or I gave altered documents intended for Senate investigators, we would be slapped with contempt citations. But obviously the official cover-up hurt no one, because it was only an investigation and the agreement had already been signed.

And in Albany, New York, the excuses for lawbreaking reached their apogee. The Republican-controlled legislature required its members to deliver their outgoing mail to the mailroom unsealed. Mailroom clerks then read the mail and returned the letters they didn't like. State Assemblyman Stephen S. Gottlieb, a Manhattan Democrat, found four hundred fifty letters addressed to his constituents returned to him for being "too political." Who was hurt? No one likes junk mail anyway. Gottlieb had to bring a lawsuit against State Assembly Speaker Perry B. Duryea, and two functionaries, to bar future attempts at censorship.

6

Private Crimes of Government Officials

CONFLICTS OF INTEREST: THE LAW
THAT NEVER WAS

Sir Francis Bacon, the great Lord Chancellor of England,
once penned these lines:

> The place of justice is an hallowed place, and therefore not only the
> bench, but the foot pace and precincts and purprise thereof, ought to be
> preserved without scandal and corruption.

Unfortunately for Bacon the House of Commons saw fit to impeach him
in 1621 for exacting payments from litigants in the amount of £12,230—
"a corruption so gross that one wonders how it went undetected for
three years." He used to threaten litigants with imprisonment unless he
were paid off, and more than once he accepted payment from both sides
in a dispute. "Not only gifts of gold buttons, suits of hangings, valuable
cabinets, and diamond rings, but also loans and gifts of currency flowed
into Bacon's coffers. Bribes reached him in minute driblets as well as in
sizable packages."

When he was presented with the sole alternative of trial by the House
of Lords, of which he was a member, Bacon confessed. His defense was
that the bribes did not affect his judgment—an excuse still used occasionally today when a judge is caught with his hands in his litigant's till.
Abe Fortas was said to have believed that his acceptance of a fee while
on the High Bench would not influence his judicial demeanor. Of
course there was a difference between Bacon and Fortas, for Bacon's
practice was corrupt in the extreme whereas the most anyone could ever
say of Fortas's behavior was that it presented an appearance of a conflict. There was another difference also: Bacon was fined and went to

the Tower; Fortas was forced to resign from public life. Even that result was unusual—other judges, including Chief Justice Warren Burger and Justice William O. Douglas, have accepted fees while on the Bench without recrimination.*

Sir Francis's behavior—as distinguished from Fortas's—is still considered corrupt. Many laws expressly prohibit and make criminal the receipt of money or other valuable commodities for official favors. If, however, Sir Francis had accepted payment not from litigants appearing before his court but in return for using his influence with the Crown to get the payor appointed to a royal sinecure, the judge's evildoing would have been more ambiguous. In modern terms, he would have been considered guilty of a conflict of interest.

Conflict of interest is a term that has not been and cannot be comprehensively defined. In public affairs, it is generally used to denote the conflict between a Government employee's official responsibility and his private economic interest. Thus, if a Government official owned a company that would enjoy doing business with the Government department the official headed, few would disagree that a conflict of interest existed, whether or not the official's company actually obtained Government business.†

President Eisenhower's Secretary of the Air Force Harold Talbott learned this rule the hard way when the *New York Times* printed the transcript of a secret Senate Permanent Investigation Subcommittee hearing concerning Talbott's activities on behalf of the Paul Mulligan Company, of which he was a half owner. The transcript "showed that Talbott had actively promoted the business of the Mulligan company from his Pentagon office, frequently writing letters to prospective clients on Air Force stationery. Included in the *Times* story were photographs of letters from Talbott to the businessmen, some written under Air Force letterheads, and all marked 'CONFIDENTIAL.'" Resigning under fire, Talbott was presented with the Medal of Freedom and a Distinguished Public Service award.

In 1955, when Secretary Talbott was hustling up business for his company, there were no laws expressly prohibiting his promotional activities. But partly as a result of such embarrassments as Harold Talbott, the Defense Department, following the passage of a tightened conflict of interest statute by the Congress in 1962, made it clear by regulation that Talbott's and like activities were not permissible.

* At least without successfully completed recrimination. A move to impeach Justice Douglas failed to spark much enthusiasm in the House when the matter was referred to committee in 1969.

† Generally, a conflict of interest occurs whenever a person represents or acts as agent for two or more parties whose interests diverge. For example, an automobile diagnostic center affiliated with a repair shop has a conflict of interest, or at least the appearance of one, as far as the customer is concerned.

The conflict of interest laws covering federal employees are rather obvious (if rather roundabout) proscriptions of the kinds of dubious behavior where the evil is clear to everyone except those involved. Thus, federal employees are not permitted to receive compensation from private sources for performing services for federal agencies when the United States has an interest in the proceeding; they may not have financial interests in the subject matter of official duties; and they may not be paid by anyone other than the Government for performing official duties.

These laws and their spirit are very often honored in the breach. President Eisenhower's appointees had a dramatic flair for dragging their names through the mud. The resignation of Sherman Adams capped a six-year period of seeming corruption in high places. Of course, conflicts of interest did not begin with Eisenhower, nor did they end with him. Eisenhower campaigned strongly in 1952 against scandals in the Truman administration (though Eisenhower himself was a rather shameless recipient of lavish gifts that were deducted as losses on other people's income tax returns). Fred Korth, President Kennedy's second Secretary of the Navy, was compelled to resign when it became clear that he had used his public office to secure business for a bank in which he owned stock. In connection with the TFX program he had engaged in public contract negotiations with General Dynamics, which had secured financing from Korth's bank. President Johnson's Assistant Secretary of Commerce Herbert W. Klotz resigned after suspicions arose that he had benefitted financially from inside information in the Texas Gulf Sulphur Company's copper strike in Ontario.

The conflict of interest laws are not uniformly applied. Many federal office holders have been required to divest themselves of paltry sums of stock before assuming office. Judge Clement F. Haynsworth was denied confirmation to the Supreme Court in part because he owned a few shares of stock in a company related to a case in his court. But David Packard, President Nixon's Deputy Secretary of Defense, was permitted to retain (in trust) three hundred million dollars worth of stock in his defense-oriented company on the grounds that the company did not sell directly to the Government and that he would not be entitled to the dividends paid while he held office.

Needless to say, violations of the conflicts of interest laws are not confined to federal officials. New York City's Corporation Counsel J. Lee Rankin managed to maintain a private law practice while serving as a full time lawyer for the city—in the face of a city charter provision stating: "Every head of a department or elected officer except Councilman who receives a salary from the city shall give his full time to his duties and shall not engage in any other occupation, profession or employment." As usual, when the facts were revealed to the public, the lawbreaker announced he would no longer carry on the practice but admitted no past wrongdoing. A bar committee later reported it saw no violation. The solemn lawyers obviously didn't know where to look.

The laws that apply to public employees are breathtakingly vague when it comes to prohibiting Congressmen and other legislators from engaging in identical activities. Though codes of ethics are often discussed, Congress has been reluctant to enact or enforce a code that would prevent Congressmen from engaging in even the simplest kinds of conflict of interest. Thus, lawyers in Congress maintain private practices and find that clients whose businesses they oversee on various Congressional committees seek out their firms for advice on matters related to committee business. Members of Congress with interest in banks seem to cluster suspiciously on banking committees. Members of Congress whose hobby is farming find themselves on agriculture committees.

Consider the case of Congressman Emanuel Celler, Democrat of New York, Dean of the House of Representatives, and Chairman of its Judiciary Committee. Congressman Celler maintains a law office in New York. It has two doors. The left door reads Weisman, Celler, Allan, Spett and Sheinberg. The right door omits Celler's name. Inside, the offices are the same; outside, clients with federal business are supposed to walk in the right-hand door. The subterfuge seems hardly worth the cost of the extra door.

PRESIDENT NIXON TAKES A BRIBE

Perhaps the most systematic conflict of interest in the federal Government is the funding of election campaigns, discussed earlier. Oftentimes the entire rationale of campaign giving seems to be a payment to induce future favors. It is no secret that those who donate generously often wind up as ambassadors. It is also no secret that those who buy elections for Congressmen often find Congressmen supporting their positions on the Senate and House floors.

The public got a glimpse of this usually secret process shortly after President Nixon returned from China in early 1972, when columnist Jack Anderson bared the now infamous International Telephone & Telegraph Corporation memorandum. That document linked an ITT pledge of $400,000 to San Diego for the Republican Convention with the settlement by the Justice Department of its suit against the company's multi-billion dollar merger.

Shortly after Richard W. McLaren came to the Justice Department in 1969 as Assistant Attorney General in charge of the Antitrust Division, he announced that the Department was bringing anti-merger suits against ITT. He stated publicly that he would pursue the cases through the Supreme Court to test the reach of current antitrust law, which he said he believed was sufficient to prevent mergers of giant conglomerates. Successful prosecution of such suits would go a long way toward reducing and forestalling economic concentration in several industries, which would in turn lower prices and increase business efficiency. McLaren said he would ask Congress for tougher legislation if the Supreme Court turned him down, but he said he would press to the end.

Two years later, with one of the three suits against ITT pending in the Supreme Court (the Government had lost in the lower courts), a settlement was reached, permitting ITT to retain the billion-dollar Hartford Fire Insurance Company (with its enormous cash resources) if it sold Levitt & Sons, Canteen Corporation, Avis Rent-a-Car, one division of Grinnell Corporation, and two smaller insurance companies, the acquisitions of which were the subjects of other suits.

Although the settlement puzzled some lawyers, politicians, and editorialists when it was announced in July, 1971, still there had been antitrust settlements before, and the courts duly approved the deal. But the uproar surrounding the Anderson revelation led to the request of Deputy Attorney General Richard G. Kleindienst that the Senate Judiciary Committee reopen its hearings on his nomination as Attorney General, and prompted a series of events so ludicrous that for a while the ITT affair became the nation's leading comedy relief.

A physician of Dita D. Beard, the ITT lobbyist and alleged author of the memorandum, testified that his patient was an excessive drinker and was irrational. It turned out that the physician's wife, also a doctor, was being investigated by the Justice Department for Medicare fraud. Curiously, the lobbyist's doctor stopped by the Justice Department before his Judiciary Committee appearance.

Mrs. Beard took nearly a month to deny the authenticity of the memorandum—apparently she required some time to realize the memorandum was, in her words, a "false and salacious document." One of Mrs. Beard's former assistants then came forward to state that she recalled typing portions of the disputed memorandum.

Immediately after the company learned that Anderson had the memorandum in his possession, but shortly before he released it, ITT's Washington office shredded "many sacks" of documents that might "be misused or misconstrued" or that would otherwise cause "unwarranted embarrassment" to the company, in the words of ITT general counsel Howard J. Aibel. But, like a good medieval scholastic, he offered a hairsplitting defense of the destruction. None of the employees involved in the shredding knew of any papers linking the settlement to the pledge, he said. He did admit that some of the shredded papers discussed the settlement, and others the pledge, and he apparently refrained from *denying* that there was any link contained in the ravaged documents.

Even though corporate political contributions are illegal, a letter from the Justice Department turned up, stating that contributions to the Republican Convention, if made via a non-profit intermediary, would be tax deductible if the donations were made primarily with the "reasonable expectation of financial return to the contributor." (The pledge was made by ITT's Sheraton Hotel subsidiary, which would gain from convention business.)

Central to the credibility gap was the performance of the three Justice Department principals—Attorney General Mitchell, Deputy Attorney General Kleindienst, and Assistant Attorney General McLaren (since named a federal judge). Mitchell first said he had no contact with the case because his former law firm had represented ITT. Later, before the Senate Judiciary Committee, he admitted that during the pendency of the suit he had had a chat with ITT President Harold S. Geneen about the Department's antitrust policies. He said they didn't talk about the specific case, but he also said, casting doubt on his general credibility, that he did not know who was responsible for picking the Republican Convention site—as if President Nixon's campaign manager could be so ignorant.

In a letter to Democratic Party chairman Lawrence F. O'Brien two months before the controversy arose, Kleindienst said that McLaren had had exclusive responsibility for the case. However, he subsequently admitted to the Senate Committee that he had initiated a series of meetings between McLaren and an ITT director that led to the eventual settlement. Crucial to this settlement was an economic analysis hurriedly prepared by a private financial advisor recruited through White House aide Peter M. Flanigan.

Strangest of all was McLaren's role. As a highly respected private antitrust lawyer and a former chairman of the American Bar Association's Antitrust Section, he was widely regarded as one of the President's most professional appointments. His public antitrust stand supported a myth, still circulating, that Republicans are more vigorous antitrust enforcers than Democrats. The evidence is not persuasive that either party is particularly vigorous, and the evidence of McLaren's perspicacity is also negligible, in view of the fatal flaw in his attempted justification of the settlement.

The crux of McLaren's justification was grounded in a fallacy so clear that it is not uncharitable to reject the argument outright as a desperate after-the-fact rationalization by a subordinate who had been subjected to overwhelming political pressure.

The settlement was prompted in large part, according to McLaren's testimony at the hearing, because the economic analysis provided by Flanigan's outside financial expert indicated that the economy would suffer greatly (stock market distress, among other factors) if the Government forced ITT to divest itself of Hartford, with its cash. But McLaren had already considered those factors and rejected them as a reason for not filing suit. No new evidence ever turned up. Moreover, *the argument presumes, and throughout the debate everyone assumed, that a court decision favorable to the Government would have required divestiture. That assumption is incorrect.*

The Clayton Act, the anti-merger law under which the ITT cases were being tried, does not require a court to order divestiture in every case—or in any case. The court may order any relief it deems proper under the circumstances. As a practical matter, divestiture is the only sensible remedy in such cases, else why bring an anti-merger case? But the same "evidence" that convinced McLaren of the folly of divesting Hartford might well—undoubtedly would, at McLaren's urging—have convinced the Supreme Court, had it agreed with his contention that conglomerate mergers are prohibited by the law, that the cases should have been consolidated, that partial divestiture be ordered, or that delayed divestiture be required.

By pressing the appeal, McLaren might thus have achieved what he got with the settlement—and also obtained the ruling he wanted from the Supreme Court: that the Clayton Act does indeed apply to conglomerate mergers. It is the express purpose of the antitrust laws to prevent massive and potentially injurious economic concentration. With a Supreme Court ruling, similar future mergers might have been preventable. Of course, the Government might have lost the suit altogether, but then McLaren could have followed through on his original intention of asking Congress for tougher legislation (no request for such legislation has been made).

As it stands, the settlement resolved none of the legal issues. The settlement is not precedent for anything—unless it be for the suspicion that there are political ways around uncomfortable suits. Some very serious doubts have been raised about the integrity of the highest officials of the Government. McLaren called the Senate Judiciary Committee's questioning of him "outrageous," adding in a self-righteous manner that the Committee seemed to be "attacking" his "judgment." More people ought to.

The pressuring of Richard McLaren, however, does not add up to corruption, and bribery has not been proved in this case. But in an unrelated incident occurring four months before the announced ITT settlement, Presidential bribery is plain.

In 1971, organized agricultural interests persuaded President Nixon to boost their members' annual income by between $300,000,000 and $400,000,000 in return for a donation of a few hundred thousand dollars. On March 12, Secretary of Agriculture Clifford Hardin anounced that milk price supports would remain at the same level as the previous year. Upset at the prospect of losing the revenues that higher support would have brought, industry spokesmen put on an intensive lobbying effort that landed them in the Oval Room of the White House on March 23. (The day before, the dairy industry happened to contribute $10,000 to Republican party committees.) President Nixon, along with Secretary Hardin and representatives of the Office of Management and Budget, listened to the delegation for fifty-eight minutes. The next day, March 24, an additional $25,000 was donated.

On March 25, Secretary Hardin reversed his thirteen-day-old decision and announced that "new evidence" had been discovered that justified raising the price support level of milk. In his March 12 statement, Secretary Hardin had gone into a detailed list of reasons why the price support level did not need changing. On April 5, reports later showed, the same dairy organizations that had met with President Nixon gave $45,000 in $5,000 lots to nine Republican party committees.

No great cry went up from anyone because clever strategists had previously contributed $60,000 to the 1970 campaigns of twelve leading Democratic Senators, including Hubert H. Humphrey and Edmund Muskie. Only one Republican candidate, Ted Stevens of Alaska, received dairy money. Other Republicans doubtless got campaign money through regular campaign committees. Of fifty-one House members who received money in 1970 directly from dairy committees, thirty-seven were Democrats (and they received $112,000, as compared to $12,000 that went to Republican Congressmen). Just to make sure things stayed quiet, the dairy industry paid out $16,000 to Democratic Party coffers from February to May.

These contributions were dwarfed by the $332,000 donated to Republicans after March and through December, 1971. Rather than give it openly, however, dairy interests established scores of dummy political committees to receive the money. The only thing remarkable about them, aside from their number, was their habit of listing as addresses suburban Washington homes of people who had no connection with them whatsoever. None of the committees bothered to file the reports required of them by the Corrupt Practices Act.

There can be little question that the March "contributions" to the Republican Party were illegal bribes. At the 1971 trial of Robert T. Carson, Senator Hiram L. Fong's administrative assistant, for bribery, perjury, and conspiracy in connection with stock manipulation, Richard G. Kleindienst testified that Carson had privately offered $100,000 for the 1972 Republican campaign if Kleindienst would agree to help quash an indictment in the case. Kleindienst rejected the offer, and when he discovered one week later that Carson was himself under investigation, Kleindienst reported the incident to the Attorney General as a bribery attempt. (Kleindienst was too slow-witted to regard the offer as a bribe when made.) If a contribution in return for help in quashing an indictment is a bribe, there is no apparent reason why it is not also a bribe for agricultural interests to make their contributions under the circumstances present in March. Payments for any kind of official favors are unlawful. Clifford Hardin and Richard Nixon ought to be in jail.

And even Francis Bacon would have agreed.

Conflict of interest is a fact of political life. Though its content may vary from era to era, its existence is never very much in doubt. At some levels, of course, conflicts of interest are not representative of the Government but of the officeholder. The closer the gain is to strictly private interests, the more likely we are to characterize the behavior as corrupt. As the next section points out, corruption may or may not be a part of official policy. Usually it is not. But whatever the gain, the pervasive fact of conflict of interest cannot be ignored.

Nonofficial lawbreaking is very often the basis for official lawbreaking. When the same Government officers see how easily they can get away with corrupt or legally dubious activities, they realize they have little to fear from remote illegalities—remote in the sense that the illegal acts do not touch their private pocket books. Just as the parent with no respect for the law will teach contempt for it to his children, and just as corrupt policemen give no motive to others to uphold an honest way of life, so the Government can, and often does, corrupt itself.

CORRUPTION

The central concern of this book is public, not private, lawbreaking, and any discussion of political corruption here must be brief. It is important to note that Governmental lawbreaking and political corruption are by no means unrelated and they may even at times be identical —as when an entire police department, say, is involved in an elaborate policy of graft, extortion, kickbacks, and theft. When an entire governmental body is corrupted, the incidence of nonenforcement of the laws is great. When the police thrive on gamblers' earnings, gambling laws are necessarily unenforced. And the situation is similar with other vice or morals statutes.

"Corruption" is a term possessing many meanings. In its usual sense, perhaps, corruption is meant to imply the abuse of public power for some private and personal end. Traditionally, in a modern society, that end is money; but it seems artificial to limit the payoff to money alone. The granting of governmental favors to secure a job or to benefit one's relatives should equally be considered a form of corruption, and it is here that the concept of conflict of interest subtly shades into more condemned activities.

It is a tiresome truism that corruption is as old as the state; where there are benefits to be gained from an official power that can disburse favors and monopolies—licenses, contracts, permission to violate the law —there will be the tempters and the corrupted. If corruption antedates the Republic, there is evidence that the Founding Fathers were men of rectitude. But the pattern of corruption set in early, and the development of urban machine politics made corruption a permanent fixture in American political life.

Corruption is supposed to be on the downswing in the America of the Sixties and Seventies. This is wishful thinking, for the modern state has more favors to grant, not less. In Chicago in 1960, scandals forced the reorganization of the entire police force. In Denver in 1961, fifty-two policemen were dismissed for varying degrees of complicity in a burglary ring. In 1968 the federal Bureau of Drug Abuse Control and the Bureau of Narcotics were merged in the Federal Bureau of Narcotics and Dangerous Drugs, and the reconstituted agency was placed under the jurisdiction of the Department of Justice. Some months later, according to Ramsey Clark, "more than fifty agents were discharged and over a dozen indicted for selling narcotics or accepting bribes."

In 1971, the Justice Department announced that a three-year effort to root out official corruption linked to organized crime had resulted in the convictions or indictments of 170 state and local public officeholders, including judges, mayors, councilmen, law enforcement officers, and purchasing agents. That same year, Judge Otto Kerner of the U.S. Court of Appeals in Chicago was indicted on nineteen charges of bribery, perjury, mail fraud, tax evasion, and conspiracy in connection with a race track scandal. Only three other federal judges have ever been indicted for criminal offenses, and only one, Martin T. Manton, was ever convicted (of selling his office to litigants in a patent case). Dan Walker, author of the Walker Report to the President's Commission on the Causes and Prevention of Violence and long an acquaintance of Kerner's, remarked that Kerner's "unblemished record was broken by his inability to withstand the enormous pressures of evil that descend upon the person who sits in the Governor's chair."

But the most revealing exposé of official corruption is the Knapp Commission's investigation of New York City police. Investigators for the Commission (named after its head, attorney Whitman Knapp) dug up evidence of police corruption so widespread that Michael Armstrong, the Commission's chief counsel, suggested as hearings opened in 1971 that the question was not of "a few rotten apples in a barrel" but "the barrel itself." Graft was shown to be rampant. The corruption touched gambling, prostitution, narcotics, theft rings, protection rackets, and payoffs (in the construction industry, by bars, cabarets, hotels, and many other businesses) to police, judges, and prosecutors.

In one noted instance, a police unit's inability to find an illegal Harlem "bottle club" when special corruption investigators found it "almost immediately," resulted in the suspension of six officers and the transfer of fourteen patrolmen, in accordance with Police Commissioner Patrick V. Murphy's policy of holding higher-ranking police officers responsible for the failures of the men they commanded. The bottle club had been specifically identified with an address, in complaints, but an official report stated that a thorough investigation had been made and the club could not be located. An investigator for the Confidential Investigating Unit found the club at the reported address and spent three hours counting "91 persons entering the building and 210 leaving, many staggering either from drink or drugs." It was reported that a patrolman had held his wedding reception in the club.

The Knapp Commission investigations in New York stemmed from the honesty of Detective Frank Serpico and Detective Sergeant David Durk, who refused to go along with the rampant bribery and shakedown system that reportedly brought commanding officers as much as $1,200 per month. Serpico offered his information to city officials, including aides of Mayor Lindsay. Finally, after eight hours of revelations were recorded by a *New York Times* tape recorder, the Mayor felt obliged to launch an official investigation.

One after another, top officials within and without the Police Department were shown to have ignored the evidence that Serpico and Durk brought to light. A police captain in charge of a city investigating unit told Serpico to forget his allegations if he did not want to wind up "floating face down in the river." Arnold G. Fraiman, Commissioner of Investigation from 1966 through 1968 (when he was appointed a state supreme court justice), admitted talking to Serpico about widespread police graft. Fraiman acknowledged that he had sat on the report without referring it to anyone for further investigation. John F. Walsh, First Deputy Police Commissioner from 1961 through 1970, told the Commission he had also received the report but had forgotten to follow it up. It "left my mind," he said.

It took Serpico eight months to convince Inspector Cornelius Behan that specific charges of corruption in the city's Seventh Division should be investigated. Behan apparently acted only because Serpico said he would go to Behan's boss, Inspector Phillip Sheridan. As a result of the investigation ordered by Sheridan, ten policemen were indicted and eleven others charged with violations of departmental regulations.

Former police commissioner Howard R. Leary complained to the Knapp Commission that no one bothered to tell him of Serpico's charges for half a year or so, but Leary did not bother to tell the Commission why, when he did learn of the charges in October, 1967, he did nothing more about them than follow Sheridan's investigation from a distance.

Most astonishing of all, Jay L. Kriegel, a close advisor to Mayor Lindsay and a friend of Durk, testified first that he had advised the Mayor of Serpico's and Durk's reports and then that he had not told the Mayor. Kriegel did not explain the contradiction, but the denial was issued after Lindsay had become a candidate for the Democratic Presidential nomination.

The political cowardice of high officials is apparent and helps explain how the city government was encouraged to break the law.

Corruption does not exist at police levels only. Sensational federal conspiracy and extortion trials have resulted in the conviction of Mayor Hugh Addonizio of Newark, Mayor Thomas J. Whelan and City Council President Thomas Flaherty of Jersey City, and many others including the Hudson County, N.J., Democratic Chairman, the County Treasurer, the County Police Chief, and a commissioner of the New York Port Authority during 1970 and 1971. New York State judgeships are commonly said to be sold to politicians with the right amount of cash.

Paul Powell, the longtime Illinois Secretary of State, was discovered after his death in 1970 to have been the happy recipient of hundreds of thousands of dollars in political payoffs, much of the cash having been stuffed into shoeboxes. Major General Carl C. Turner was Provost Marshall of the U.S. Army between 1964 and 1968, and following his retirement he served as Chief U.S. Marshall for seven months in 1969, until he resigned under fire; he was eventually convicted of stealing 136 firearms the Chicago police had turned over to him for Army use.

The General's name came to prominence in connection with an Army-wide scandal and Senate probe into the misuse of funds belonging to noncommissioned officers' clubs. Even more dismaying was the revelation that systematic graft of heroic proportions was rampant in the Army's worldwide PX system. Private companies bribed purchasing officers with kickbacks, free housing, entertainment, and sex to buy their goods, and PX personnel did so, even to the extent of offering diamonds and fur coats for sale in the war zone. So staggering was the extent of the corruption that the Army, apparently on its own initiative, demoted and retired a Brigadier General, Earl F. Cole, who figured prominently in the Senate investigation.

But the Army was generally uncooperative during the course of the Senate inquiry. Senator Abraham Ribicoff of Connecticut, the investigation subcommittee chairman, wrote to Defense Secretary Laird, as follows:

> The Subcommittee's staff has reported to me that they have experienced a considerable and disturbing lack of cooperation by officers in

certain military installations in relation to the Subcommittee's investigation of improprieties and corruption in the use of non-appropriated funds in the United States and abroad.

You will recall that Senator Gurney wrote to you on November 24, 1970, about this problem shortly after he had returned from Southeast Asia. He reported then that Subcommittee staff members had not received cooperation from military officers, particularly in gaining access to Army CID files, both open and closed.

The staff members also reported to me that they were denied access to records which had been requested in advance of their trip, in a joint Department of State and Department of Defense dispatch to all pertinent commands, datea October 29, 1970. . . .

The Subcommittee cannot conduct its investigation effectively while such roadblocks are placed in its way. We cannot oversee government operations if we are denied access to information and documentation. In fact, the refusal of representatives of the Department of the Army to cooperate with the Subcommittee directly contravenes Title 5, U.S. Code, Section 2954, as well as the Presidential Memorandum for the Heads of Executive Departments and Agencies dated March 24, 1969. I believe that the refusal to cooperate also is contrary to your policy on these matters, as stated to me in our correspondence last year relating to the Subcommittee's inquiry into operations of military clubs and messes.

Our investigators have advised me that the Department of the Navy cooperated completely with them, and they have received cooperation from the Department of the Air Force. However, Army officers in overseas commands have refused such cooperation, in spite of the jurisdiction and responsibility of the Subcommittee which I have stated and which is defined in the Legislative Reorganization Act of 1946, as amended.

Laird was displeased with the laxity Ribicoff complained of, and he ordered a reorganization of the Army's Criminal Investigation Division (CID), which was implicated in the Army's attempt to hush up incidents and to prevent the disclosure of the names of high-ranking officers.

The temptation to turn over federal funds to the private uses of state officials has already been discussed.* One other example underscores the point: Florida Governor Claude R. Kirk, Jr., was discovered to have wasted $475,000 in Federal Law Enforcement Assistance Administration funds, some of it having been spent in Miami on a thousand banquet dinners at the Hotel Fontainebleau.

Elected federal officials have been caught from time to time in acts of petty corruption: the unseating of Congressman Adam Clayton Powell and the censure of Senator Thomas Dodd for illegal expenditures and padding of official bills come readily to mind. Congressman John Dowdy of Texas was convicted in December, 1971, in federal court for accept-

* See pp. 174-5.

ing a $25,000 bribe to use his influence to have a federal prosecution involving a mortgage scandal called off.

The innumerable cases of conflicts of interest at the federal level represent the grave potential for corruption. Campaign practices that put money in the pockets of Congressmen who vote right are really nothing more than a polite form of public bribery; proof for this is seen all too clearly in the secrecy and subterfuge used by Congressmen to disguise their pecuniary tributes.

Despite denials, corruption flourishes in every American city and out in the countryside as well. After all, if crooks can break the law, why can't office holders?—and much more successfully at that.

7

The Government Responds or How to Spot a Lawbreaker

THE GOVERNMENT and its officials are aware of their crimes. Though they often prefer to remain silent, public officials make many statements that indicate clearly their understanding that laws have been violated, but only in the rarest case will the Government openly admit that its actions were unlawful. These admissions are prompted almost always by a high official's realization that the lawbreaking was the result of activities of a much lower-ranking official for whose conduct his superior could not possibly be held accountable (except perhaps in some extremely technical sense).

Secretary of the Navy John Chafee, for example, admitted violation of federal pollution laws when bilge oil was dumped at sea. But, he added in testimony to the Senate Air and Water Pollution Subcommittee, "if we had known this was going on it wouldn't have been going on." Secretary Chafee obviously was not to blame, and this was not a personal admission of guilt. Likewise, President Nixon described the Coast Guard's bungling of the affair of Semas Kudirka, the defecting Lithuanian sailor, as "outrageous," but no one could seriously believe that the President was responsible for the stupidity of a Rear Admiral, his Chief of Staff, and a mere commanding officer aboard an obscure Coast Guard cutter. The Government is a big place, and it is difficult, if not impossible, to prevent mistakes from happening, even if they result in illegal actions.

But even these admissions are all too rare. A debater might point out that ordinary criminals have scores of devices at their command to avoid pleading guilty and to contest criminal charges. Yet in some states, at least 90 percent of all convictions result from guilty pleas, and while this does not mean that 90 percent of all criminals plead guilty (not by a wide margin) it is a wonderful improvement on the Government's record.

Aside from the rare admission of guilt, the Government or its officials have at least nine basic means of responding to charges that they have violated the law in one way or another. Many of these means have been documented throughout these pages in connection with the incidents of lawbreaking described. It is useful to summarize briefly these responses by type. They are as follows: (1) deny the charges; (2) confuse the issue or evade the charges; (3) promise action or investigation; (4) assert necessity; (5) accuse the accuser; (6) assert the difficulty and unfairness of enforcement; (7) cite a duty; (8) show an obscure lawful purpose; and (9) assert that the lawbreaking is a mere aberration confined to lower-ranking officials.

DENIAL

Practically every example of lawbreaking in this book was accompanied by some kind of official denial that any wrongdoing had occurred. Candidates for office regularly deny that any of their financial activities are tainted, no matter how gross the suspicion or the reality. Officials of all descriptions in administrative agencies regularly deny that anything they do (or don't do) is wrong; everything is according to law. The President denies, through his assistants, that he violates the Constitution when he withholds funds authorized and appropriated by Congress to be spent; Congressmen and Executive officials will never admit they engage in conflicts of interest (none of the many officials from Sherman Adams on down who were forced to resign from positions of importance in the Eisenhower Administration ever admitted that what they were doing had even the appearance of a conflict); and police chiefs continue to deny that any of their men are corrupt or that they occasionally beat up a suspect. Indeed, in St. Louis it has happened that when citizens make official complaints against the police for misconduct, the citizens have been investigated by the FBI for filing false charges.

The denial response is illustrated by a minor cause célèbre concerning the police shooting of a twenty-eight-year-old collector of antique guns. Kenyon F. Ballew, a resident of Silver Spring, Maryland, found some people—police, it turned out—breaking into his apartment the night of June 7, 1971. As the first wave of a twenty-seven officer raiding party burst into his door, Ballew grabbed an antique cap and ball gun to defend himself and at the same time was shot in the head. Ballew's wife, who was standing next to him when he was shot, said she and her husband thought the intruders were "hippies" or "racketeers" when they first entered. The first three men who rushed into the house with guns drawn were wearing short sleeved, brightly-colored sweat shirts and polo shirts, and they sported long mustaches and side burns. Only one officer entered the apartment in uniform, and he was not among the first to go in.

The reason for the raid was this: agents of the U. S. Treasury Department's Alcohol, Tobacco, and Firearms Division and Montgomery County police had obtained a warrant, on the basis of questionable information, to search Ballew's apartment for illegal hand grenades. The police and Treasury agents actually found four inert hand grenades and many antique guns. The Treasury agents refused to reveal who their informants were, but Ballew's attorney later said that the only source of information was a juvenile charged with housebreaking. The police did admit that owing to their faulty record-keeping, they had also raided another, and wrong, apartment that same evening, seeking Ballew. In both cases, police burst through the doors with a battering ram. Inside the Ballews' home, they found Ballew nude and his wife wearing only underpants, which explains why the couple did not open the door very quickly when the police knocked and announced their presence outside.

Despite the fact that the Treasury agents and police violated the most elementary rule of police work by breaking into a house in clothes that would not identify them as policemen (especially when there were uniformed men available), thus greatly increasing the risk of physical harm, Montgomery County Executive James P. Gleason said the raid was "justifiable." The only fault he found at all was in raiding the wrong apartment earlier.

A report prepared for Gleason said: "Apologies should be in order and payment should be made for the broken door." Gleason stated that Ballew's gun had been fired accidentally after police had shot him in the head, but, according to Gleason, "when you take all the circumstances in the case, it was justifiable. There isn't anything that could have been done differently; it was a dangerous situation." He did not add that the danger was caused by the police conduct, not Ballew's.

Two weeks after the Montgomery County report, the Treasury Department issued its own, finding "administrative and supervisory deficiencies" but holding that the raid was "legally proper under the circumstances." The Treasury report stated that the agents' supervisors were sitting outside in a car while the raid was in progress, showing little inclination to supervise, and it also stated that "no files or formal documentation" was on hand before the search warrant was drawn up.

The questions as to why twenty-seven agents and policemen were necessary to carry out the raid, why the first to break in through the door was required to wear outlandish clothes in a Washington suburb, and why nine shots were fired at Ballew, one causing possibly life-long paralysis, were never answered. Nor was it ever explained why the police were in such a hurry to enter the apartment, since it is beyond the imagination of even the police that a gun collector would have been able to dispose of the grenades and the gun collection while the police stood idly by outside.

An even clearer example of official denial occurred in the murder trial of Lloyd Eldon Miller. Following the Supreme Court's reversal of his murder conviction on the ground that the prosecution had deliberately misrepresented the nature of the red stain on the undershorts, the Illinois Bar Association Grievance Committee conducted an investigation "to determine whether disciplinary action should be taken against the prosecutors." The Grievance Committee exonerated them fully. Part of the whitewash is reprinted here.

It became apparent to the Committee early in its investigation that the United States Supreme Court had misapprehended the facts of the case. . . .

The Committee found no reason to doubt that there was blood on the shorts at the time of the trial and no reason to doubt that the prosecutors in the case believed there was blood on the shorts. Accordingly, the Committee found that there was no basis for the view of the United States Supreme Court that the prosecution had been guilty of a misrepresentation when it asserted as a fact that the shorts contained blood.

The Committee investigation further disclosed that, in addition to the blood, there was paint on the shorts. It is clear that the prosecution knew, or at least assumed, there was paint on the shorts as well as blood, and the prosecutors contend that the difference was apparent.

The question before the Grievance Committee, then, was not whether the prosecution misrepresented the fact that there was blood on the shorts, because clearly its statement to this effect was not a misrepresentation. Instead the question was, assuming the defense did not know of the paint, whether the prosecution was guilty of unethical conduct in failing to disclose its presence to the defense. The resolution of this question depended, in the judgment of the Grievance Committee, upon whether there was any reason to believe that the prosecution felt the facts concerning the paint would have been helpful to the defense and, knowing of its relevance, nonetheless concealed it. The Grievance Committee determined that the presence or absence of paint on the shorts was not a material question in the case. . . .

The final allegation against the prosecutors is that they improperly informed the defendant's landlady that she had a "constitutional" right to decline an interview with the defense attorneys. In a pardon hearing conducted seven years after the trial, there was testimony by several witnesses tending to establish an alibi for the defendant at the time of the crime. The Committee found no evidence that the prosecutors had been guilty of any impropriety with regard to these witnesses. There is no evidence that the prosecutors did anything other than inform one witness—the landlady—that she was not required to discuss the case with the defense. While the Committee believes that it was not technically accurate to inform the landlady that she had a "constitutional" right to refuse the interview with the defense, it is nonetheless true that, in a criminal case, the defense has no legal right to require a witness to submit to a pretrial interview. Moreover, the Grievance Committee felt that it was inconceivable that these "alibi" witnesses would not have come forward at the time of the trial if, in fact, they could have established the alibi later asserted. The crime was committed in a small town and was obviously a major topic of discussion at the time.

A variant of the simple denial is the additional and more heated retort: "I'm not the only criminal around here; the other guy did it too!" This response puts a Presidential administration in a somewhat embarrassing posture, since it must claim support in the past practices of administrations of the other party to blunt partisan attacks. This is not called "me-tooism," however; it masquerades under a more comfortable label—"precedent."

When unapproved wiretapping is sought to be approved, the ancient memoranda of Presidents Roosevelt and Truman are dusted off; "let me point out," said Attorney General Mitchell, "that national security wiretapping without a court order has been used . . . at least since 1940." When a future President wishes to conserve funds already appropriated, he can turn to a history of conservation dating back to the early 'Forties as well)

EVASION

The need to justify is characteristic of most people. It is the rare person—President, legislator, judge, bureaucrat, dictator, demagogue, or even madman—who will not try to explain what he is doing and assert that the proof that satisfies him ought to satisfy others. A concomitant of this tendency to justification, at least in America, is the enactment of all sorts of laws that fool us into thinking evil has been corrected. Built into the law, however, are sufficient numbers of loopholes through which those affected by the law, and without whose grace the law would never have been passed, can escape. This is the typical American solution to conduct that is deemed politically and socially necessary: we make the general evil unlawful and then declare that numerous toeholds, unmarked trails, and indirect roads are not the same since they are not *identical* and that they are therefore not unlawful.

There is an old story about a devout man who also happened to fancy tobacco. One day he asked his priest whether he might smoke while he offered his prayers to God. Horrified, the priest said that to do so would be next to blasphemy. "Well then," asked the penitent, "would it be permissible for me instead to pray while I smoke?" That, the priest allowed, was perfectly safe. Just so, the Government seeks to avoid its responsibility for breaking the law.

The massive failure of the states and the federal Government to insure black citizens equality under law is replete with evasive responses. The history of race litigation is as tortured as it is because the Government (and lawyers) responded at every turn that their next step was perfectly legal. The evaders distinguished each new case in the pantheon of civil rights litigation from its predecessor on the basis of an irrelevant difference. The process in the area of race relations is too well known to require detailed examples, but an interesting twist was Attorney General Mitchell's response in refusing to veto Mississippi's so-called "Evers Law" that eliminated party primaries and foreclosed the possibility that a black candidate running ahead of many white candidates could be elected to state office. Under the Voting Rights Act of 1965, the Attorney General has the power to veto laws enacted after 1965 in the South if he finds that the laws would affect the right of blacks to vote. The Justice Department's decision not to strike down the Mississippi law was made, according to Assistant Attorney General Jerris Leonard, because the facts "do not *conclusively establish* that the present acts are afflicted with a racial purpose."

The very process of evasion permits many Government crimes to go unproved because they get so fuzzy that no one can show or attempt to show a violation without being subjected to at least verbal abuse; the Government's response to the Kent State shooting, to the Chicago raid against Black Panther leaders, to the slaying of students at Jackson State, and to the issue of the legality of the war in Vietnam are all examples.

When the Justice Department released letters to be used as evidence in the conspiracy trial against the Rev. Philip S. Berrigan and five others, Department lawyers said that it was "not an uncommon practice" to release such evidence in connection with the indictments. Asked to name any other incidents in which such evidence had been released a Department spokesman admitted he could name none. The explanation, however, was simple: the spokesman sidestepped the entire issue by stating simply that "a book of approved forms that U.S. Attorneys use in drafting indictments" had been followed in the Berrigan indictment.

The net of this Government response is to keep the ordinary citizen from believing that the Government shares any responsibility for a host of problems. It is a powerful technique, often turned to the Government's advantage.

PROMISING ACTION OR INVESTIGATION

Occasionally, Government officials will implicitly admit the possibility of lawbreaking and promise a thorough investigation of the particular incident. Thus, New York City officials promised to investigate the police attack on Black Panthers in a Brooklyn courtroom, though nothing ever came of the investigation.

Another illustration of this process was the reaction of public officials to the raid on the home of Dr. Lykken.* Following the raid, many officials spoke up. Robert C. Renner, U.S. Attorney in Minnesota, said an investigation would begin immediately. Assistant Attorney General Leonard announced the federal investigation from Washington. Hennepin County Attorney George M. Scott indicated his office "will look into [the matter] thoroughly and then report the results of the investigation to the Hennepin County Grand Jury." Hubert H. Humphrey, then campaigning for his return to the Senate, and Minnesota Congressman Donald Fraser asked prompt action from the Justice Department. But no report was issued and no action was taken against the local police, nor did the call for action seem to influence the Minneapolis police.

NECESSITY

The argument for a good many unlawful actions stems from that vague but compelling concept "necessity." Whenever there is no other reason for an action than that the Government wishes to do it anyway, it finds a stunning justification in the necessity to do whatever was done. Unlawful wiretapping has been justified by many senior federal and state officials on the ground that the danger being countered was great and that no other way to forestall it existed.

"Military necessity" is such a well-recognized concept that it is an explicit exception to many laws of war prohibiting various acts of brutality against the enemy and the civilian populace. State actions that illegally cut off welfare benefits are often justified only by the argument that the state was facing financial crisis and it was necessary to act. Whenever the federal Government has taken over Indian lands or otherwise interfered with Indian rights, there is then always, of course, a "necessity." Prosecutors and police have long argued that the "third degree" is sometimes necessary to extract the proper confession to secure the necessary conviction.

The argument for necessity is often all too easily accepted. Edward

---

* See pp. 79 ff.

S. Corwin, the constitutional scholar, described President Roosevelt's proclamation of his

> intention and his constitutional right to disregard certain provisions of the Emergency Price Control Act unless Congress repealed them by the following October 1. "The American people," said he [on September 7, 1942], "can be sure that I will use my powers with a full sense of my responsibility to the Constitution and to my country. . . . When the war is won, the powers under which I act will automatically revert to the people—to whom they belong."

Corwin adds:

> While the situation which the President foreshadowed did not materialize, thanks to a Congress's compliance with his demand, albeit a day late, yet any candid person must admit the possibility of conditions arising in which the safety of the republic would require the waiving of constitutional forms. What is not so easily conceded is the President's apparent assumption that the Constitution lodges the power solely in one man to decide that such a situation has arisen, and by so deciding to invest himself with the role of dictator.

Corwin would permit the Constitution to be "waived" or "suspended" if *both* the President and Congress agreed—which is still not a very satisfying check against the temper of "necessity."

ACCUSING THE ACCUSER

One handy retort to a charge of illegality is to accuse your accuser of greater wrongdoing. The entire thrust of the Nixon administration's attack on the news media has been to divert public attention from what the newspapers and broadcast media were revealing.

Congressional committees have been no less bold. When CBS Television News broadcast its documentary "The Selling of the Pentagon," picturing for the viewer many instances of questionable and sometimes unlawful promotional activities by the Defense Department, a House Committee investigated not the Department but CBS-TV News for improper editing of filmed interviews. Committee Chairman Harley Staggers commented that if the House of Representatives refused to uphold a contempt citation against CBS President Frank Stanton, who had refused to turn over "outtakes" (unedited film footage) in response to a committee subpoena, Staggers would interpret the House denial as a personal "injustice" to himself. The House turned Staggers down.

Similarly, questionable activities of the police are constantly defended by reminding the interested citizen that the police, after all, are dealing with criminals. In a speech in the summer of 1971, Attorney

General Mitchell even went so far as to declare that "preoccupation with fairness to the accused" had gone too far and should be reversed. General Lewis B. Hershey, the Selective Service Director, defended his "suggested" guidelines to draftboards for speeding up inductions of certain kinds of radicals. He could not understand why so much concern was being shown for those whom *he* would classify as delinquents.

In a desperate effort to head off indictment, Illinois State's Attorney Edward V. Hanrahan charged that the special prosecutor who had conducted the grand jury probe against Hanrahan in connection with the Chicago Black Panther raid was himself guilty of unlawfully coercing the jurors into handing down an indictment. But the Illinois Supreme Court, by a 4 to 3 vote, ruled that the special prosecutor's actions could not be questioned and the indictments against Hanrahan and other officials were issued.

DIFFICULTY AND UNFAIRNESS
OF ENFORCEMENT

This curious response is usually heard in connection with the failure to enforce laws that by common consent of the community exist as showpieces only. The Justice Department's refusal to enforce the federal campaign laws for more than forty-five years is based on this excuse. It is also the favorite response of every administrative regulatory agency, whether its members have been bribed, or are lazy, or are merely dull-witted, when the agency refuses to take action against corporate and individual violators of thousands of laws and regulations intended to protect the consumer, the taxpayer, and the citizen.

In 1971, the Federal Communications Commission called off an investigation of AT&T on the grounds that the Government agency could not afford to study the telephone monopoly it is supposed to regulate (only to reinstate the investigation one month later under heavy pressure).

DUTY

A few days after the Supreme Court announced its decision in May, 1971, permitting the *New York Times* and the *Washington Post* to publish secret war documents, President Nixon said that the federal Government was moving against the newspapers because it is against the law to publish classified documents, and he believed his credibility would suffer with the people if he did not do his plain duty by enforcing the law.

The President omitted to call attention to the wide discretion given all prosecutors as to whether or not to proceed against the newspapers. Nor did he note his own failures to prosecute campaign law violations or to bring indictments against National Guardsmen in Ohio in order to test whether or not they were guilty of homicide against students at Kent State.* He did not explain why he had refused to permit his Attorney General to sign an indictment handed down by a Baltimore grand jury that would supposedly have required Senator Russell B. Long of Louisiana and other politicians to stand trial for bribery in connection with a construction scandal.

The "duty" argument is often used where there is a strong suspicion that the Government had other than pure motives for bringing a criminal prosecution or for some other action. Thus, the Government argued in the case of Reuben G. Lenske that regardless of the Government's motives, Lenske was, after all, a tax evader. In Alabama's case against William K. Powell,† the prosecutor unlawfully withheld pertinent information from the defense because, according to Powell's attorney R. Clifford Fulford, of "his good faith belief that he had a duty to be 'hard nosed' in his performance as a prosecuting attorney. Even though I disagreed with him sharply and gave him a hard time on the witness stand, I have always considered it to his credit that he faced the issue with commendable candor and even helped bring it into focus." The Fifth Circuit Court of Appeals upheld defense attorney Fulford in ruling that the prosecutor had had an overly expansive view of his "duty" —in fact, said the court, his duty was just the opposite of what he took it to be. But that was news to the prosecutor: "The Fifth Circuit's decision was widely regarded as revolutionary and was reportedly once cited by Alabama's Chief Justice as an example of the federal burden being placed upon state procedures in criminal cases."

Finally, whenever the Government prosecutes one class of offenders and not another—under flag desecration laws, for example—the Government retort is invariably that it is only "doing its duty"—toward the class of offenders prosecuted.

---

* The Scranton Commission on Campus Disorders found that the killings at Kent State were "unnecessary, unwarranted, and inexcusable." Photographs and other evidence showed that despite the lack of fire at the Guardsmen (they had claimed snipers were shooting at them), the rifle squad went to ground higher than the protesting students, turned and took dead-level aim, and twenty-eight Guardsmen almost simultaneously fired sixty-one shots within thirteen seconds at students three hundred feet away. The evidence is strong that the squad was under orders to act in this co-ordinated way. Yet despite the mass of evidence assembled by the Scranton Commission, the FBI, and others, the Attorney General refused to present any of it even to a grand jury.

† See pp. 55 ff.

THE OBSCURE BUT LAWFUL PURPOSE

Occasionally, the Government surprises everyone with the assertion that its action did not break the law at all but was intended to serve some obscure and hitherto unknown purpose. In El Paso, legal assistance attorney Stephen Bercu told the Senate Subcommittee to Investigate Juvenile Delinquency what usually happened following the arrest of juveniles:

> Once arrested, the procedures by the police are the procedures most likely to intimidate and abuse the child. All children are taken to the police department and have their fingerprints taken, whether or not they have committed an offense that would be punishable as an adult and in fact whether or not they have committed an offense. . . . [T]he police department and the city indulged in the verbal fantasy of justifying the fingerprinting of juveniles by saying that these fingerprints would be useful in case of a disaster at the detention home, but that they were not used for purposes of identification. . . . [But] there appear to be no provisions for destruction of these fingerprint cards if in fact no charges are brought against the juvenile or, following the reasoning of the police department, if the juvenile is not in fact detained in the detention home or if the juvenile is released from the detention home or if the juvenile is found not to be delinquent. The *only* justification that I can see for fingerprinting juveniles is to take them to the police department and to intimidate them and to "give them a lesson."

And when the Air Force fired Ernest Fitzgerald for his outspoken statements in connection with the C–5A scandal, it sought to justify the move by claiming that for reasons of economy Fitzgerald's job had been abolished. But high-level jobs are not abolished in the federal Government except as part of a general organizational restructuring, and in any event the statement turned out to be untrue, since a high-priced consultant was hired to perform many of Fitzgerald's duties.

ABERRATION

When nothing else can be done but to admit that something was seriously wrong, the Government seeks to pin responsibility on the lowest possible operating level. For instance, the war-crime trials for the massacre at Mylai involved no one higher in rank than an Army Captain; a colonel was tried for covering up (and acquitted), but similar charges against generals had been dropped earlier, and the entire episode was said to be inconsistent with and not representative of Army or United States policy.

This is not to say that low-level bureaucrats do not often take actions that are not consistent with higher policy; perhaps, statistically, that is the primary cause of Governmental lawbreaking. But whenever the higher official points the finger at his subordinate, the citizen should think a little deeper and look a little farther before accepting the explanation.

*   *   *   *

The various responses described do not occur in a vacuum, and often a collection of them are uttered together. The May Day arrests in Washington, D.C.,* illustrate the principle of multiple responses. The Government denied that it had violated anyone's rights. The President accused his accusers of being "vandals and hoodlums and lawbreakers," saying "they should be treated as lawbreakers." At a press conference on June 1, 1971, the President first tried to confuse what actually happened; when he was repeatedly queried by inquisitive reporters, he then pleaded necessity and duty. The President's remarks at the press conference follow:

Q. Mr. President, it has been about a month now since the May Day demonstrations. In that period, several people have raised questions as to whether the police handled it properly, and also the charges against something more than 2,000 people arrested on that Monday have been dropped.† I wonder with that perspective of the month whether you think the police handled it properly, and the broad constitutional question involved of protecting the individual rights in a difficult situation of control.

A. Mr. Kaplow, yes, I believe the police in Washington did handle the question properly with the right combination of firmness and restraint in a very difficult situation. Let us separate the question into what we are really dealing with.

First, there are demonstrators. The right to demonstrate is recognized and protected, and, incidentally, has been recognized and protected by the Washington police. Thousands of demonstrators have come down here peacefully and have not been, of course, bothered. They have been protected in that right.

But when people come in and slice tires, when they block traffic, when they make a trash bin out of Georgetown and other areas of the city, and when they terrorize innocent bystanders, they are not demonstrators, they are vandals and hoodlums and law breakers and they should be treated as law breakers.

Now, as far as the police are concerned, they gave those who

* See pp. 115 ff.

† Subsequently, charges against more than 99 percent of those arrested were dropped or dismissed by the courts. Fewer than 100 of the 12,000 persons arrested were ultimately convicted.

were in this particular area, and who were engaged in these activities, approximately 15,000 in all, an opportunity to disperse. They did not. They said they were there to stop the Government from operating.

I have pledged to keep this Government going. I approve the action of the police in what they did. I supported it after they did it. And in the event that others come in, not to demonstrate for peace but to break the peace, the police will be supported by the President and by the Attorney General in stopping that kind of activity.

This Government is going to go forward, and that kind of activity which is not demonstration, but vandalism, law-breaking, is not going to be tolerated in this Capital.

Q. Mr. President, regarding the mass arrests. I wonder—you seem to have thought that closing down the Government and keeping it running, in other words, was so important that some methods such as suspending constitutional rights was justified. Was it that important? Do you think it was?

A. I think when you talk about suspending constitutional rights that this is really an exaggeration of what was done. What we were talking about here basically was a situation where masses of individuals did attempt to block traffic, did attempt to stop the Government. They said in advance that is what they were going to do. They tried it and they had to be stopped without injuries of any significance. They were stopped, I think, with a minimum amount of force and with a great deal of patience. And I must say that I think the police showed a great deal more concern for their rights than they showed for the rights of the people of Washington.

Q. Mr. President, if I may follow up, if that is true, then why are the courts releasing so many of the cases and so many of the people that have been arrested? If they were lawfully and properly arrested, why are the courts letting them out?

A. It is because, of course, Mr. Ter Horst, as you know, that arrest does not mean that an individual was guilty. The whole constitutional system is one that provides that after arrest an individual has an opportunity for trial. In the event that the evidence is not presented which will convict him, he is released. I think that proves the very point that we have made.

Q. Mr. President, they are not being released on the grounds that guilt isn't proved. They are being released on the grounds that they weren't properly arrested.

A. It seems to me that when we look at this whole situation that we have to look at it in terms of what the police were confronted with when those who contended they were demonstrators, but actually were lawbreakers, came into Washington. They were confronted with what could have been a very difficult crisis. They dealt with it, it seems to me, with very great restraint and with necessary firmness. I approve of what they did, and in the event that we have similar situations in the future, I hope that we can handle those situations as well as this was handled. I hope they can be handled that well in other cities so that we do not have to resort to violence.

Governmental "law and order" is a serious issue, but it is not one that candidates like to run on in election years. Presidents ought to be unembarrassed by the issue; they ought to point to all the wonderful policies and administrative mechanisms they have fashioned to reduce and forestall the extent of Government lawbreaking. After all, every President inherits the lawless Leviathan from someone else, and no one can blame him for not rooting out every vestige of illegal behavior.

Opposition candidates ought to run on the lawlessness issue, too. Sometimes they do so, of course, but more often they prefer to deprecate in a more generalized way; they decry joblessness and defense weaknesses, or unwise and immoral war fevers, but they are leery of complaining that the Government has the capacity to act unlawfully. After all, they want to inherit it.

The citizen's power to check Governmental lawlessness is limited. Civil disobedience, the powerful method of opposing some kinds of oppression, is virtually impotent to halt many of the kinds of lawlessness portrayed on the preceding pages. You cannot disobey the prosecutor, especially when what is at issue is discriminatory law enforcement. You cannot disobey the Government by staying in a job from which you have been fired. And lawsuits cost money.

The issue must be raised, therefore, by the candidates themselves. As an issue, "law and order in Government" can be a powerful antidote to the problems raised by people who cry for "law and order" generally. Of course, the issue can be corrupted by racist and other politicians labeling everything the federal Government does as illegitimate usurpation. Respectable politicians must seize the initiative and make the issue a respectable response to the unlawful activities plainly around us.

8
Causes and Effects

CAUSES

IT OUGHT TO BE obvious that there are many different causes of Governmental lawbreaking. Just as we may ascribe to the private crimes of individual citizens many different motives, so too the reasons for the Government to disregard the law are complex. Though different strands of explanation can be described, they do not individually explain Government lawlessness, any more than individual strands explain the strength of braided rope. To varying degrees, the causes fit together.

Lawlessness Generally

The primary, underlying cause for the lawlessness of the Government in modern times is that in a very direct sense it is without law. Its power is delegated from legislative bodies, and such delegation in the Twentieth Century has been almost entirely standardless. That is, Congress has transferred power to the Executive Branch without prescribing how that power is to be used. Regulators and administrators are free to carry out "public policy" on their own.

In the absence of strict legal controls, the classic American response to the potentiality of dictatorial power is to co-opt it. As has often been observed, administrators tend to be captured by those they oversee. Tough policy at the enactment stage cries out for soft policy at the enforcement stage.

But actions undisciplined by explicit standards can become lazy and slovenly habits; and when the administrator sees he has nothing to fear by cooperating with his wards, he becomes by degrees bolder when his actions and their interests hurt others. So powerful does the habit become that he can close his eyes when he or his minions cross the line into illegality; so automatic is the reflex that his response unvaryingly tells us he has rationalized again. Without standards, rationalizing is easy, and the administrator may actually believe he has done right or at least not done wrong. The sincere lawbreaker—especially when he is cloaked with the governmental imperium—is hard to beat.

Kenneth Culp Davis, a scholarly observer of the bureaucracy, has concluded that "perhaps 80 or 90 percent of the administrative process involves discretionary action in the absence of [the safeguards of hearings or judicial] review." The armed forces process hundreds of thousands (and sometimes millions) of soldiers, sailors, and airmen every year. Senior officers make millions of decisions affecting their lives under sweeping regulations that provide little scope of review.

Regulatory agencies of all types are likewise required to pass upon enormous numbers of applications, cases, and other matters and to dispose of them under the vaguest of guidelines. As Davis has noted:

> For the fiscal year 1969 the SEC passed upon 4,706 registration statements, but it had only 103 formal cases. It probably issued about 5,000 no-action letters. For the same year the FCC disposed of more than half a million transmitter applications, but it had only 197 formal cases. The Immigration and Naturalization Service handled the huge number of 20,109 formal cases, but it disposed informally of 993,324 applications. The Social Security Administration passed upon 4,600,000 claims for benefits, but it had only 24,048 formal cases; the number of persons covered by insurance increased to 101,000,000. The Internal Revenue Service received 110,000,000 tax returns and examined 2,544,000; it recommended 1,049 prosecutions (in each instance making a very important determination), but it decided only 37 formal cases.

As the discretionary powers of Government increase in number, the burden of regulation and enforcement increases correspondingly. As bureaucracies grow larger, increasing amounts of time are required to be devoted to internal housekeeping, management, and liaison. The substantive, underlying regulatory goal is often lost. Also, the increase in the number of bureaucrats diffuses the responsibility for decision-making (and multiplies instances of lawbreaking).

Administrative errors are rarely one person's fault. The seizure of the U.S.S. *Pueblo* by the North Koreans showed just how diffuse accountability had become in the United States Navy, where theoretically each higher rung of the chain of command is responsible for mistakes of the lower rungs. But precisely because responsibility ran up a chain of command, the Navy was reluctant to assign blame to any one person or any particular level. The top man, Admiral Thomas H. Moorer, Chief of Naval Operations, was later rewarded with a promotion to the chairmanship of the Joint Chiefs of Staff.

In the common-sense view of things, we usually blame the man who pulled the trigger, not the many people in the deviant's past who one way or another helped fashion the criminal personality. But in the case of Government, where each level of bureaucracy is merely "following orders," the lack of an accountable boss and the possibility of pleading that any action taken was within the lawful discretion of the administrator very often means that anything goes. Thus, practices deriving from lawful bureaucratic activity may become agency policy even though they are unlawful.

Administrative discretion does not mean that the Government always violates the law out of malice or vindictiveness; far more often it means that sloppy staff work, laziness, and lack of the necessary follow-up—all conducive to unlawful acts—flourish in the discretionary wilderness. The need and prerogative of discretion become so thoroughly ingrained in Government that when there are signs of trouble administrative agencies usually permit an investigation by their own investigators only, which is something like the Attorney General's asking the Mafia to engage in a little "self-regulation."

Discretion can, of course, breed contempt for the law directly. Someone long accustomed to having his own way is not often inclined to permit others to test his actions, and malice works best under cover.

Administrative discretion poses the same difficulty for the investigator that an impenetrable jungle provides for the explorer. Justice Brandeis's statement to the effect that sunlight is the best disinfectant is often quoted; but in a modern state with tens of thousands of ordinances, regulations, statutes, and judicial decisions, the difficulty of uncovering lawbreaking, much less of making it public, is immense. As one essayist has put it:

> Like so much else in the bureaucracy, its illegality is strikingly devoid of flair, of passion, and of individuality. If it is hidden from the public, it hides not behind a well-constructed shield of secrecy, but behind a camouflage of boredom. Federal lawlessness is the result of a systematic series of decisions that become impersonal and eventually uninteresting, except to the victims. It is no thrill; it is a sure thing, accomplished from nine to five, with regular coffee breaks.

When occasional examples of corruption or lawbreaking are revealed, they are more often than not passed over with nonchalance or perhaps "deplored," with no further action being taken.

Moreover, standardless legislation means that social policies can be defeated as easily, and sometimes far more easily, at the enforcement stage than at the enactment stage. The prelude to legislation is highly visible: the arguments pro and con are discussed volubly, and the news media focus popular attention on legislative deliberations. Most new laws will be effective over a very broad spectrum of society because legislation by nature is general; the statute (usually) establishes broad precepts or commandments. And once a law is enacted, it is recorded for all who know where to find it to read.

Enforcement of the laws, to the contrary, is not universal; it is particular. It is not a one-time declaration; it is a never-ending process. Legislation is centralized; enforcement, decentralized. Enforcement is not open, visible, and voluble; at least, it need not be. It is often hidden, difficult to find, and lacking in pattern. Reporters find it more difficult to write about the lack of law enforcement—because it is difficult and dangerous to prove that criminal activities are taking place in the enforcement area—than to write about the passage of laws, news of which is usually handed to them in a press release by a proud President or legislator.

Furthermore, the effort to promote general legislation or to defeat it is very expensive because so much is being bought; the cost of corrupting an administrator to deter him from enforcing a law in a particular instance is far cheaper, because protection for everyone is not necessary. The promise of a $30,000-a-year industry job is obviously cheaper than a million-dollar advertising campaign. Finally, vague policies may slip by and become law; application against a particular offender is invariably objected to. That is why policies in the public interest occasionally become law and are then rarely enforced: witness campaign laws, pollution laws (at least until lately), and other laws regulating health, safety, and welfare.

Special interest groups have economic and other motives for attempting to influence bureaucrats. But the public's interest is too diffuse even to demand effective implementation and administration of the many regulations to warrant the time and money it costs to monitor the Government.

Read through Title 32, Chapter XVI, of the Code of Federal Regulations—the rules dealing with the Selective Service System—and you will be struck immediately by the gap between the promises on paper and the personal experiences of husbands, sons, and brothers before their draft boards. The names of board members, for instance, are supposed to be posted. Yet there are dozens of examples in the burgeoning legal litertaure of selective service law of board members unaware or contemptuous of the regulations, who refuse to give out their names, especially after having made an unlawful, unwise, or impolitic comment at a hearing. Their reactions are perfectly understandable even if they are often unlawful. But who can monitor all these examples of petty illegality by petty officials and hold them to account?

The American political system tolerates bad laws passed openly (no matter how difficult the legal language in which they are couched). It does not, however, formally tolerate the cheaper alternative of private control over law enforcement. When the Government is implicated, the unlawful activity must be justified as within the bounds of administrative discretion. Doing this is usually an easy matter because of the inflexible operation of Lieberman's Law.

Lieberman's Law

The Law explains the paradoxical fact that the lack of law in the administrative process is due largely to the superabundance of law. The Law runs as follows:

Legal rules proliferate to support their loopholes. The Law perceives the increase in legal rules as a dynamic tendency: the lack of law produces more law, and when there is too much law there is no law at all.

Description of the Law. The rule can best be described as a wall of lattice-work: the thin strips of wood represent all of our legal rules, but the pervasive holes are very prominent; indeed, but for the holes there would be no design at all.

Quantitative Formulation. The rate of expansion in laws is at least geometrical. That is, let us say a rule is created and four loopholes in it are discovered. So another rule is promulgated, with four parts, one to plug each hole. But in order to pass the new rule, other rules have to be announced to prevent misuse of the four-part rule. Each of these new rules and each part of the four-part rule are then discovered to have their own loopholes. So the process begins again, with ever increasing rapidity.

Personnel. The system of creating rules, applying them, and attempting to plug the loopholes (usually called regulation or law enforcement) requires personnel—called bureaucrats—for its operation. Laws are not self-executing. The human agencies required to implement every regulatory scheme may abuse their power, so an ever-lengthening set of rules is concocted to control the power. But these controls are not self-executing either so more agencies and divisions and subdivisions are necessarily created to act as counterweights (appeal boards, advice boards, offices of general counsel, public relations and information offices, liaison offices) to insure that each office talks to the others. More rules, internal rules, are promulgated to ensure that these offices all get along.

The ratio of bureaucrats to rules (B/R) has never been systematically explored. So hazy is our understanding, in fact, that we have two common contradictory versions: the first has it that the country is crawling with bureaucrats whose number far outstrips the demand created by legal rules and who, consequently, wind up shuffling papers. The second version has it that there are an overwhelming number of rules whose enforcement is greatly impeded by the paucity of monitoring officials.

These versions can be reconciled by the simple corollary to the Law that *creating rules is far more important than enforcing them.* This corollary follows because enforcement is conceived of as a method of plugging loopholes and, by the Law, Americans plug loopholes by creating more rules.

One example of the Law in operation should suffice. The coal mining industry in the United States has neglected the welfare of its workers for years. The Federal Coal Mine Health and Safety Act of 1969 was supposed to change all that. The measure permitted stiff fines of up to $10,000 to be assessed against violators. Because previous laws had rarely been enforced, the Bureau of Mines in early 1971 published a "fee schedule" listing the range of fines (between $5,000 and $10,000) it said would be imposed on operators whose mines are ordered closed because their violations pose an "imminent danger." But the Bureau also established two loopholes for the one rule:

> If it is determined (A) that the operator did not or could not, with the exercise of reasonable diligence, know of the violation, or (B) did not or could not have available to him at the time of inspection the equipment, material, personnel or technology to avoid the violation

the penalties would not be assessed. Translated, the rule means this: the operator is immune from penalty for subtle safety violations; he is also immune, by the second part of the rule, from penalties for gross violations. Whether anything falls in between is up to the benevolence of the Bureau of Mines, which had failed to enforce the law before and had established these new regulations ostensibly to overcome the bureaucratic difficulty of making a choice. Lieberman's Law leads ineluctably to the conclusion that the only way to get respect for law is to wipe out most of our laws.

Administrative discretion does not explain all of governmental lawlessness. Human activity springs from a variety of motivations, and institutional arrangements are subject to deterioration and decay from a variety of causes. Some of these are briefly discussed below.

Inability to Admit Mistakes

The typical politician has a congenital indisposition to heed Cromwell's injunction to think that he may be mistaken. When President Nixon pronounced guilt on Charles Manson, then being tried in California for the sensational slaying of movie actress Sharon Tate and others, the headlines were quick to point out the error. The President was equally quick in backtracking. The President and his aides "explained" what he earlier "meant" or "intended."

The President's original statement follows:

I think the main concern I have is the attitudes that are created among many of our younger people and also perhaps older people as well, in which they tend to glorify and make heroes out of those who engage in criminal activities. This is not done intentionally by the press. It is not done intentionally by radio and television, I know. It is done perhaps because people want to read or see that kind of story. I noted, for example, the coverage of the Charles Manson case when I was in Los Angeles, front page every day in the papers. It usually got a couple of minutes in the evening news. Here is a man who is guilty, directly or indirectly, of eight murders without reason.

Shortly after these remarks were delivered to journalists at a Law Enforcement Assistance Administration (LEAA) conference in Denver, Ronald Ziegler, the press secretary, personally "clarified" the "intent of the President's remarks":

The President, in his remarks to you in this room earlier, was, of course, referring to the focus of attention and the dramatics that are oftentimes put on various criminal acts, alleged criminal acts. Quite obviously, the President in his remarks regarding the trial now underway was referring to allegations that had been raised and are now in a court of law. If you take the President's remarks in the context of what he was saying, there is no attempt to impute liability to any accused. The gist of his statement was just the contrary. I think when he concluded his statement in reference to the system, including his remarks to you, he made it very clear that it is important in our system, as it does exist, that individuals have the right of fair trial, although, apparently, many of you understood it to mean something other than the President intended it in his total remarks, to suggest that he was referring to something other than the obvious, and that is the fact that he was referring to the allegation against Mr. Manson and the others on trial in Los Angeles.

That clarification, inarticulate because of haste in making it, was further refined by the President as he returned to Washington; a statement was prepared aboard the Presidential plane and distributed to reporters as the passengers disembarked at Andrews Air Force Base:

I've been informed that my comment in Denver regarding the Tate murder trial in Los Angeles continues to be misunderstood despite the unequivocal statement made at the time by my press secretary. My remarks were in the context of my expression of a tendency on the part of some to glamorize those identified with a crime. The last thing I would do is prejudice the legal rights of any person, in any circumstances. To set the record straight, I do not know and did not intend to speculate as to whether the Tate defendants are guilty, in fact, or not. All the facts in the case have not yet been presented. The defendants should be presumed to be innocent at this stage of their trial. To repeat what I said at the LEAA conference in Denver, our American system of justice requires the constant support of every citizen, to insure a fair trial for the guilty and innocent alike.

The "mistake" was thus explained away as a semantic misinterpretation.

Four months later the President finally owned up to the mistake. At a news conference the following colloquy took place:

> Q: Mr. President, at a previous news conference you said that what happened at Mylai was a massacre. On another occasion, you said that Charles Manson is guilty. On another occasion, you mentioned Angela Davis by name and then said that those responsible for such acts of terror will be brought to justice.
>
> My question concerns the problem of pretrial publicity and the fact that it could jeopardize a defendant's rights at a trial. How do you reconcile your comments with your status as a lawyer?
>
> THE PRESIDENT: I think that's a legitimate criticism. I think sometimes we lawyers, even like doctors who try to prescribe for themselves, may make mistakes. And I think that kind of comment is probably unjustified.

This humble confession of error has not signalled any willingness on the President's part to subscribe to the cognate necessity of keeping an open mind. He has said, for instance, that he would pay no heed to any recommendation of his National Commission on Marijuana and Drug Abuse that marijuana be legalized, even though the Commission was only beginning to undertake a study of the problem when the statement was made.

The statement about Manson's guilt is a relatively trivial, though prominent, example of the failure of our political and legal institutions to be able gracefully to admit errors and mistakes. A component of the prosecutor's decision to suppress evidence in the case against Lloyd Eldon Miller was his fear that an acquittal would show a mistake had been made. Jim Garrison, the notorious district attorney of New Orleans, charged Clay Shaw with perjury after his acquittal in a Kennedy conspiracy trial in order to cover up Garrison's shenanigans. The cover-ups by high-ranking Army officials in connection with the massacre at Mylai stemmed in part from the same impulse.

After the May Day demonstrations in Washington, Police Chief Jerry V. Wilson denied that false arrests had been made: "The fact that we cannot in every case prove the case in court does not make it a false arrest," he said; "I don't think I would agree that we violated [the demonstrators'] civil rights." It would not have been difficult or even very damaging in terms of his public posture to admit that in the heat of the moment some arrests may have been made without cause. Chief Wilson might have pledged an "investigation" and later exonerated his men; but somehow he and the Attorney General knew almost before the demonstrations had ended that police abided by the law one hundred percent of the time. Babe Ruth himself never hit above .400. Wilson said after the arrests that the only alternative would have been "martial law, which is much worse, because the individual doesn't even get released." Whatever the merits of that legal argument, declaration of martial law would at least have told innocent bystanders and gawking spectators to stay off the streets.

The deeply ingrained and all-too-human reluctance to confess error permits minor mistakes and infractions of the rules to develop into full-blown unlawful policies.

Corruption

Ward politicians brought up on a diet of corruption and conditioned to blink at the law are not readily convinced, once they are elected to high office, that they should always abide by the law. Moreover, the example of officials who blink at or ignore the law is not wasted on their subordinates. Much police corruption stems in part from the tacit understanding that superior officers at the station house will pretend not to see what is going on about them.

The temptation to corruption is understandable, as one policeman explained to an investigator for the President's Commission on Law Enforcement and Administration of Justice:

> These people really work on you. They make it seem so logical—like you are the one that is out of step. This bookie gave me this kind of line: "It's legal at the tracks, isn't it? So why isn't it legal here? It's because of those crooks at the Capitol. They're gettin' plenty—all drivin' Cads. Look at my customers, some of the biggest guys in town—they don't want you to close me down. If you do they'll just transfer you. Like that last jerk. And even the Judge, what did he do? Fined me a hundred and suspended fifty. Hell, he knows Joe citizen wants me here, so get smart, be one of the boys, be part of the system. It's a way of life in this town and you're not gonna change it. Tell you what I'll do. I won't give you a nickel; just call in a free bet in the first race every day and you can win or lose, how about it?"

Sometimes the laws directly incite corruption in the administrative agencies created to implement policy. The Texas Youth Council, for example, administers a program whose budget depends directly on the number of children condemned to its reformatories. The budget was established at approximately ten thousand dollars per child in 1969 and 1970; when newspaper revelations of the "agreed judgment" technique for sending children to schools operated by the TYC caused an outcry in El Paso, the TYC revoked the paroles of a much higher number of children than usual to make up for the decrease in the number of those sent directly to the schools for the first time. Thus the budget level was roughly maintained.

Political Pressure

Closely related to rank corruption is the distortion of the legal process caused by political pressures. Even obvious violations of the law are covered up by the apparent governmental policy of firing employees who reveal violations. Thus Ernest Fitzgerald.

Thus, also, the difficulties of the New York State Division of Human Rights (SDHR), which has been almost totally lethargic in enforcing that state's tough antidiscrimination law in the construction trades. An official of the Division said: "I won't say if we're really meeting the problem because if I answer that I'd lose my job." Moreover:

> It was no black militant, but still another official of the SDHR, who said that only the political power of the construction trade union, or fear of it, prevented action. It was a young attorney in the office of the attorney general who told us nothing is being done because of the "political climate," that his superior is a "politician" and that action against discrimination would be unpopular because the electorate is composed of what he called "Procaccino's people." It was an official of the State Department of Labor who stated that the department did not "tangle" with the labor unions, because if it did "its appropriations would be cut off."

The dismal record of the United States Bureau of Mines in policing mines and insuring their safety can be traced in part to the appointment of officials who lack any qualifications whatsoever. The Federal Coal Mine Health and Safety Act of 1969 required that the Interior Department Advisory Committee on Coal Mine Safety Research consist of persons "who are knowledgeable in the field of coal mine safety research." In February, 1971, Acting Secretary of the Interior Fred J. Russell unlawfully appointed to the thirteen-member Committee seven persons without any mining experience. Mrs. Jo Anne Gray, Republican National Committeewoman from Colorado, was put on the committee because "Mrs. Gray's mother's folks were coal miners." Mrs. Sara Abernathy, the widow of a doctor and an employee of Republican Senator Henry L. Bellmon of Oklahoma, was named to the post, according to an Interior Department spokesman, "because a doctor's wife knows a lot about medicine." Two of the new appointees were officials of the two mining companies whose safety policies were so poor that they had the highest death rates due to safety-related defects in the 1960's.

Mr. Russell appointed these people from a list prepared for him by an aide to the Assistant Secretary for Mineral Affairs. The aide had worked for the Colorado Mining Association, a trade association, before his appointment to the Interior Department. The annals of American politics are filled with similar examples of bypassing professional qualifications in choosing personnel.*

Stupidity, Insensitivity, and Oversight

Stupidity, insensitivity, and oversight are sometimes the causes for lawbreaking, but the surface appearance may be a mask for cunning. In 1971, for example, the Attorney General justified "national security" wiretaps without first applying for court authorization by claiming "by the time enough evidence is obtained to show probable cause, it may well be too late." He added, however, that "when the national security is threatened, prevention is the first consideration. We first need intelligence on the movements of suspected conspirators, not formal evidence on which to convict them." The shift between "probable cause" and "formal evidence" may be a matter of stupidity, insensitivity, or oversight; in all events, it heightens the dramatic tension.

The Attorney General went on to claim that if "enough evidence to show probable cause for a court order to wire tap" existed "we could probably prevent the threat in question without needing a wiretap." That statement, in turn, leaves dangling the question why wiretaps are ever needed when there are legal grounds to get them; but his audience was not enlightened.

In 1970, the new Chief of Naval Operations, Admiral Elmo R. Zumwalt, had issued sixty-seven of his famous "Z-grams," which laid down broad guidelines for modernizing the naval service. A few days before Christmas, the Admiral's military lawyer called over to his counterparts in the Office of the Judge Advocate General, asking them to read over each of the sixty-seven Z-grams in one afternoon to determine whether they were in every respect consistent with Navy Regulations. If they were not consistent, he said, a new Z-gram would be promulgated stating that all the other Z-grams would take precedence over the Navy Regulations. Of course, the Regulations were issued by higher authority even than Admiral Zumwalt, and his Z-grams could have no such legal effect. But it is this kind of oversight and failure to think things through at the proper time that is capable of producing many acts against the law.

---

* Many other advisory committees, operating partly with Government funds, have only industrial representation; for instance, the short-lived Civil Aeronautics Board Finance Advisory Committee and the National Industrial Pollution Control Council. When an occasional advisory group is required by law to contain certain kinds of members, the President has been loath to appoint them. The Advisory Council on Environmental Education, established by the Environmental Educational Act of 1970, required among its members ecologists, students, academicians, and medical, legal, and scientific representatives. A year after the Act was signed into law by President Nixon, he had appointed no one to its membership.

Mistakes and Ignorance

There are so many laws that it is impossible for any Government official to guarantee that his department or agency will not violate one. Sometimes the laws make sense and other times they are hopelessly muddled. It has been said that the Interior Department's Indian Affairs Manual "fills 33 volumes that stack some six feet high and contains more than 2,000 regulations, 389 treaties, 5,000 statutes, 2,000 federal court decisions and 500 opinions of the Attorney General." It is inevitable that the Government will often react to situations out of ignorance or by mistake.

Sometimes the mistake is that of a junior official who understands neither his own function nor the political subtleties that surround him. When Yehudi Menuhin, the world-famous American violinist, accepted honorary Swiss citizenship, he was informed by letter from the American consulate in Berne that a "preliminary decision" of the State Department had been made that his acceptance revoked his birthright.

A stinging letter from Menuhin to Secretary of State William R. Rogers brought forth the reply that "a preliminary finding" had not been reached. Nevertheless, Winifred T. Hall, chief of the consular section of the American Embassy in Switzerland, had written Menuhin that "the Department of State requested us to inform you that your obtention of naturalization as a Swiss citizen is regarded as highly persuasive evidence of your intention to relinquish United States citizenship. The surrounding circumstances and purposes are not considered to negate such intent. Consequently, the Department of State holds that you expatriated yourself. . . . This decision by the Department of State that you have lost your United States citizenship is a preliminary one. The final decision will be made by the Department of State in the next several months."

Switzerland does not award medals or other honors to those it holds in high esteem; its only "form of public honor," according to Menuhin, is the granting of honorary citizenship. In that spirit, Menuhin said, he had been honored to accept the grant. Upon learning of the "preliminary decision," Secretary Rogers ordered that the incident be "investigated promptly" and said he was "distressed" to hear of the Department's letter. Officials noted the next day that the "routine" procedure would be altered to avoid future misunderstandings.

Under the law, the Government must prove that a citizen has voluntarily relinquished his citizenship before it can deny him a passport; there is no legal procedure by which the Government can strip a person of his citizenship. Shortly thereafter, Rogers wrote Menuhin that "your acceptance of an honorary citizenship did not place your United States citizenship in jeopardy."

Mistakes can also result from insufficient or sloppy methods of administrative organization. Examples of loose auditing procedures presented elsewhere in these pages illustrate the problem.

Lack of Professionalism

Many times Government officials break the law and are permitted to break the law by their superiors because they are insufficiently professional. American policemen are consistently underpaid and undertrained; the temptations leading to corruption are abundant. Frequently law enforcement officials perceive their roles along narrow institutional lines and do not sense the larger public interest they are supposed to serve.

Police are supposed to make arrests and "bring criminals to justice." The jurisprudence that says they must make their catch in certain ways only is dismissed as a technicality. The same police department in Minneapolis that conducted the raid on Dr. Lykken's home interrogated a college graduate who sought a job on the force and who had received a grade of 96 on the written civil service examination with such questions as "What do you think of Margaret Mead?" Not surprisingly, he failed the oral examination and was put on probationary status in a suburban department. The fear of educated policemen is a significant deterrent to the staffing of a professional force.

The lack of professionalism is widespread. The lower substratum of judges is almost uniformly inferior. There never has been a professional civil service class in the United States from which could be drawn the thousands of officials who serve in policy-making positions. Instead of men and women who put the public interest first, federal agencies are frequently staffed with political hacks.

Even when top jobs go to extremely able people, the danger of conflict of interest is always present. Traditionally, conflict of interest has meant a conflict between private interest and public trust. Of late, the term has come to mean in addition "confluence of interest"; thus, retired military officers work for defense contractors and tax lawyers get important posts within the Internal Revenue Service, not because they have bribed someone or worked out compelling financial arrangements that can be augmented by official positions, but because the old and new jobs are complementary and call on the same body of knowledge and experience.

The "conflict of interest" is often simply a shared mutual interest. The mutuality of interest means, however, that private industry can seduce the civil servant to return to the fold; since partisan politics dominates the selection process, the public servant becomes expert in one substantive area but rarely in the art of government. The lawyer or businessman does not go from one agency to another but from private industry to government and back to the same industry. The implications of such a system are well known: no person who has a stake in a particular industry is likely to devote his entire energies to devising rules that may decrease that industry's profitability.

Even in the few areas of American Government where a career class has developed—such as in the military—the extent of professionalism leaves much to be desired. A Coast Guard Rear Admiral, who presumably received training in the things that can happen to, on, or near the American coasts, apparently was never told about the rules governing defectors—or else he forgot. The few officials on duty in the State Department were similarly unresponsive. And after the Mylai exposure, the Army began beefing up its training sessions on the laws of war—in the belief that the learning was relevant and maybe officers-to-be and soldiers would learn it.

Lack of Resources

In any human "system" there are always more jobs to be done than time and resources will permit. The "Noble Experiment" of Prohibition was a failure because no sound enforcement program was ever devised. Ramsey Clark relates that for a good part of the 1960's only two narcotics inspectors were responsible for patrolling the entire United States-Mexico border. Inspection programs under the Walsh-Healy Act, which is supposed to protect the safety of workers in factories with federal contracts, is so poorly funded that inspectors cannot hope to examine more than two or three percent of the thousands of federal contractors covered. The United States Geological Survey, which has jurisdiction to police the oil drilling industry, has seventeen inspectors who watch over forty-five hundred oil wells. The Federal Renegotiation Board, responsible for overseeing more than $60 billion worth of government contracts, has a staff of fewer than two hundred people; according to Vice Admiral Hyman Rickover, who has documented its failures in protecting the taxpayer, the Board "is about as effective as putting a Band-aid on cancer."

The Office of Corporation Counsel in Washington is so understaffed that its former chief reported to a City Council budget hearing that "literally no enforcement" of the city's fair-housing and employment statutes was possible with its present manpower and that only "minimal" enforcement of the housing code and tax laws could be carried out. Former Corporation Counsel Charles T. Duncan noted in his report that three-quarters of his enforcement division's time was devoted to prosecuting traffic offenses, which require little effort or energy to prosecute—with a like effect on the offenses. He said that "assistants do not have adequate time to prepare for trial or research points of law. . . . Enforcement of various regulations necessarily is haphazard and takes place, if at all, on a time available basis. There is literally no enforcement of the regulations relating to fair housing and fair employment simply because staff is not available to engage in the extensive preparation which those cases require."

The problem there, as elsewhere, is a severe shortage of money. There are so many laws in the United States and so many ways to avoid them that adequate enforcement funding might take the entire budget. Of course, if the federal Government, not to mention every other government, ever became serious about enforcing laws, the culture of industrial lawbreaking, at least, might be changed.

The lack of money is reflected in other kinds of lawbreaking as well. Perhaps the best example is the constant and nationwide attempt to cut welfare expenditures, legally or not. Full enforcement of the welfare laws, it has been estimated, would double the number of people on welfare and would require an increase in the payments to many people now on the rolls. The incentive to break the law in order to hold down the budget is evident.

The Inoperative Personal Belief Syndrome

A perversity of the human spirit permits many people to avoid practicing what they preach. Many rail against vice but commit immoral and evil acts, like the politician who frequents private gambling clubs but calls on the police to stop his poorer neighbors from rolling dice in the streets.

The discrepancy between practice and belief is not always easily explained. Sometimes the discrepancy springs from ignorance; Havelock Ellis told the story of the prim lady who for years inveighed against certain private practices of adolescents only to discover in one horrifying moment that she was no stranger to the secret sin herself. Ellis's example is an extreme one, but the Victorian mood that produced it has tenacious roots and its continued growth gives the Government great opportunity to break the law.

Thurmond Arnold put it best when he wrote in 1935 that "most unenforced criminal laws survive in order to satisfy moral objections to established modes of conduct. They are unenforced because we want to continue our conduct, and unrepealed because we want to preserve our morals."

This contradiction between behavior and expressed belief may be called the "inoperative personal belief syndrome," because the belief, though expressed, does not operate to restrain its holder. The cause of the syndrome is multifaceted. Part of the cause lies in the differing moral beliefs of the community. Some people honestly believe that prostitution, vagrancy, gambling, and other vices are immoral. Others are not so persuaded or do not care. Another part lies in the weakness of the human flesh and spirit (else there would be little use for moral codes).

Many people, therefore, do what they know to be wrong, immoral, or dissolute. The politician, who must get himself elected at regular intervals, can rarely discuss openly and honestly his personal beliefs, for popular beliefs in matters of vice and immorality seem to exist, ghostlike, separate and apart from the men and women who espouse them. Legislators must refer to this assumed moral standard, which endures because each person thinks the other person will refer to it. Though no one may really believe in the necessity for a given rule, the belief that another may believe it reinforces it. This can be expressed mathematically by the equation: $0 + 0 = 2$.

What gets enacted by legislators as a result of this syndrome is a set of laws that characterizes as criminal many popular forms of behavior. To protect the legislators themselves, the laws give the police and other law enforcement officials the widest latitude in interpreting the criminal codes. People without influence can be arrested for a variety of petty or harmless offenses; the police often use their discretionary power to enforce these laws in a grossly discriminatory way.

Vice laws invite discrimination. Police often makes arrests in ghetto areas for vague offenses such as "failure to obey a police officer's order to move on" and for using the same profane language toward a police officer that police officers use among themselves back at the precinct.

Police make gambling raids in some areas of town and leave others wide open. In one flagrant instance, police in Pasadena, California, conducted a series of gambling raids in the black ghetto. In 1957, of 292 people arrested for gambling, only 16 were white. Of 91 arrested in 1958, only 9 were white. In 1959, no whites were arrested at all, despite the fact that the police had actually found some whites engaged in illicit gambling. The police had special patrols in black neighborhoods but none in white ones. The Pasadena Chief of Police belong to an Elks Club that maintained a semisecret card room in which a "key card" was necessary to gain entrance; two other private clubs also had gambling facilities. At a gambling trial of blacks picked up in a raid, the defendants sought to introduce evidence of these facts to show a pattern of discriminatory enforcement. The "keeper" of the card room refused to testify on the grounds that he might incriminate himself.

Another type of law supported by the inoperative personal belief syndrome is the Sunday closing law. Enacted in a more religious time and upheld as recently as 1961 by the Supreme Court, the Sunday closing laws are nothing more than an invitation to corruption. It has been estimated that to forestall prosecutions police in New York City take more than $6,200,000 a year in bribes from ten thousand Puerto Rican shops. Police graft extracted from delicatessens and other shops open on Sunday in New York is reported to be equally widespread.

Evidence of this kind of corruption is exceedingly elusive and difficult to gather; one concrete case of a two-dollar payoff received by a policeman from a Brooklyn grocery store owner was documented by Detective Frank Serpico, who made a tape recording of a conversation in which the bribe-taker admitted the act to another policeman. The grocery store owner was Serpico's brother; the policeman taking the money was dismissed from the force.

Police latitude in enforcing unenforceable law is often explicitly approved by the courts. The Arkansas Supreme Court once upheld the police practice of prosecuting only grocery stores under the Sunday closing laws. Drug stores, hotels, filling stations, restaurants, funeral homes, bakeries, tourist courts, bus stations, city park concessions, and sporting goods stores operated on Sunday without arrests or prosecutions. In spite of the fairly clear evidence of discrimination here, the Arkansas court affirmed a directed verdict of guilty. The court found the constitutionality of the discriminatory practice in the answer to the question: "If the state statute applied by its terms to grocery stores alone, would it be valid?" The answer to that question, the court said, was clearly in the affirmative, since the legislature is empowered to make classifications in its criminal law. Just so, but traditionally that power is presumed to be in the legislature alone; by its decision the Arkansas Supreme Court permitted the police themselves to make the criminal law of the state.

The use of these laws does not prevent white-collar and Government officials from engaging in the same activities. The common streetwalker is often arrested, but the expensive call girl who may spend a few days with a Congressman or high official on a yacht or in a private suite is rarely charged. The police did not devote an inordinate amount of attention to social drinking by influential people during Prohibition, nor does respectable gambling run much risk of finding itself abated.

The morals statutes, illness statutes (such as those condemning alcoholism or drug addiction), and nuisance laws (vagrancy, loitering, and others) have been said to represent the practice of "overcriminalization" prevalent in American society, but they are not the only manifestation of the inoperative personal belief syndrome. The widespread disregard of Supreme Court decisions against prayers in public schools represents a different aspect of the syndrome. Teachers and administrators, as well as private citizens, have ignored the Court's decisions. Few of the parents who protest the loudest believe in the efficacy of morning prayer; otherwise prayers at the breakfast table would serve as well as public requests for absolution one hour later. Moreover, the parents undercut their own position by admitting the blandest and most nondenominational prayers would satisfy them. Nevertheless, they cannot admit to friends and neighbors (and perhaps to themselves) that their heated protests against the Supreme Court spring more from a desire to look respectable in the eyes of the community than a heartfelt and devout wish that their children learn the lesson of personal and daily supplication to that mysterious (but nondenominational) omnipotence that rules us all.*

Crisis

The Government's perception that an incident or problem has reached a crisis and cannot be handled routinely may determine whether or not the Government will break the law. Official conduct that would not be contemplated in the absence of an emergency is often felt to be compelled when a crisis is at hand. The more politicized the issue the more likely that the Government will interpret the situation as a crisis requiring strong measures that may overstep the bounds of law. Sometimes the overstepping is deliberate and sometimes it is the inevitable result of the lack of time to ponder the best course.

The "necessity" that attends any crisis can naturally be overworked. "Military necessity" is a catch phrase that permits nations to avoid calumny (they think) or legal responsibility for acts that would otherwise be war crimes; similarly, the Government has argued, unsuccessfully, that domestic security permits it to adopt measures that would be unthinkable in the absence of a crisis. The threat of war or its actuality is the most frequently heard excuse for extensions of governmental power. President Roosevelt in 1942 invoked the war power to "suspend" certain laws, and he herded Japanese-Americans into concentration camps and got away with it. President Truman seized the steel mills pursuant to the same claim. President Roosevelt permitted the writ of habeas corpus to be suspended during World War II (although the Supreme Court ruled after the war that the suspension was illegal).

The cold war has produced other kinds of crisis—real or imagined— and the argument for unauthorized wiretapping and other spying stems from the same theory. Whether the crisis is rhetoric or reality is usually difficult to discern and the bipartisan spirit that usually hovers over

---

* This is not to argue that lawbreaking caused by the overcriminalization statutes is the same as that caused by the Supreme Court's prayer decisions. The first type of law creates black markets and establishes an enormous potential for public corruption; the second type of law does not create malfeasance, at least overtly. The first type of law is maintained and supported by the inoperative belief syndrome; the second type is violated because of that syndrome. But in both situations, the syndrome is responsible for lawbreaking by public officials.

issues of war and peace quite frequently permits the Government to do what it wants.

Crisis is not perceived alone in the eyes of the Government. The ultimate fact for America is that the Government is sustained by the beliefs of the population at large. And the conclusion is inescapable, therefore, that the Government often breaks the law simply because the people want and expect it to do so. The crisis of crime in the late 'Sixties was clearly a real fear in the minds of a substantial number of the population. Politicians did not invent the crisis, but they inevitably played upon it. The off-duty policemen who attacked black citizens in a New York courthouse were doubtless responding as a good portion of the electorate would have had them respond—somehow their action was helping counter "crime in the streets." When a fearful but dominant majority wants action, the lawless solution is usually the quickest.

Absurdity of the Laws

One short answer to the why of some Government lawbreaking is that some of the laws officials are bidden to obey are manifestly absurd. In almost every political jurisdiction district attorneys are commanded by law to prosecute every infraction of the law ("The district attorney *shall* prosecute . . ."). But even if it were possible, why would the police want to arrest every jaywalker when it is far safer, in most cities, to cross the street in the middle of an empty block than at a crowded and irrational intersection? Why should the police try to enforce laws prohibiting the sale of contraceptive devices? Why should they arrest people on the streets, otherwise quiet, who don't "appear" to have "gainful employment"? Many of these laws present so many administrative headaches that the police need no excuse to ignore them.

The 1970 Policeman of the Year, Sgt. Paul E. Fabian of Rotterdam, New York, was named jointly by the International Association of Police Chiefs and *Parade* Magazine for his effective fight against drug addiction. His method was simple: instead of arresting suspects, he pledged them immunity from prosecution if they promised to do nothing more than talk to him honestly about their problems and perhaps tell the names of their pushers. According to a news account: "the sergeant, along with his chief, Joseph S. Dominelli, and the Schenectady County District Attorney, Howard A. Levine, readily admits that his informal administration of immunity is both unusual and illegal. But all of them agree that it has produced remarkable success in keeping a growing narcotics problem in Rotterdam from turning into an epidemic."

If at the stationhouse, so too—perhaps—at the White House. From the perspective of the Presidency, Congress enacts many downright foolish laws the country would be far better off without. If he can, the President will veto them. Lamentably, however, the Constitution provides him with no item veto, and Congress has the unfortunate habit of joining in one single bill many unrelated items—some worthy, some laughable or harmful. If he does not want the latter he cannot afford to veto the former. What can he do? Sign the bill and refuse to spend money on a wasteful weapons system the country does not need?—that is sometimes the only possible political response to an absurd and unnecessary law.

Sometimes, that is, the matter is too clear for doubt, and if it bothers the purist, that is the purist's problem. So says the Government.

EFFECTS

The general effects of Government lawlessness are obvious: Government lawlessness, as Justice Brandeis said, breeds contempt for law; it creates gross injustice in particular cases; it is responsible for enormous monetary expense, both in the waste of taxpayers' dollars and in the failure to redress the overwhelming distortions that private business introduces into the "free market"; it brings further crime and violence in its wake; and, finally, it may lead, paradoxically, both to dictatorship and anarchy.

Contempt for law is written in the acts of those who disobey it. When people see that Government officials who break the law are treated leniently—and the higher the rank the more lenient the treatment—they become skeptical of the belief that respect for law is of vital importance to a free society. When a two-star general loses one star but is not court-martialed for his role in covering up grievous American war crimes, but junior officers and enlisted men are subjected to the possibility of the death penalty, the prospect of law seems nothing but the prospect of brute force. When a Congressman convicted of crimes is given a light sentence but possessors of marijuana draw years in jail; * when police officers are rarely charged and even more rarely convicted for homicide, harassment, and corruption; when those who commit crimes against members of minorities are not even indicted; when people are fired from Government jobs for telling the truth on behalf of the taxpayer; when prosecutors fabricate evidence to maintain their own

---

* In 1970, a philosophy professor, to protest the war, filed a false claim of twenty exemptions on his income tax return. The Government brought a criminal suit (it could have instituted a civil case to recover the taxes owed), and the protester was sentenced to a year in jail. A year later, former Congressman (and a past national commander of the American Legion) Martin B. McKneally of Newburgh, New York, pleaded guilty to a charge of filing no return in 1965. In return for the plea, the Government dropped charges of failing to report a total of $54,000 in 1964, 1966, and 1967. His one-year sentence was *suspended,* though he was fined $5,000.

reputations; when judges violate law to teach men humbled before them to respect it; when legislators ignore constitutional requirements and when they engage in the most obvious conflicts of interest—then legal institutions are demeaned and undercut. The incentive to obey the law is reduced to a game of "doing whatever you can as long as you can get away with it" and we return in no small measure to the natural state that Thomas Hobbes saw for humankind: "solitary, poor, nasty, brutish, and short."

Since a democracy is premised on a series of governmental checks and balances, the lawbreaking of one branch of the Government may be expected to produce a reaction from another. The open violation by state governments of constitutional policies against racial segregation has led directly to intimate federal supervision over large areas of what was once considered the province of state legislatures. The open display of contempt by state legislatures toward their own constitutions has led to direct judicial supervision of their apportionment process. The sustained example of police lawlessness in certain areas of the criminal process has likewise brought stern rebuke from the courts.

But the courts are not structured or intended to do the jobs of other organs of Government. Necessarily, therefore, the attempt by courts to control other governmental lawbreaking will itself be an overreaction, in turn requiring a response from the agencies they are attempting to control. The curious spectacle of one branch of Government hurling accusations of wrongdoing at another can only confuse the citizen and bring the law into further disrepute. Moreover, it can often lead to ludicrous results; for instance, President Nixon first campaigned against judicial interference in the criminal process, raising the hopes of the police that he would return the nation to their nostalgic vision of its (misremembered) former quiescence, but he later declared that he would not move to end de facto segregation because the courts had not yet required him to do so.

Nothing need be added here about individual injustices caused by Government lawlessness. The effects are explicit in all the examples presented in these pages, and it may be admitted in passing that the chapter titles in this book are obviously artificial: an injustice to one person is a grave potential threat to all of us. Similarly, the high cost to everyone of Government crimes needs no further elaboration.

Government lawlessness can breed hostility that turns to violence. A Government that refuses to enforce its proscriptions and that violates its own prescriptions cannot expect to remain unscathed; a society that permits its Government to break the law cannot expect to remain unharmed. Civil disobedience is almost a corollary to Government illegality, and criminal disobedience is certain, for the art of skillful retaliation is subtle and rage can be expressed best by hostility. As the authors of a study of New York's failure to enforce its antidiscrimination policies concluded:

> Thus far, the only progress that has been made in the hiring of blacks in the construction trades has been as the result of confrontation and nearly open conflict. Not until students at the State University of Buffalo picketed the campus was construction there halted, and effort to achieve improvement begun. Now, even as confrontation has eased, the state has begun to delay and hamstring local efforts to hire the unemployed for state-financed construction there. A high official of the State Division of Human Rights put it to us succinctly: "The only time the Division can act," he said, "is when pressure is brought from outside." Thus the entire policy of the state is directed at inviting confrontation by not acting in its absence; and further, encouraging confrontation by responding to the pressure it brings. The result is to invite in New York and Buffalo, in Albany and elsewhere across the state precisely that kind of racial confrontation which has so severely divided this country and this state already. It is a prescription for disaster.

That Government lawlessness can lead to a dictatorship is almost a truism. A classic statement of the proposition that the law can be ignored when greater purposes are to be served—that the Government ought to engage in civil or criminal disobedience—was Congressman F. Edward Hebert's celebrated 1967 advice to the federal Government that it ignore the First Amendment and induct vocal antiwar demonstrators into the Army. Said Hebert: "Let's forget the First Amendment. . . . I know this [prosecution] would be rescinded by the Supreme Court but at least the effort should be made. It would show the American people that the Justice Department and Congress were trying to clean up this rat-infested area." In response to a flurry of criticism, Congressman Hebert a few days later provided a gloss on his remarks: "It's not that I love the First Amendment less; it's that I love my country more." This was candid advocacy of the "chilling effect": damn the law, prosecute anyway.

Human rights are fragile and abstract notions. When disregarded or toyed with they have a tendency to shatter or dissolve. The logical extension of Hebert's assertion that governmental lawlessness is occasionally proper is to put everyone in jail and let the courts decide who should not be there.

The vesting of broad discretionary powers in all public officials leads to the possibility of dictatorship. It is a standard rule of constitutional law that vague statutes—*e.g.*, "disloyalty to the state," or "immoral behavior"—cannot be used as the basis for criminal sanctions. But the evil is the same if a panoply of laws permits the police to pick and choose the laws they want to enforce and the people against whom they wish to enforce them.

Finally, Government lawlessness may lead even to anarchy. When the bureaucracy avoids individual responsibility by diffusing all responsibility throughout a bloated hierarchy, the lack of accountability is precisely the same anarchy feared in the private sector. Anarchy is chaos or the lack of order; it presupposes no restraints, force, or regulation. Precisely this situation may occur in bureaucracies operating under regulations that permit them to go in both directions at once or to ignore their legal responsibilities altogether. And when that happens often enough, we may reasonably expect that crime, inflation, unemployment, poverty, war, pollution, environmental decay, racism, consumer fraud, and monopoly will result.

9

Bringing the Government to Account

THE CASE STUDIES are at hand; the reasons for our being victimized by the Government are tolerably clear. What, then, is to be done?

The difficulty with most proposed solutions to political problems with deep roots is that the "solutions" are usually restatementts of the problems. If, for instance, the problem is that the police do not always obey the law, it is hardly a solution to suggest that the police should obey the law. But all too often, this facile kind of suggestion is put forward as some kind of moral exhortation. General Matthew B. Ridgway, former Army Chief of Staff, commenting on the low esteem to which the Army had fallen, noted that

> the [indictment] of the Army's Sergeant Major . . . and that of several other senior noncommissioned officers by a Federal grand jury on charges of embezzlement of N.C.O. club funds overseas; the award of battlefield decorations for acts never performed; the pending charges against the former Provost Marshall General of the Army; and most damaging of all, the Mylai court-martial, are grievous blows.

General Ridgway's solution to the problem of restoring to the "American people our unshakable faith in the validity of the principles by which we were trained" was elemental:

> I know of but one way and that is by an undeviating adherence within the corps of cadets to the West Point code—a scrupulous regard for the sanctity of one's word and the integrity of one's acts, and then an unceasing effort to imbue our associates in the officer corps with comparable standards of conduct.

Reforms will be practical (meaning, in part, politically feasible) to the extent that they are general and indirect. Reforms that would cover only specific large areas of the Government would require enormous expenditures of energy because so many of them would be required to correct the abuses described in this book. Reforms aimed directly and specifically at particular abuses would likewise be extremely costly because they would be so strenuously resisted. Real reforms must affect the entire operation of the Government, by changing its structure and its motivations.

OPENNESS AND SECRECY

Lawbreaking does not flourish in the open. The exposure of a large number of acts of official wrongdoing has resulted in shake-ups, recriminations, prosecutions, and electoral defeat. Often the reaction has been in direct proportion to the success in covering up unlawfulness, and if officials had been more open, there would have been less inclination to overreact later on the side of rectitude.

Publicity is a powerful force in a democracy for bringing the Government to account. Much that transpires in darkness would not and does not survive in daylight. That is why a completely independent press is an absolute necessity and why the Government's attempts to muzzle the press are dangerous.

The press has unearthed and reported many notable stories, but the more deeply the stories probe into the inner workings of the Government the more likely it is that they came to light from a "leak." The "Pentagon Papers," the publication of which prompted, it is said, the first attempt by the federal Government in history to enjoin a newspaper from publishing, were handed over to the *New York Times* by an extremely disaffected former federal employee. The revelations, like Daniel Ellsberg's sense of desperation, were directly proportionate to the importance of the issue.

Lesser issues do not seem to attract as many "whistle blowers," although Government employees acting on the concept popularized by Ralph Nader have been responsible for some notable scandals being brought to light—witness Ernest Fitzgerald, John McGee, and Frank Serpico.

But the whistle-blowing method of gathering information for the public is at best random. The press needs a much more dependable process. In 1967, the Freedom of Information Act, pushed through Congress largely with newspaper and broadcast pressure, seemed to promise a new day in the gathering and reporting of information about the inner workings of the Government.

The hope has proved so far to be an illusion. The Act, its sponsors believed, would open Uncle Sam's file drawers "to the public," except for records that fall within nine categories of exceptions, ranging from the usual "national defense or foreign policy" requirements of secrecy to the highly particularized exemption for "geological and geophysical information and data, including maps, concerning wells." The exceptions do not require the Government to withhold information; they merely permit it to do so. But large categories of information, previously difficult to obtain, like final opinions and orders, internal rules that were intended to guide general policy, were opened to any person who desired to read them.

If the Act worked, it could have a large impact on the incidence of governmental lawbreaking. Administrative agencies, required to reveal final orders—such as directives refusing to permit prosecutions or investigations—would have provided enterprising newsmen (and lawyers) with a wealth of information (and precedent) that would seriously undermine an agency's ability to enforce the law in an arbitrary and discriminatory manner.

Unfortunately, the Act has consistently been undermined by a Government never enthusiastic about its existence. Shortly after the Act became effective, Attorney General Ramsey Clark agreed with the arguments of resistant agencies and in an official memorandum put a narrow interpretation on what was required to be revealed. This should not have been surprising, for the Act was in form an amendment to the Administrative Procedure Act, the basic charter of administrative fair play, a law not always scrupulously regarded by the executive agencies it is supposed to guide. The abysmal record of the U.S. Parole Board has already been noted; that agency has consistently refused to abide by the Act's requirement to give reasons when it denies parole applications.

So, too, the Freedom of Information Act is constantly abused. For example, this Act requires "statements of policy and interpretations which have been adopted by the agency" to be open to inspection by any member of the public. The Army doesn't like this provision. When I sought from the Judge Advocate General his opinion in a case concerning an officer holding a civil office,* he refused to release it to me, citing among other things one of the Act's exceptions for "intra-agency memorandums." This was an incredible claim on the face of it, since I had first seen a reference to the opinion in an official digest of opinions of the Judge Advocate General, published by the Army and available to the public. The opinion was clearly being discussed as an Army interpretation of federal law.

After a bizarre telephone call to a colonel in the Pentagon—prompted by a line in the Army's letter saying that if I wished to appeal the refusal

---

* See pp. 164 f.

I should make it to the Judge Advocate General, the very office denying my request *—I discovered that the fear was that I might be representing someone and might misuse the opinion. Upon my assurance that I had no client and needed the opinion solely for research, it was duly mailed to me.

The original refusal, in light of the subsequent release, was a blatant violation of the Information Act, since the purpose to which the information is to be put is irrelevant under the terms of the Act. (I have since been informed that the hostile treatment I first received was not due to my civilian status. Army lawyers say that they, as uniformed officers, have been denied a look at Army JAG opinions when they requested them from the "field." The Judge Advocate General of the Army, it seems, is desperately afraid that his subordinates might rely on what he has said. Official opinions are thus denied precedential value.)

Citizen, consumer, and other interest groups ought to press for an end to secrecy of this type everywhere that it occurs. The Information Act should be amended to plug many obvious loopholes that now exist. The rules and reasons that Government agencies use to justify their actions, or nonactions, should be known to anyone who cares to look.

The principle of openness could be usefully extended to all agencies everywhere. For example, guidelines for enforcement of the laws ought to be plainly published because publication (1) would force the Government to write guidelines, (2) would greatly simplify the task of monitoring the Government to see that it abides by its own reguations, and (3) would inform people what the law really is.

Equally crucial is the requirement that reasons accompany official decisions. The simple act of giving reasons is one of the hallmarks of civilization and the requirement is a great advance over the use of naked power. The requirement of stated reasons usually checks the range of arbitrary action. To require reasoned decisions publicly stated is not a panacea but an improvement that might considerably lessen the great number of illegal, hidden Government administrative activities.

When the Food and Drug Administration investigates a new drug, its findings ought to be released. When a study is made of the effects of supersonic flight on the atmosphere, there should be no hesitation in releasing it to the public, and if political considerations intervene, the public ought to have an easy method of obtaining it through court order, with all costs to be paid by the Government agency that refuses to release it. When Government advisory councils meet, their deliberations ought to be spread out on a public record. When the Attorney General refuses to bring an antitrust case recommended by his antitrust chief,

---

* The colonel informed me when I expressed my incredulity at this appeal arrangement that "I have my reasons, which I'm not going to tell you."

reasons ought to be on the record. Discriminatory enforcement and non-enforcement of the laws can be drastically reduced by requiring justification.

Compelled disclosure of reasons for acting or not acting is not the whole answer to Government illegality, nor will it be possible to write laws to force the Government to reveal the reasons for all decisions. Suppose it is not the Attorney General who refuses to bring an antitrust case, but the antitrust chief. Unless it were known what investigations he was pursuing, there would be no way to know to press for his reasons. Moreover, there could not be a requirement that the Department reveal all cases being investigated, for that requirement could well destroy many an investigation.

The *process* of Government, in areas like law enforcement, cannot work successfully in a fishbowl. But the *decisions* of Government, even the refusal to prosecute a case where the public has knowledge that the case is being investigated, ought to be explained. Secrecy shields the Government from truth as much as from public wrath, for without the possibility of an accounting, of being caught in error, there is no chance for easy correction.

PRODDING

It is symptomatic of the myth that the Government obeys the law, that "the law" itself provides precious few remedies to victims of Government lawlessness. Even where there are remedies, it is often excruciatingly difficult to secure them from the courts, the public agency most adapted to recognizing and maintaining the right of the citizens against the Government itself. An impressive array of legalistic doctrines has in the past deterred the courts from considering the merits of a citizen's claim against his Government.

The most substantive aspect of these doctrines is their names. Preeminent among them are three: "standing," "sovereign immunity," and "unreviewability." It is unnecessary here to rehearse the legal growth and depth of these doctrines, but a short statement of their scope will indicate that one method of bringing the Government to account is to permit citizens direct access to the courts to contest illegality in individual cases.

"Standing" is a doctrine that only those people with a certain direct interest in a concrete controversy may be heard by the courts. The Supreme Court has said of the law of standing that it is "a complicated specialty of federal jurisdiction." Ultimate definition of the rule can be perceived only through some mystical cloud because the rule has historically been applied fitfully and inconsistently.

Nevertheless, one classic version of the rule emerged from the Supreme Court in 1923 when it ruled that a taxpayer in Massachusetts could not attack in court the constitutionality of a law that would have provided federal funds for expectant mothers. The woman's interest in the legal issue was held to be too remote because she was merely one of millions of federal taxpayers. That rule was partially overturned by the Court in 1968, when it ruled that taxpayers may bring suits to challenge under specific clauses of the Constitution the legality of federal expenditures. (In the 1968 case that issue was expenditure of funds under the Elementary and Secondary Education Act of 1965 for religious schools.)

This upheaval in the law of standing suggests that many cases previously nonjusticiable may now be brought to the federal courts. In the case of *Reservists Committee to Stop the War* v. *Laird,* Federal District Judge Gerhard A. Gesell ruled that present and former reservists have standing as citizens of the United States to litigate the question of whether Congressmen who hold reserve commissions in the armed forces of the United States are unconstitutionally holding executive office.* The Judge was reasoning from the language of recent Supreme Court decisions stating that the test for standing is "whether there is a logical nexus between the status asserted and the claims sought to be adjudicated" and "whether the interests sought to be protected by the complainant are arguably within the zone of interests to be protected or regulated by the statute or constitutional guarantee in question."

He ruled that although "there are undoubtedly very few instances in which plaintiffs who assert merely the undifferentiated interest of citizens have a personal stake in the outcome sufficient to support standing in the constitutional sense," citizens simply asserting their interests as citizens could bring their cases before him for four reasons: (1) "While any injury which might result from Congressmen holding reserve commissions is hypothetical, the hypothesis is not by [the citizens] but underlies the constitutional provision itself. Like a conflict-of-interest statute, the constitutional bar addresses itself to the potential for undue influence rather than to its realization." (2) "The issue tendered is a narrow one and involves a precise self-operative provision of the Constitution." (3) "The interest in maintaining independence among the branches of government is shared by all citizens equally, and since this is the primary if not the sole purpose of the bar against Congressmen holding executive office, the interest of plaintiffs as citizens is undoubtedly one which was intended to be protected by the constitutional provision involved." (4) "There can be no doubt that this is a 'case or controversy' in the common meaning of those words; the parties sharply conflict in

* See page 166 f.

both their interests and their views and the case was ably briefed and argued."

Much generalized governmental lawbreaking has been premised on the heretofore widely held belief that the doctrine of standing would prevent anyone interested in good government from going to court to sponsor it. The future willingness of courts to pierce this archaic doctrine is one important step toward permitting citizens to reassert their control over the actions of their Government.

Judge Gesell's decision is being appealed, but regardless of the eventual outcome of this particular case, it is clear that something like his rule of standing is necessary to test the legality of governmental activity.

Persons clearly, directly, and personally injured by government lawlessness have not heretofore been barred from bringing their case to court by the doctrine of standing. But very often private litigants are barred from proceeding further with their claims by the doctrine of "sovereign immunity." Again, it is unnecessary to outline that doctrine's contorted and tortured history; it is sufficient to point out that it is usually believed to rest on ancient British precedents, summarized by the statement that since the King could not be sued in his own court, neither could his agents. The classic American statement of the rule was Justice Holmes's in 1907: "There can be no legal right as against the authority that makes the law on which the right depends."

That is simple sophistry, but the sophistry has worked real harm in the past and threatens to continue to do so. Suppose, for example, the United States has unlawfully assumed title to a thousand acres of oil-producing land and is collecting royalties on oil obtained. When the true owner attempts to go to court to prove that the United States does not have legal title he is met with the argument that he will not even be permitted to prove his case. The Government is immune, the court will say, and suit against the Secretary of the Interior (whose department claimed the land) was merely "an unsophisticated attempt to avoid the defense of governmental immunity by naming as defendants the officers of the particular government agencies alleging that these officers acted beyond their authority." That is what the United States Court of Appeals for the Fifth Circuit said in 1968, following an old line of Supreme Court decisions. The net of these decisions—and the underlying meaning of the doctrine of sovereign immunity—is that the federal Government may take your land whenever it feels so inclined and if you are too slow to prevent federal agents from moving in, you will never be able to move them out—at least not in a civilized fashion.

The "sovereign" may undo this mischief by consenting to be sued. In various statutes from time to time, Congress has in fact waived the doctrine of sovereign immunity and permitted the United States to be sued in the federal courts for a variety of misdeeds. The Administrative Procedure Act, for instance, provides the manner by which any injured person may contest in court adverse decisions of federal administrative agencies.

But there is one significant area in which sovereign immunity still remains a viable doctrine: persons injured by willful and malicious acts of governmental officers may not sue the United States (though suits when officials *negligently* cause injuries are permitted). This anomaly is based on the false presumption that the Government will not deliberately harm its citizens and that such injuries must therefore result from officials acting outside the scope of their employment. Since they were acting without the authority of their office they should not, for those purposes, be considered governmental agents, and the Government should therefore not be sued. That is the argument, and if the logic seems a little shaky, it is.

If officials acting wantonly and maliciously are outside the scope of their employment, the thought may occur that they could be sued in their individual capacities as private citizens. For many years the answer was that they could not be sued. The reasoning stemmed from the principle underlying the absolute immunity of judges from civil suit for courtroom conduct.

As early as 1871, the Supreme Court said that "it is a general principle of the highest importance to the proper administration of justice that a judicial officer, in exercising the authority vested in him, shall be free to act upon his own conviction, without apprehension of personal consequences to himself. . . . The principle . . . obtains in all countries where there is any well-ordered system of jurisprudence."

In 1896, in connection with a case concerning alleged defamation by the Postmaster General, the Supreme Court said that "the same general considerations of public policy and convenience which demand for judges of courts of superior jurisdiction immunity from civil suits for damage arising from acts done by them in the course of the performance of their judicial functions, apply to a large extent to official communications made by heads of Executive Departments when engaged in the discharge of duties imposed upon them by law."

Following these precedents federal courts have held on various occasions that the Secretary of the Interior may maliciously defame persons in a press release dealing with official business and the Secretary of the Treasury cannot be held to account for "arbitrary, wanton, capricious, illegal, malicious, oppressive, and contemptuous" actions. Thus the Government cannot be sued when its agents commit willful and unlawful injuries (because they are then to be presumed to have acted outside their employment), and the agents cannot be sued either (because the fear of suits might prevent them from doing their duty).

In a significant turnabout in 1971, the Supreme Court ruled for the first time that federal officers, though acting pursuant to a claim of legal authority, may be sued for civil damages when it is alleged that they violated a citizen's constitutional right against unreasonable searches and seizures. In the particular case, the claim was made that agents of the Federal Bureau of Narcotics, without warrant or probable cause, entered a man's "apartment and arrested him for alleged narcotics violations. The agents manacled [the man] in front of his wife and children, and threatened to arrest the entire family. They searched the apartment from stem to stern." The Supreme Court reversed the lower court's decision that the man had no right to bring his suit.

The case is as important for the problems it raises as for its conclusion. For there is a good deal of merit in the old belief that officers of the Government may not act effectively if they fear the consequences, though the precise reach of the fear is scarcely quantifiable. In dissent, Justice Harry A. Blackmun expressed his feeling that the Supreme Court's decision "opens the door for another avalanche of new federal cases. Whenever a suspect imagines, or chooses to assert, that a Fourth Amendment right has been violated, he will now immediately sue the federal officer in federal court. This will tend to stultify proper law enforcement and make the day's labor for the honest and conscientious officer even more onerous and more critical."

This is the oft-heard cry that the creation of new rights will "open the floodgates." "It is worth noting," the majority said in answer to Justice Blackmun's complaint, "that a survey of comparable actions against state officers under [a federal statute] found only 53 reported cases in 17 years (1951–1967) that survived a motion to dismiss. Increasing this figure by 900% to allow for increases in rate and unreported cases, every federal district judge could expect to try one such case every 13 years."

In a separate dissent, Chief Justice Burger expressed the view that both methods of deterring unlawful police conduct—the judicial suit for money damages authorized by that day's decision and the so-called "exclusionary rule" were inadequate. The exclusionary rule says that evidence unconstitutionally gathered by Government officers must be excluded from the trial, even if it means that a clearly guilty defendant must go free. The doctrine has been severely criticized, the analysis usually beginning with the words of Justice Benjamin N. Cardozo (then the Chief Judge of the New York Court of Appeals): "The criminal is to go free because the constable blundered." Justice Cardozo's otherwise reasonable assumption becomes a subtle evasion of the truth when the Government's activity is more than mere "blundering." Constitutional restraints on Government agents become meaningless if they may be disregarded at the whim of the Government.

The Chief Justice proposed a third alternative: a federal statute that would waive sovereign immunity, that would permit suit against the Government rather than against the individuals breaking the law, that would provide an independent tribunal to hear claims under the statute, and that would abrogate the exclusionary rule. In effect, the Chief Justice would permit evidence unconstitutionally seized to be used but would also permit those injured by the unconstitutional conduct of federal officials to sue.

The Chief Justice did not make it clear in his dissent whether a person convicted in part on the strength of evidence unconstitutionally gathered would be considered to be "injured" for purposes of the remedy. If so, any person jailed or fined through the use of such evidence would be able to collect the entire amount of the fine and the reasonable value of the stay in prison. If he did not mean that, then the thrust of the Chief Justice's opinion must be that only those acquitted would be permitted to sue, a circumstance that could produce a number of undesirable results as well—for instance, an upsurge in unlawful Government acts. The net of it is that there is no perfect remedy, but the refusal even to permit courts to hear allegations of official misconduct must surely be too extreme.

A third broad doctrine that prevents courts from inquiring into official misconduct can be termed "unreviewability." This doctrine has it that many issues are simply not fit for judicial review, since the power to take action complained of is vested by Congress in the "discretion" of the miscreant.

A classic statement of this position was that given by then Circuit Judge Warren Burger in 1967, in a case concerning a prosecutor's unequal treatment of codefendants. Two men were charged with housebreaking and petty larceny. One of them was permitted to plead guilty to petty larceny and *attempted* housebreaking, both misdemeanors. But the United States Attorney refused to accept the same plea from the other defendant, forcing him to stand trial on the more serious charge. Following his conviction on that more serious charge, the defendant appealed on the ground that the disparity of treatment was unconstitutional. The Court of Appeals for the District of Columbia Circuit dismissed the appeal. "Few subjects," Judge Burger wrote, "are less adapted to judicial review than the exercise by the Executive of his discretion in deciding when and whether to institute criminal proceedings, or what precise charge shall be made, or whether to dismiss a proceeding once brought."

At the close of his discussion, Judge Burger made the following remarks:

It is assumed that the United States Attorney will perform his duty and exercise his powers consistent with his oaths; and while this discretion is subject to abuse or misuse just as is judicial discretion, deviations from his duty as an agent of the Executive are to be dealt with by his superior.

The remedy lies ultimately within the establishment where power and discretion reside. The President has abundant supervisory and disciplinary powers—including summary dismissal—to deal with misconduct of his subordinates; it is not the function of the judiciary to review the exercise of Executive discretion whether it be that of the President himself or those to whom he has delegated certain powers.

This bald statement should be rejected. The President of the United States will not likely dismiss summarily or take any other action against a United States Attorney in mundane circumstances such as these. The convenient description of acts not to be reviewed by the courts as "discretionary" begs the question.

Of course, Judge Burger may have been saying simply he saw no facts that would lead him to conclude that the United States Attorney did not have a good reason to do what he did. In other words, Judge Burger may have been trying to say that the defendant had the burden of proving that the unequal treatment was not well grounded. A concurring opinion in the case so suggested. Yet Judge Burger took exception to that line of reasoning. He noted that "the concurring opinion would reserve judicial power to review 'irrational' decisions of the prosecutor. We do our assigned task of appellate review best if we stay within our own limits, recognizing that we are neither omnipotent so as to have our mandates run without limit, nor omniscient so as to be able to direct all branches of government. The Constitution places on the Executive the duty to see that the 'laws are faithfully executed' and the responsibility must reside with that power."

Judge Burger seemed to have been saying that a court should never be permitted to review unequal treatment by a United States Attorney. This same conclusion would deny the unconstitutionality of a Governor's pardoning all white criminals and refusing to pardon all black criminals; but whether or not the power to pardon is "discretionary" should be irrelevant, given the context of the use of the pardon power.

We need articulated reasons, not statements that cut off discussion, whenever courts decline to pass judgment on executive action. No court would ever compel the President to select one person rather than another for a cabinet post; conversely, no court would decline to compel the President or other federal administrator to rehire a person discharged from federal employment solely on the basis of race or religion. Between those extremes of total discretion and nondiscretion lies a vast middle ground of executive power, the abuse of which courts ought to strive to remedy.

The power to investigate and prosecute has traditionally been held to be wholly discretionary. The Michigan Supreme Court once upheld the power of the state to prosecute one group for playing bingo (prohibited by the state lottery law), while refusing to prosecute many others: "A right to violate the law can never be conferred by laxity in its enforcement as to others. . . . If peace officers are derelict in their duties as herein charged, we cannot adjudge that complaint within the confines of the instant case."

Some courts, however, have begun to recognize that their duty extends beyond the traditional quick glance to see whether any obvious abuses of discretion are apparent. California law permits a deeper look at allegations of discriminatory law enforcement. In the case of the Pasadena gamblers discussed earlier * the courts permitted the defendants, each of whom conceded that he was gambling or present while the gambling occurred, to present evidence that the city ordinance was being enforced in a discriminatory manner. Among the evidence presented by the defendants was, as has been described, testimony showing that an Elks Club knowingly permitted gambling in a back room, to which the Chief of Police occasionally repaired. A retrial of the case resulted in a hung jury, and the trial judge, Donald R. Wright, since named Chief Justice of the California Supreme Court, dismissed the case.

It is not enough to annul the restrictive doctrines that have mired the courts in needless formalisms. Lawsuits cost money, and even if a potential litigant were free from the present doctrinal limitations on his ability to sue, the staggering costs of bringing the Government to heel might well—and often do—deter him.

One method of meeting the Government's large—though not limitless—pocketbook is the "class action," which enables a small number of people representative of a common class (such as taxpayers, consumers, and the like) to fund suits against the Government by subscription and other public donations. The objection to class actions, like the objection to any device that permits suits that were formerly prohibited, is that the Government may be stopped in its tracks.

The short answer must be that courts are adept at dismissing purely frivolous suits, and cases with legal merit should be permitted, no matter what the consequences, so long as we continue to profess our belief in the rule of law. William Goodrich, former General Counsel of the Food and Drug Administration, has said that "many of these suits make us carefully examine our policies in an effort to defend them; if we can't

---

* See p. 248 ff.

defend our policies, they ought to be changed." That notion is a sensible one, though it is still most often resisted by bureaucrats who find it intolerable that the public should express an interest in governmental functions and ask for explanations of those things that don't seem right.

Lawsuits ought to be one major way of challenging unlawful Government activity, since almost by definition the courts are the agencies through which law violations are determined. The constant threat of litigation ought to insure a greater willingness by the Government to abide by the law. In the long run, however, litigation may not prove to be the people's most enduring recourse against an unlawful Government. In a remarkable speech in 1971, the Chief Justice of the United States suggested that young lawyers and other zealots should not look to the courts for reform. Law must be changed by the legislature, he said.

No matter how disheartening his words may have been for idealists who believe the best way to reform is through the law, the Chief Justice ascribes a meaning to legal action different from that imputed to it by a more recent generation. Political protest and action, he seemed to be saying, is the only lasting way of achieving legal reform.

LESS BUREAUCRACY: CONSOLIDATION AND REPEAL

As has earlier been suggested, the Government violates legal strictures because there are too many laws and there is too much uncontrolled discretion. The answer for some kinds of official lawbreaking, therefore, must be that excessive laws should be repealed. In an important step in that direction in 1971 the Supreme Court by a narrow five to four vote overturned a loitering law as unconstitutional. A Cincinnati municipal ordinance prohibited people from loitering in public in an "annoying" manner. Since an arrest and prosecution "may entirely depend on whether or not the policeman is annoyed," Justice Potter Stewart wrote for the majority, this circumstance makes the law an "invitation to discriminatory enforcement." In February, 1972, the Supreme Court removed any lingering doubts about the constitutionality of loitering laws when it unanimously voided a Jacksonville, Florida, ordinance that prohibited "strolling around from place to place without lawful purpose or object."

The contraction of laws that tempt prosecutors and police—whether at the local or federal level—into corruption and lawbreaking can only have a salutary effect on society at large. The laws that should be repealed are those prohibiting nonviolent consensual conduct that by and large offends the esthetic sensibility of the citizenry. The inoperative personal belief syndrome must be understood and cured.

It is a fundamental fact that the existence of discretion in Government provides the Government with a cloak behind which it can engage in unlawful activities. Discretion is a self-executing multiplier of related, and eventually unrelated, actions not consonant with law. The existence of discretion permits wide-ranging excuses, rationalizations, loopholes, and avoidance.

To reduce lawbreaking, discretion, in the words of Kenneth Culp Davis, must be confined, structured, and checked. Methods must be found to narrow the bounds of the overample discretionary power that exists within federal and state governments today, to force administrators to regularize their discretion and to abide by their own regulations, and finally to promote the idea that reviewing courts can and should require administrators and their agents to justify their deeds.

One of the cheapest and most efficient means of checking discretion is the requirement that courts may easily impose upon administrators to state reasons for activities that have a discriminatory or other unfair appearance. In some cases this may mean nothing more than that the courts should require agencies that are now consistently breaking the law to state the reasons for their decisions.

If we cannot do away with administrative agencies and bureaucracy—and it seems that we cannot—we must bring them under control. The first steps have only recently been attempted. We must mount a massive inquest into the workings of our public bureaucracy, to substitute the realities of its operations for the shibboleths that we now take to be our understanding of the "system." We must fundamentally change the motivations of the bureaucracy. We must rethink our jurisprudence.

MORE BUREAUCRACY: THE OMBUDSMAN AND OTHERS

It is a curious fact that Americans speak in absolute terms about very relative things: the same person who deplores the federal regulatory bureaucracy and denounces it as dictatorial for its interference in his corporate life may be more willing to give high marks to draft boards and to disbelieve that any of their activities are unlawful or to disregard those unlawful acts as trivial or necessary. Too, reformers who clearly see the abject failure of the administrative process to achieve its ends and for whom existing agencies hold no enchantment very often propose new agencies as solutions. In *America, Inc.,* for example, Morton Mintz and Jerry S. Cohen catalogue a seemingly limitless tale of governmental malfeasance in regulatory corporate activities, only to propose in their final chapter a federal agency to charter and regulate corporations.

Americans have an inexhaustible ability to favor as a remedy the very evil they deplore.

But if it is a paradox, this American predilection for opposites may be a necessary one. Three proposals are, therefore, put forward. First, administrators should be required to develop and make public rules that state their understanding of the statutes under which they operate. Many agencies have rules that they now keep secret; many agencies float in a void, picking and choosing conduct to prosecute as the broad and vague categories of their organic statutes permit. The resulting proliferation of rules would permit the courts to hold an administrator to his own rules and regulations, would greatly reduce discriminatory enforcement because of the very openness of the rules, and would more likely than not act as a self-operating brake upon Government lawlessness, reducing rather than increasing the necessity for citizens to go to court.

Second, there is a philosophy that a corporation or a public agency—"the system"—does things wrong, but its managers are innocent. Thus, almost never are corporate managers convicted, fined, or jailed for activity that is not only morally condemned but violates public law. But *people* are responsible for the shortcomings of their "systems," and certain types of "bad management" ought to be a criminal concept. President Nixon announced that any of his officials ordering more than "minimal" busing in connection with school integration would be fired. If he thinks that he can enforce that philosophy, a "bad management" philosophy and an accompanying edict against real lawbreakers is eminently in order.

Third, a great deal of administrative sloppiness, laziness, and fear that results eventually in lawbreaking occurs in the absence of any efficient administrative checks on executive power. William Rehnquist's belief in the "self-discipline of the Executive branch" is absurd. It is a frustrating fact that all too often administrative investigation and audits that are designed to detect and uncover questionable and unlawful behavior are conducted by the very agencies accused of that behavior.

Rarely, if ever, do executive departments permit truly independent investigations by their own personnel; the fates of Ernest Fitzgerald and John McGee are suggestive of the cover-up mentality that necessarily exists in the absence of an independent investigative agency. So thoroughly frightened are the heads of agencies that the detective work of their underlings might produce damaging information that in one celebrated case—the Army's investigation into the activities of Brigadier General Earl F. Cole in connection with the PX scandal—the Provost Marshall of the Army, Brigadier General Harley L. Moore, was required to obtain explicit permission from General William Westmoreland, Army Chief of Staff, before he could follow "investigative leads in the

United States." Some independent check is required within the bureaucracy itself.

One possible solution, rapidly coming into the public consciousness, is the "ombudsman," a public official who investigates citizen complaints but who is not subject to direct supervision by other administrative officials. Of course, the solution is far from perfect, since any new agency under an ombudsman—or what might be a more descriptive title, the Inspector General of the United States—charged with investigating all suspect governmental activity at the behest of complaining citizens would be a bureaucracy as wonderfully large and complex as the Government itself. The ombudsman or Inspector General should not be empowered to make arrests or to prosecute; his entire function should be to investigate and bring to public and the Government's attention unlawful or oppressive Government actions. His subpoena power, however, should be nearly coextensive—if not fully coextensive—with the population of the United States.

An ombudsman-like agency now exists—the General Accounting Office, headed by the Comptroller General of the United States. This is not an executive agency but is, instead, a creature of Congress and legally accountable only to Congress. The success of the GAO in recent years in uncovering at congressional request many examples of governmental fiscal irregularity is suggestive of the possibilities if the American people had a full-time independent investigator to probe beneath the surface of officialdom.*

In the short run, it would be helpful to establish three national commissions. The task of the first would be to uncover the extent of official lawlessness, from the President of the United States down to the Fulton County (Illinois) prosecutor—with amnesty for all, of course. The task of the second would be to put into perspective a related evil —official corruption. We need a much greater historical perspective than we now have. What has been the variable content of corruption since before the birth of the nation? How do practices and conditions that once seemed unexceptionable come to be reviled as corrupt? Third, we need a commission to attempt some understanding of the extent and nature of Governmental discretion and how the exercise of that discretion is affected by the competence or incompetence we have come to expect at various levels of the bureaucracy and judiciary.

---

* The GAO occasionally succumbs to industry blandishments. For example, the Defense Industry Advisory Committee (with the exception of the Secretary of Defense, composed entirely of corporation heads) pressured the GAO in 1971 to temper a report showing that in 146 defense contracts examined, the average profit to private industry was 56 percent (based on equity in the contract). The Advisory Committee supplied new statistics and induced the GAO to rewrite the report to reflect profits of "only" 21 percent.

These commissions could be public, but one may legitimately doubt the perspicacity of one who studies himself. A private group would obviously be more limited in its ability to uncover information, but an honest inquiry even by the normally conservative and cautious American Bar Association, such as the one it conducted during the early thirties into police lawlessness, would be highly revealing and in all probability productive of popular indignation that might well, in the present climate, spur needed reform.

Government lawlessness is not the sum of official injustice. To conclude that the Government on many occasions follows the law does not necessarily indicate a benevolent or humane society. Laws can be rigged; indeed, they often are—by those with access to the lawmaking institutions. Traditionally, for example, landlords have had far more legal power over tenants than tenants over landlords. Rent strikes are quite typically unlawful, though judicially sanctioned evictions are entirely proper, no matter how unconscionable landlords' policies have been. The even-handed administration of inherently oppressive laws may be in a formal sense "legal," but unjust laws are no less divisive than unjust application of the laws.

But if Governmental law-breaking is not the sum of official injustice, it is responsible for creating a climate in which the ideal of justice under law has been greeted with derisive laughter and in which the hope of peaceful settlement of grievances has turned to despair. "Law" has come into disrepute not merely because there are bad laws but also and more importantly because the Government has failed to abide by and enforce a very large number of good laws. The statute books are filled with laws that speak of impartiality and justice; the Constitution is a powerful (written) weapon against lesser laws that do not. But laws require a Government to operate them.

To those, like Chief Justice Burger, who abhor turning every cause into a legal issue and every legal issue into a constitutional question, there is one answer: change "the system" where it operates. The Chief Justice recognizes the need for change and advocates it, in principle, through Congress and the state legislatures.

Unthinking proponents of the theory that the Government can do no wrong—in certain areas, at least, like criminal investigations and prosecutions, foreign policy, civil rights and liberties—ought to take heed. Even the Chief Justice will not be able to withstand the onslaught of the reformers' fury if change is not permitted to work its wonders through Congress and the Executive.

Let the Government obey the law, and reform will be more orderly and less costly. Let the Government continue in its lawless ways and there will be bloodshed. I do not deny that ours is a particularly stubborn, confident, or cocky society with an astonishingly renewable capacity for corruption, nor that ordinary citizens commit with depressing regularity the most heinous crimes. But it is no less true that these same citizens, elevated to offices of public trust, do not change their personal quirks overnight.

Without Governmental willingness to abide by the law there can be no justice. Without justice there can be no peace. Think on it.

Appendix: The Comptroller General Responds

A DRAFT OF pages 160 through 166 in substantially the form printed was submitted to the Comptroller General of the United States for reply to the allegation that regular military officers have been and are holding "civil office" in violation of the *United States Code*. His response is printed verbatim (except for the omission of the list of names on page 160-1).

COMPTROLLER GENERAL OF THE UNITED STATES
WASHINGTON, D.C. 20548

B-174218

Nov. 26, 1971

Dear Mr. Chairman:

Further reference is made to your letter dated September 27, 1971, in which you request our comments on an enclosed copy of a draft of ,chapter 4, from a book by Mr. Jethro K. Lieberman, which refers to decisions of this Office concerning regular officers of the armed forces holding civil offices. You specifically request our opinion as to whether nine officers listed in Mr. Lieberman's book have violated or are violating the law by holding civil offices. You also requested as extensive a list as possible of military men holding statutory civil offices.

The point of chapter 4, entitled "Crimes Affecting Everyone," seems to be that the provisions of section 973(b) of title 10, United States Code, are being violated in that certain officers of the regular components of the armed forces are holding what Mr. Lieberman considers to be civil offices.

The current United States Government Organization Manual (1971/ 72), pages 119-121, indicates that the position of Deputy Assistant Secretary (Inspection Services) has been eliminated. The position of Deputy Assistant Secretary, Environmental Quality, has been established with Colonel Maurice G. Patton, USA, acting, in that position. In addition it appears that Lieutenant General Robert C. Taber, USA, is now Principal Deputy Assistant Secretary, Manpower and Reserve Affairs, replacing Vice Admiral W. P. Mack, USN. Also, Major General George M. Seignious, II, USA, apparently replaced Lieutenant General Robert H. Warren, USAF, as Deputy Assistant Secretary, Military Assistance and Sales.

On similar grounds Mr. Lieberman also questions the propriety of Vice Admiral John M. Lee, USN, holding the position of Assistant Director, Weapons Evaluation and Control Bureau, United States Arms Control and Disarmament Agency.

Section 973(b) of title 10, United States Code, provides as follows:

> "(b) Except as otherwise provided by law, no officer on the active list of the Regular Army, Regular Navy, Regular Air Force, Regular Marine Corps, or Regular Coast Guard may hold a civil office by election or appointment, whether under the United States, a Territory or possession, or a State. The acceptance of such a civil office or the exercise of its functions by such an officer terminates his military appointment."

Section 973(b) was derived from the act of July 15, 1870, ch. 294, section 18, 16 Stat. 319, section 1222, Revised Statutes, which as originally enacted applied only to officers "of the Army on the active list." It was recodified and extended to include regular officers on the active lists of the Army, Navy, Air Force, Marine Corps and Coast Guard by the act of January 2, 1968, Pub. L. 90-235, section 4(a)(5)(A), 81 Stat. 759, 10 U.S.C. 973(b).

The questions presented as to the officers which Mr. Lieberman lists appear to be: Are the positions which they occupy "civil offices" within the meaning of 10 U.S.C. 973(b), and, if so, is there "otherwise provided by law" authority for them to hold such offices so as to prevent the termination of their commissions?

As Mr. Lieberman indicates, the term "civil office" as used in section 973(b) has not been statutorily defined. In our decision 29 Comp. Gen. 363 (1950), copy enclosed, to which Mr. Lieberman refers, we considered the question as to whether a Regular Army officer vacated his commission by accepting appointment by the Secretary of the Interior to the position of Commissioner of Roads for Alaska, a position which was administratively created by the Secretary.

In that decision we concluded after a lengthy discussion of our previous decisions on the subject as well as decisions of the Comptroller of the Treasury, the Attorney General, the courts and other authorities, that the term "civil office," as distinguished from "military office," is synonymous with "public office" and is usually defined in much the same terms. Also, in that decision we quoted judicial decisions to the effect that the chief elements of a "public office" are: the specific position must be created by law; there must be certain definite duties imposed by law

on the incumbent, and they must involve the exercise of some portion
of the sovereign power. Since the position in question in that decision
did not meet these criteria, we concluded that it was not a civil office
which would cause the Army officer's acceptance of it to vacate his
Army commission.

In our decision 44 Comp. Gen. 830 (1965), copy enclosed, to which
Mr. Lieberman also refers, we considered the question of whether a
Regular Army officer accepted a "civil office" so as to terminate his appointment in the Army by accepting a temporary appointment as a
special policeman in the Library of Congress while participating in an
excess leave program attending law school. In that decision we held that
since the positions of special police appointed by the Librarian of Congress were created by a statute which defines their duties and that such
police exercise some of the powers of the sovereign, the acceptance of
such a position was the acceptance of a civil office.

It was also held in that decision that the fact that the officer was on
excess leave at the time he accepted the office provided no basis for
viewing his acceptance as not terminating his appointment as a Regular Army Officer since, quoting from 25 Comp. Gen. 377, 381 (1945),
"The statute makes two positions incompatible as a matter of law,
without qualification and without regard to any showing of compatibility
in fact by reason of leave of absence, or otherwise, with respect to a
particular officer and a particular position."

Also, in the 1965 decision we cited 29 Comp. Gen. 363, *supra,* to the
effect that whether a particular position is a "civil office" is not determined solely by the level of importance of the duties of the Office. In
this connection the case of *Martin* v. *Smith,* 1 N.W. 2d 163 (1941), was
cited wherein the court concluded that the President of the University
of Wisconsin who was elected by the Board of Regents of the University and subordinate to them did not hold a public office while a
justice of the peace or a notary public is a public officer.

Title II of the National Security Act of 1947, 61 Stat. 499, created
the National Military Establishment with a Secretary of Defense as its
head. Included in the National Military Establishment were the Departments of the Army, Navy, and Air Force and all other agencies created by
title II. Section 4 of the National Security Act Amendments of 1949, 63
Stat. 579, converted the National Military Establishment into the Department of Defense as an executive department of the Government with the
Departments of the Army, Navy, and Air Force as military departments
within the Department of Defense. Similar provisions of law are now
codified in 10 U.S.C. 101(5), (6), (7) and 131. The character of the
Department of Defense as a military establishment remains unchanged.

Under such statutory provisions, it is our opinion that offices and
positions in the Department of Defense must be viewed as essentially
military offices and positions and not public offices of a civil nature. In
this regard, while requiring that the Secretary of Defense and three
special assistants to advise and assist him be appointed from civilian
life, the law specifically provides that officers of the armed services could

be detailed for duty as assistants and personal aides to the Secretary of Defense. Any officer so detailed continued to serve in his respective military service and capacity.

The mentioned provisions of title II of the National Security Act are now codified in title 10 of the United States Code and as codified provide for a Secretary of Defense (section 134), eight Assistant Secretaries of Defense and a Deputy Assistant Secretary of Defense for Reserve Affairs (section 136) to be appointed from civilian life. None of these secretarial positions is occupied by a military officer and we are not aware of any military officer serving in any other position in the Department of Defense which is required by law to be filled from civilian life.

As provided in the 1947 statute, section 718 of title 10 of the United States Code authorizes the detail of officers of the armed forces for duty as assistants or personal aids to the Secretary of Defense. In view of that specific authority and considering that the Department of Defense is a military as distinguished from a civilian establishment, there would appear to be no sound basis for viewing the officers listed by Mr. Lieberman as subject to the provisions of 10 U.S.C. 973(b) by virtue of their Department of Defense assignments. With the exception of those offices created by statute and required by law to be filled from civilian life, a similar conclusion is required with respect to any other office in the Department of Defense.

The Arms Control and Disarmament Act, approved September 26, 1961, Pub. L. 87-297, 75 Stat. 631, as amended (22 U.S.C. 2551, *et seq.*) established the United States Arms Control and Disarmament Agency with a Director as its head who, under the direction of the Secretary of State, has primary responsibility within the Government for arms control and disarmament matters. There is also provided a Deputy Director who, under certain circumstances, may exercise the powers of the Director.

Title II, section 24 of the act (22 U.S.C. 2564) as amended by section 305 of the Federal Executives Salary Act of 1964, approved August 14, 1964, Pub. L. 88-426, 78 Stat. 424, provides for Assistant Directors of the Agency as follows:

"Not to exceed four Assistant Directors may be appointed by the President, by and with the advice and consent of the Senate. They shall perform such duties and exercise such powers as the Director may prescribe."

In addition, title IV, section 41 of the act (22 U.S.C. 2581) provides in pertinent part that:

"In the performance of his functions, the Director is authorized to—

"g) delegate, as appropriate to the Deputy Director or other officers of the Agency, any authority conferred upon the Director by the provisions of this Act; * * *."

Section 303(c)(75) of the Federal Executives Salary Act of 1964 (5 U.S.C. 5316(75)) establishes the compensation of such Assistant Directors at Level V of the Federal Executive Salary Schedule.

Accordingly, it appears that the position of Assistant Director of the United States Arms Control and Disarmament Agency is a civil office within the meaning of 10 U.S.C. 973(b), in that it is specifically created by law and has or may have definite duties imposed upon it which involve exercising a portion of the sovereign power. See 29 Comp. Gen. 363 (1950) *supra,* and 44 Comp. Gen. 830 (1965) *supra.*

The annual reports of the Arms Control and Disarmament Agency show that during most of that agency's approximately ten years of existence, the position of Assistant Director, Weapons Evaluation and Control Bureau, has been filled by a military officer. The present incumbent, Vice Admiral John M. Lee, USN, was appointed by the President and confirmed as Assistant Director by the Senate on April 6, 1970.

The Arms Control and Disarmament Act, *supra,* and its legislative history indicate that one of the purposes for the creation of the Arms Control and Disarmament Agency was to create an agency with the "capacity to provide the essential scientific, economic, political, military, psychological, and technological information upon which realistic arms control and disarmament policy must be based." See section 2 of the act (22 U.S.C. 2551). To enable the agency to obtain the varied resources and personnel necessary to its functioning, various provisions were made in the act to allow the agency to obtain personnel from other Government agencies. In this regard section 41(c) (22 U.S.C. 2581(c)) of the act provides that in the performance of his functions the Director is authorized to—

> "(c) enter into agreements with other Government agencies, *including the military departments through the Secretary of Defense,* under which officers or employees of such agencies may be detailed to the Agency for the purpose of service pursuant to this Act *without prejudice to the status* or advancement of such officers or employees within their own agencies." (Underscoring supplied.)

Such provisions expressly provide for the detailing of a regular military officer to the Arms Control and Disarmament Agency for service pursuant to the Arms Control and Disarmament Act and we do not believe that the fact that the position in which Admiral Lee is serving is a public office to which members are required to be appointed by the President with the advice and consent of the Senate removes it from the scope of section 41(c). In our opinion, section 41(c) clearly constitutes an exception to 10 U.S.C. 973(b) so as to prevent the termination of the military commissions of officers detailed pursuant to its provisions. Accordingly, it appears that Vice Admiral Lee's commission and the commissions of the other officers who previously held the position of Assistant Director, did not terminate upon their acceptance of that position.

Information relative to your request for a list of military officers holding statutory civil offices is being developed and will be forwarded to you when it is received. Since it may take some time to obtain that information, it appeared that your question regarding the officers listed in Mr. Lieberman's book should be answered prior to the submission of that information.

We hope this, together with the data to be submitted later, will serve the purpose of your inquiry.

Sincerely yours,

(Signed)   ELMER B. STAATS
Comptroller General
of the United States

Enclosures

The Honorable William Proxmire
Chairman, Joint Economic Committee
United States Senate

The curious aspect of this citation-studded opinion is that the two critical conclusions are supported by nothing other than personal opinions devoid of any legal authority logically supporting them. After reciting past opinions for four pages, the Comptroller General glibly asserts that military officers may be detailed as assistants (in the sense of personal aides) to the Secretary of Defense and the military Secretaries and that positions within the Department of Defense are military rather than civil. Therefore, he says, regular military officers may hold the positions of Deputy Assistant Secretary.

But the detailing of an officer to serve in an office is not the same as appointing him to a position. A personal aide or an assistant at some low level is scarcely the same as a Deputy Assistant Secretary. Moreover, the Comptroller General cites no authority whatsoever for the astonishing proposition that "civil" is now to be interpreted in the sense of "civilian"; he makes up the argument on the spot. And he ignores an opinion of the Attorney General dating back to 1873 that General William T. Sherman would forfeit his commission if he performed "the duties of the Secretary of War during the temporary absence of that officer." The office of Secretary of War, the Attorney General ruled, was civil, not military, in nature.

The argument on behalf of Vice Admiral Lee is even sillier. The Comptroller General concedes that the position of Assistant Director of the U.S. Arms Control and Disarmament Agency is a civil office. He then cites a law permitting the Director to enter into "agreements" with departments, including the military departments, under which officers may be "detailed" to the agency. From this law he reasons that Admiral Lee has been so detailed.

But Admiral Lee was not "detailed" pursuant to an "agreement." He was appointed by the President of the United States and confirmed by the Senate. Nobody can enter into an "agreement" with the President of the United States and the United States Senate that a particular officer will be appointed to a public office, nor could a public law be so interpreted. The conclusion that the "agreement" provision is an explicit exception to Section 973(b) is wholly without merit.

The opinion does represent the honest effort of a clever staff lawyer to construct some chain of reasoning leading to a conclusion consonant with the preordained position of his boss. In that sense, the opinion is a model of the genre.

Notes and References

$\mathcal{N}$otes and References

ALTHOUGH MUCH HAS been said about individual aspects of Government lawbreaking, little has been written about the whole of it. What follows is a brief list of books dealing with significant parts. Theodore L. Becker and Vernon G. Murray, eds., *Government Lawlessness in America* (New York: Oxford University Press, 1971), is a collection of articles, arranged according to the governmental unit breaking the law—*viz.*, the police, the military, prison officials, judges, bureaucrats, and elected local officials. Robert K. Murray, *Red Scare* (New York: McGraw-Hill, 1964), is a vivid description of federal lawlessness during a period of national hysteria. Zechariah Chafee's *Free Speech in the United States* (Cambridge: Harvard University Press, 1941), a brilliant exploration of governmental infringements of the First Amendment, has been reissued in paperback (New York: Atheneum, 1969). Leon Friedman, ed., *Southern Justice* (Cleveland: Meridian Books, 1967), and James W. Silver, *Mississippi: The Closed Society* (New York: Harcourt Brace Jovanovich, 1964), contain corruscating descriptions of the subtle and not so subtle processes of evading civil rights laws. Kenneth Culp Davis, *Discretionary Justice* (Urbana: University of Illinois Press, 1971), and Theodore J. Lowi, *The End of Liberalism* (New York: W. W. Norton, 1969), are essential on the problem of discretion in a government of supposed checks and balances. Police lawlessness is ably chronicled in Paul Chevigny, *Police Power* (New York: Vintage, 1969), and in the spate of presidential commission reports and in the reports of their various task forces. Also valuable for historical data are the *Wickersham Reports* of the early thirties, reprinted in a multivolume series (Montclair, New Jersey: Patterson Smith, 1968). Richard A. Falk, Gabriel Kolko, and Robert Jay Lifton, editors of *Crimes of War* (New York: Vintage, 1971), have put together an astonishing array of documents and articles concerning this rapidly expanding and difficult problem.

The notes that follow collect a number of other books and articles on one or more aspects of the problem of Government lawbreaking, but only as they relate to the discussion in the text. They are not meant to be exhaustive.

9 Gallup Poll: Albert H. Cantril and Charles W. Roll, Jr., *Hopes and Fears of the American People* (New York: Universe Books, 1971), p. 51.

17 Thurmond, *Washington Post,* August 11, 1970, p. A1.

18–19 Eisenhower: *Public Papers of the Presidents of the United States,* 1954 (news conference of May 19, 1954), p. 491.

19 Eisenhower footnote: *Id.* at p. 700 (news conference of August 11, 1954). Nixon: *Id.* (1969), p. 1010 (news conference of December 8, 1969).

20 LaPalombara: Address to Yale Club of Washington, February 19, 1971, Washington, D.C.

24 Less conservative advocates: Howard Zinn, *Disobedience and Democracy* (New York: Vintage Books, 1968), p.8.

25 Law student book review: Bob Hernandez, " 'Law Against the People': Radicals Within the System?" *Harvard Law Record,* December 10, 1971, p. 16.

26 Selective conscientious objection: *Gillette v. United States,* 401 U.S. 437 (1971).

27 The desegregation decision is, of course, *Brown v. Board of Education,* 347 U.S. 483 (1954).

29 The code provision is Section 1505 of Title 18 of the United States Code (hereafter code sections are cited as follows: 18 U.S.C. §1505).

29ff. The hearings at which Fitzgerald testified are published in Hearings Before the Joint Economics Committee (November 1968–December 1969); excerpts are reprinted in Theodore L. Becker and Vernon G. Murray, eds., *Government Lawlessness in America* (New York: Oxford University Press, 1971) pp. 249–65. The affair is discussed in William Proxmire, *Report from Wasteland* (New York: Praeger, 1970), Ch. 2. The Fitzgerald affair is also discussed and materials are collected in the *Congressional Record,* vol. 115, pp. 4524–25 (May 5, 1969); pp. 9164–66 (August 5, 1969); pp. 11938–40 (November 24, 1969).

30–1 The Lang memorandum is reprinted in Becker and Murray, *op. cit.,* pp. 262–63.

33 Fitzgerald's appeal: *Washington Post,* December 2, 1971, p. K2.

33–4 The Nixon speech is published in the *Congressional Record,* vol. 97, pp. 4393–94 (April 26, 1951).

35 First Walker case reversal: *People v. Walker,* 14 N.Y. 2d 901, 252 N.Y.S. 2d 96, 200 N.E. 2d 779 (1964); second Walker case reversal: *People v. Walker,* 50 Misc. 2d 751, 271 N.Y.S. 2d 447, 448 (App. Div. 1966). The case is noted in 78 *Harvard Law Review* 884 (1965).

35ff. The discussion of the *Miller* case is taken from a variety of materials, including the published opinions, the trial transcript, the parties' briefs, and letters from individual counsel in the case. The principal cases are five: (1) the Illinois Supreme Court's affirmance of the conviction: 13 Ill. 2d 84, 148 N.E. 2d 455 (1958); (2) the U.S. Court of Appeals' decision affirming the conviction: 300 F.2d 414 (7th Cir. 1962); (3) the second federal district court's granting of habeas corpus: 226 F. Supp. 541 (N.D. Ill. 1963); (4) the U.S. Court of Appeals' reversal of the preceding decision, reinstating the conviction: 342 F.2d 646 (7th Cir. 1965); and (5) the Supreme Court's ultimate reversal on constitutional grounds: *Miller v. Pate,* 386 U.S. 1 (1967).

37 The quotation from the state Supreme Court: 148 N.E.2d at p. 463; the quotation from the Court of Appeals for the Seventh Circuit: 300 F.2d at p. 418.

40 Quotations from state Supreme Court: 148 N.E.2d at pp. 466, 467, 469.

41 The outcome of the Malmgren contempt citation: letter of June 25, 1971, from Malmgren to the author.

41–2 Quotation from state Supreme Court: 148 N.E.2d at p. 469.

42 Second try in Illinois Supreme Court: *Miller v. People,* 23 Ill. 2d 420, 178 N.E.2d 355 (1961).

42–3 Quotations from federal district court: 226 F.Supp. at p. 545.

43 Rosenfield's interest: according to *Variety,* February 22, 1967, p. 38.

43–4 Seventh Circuit's explanation for hair in vagina: 342 F.2d at pp. 651–52.

44 For response to Seventh Circuit's suggestion, see Brief of Radio Station WAIT and the Illinois Division, ACLU, as Amici Curiae, *Miller v. Pate,* p. 7.

44–5 References establishing various contradictions and latter exculpatory evidence are given in Brief of Radio Station WAIT, *op. cit.,* pp. 8–11.

45–6 Chemist's testimony quoted in 386 U.S. at p. 4.

46 Prosecutor's remarks quoted in *ibid.*

46 Illinois Supreme Court's remarks concerning the "bloody shorts": 148 N.E.2d at pp. 458 and 467; state's contention at federal hearing quoted in 386 U.S. at p. 6, fn. 13.

46–7 Supreme Court's statement concerning probative value of shorts: 386 U.S. at p. 6.

47 Friedman's remarks: Quoted in Motion and Brief of Radio Station WAIT and the Illinois Division, ACLU, as Amici Curiae, *Miller v. Pate,* No. 1780 Misc. U.S. Supreme Court October Term 1967, pp. 5–6. Malmgren's opponent's platform: William Malmgren letter to author, *op. cit.* Seventh Circuit's ringing declaration: *United States ex rel. Miller v. Pate,* 429 F.2d 1001, 1002 (7th Cir. 1970).

48 Exoneration: see *Illinois Bar News,* June 1968, pp. 6–7. Avoid the eye of the camera; Motion and Brief, *op. cit.,* p. 5.

48ff. *The Mooney Case* (Stanford: Stanford University Press, 1968); Zechariah Chafee, Jr., Walter H. Pollak, Carl S. Stern, *The*

Mooney-Billings Report, submitted to the National Commission on Law Observance and Enforcement, June 1931, reprinted as Vol. 15 of the *Wickersham Reports* (Montclair, N.J.: Patterson Smith, 1968).

53   Supreme Court quoted: *Mooney v. Holohan,* 294 U.S. 103, 112 (1935).

53–4   Alcorta case: *Alcorta v. Texas,* 355 U.S. 28 (1957).

54   Texas' Outstanding Prosecutor: *Time* magazine, March 31, 1967, p. 73.

54–5   Jackson case: *United States ex rel. Jackson v. Rundle,* 219 F. Supp. 538 (E.D. Pa. 1963).

55–6   Powell case: *Powell v. Wiman,* 287 F. 2d 275 (5th Cir. 1961).

56   Race of defendants and victims: Letter of May 18, 1971, from R. Clifford Fulford, attorney for William K. Powell, to author.

57   Quotation of Chief Judge Thomsen: *Smallwood v. Warden, Maryland Penitentiary,* 205 F. Supp. 325, 330 (D. Md. 1962). Ample grounds to support doubt: For other cases holding government willfully violated defendants' rights, see: *Turner v. Ward,* 321 F. 2d 918 (10th Cir. 1963) (failure to disclose nature of sexual assault); *Ashley v. Texas,* 319 F.2d 80 (5th Cir. 1963) (failure to disclose mental incompetence of defendants); *Application of Kapatos,* 208 F. Supp. 883 (S.D.N.Y. 1962) (suppression of exculpatory evidence); *Curran v. Delaware,* 259 F.2d 707 (3d Cir. 1958) (perjury by police detective); *United States ex rel. Meers v. Wilkins,* 326 F.2d 135 (2d Cir. 1965) (failure to call material witnesses unknown to defendants); *Barbee v. Warden, Maryland Penitentiary,* 331 F.2d 842 (4th Cir. 1964) (suppression of police report).

57–9   Walsh incident: *United States v. Keith,* Criminal No. 1411–69, trial transcript, pp. 33–38.

60–1   Minor derelictions: Examples and quotations are from Harvey Katz, "Some Call It Justice," *The Washingtonian,* September, 1970, p. 46.

61   Embrey's removal from criminal court: *Washington Post,* December 30, 1971, p. A1.

62   *Jenkins v. United States,* 307 F.2d 637 (D.C. Cir. 1962).

63–5   Facts and transcript from: *United States v. McNeil* (D.C. Cir. No. 24,263, August 28, 1970.

66   Quotations concerning Judge Curran: Chief Judge David L. Bazelon, concurring in *McNeil,* pp. 15–16. Footnote: Information from Mrs. Barbara Allen Bowman, Director, Public Defender Service for the District of Columbia, letter of October 5, 1971, to the author.

66–70   Lenske case: *Lenske v. United States,* 383 F.2d 20 (9th Cir. 1967).

70   Bazelon quotation: *Scott v. United States* (D.C. Cir. No. 20,954, February 13, 1969), footnote 2. See also, Sandor Frankel, "The Sentencing Morass," 3 *Criminal Law Bulletin* 365 (1967). The discussion on pp. 70–72 is based on the decision in *Scott.*

72   On remand: I am indebted to the prosecutor for the details of the resentencing.

72   Plea bargaining: See D. J. Newman, *Conviction: The Determination of Guilt or Innocence Without Trial* (Boston: Little Brown, 1966).

73   Yankee Independence; quotations: Stephen R. Bing and S. Stephen Rosenfeld, *The Quality of Justice in the Lower Criminal Courts of Metropolitan Boston* (Boston: Lawyer's Committee for Civil Rights Under Law, 1970), pp. 83, 87, 91.

74   Rolph quoted in Richard H. Frost, *The Mooney Case* (Stanford: Stanford University Press, 1968), p. 469; as quoted in *San Francisco Chronicle,* November 28, 1933. Vigilante Movements: See Richard Hofstadter and Michael Wallace, *American Violence* (N.Y.: Alfred A. Knopf, 1970).

75   Comment on Internal Security Act: Leonard B. Boudin, "How Just Was Ramsey Clark?" *New York Review of Books,* January 28, 1971, p. 41.

76-7   Chicago raid on Black Panthers: See Lillian S. Calhoun, "The Death of Fred Hampton." 2 *Chicago Journalism Review* 13 (December 1969); reprinted in Becker and Murray, *op cit.,* pp. 34–47. Independent Commission: *New York Times,* March 17, 1972, p. 17.

78   Leary's statement: *New York Times,* September 6, 1968, p. 49.

78-9   Walker Report quotations: *Rights in Conflict* (N.Y.: Bantam Books, 1968), p. 10.

79-81 Disorderly house: The discussion is based on information in letter of June 9 from Dr. Lykken to the author; his article in *Pro/Con Magazine* of April 1971, p. 5; and the opinion of Judge Leslie in *Minnesota v. Lykken,* Case Nos. 423325–42344 (Municipal Court, First Division, Minneapolis, 1970); *Minneapolis Tribune,* May 11, 1970, p. 22; May 12, p. 20; *Minneapolis Star,* May 11, 1970, p. 9A.

81   "Normal . . . arrest": *Minneapolis Star,* May 13, 1970, p. 7A.

82   Telluride: *New York Times,* May 20, 1971, p. 20.

82-3   The cases: *New York v. Kane and De Leon;* in Alabama, there were 182 separate cases. Information from letters of Tom Rubillo, ACLU Department of Information, to author, January 27, 1972.

83   Metzger case: Nicholas Pileggi, "From D.A. to Dope Lawyer," *New York Times Magazine,* May 6, 1971, p. 34.

84   Justice Department spokesman: *New York Times,* May 6, 1971, p. 21. Judge Boldt: *Washington Post,* December 29, 1970, p. A15.

84-5   The Judge Rea story based on information supplied by defense counsel.

85   *Olmstead v. United States,* 277 U.S. 438 (1928). Justice Brandeis' dissent is at p. 471.

86   Federal Communications Act: 47 U.S.C. § 151 *et seq.* Act covers Government: *Nardone v. United States,* 302 U.S. 379 (1937). Directive to Murphy and Clark's memoranda: from letter of Deputy Attorney General Richard G. Kleindienst, *Washington Post,* February 24, 1971.

86-7   Clark's distinction: Ramsey Clark, *Crime in America* (New York: Pocket Books, 1971), pp. 274–76.

87–8   *Coplon v. United States,* 191 F.2d 749 (D.C. Cir. 1951); 185 F.2d 629 (2d Cir. 1950). See also *New York Times,* November 22, 1953, p. 26.

88   Unlawful state evidence in state trials: *Schwartz v. Texas,* 344 U.S. 199 (1952); unlawful state evidence in federal trial: *Benanti v. United States,* 355 U.S. 96 (1957). *Olmstead* overruled: *Katz v. United States,* 389 U.S. 347 (1967). *Schwartz* overruled: *Lee v. Florida,* 392 U.S. 378 (1968). Another 1967 case: *Berger v. New York,* 388 U.S. 41 (1967).

89   Number of prosecutions: *Alderman v. United States, Ivanov v. United States, Butenko v. United States,* 394 U.S. 165 (1969).

90   Graham: *New York Times,* March 13, 1969, p. 1.

91   Decision shortly thereafter: *Taglianetti v. United States,* 394 U.S. 316 (1969); see also *Giordano v. United States,* 394 U.S. 310 (1968). Hoover testimony: *New York Times,* May 2, 1971, p. 1; May 5, p. 33. Griswold shifted argument: *New York Times,* May 9, 1971. Footnote statistics: Tom Wicker, "A Gross Invasion," *New York Times,* December 19, 1971, p. E11.

92   Post Office: See Omar Garrison, *Spy Government* (N.Y.: Lyle Stuart, 1969), Chap. 5; reprinted in Becker and Murray, *op. cit.,* p. 215ff. Footnote: improperly authorized wiretaps: *Washington Post,* March 21, 1972, p. A6.

93   Resor: *New York Times,* February 18, 1971, Rehnquist: *New York Times,* March 10, 1971, p. 1.

95   Prize essay: Captain Robert J. Hanks, "Against All Enemies," *Naval Institute Proceedings,* vol. 96, March, 1970, pp. 23–29.

99   Albright: "Military Justice," Joint Hearings Before the Subcommittee on Constitutional Rights of the Senate Judiciary Committee and Special Subcommittee of the Committee on Armed Services, Part I, 89th Congress, 2d Session, March 3, 1966, pp. 403–23.

100   Moorer letter: Personal letter to author, of May 28, 1970.

101–2   Seizure of mail: *New York Times,* March 31, 1971, p. 5.

102   Hershey quoted: *New York Times,* November 8, 1967, p. 10.

103   Selective Service pamphlet: *Legal Aspects of Selective Service,* Selective Service System, 1969, p. 3. Hershey: *New York Times,* November 8, 1967, p. 18.

103–4   Lawlessness of draft boards: Marvin M. Karpatkin, "New Weapons to Challenge the Rulings of the Local Board," *New York Times,* October 31, 1971, p. E11.

105–6   1914 case: *Weeks v. United States,* 232 U.S. 383, 393–4 (1914).

106   *Wolf* case: *Wolf v. Colorado,* 338 U.S. 25 (1949).

107   *Mapp v. Ohio,* 367 U.S. 643 (1961). Footnote: *Stanley v. Georgia,* 394 U.S. 557 (1969). *Mapp* quoted: 367 U.S. at pp. 654–55.

108   Clark quoted: 367 U.S. at p. 660. Judge Younger quoted in Nicholas Pileggi, "From D.A. to Dope Lawyer," *New York Times Magazine,* May 16, 1971, p. 47.

109   Mosk quoted in *ibid.* New Jersey Turnpike case: *New York Times,* July 13, 1971, p. 33.

110   Crime Commission: See Albert J. Reiss, Jr., *The Police and the Public* (New Haven: Yale University Press, 1971). Quoted in *New York Times Book Review*, Nov. 28, 1971, p. 5.

111–12 Bail transcripts quoted in Jerome Skolnick, *The Politics of Protest.* (N.Y.: Ballantine Books, 1969), pp. 305–06.

112   Boyle quoted in *ibid.*, p. 305. Prostitution in Manhattan and Judge Schwalb: *New York Times*, July 7, 1971, p. 1.

113   ABA Committee, quoted in *Report on Lawlessness in Law Enforcement*, vol. 11 of the *Wickersham Reports, op. cit.*, p. 191. 1951 Survey: "The 50 States Report." Submitted to the Commission on Civil Rights by the State Advisory Committee, 1961, p. 687; quoted in "The Police," task force report to the President's Commission on Law Enforcement and Administration of Justice, 1967, p. 181. 1961 quotation: "The Police," *op. cit.*, p. 183. Task force quoted: *ibid.*, p. 181.

114   Statistics and quotations *ibid.*, p. 182.

115   D.A.'s assistant quoted in Louis Pollak, *The Constitution and the Supreme Court* (Cleveland: World, 1966), vol. 2, pp. 187–88, from *New York Times*, May 16, 1965.

115   *Miranda* guidelines are in *Miranda v. Arizona*, 384 U.S. 436 (1966).

116–20 Mayday arrests based on "Mayday 1971, Challenge to Civil Liberty?" report of the District of Columbia Human Relations Commission, June 24, 1971.

120–21 New York City arrest based on Paul Chevigny, *Police Power* (N.Y.: Vintage Books, 1969), pp. 154–58.

121   Atlanta ordinance: *New York Times*, November 29, 1965, p. 41. Askew: *Washington Post*, May 6, 1971, p. A23.

122   Tucker State Prison Farm: *New York Times*, January 19, 1970, p. 70. Mississippi County Penal Farm: *New York Times*, November 10, 1971, p. 55. Presidio case: See Robert Sherrill, *Military Justice Is to Justice as Military Music Is to Music* (N.Y.: Harper Colophon Books, 1970), Ch. 2; *Congressional Record*, vol. 116, August 6, 1970, pp. 7896–7907.

123   *Times* survey: *New York Times*, May 15, 1971, p. 1.

123–24 Mississippi prison decision: *Anderson v. Nosser*, 438 F.2d 183, 186–188 (5th Cir. 1971).

124–5   Sostre: *Sostre v. Rockefeller*, 312 F. Supp. 863 (S.D.N.Y. 1970), affirmed in part, 442 F.2d 178 (2d Cir. 1971) (en banc).

125–6   Attica: *New York Times*, Dec. 2, 1971, p. 1.

126   Davis quoted in Davis, *Discretionary Justice* (Urbana: University of Illinois Press, 1971), pp. 128–29. Footnote: 1972 announcement: *Wall Street Journal*, January 14, 1972, p. 1.

127   *Plessy v. Ferguson*, 163 U.S. 537 (1896). West Virginia case: *Strauder v. West Virginia*, 100 U.S. 303 (1880). *Civil Rights Cases*, 109 U.S. 3 (1883). Harlan quoted: 109 U.S. at p. 53.

129   Quoting C. Van Woodward, review of Alan Trelease, *White Terror: The Ku Klux Klan Conspiracy in Southern Reconstruction* (New York: Harper & Row, 1971), *New York Times Book Review*,

May 23, 1971, p. 5. Murder in Drew: *New York Times,* May 27, 1971, p. 1; May 28.

129–30   Montgomery case: *U.S. ex rel. Montgomery v. Ragen,* 86 F.Supp 382 (N.D. Ill. 1949).

131–2   Selma prosecutions: see *U.S. v. McLeod,* 385 F.2d 734 (5th Cir. 1967).

132   The statute is 42 U.S.C. §1971(b). One commentator: "Federal Protection of Negro Voting Rights," 51 *Virginia Law Review* 1051, 1054 (1965).

134   President's message: "The American Promise," *Public Papers of the Presidents of the United States,* 1965, pp. 289–90.

134–35   Colloquy: *New York Times,* March 12, 1964, p. 23.

135   28-sided city: *Gomillion v. Lightfoot,* 364 U.S. 339 (1960). Herndon: *New York Times,* December 15, 1971, p. 31; January 8, 1971, p. 21.

135–36   Schools: See *Washington Post,* November 26, 1970, p. A2; *New York Times,* March 16, 1971, p. 1.

136   Tax exemptions: *New York Times,* March 27, 1971, p. 1.

137   Title VI: 42 U.S.C. § 2000d.

137–38   See Adam Walinsky et al., *Official Lawlessness in New York State; Construction Employment, Government Inaction, and the $275 Million Cost,* 1969: excerpts reprinted in Becker and Murray, *op. cit.,* pp. 231–38.

138   Virginia miscegenation: *Loving v. Virginia,* 388 U.S. 1 (1967).

139   Miscegenation: *New York Times,* May 22, 1971. Celebrated retort: Charles Warren in *The Supreme Court in United States History* (Boston: Little, Brown, 1937) doubts that Jackson actually made the retort. Apparently the first written reference to it was in Horace Greeley's 1864 book *The American Conflict.* William Graham Sumner gave credence to it in 1899 in his life of Andrew Jackson. (Warren, p. 759, note 1.) Pp. 139–40 are based on Warren, Ch. 19.
         Right to occupancy only: *Johnson v. McIntosh,* 21 U.S. (8 Wheat.) 543 (1823).

140   Cherokee Nation case: *Cherokee Nation v. Georgia,* 30 U.S. (5 Pet.) 1 (1831). Missionary case: *Worcester v. Georgia,* 31 U.S. (6 Pet.) 515 (1832).

141   Forced march: See Thurman Wilkins, *Cherokee Tragedy* (N.Y.: Macmillan, 1971). Pickering treaty violation: According to Vine Deloria, *Custer Died for Your Sins* (N.Y.: Avon, 1969), p. 36.

142   1971 report: *New York Times,* January 13, 1971, p. 13. Court quoted: *Cherokee Tobacco v. United States,* 78 U.S. (11 Wall) 616, 621 (1871).

143   Court quoted: *The Head Money Cases,* 112 U.S. 580 (1884). Indian citizenship case: *Elk v. Wilkins,* 112 U.S. 94 (1884).

144–45   Bercu's statements: *Juvenile Confinement Institutions and Correctional Systems,* Hearings before the Senate Subcommittee to Investigate Juvenile Delinquency, 92nd Congress, 1st Session, 1971, pp. 50ff. Statistics from Bercu affidavit of March 23, 1971.

146–48   Testimony of Bill Payne, reporter for the *El Paso Times*, at Hearings, *id.*, May 3, 1971, pp. 72ff.

148–50   Affidavit: from Hearings, *id.*, p. 63f.

150   Payne testimony, *op. cit.*

151   Madison Heights ordinance: *Washington Post*, January 7, 1971, p. C5.

151–52   Nevada welfare imbroglio: *New York Times*, March 21, 1971, p. 41.

152   California suit: *Washington Post*, March 26, 1971. *New York Times*, April 3, 1971, p. 9.

152–3   New Jersey fornication law: *New York Times*, March 23, 1971, p. 21.

153   First Supreme Court decision and quotation: *Shapiro v. Thompson* 394 U.S. 618, 634 (1969).

154   New law: *New York Times*, July 13, 1971, p. 37. Struck down: *New York Times*, January 25, 1972, p. 1. Justice Minton quoted: *United States ex rel. Knauff v. Shaughnessy*, 338 U.S. 537, 544 (1950). Condemned to Ellis Island: *Shaughnessy v. United States ex rel. Mezei*, 345 U.S. 206 (1953). Paroled to American family: Walter Gellhorn, *American Rights* (N.Y.: Macmillan, 1960) p. 142.

155   Quoted language is from "Action of the Convening Authority," Letter of December 18, 1970, from the Commandant of the Coast Guard, attachment to the official report of Vice Admiral Thomas R. Sargent, Serial 5830 of December 17, 1970 ("Formal Board of Investigation into Allegations of Improper Conduct in Connection with Recent Defection of Soviet Crewmen to CGC Vigilant near Martha's Vineyard, Massachusetts, on 23 November 1970"). 1939 case: *Kessler v. Strecker*, 307 U.S. 22 (1939).

156   Supreme Court quoted: *Harisiades v. Shaughnessy*, 342 U.S. 580, 594 (1952). Justice Chase quoted: *Calder v. Bull*, 3 U.S. (3 Dall.) 386, 389 (1798).

157–58   Quotation: Neil Sheehan, "Should We Have War Crimes Trials?" *New York Times Book Review*, March 28, 1971, p. 2.

158   Telford Taylor, *Nuremburg and Vietnam* (New York: Quadrangle Books, 1970). General Rothschild's statement appears in the *New York Times*, October 13, 1970, p. 43.

157–59   Orange herbicide: *Washington Post*, October 24, 1970, p. A8; November 22, p. A17.

160   Original law: Act of July 15, 1870, Ch. 294, section 18, 16 stat. 319. Rep. Jones: *Congressional Globe*, vol. 91, p. 1852, March 10, 1870.

161   One DOD regulation: DOD Directive 1344.10 of September 23, 1969, Paragraph III.D.

162   Exemptions: See, *e.g.*, 50 U.S.C. §403; 10 U.S.C. §711. Law requiring a civilian: 10 U.S.C. §136(f).

162–63   "Public Office" defined: 29 Comp. Gen. 363, 366 (1950).

163   General Meade: 13 Op. Att. Gen. 310 (1871). Alaska roads commissioner: 29 Comp. Gen. 363 (1950). Wisconsin case: *Martin v.*

Smith, 239 Wis. 314, 1 N.W. 2d 163 (1941). Library guard case: 44 Comp. Gen. 830 (1965).

164 Footnote: *United States v. Hartwell,* 72 U.S. (6 Wall) 385, 393 (1867). Attorney General's opinion: Letter of Leon Ulman, Deputy Assistant Attorney General (Legal Counsel), to Major General James S. Cheney, the Judge Advocate General of the Air Force, October 7, 1971. *Cf.,* for directly contrary interpretation, Opinion of the Comptroller General B-127798 of June 8, 1956.

164–65 Potent weapon: Opinion of the Judge Advocate General (Army), JAGA 1970/4981 (November 20, 1970).

165 Footnote: Opinion of the JAG (Army), JAGA 1969/3878 (May 6, 1969).

166–67 Constitutionality of Congressmen's reserve commission: *Reservists Committee to Stop the War v. Laird,* 323 F. Supp. 833 (D.D.C. 1971).

167–70 The discussion is based on John H. Stassen, "Separation of Powers and the Uncommon Defense: The Case Against Impounding of Weapons System Appropriations," 57 *Georgetown Law Journal* 1159 (1969).

168 Testimony: *Hearings on Department of Defense Appropriations for 1951 Before the House Committee on Appropriations,* 81st Congress, 2d Session, Pt. I, at pp. 52–55 (1950). Eisenhower: See Samuel Huntington, *The Common Defense* (New York: Columbia University Press, 1961) p. 145.

169 1966 law: See H.R. Rep. No. 1679, 89th Congress, 2d Session (1966), p. 2. Budget bureau: Quoted in Stassen, *op. cit.,* p. 1177.

170 The Steel Seizure case: *Youngstown Sheet & Tube Co. v. Sawyer,* 343 U.S. 579 (1952). Astute commentator: Stassen, *op. cit.,* p. 1191. Clark letter: February 25, 1967, on file in Legislative Research Service, Library of Congress. Nixon impounding: *New York Times,* March 25, 1971.

171 Weinberger quoted: *New York Times,* March 27, 1971, p. 26. Weinberger dissembled: *New York Times,* March 24, 1971, p. 13. Some days after: *New York Times,* May 18, 1971.

172 Law providing new pay table: P.L. 92–129 of September 28, 1971, 85 Stat. 348, Title II. British court quoted: *Rex v. Hampden,* 3 S.T. 825 (ex. 1637).

173 Corwin: *The President: Office and Powers* (New York: New York University Press, 4th rev. ed., 1957), pp. 251–52.

173–74 COMSAT: *Washington Post,* October 21, 1971, p. A15.

174 Eidson quoted: *New York Times,* July 15, 1971.

174–75 Misuse of funds in Alabama: *New York Times,* February 22, 1971, p. 17.

175 Lindsay and Beame: *New York Times,* October 30, 1971, p. 1.

175–76 Richardson incident is related by Herbert Brucker, "Profits from Public Papers: The Government Copyright Racket," *Saturday Review,* August 11, 1962.

176 Advertisement: *Washington Post,* March 12, 1962. General Dodge

quoted: *Washington Post,* March 17, 1962. Kennedy book: Brucker, *op. cit.* Colorado UFO study: See M. B. Schnapper, *Washington Post Book World,* May 4, 1969.

177 Government Reports and the GPO: See statement of Senator Ralph Yarborough, *Congressional Record,* vol. III, October 22, 1965. Federal Corrupt Practices Act: 2 U.S.C. §241 *et seq.* Unreported funds: *New York Times,* April 11, 1971, p. 25.

178 AMA: *Washington Post,* January 10, 1971, p. A21. BankPac: *Washington Post,* January 9, 1971, p. A6.

178–79 Senator Bentsen: *Washington Post,* December 10, 1970, p. A1.

179 Federal Corrupt Practices Act quoted: 2 U.S.C. §246(a)(1).

180 Failure to prosecute: *Washington Post,* July 17, 1970, p. A1; February 22, 1971, p. A2. Boyle conviction: *Washington Post,* April 1, 1972, p. A1.

179–80 O'Neill: *Washington Post,* January 9, 1971, p. A6.

180 Ford: *New York Times,* February 12, 1971.

181 Departmental spokesman: *Washington Post,* February 22, 1971, p. A2; Morrisseau: *Ibid.,* and *New York Times,* November 22, 1970.

182 Forgiving campaign debts: *New York Times,* May 16, 1971, p. 25. See also Morton Mintz and Jerry S. Cohen, *America, Inc.* (N.Y.: Dial, 1971), p. 161. Rooney: Mintz and Cohen, *id.,* pp. 223–24.

182–83 Alabama Air National Guard: *New York Times,* February 20, 1971; March 26, 1971, p. 26.

183 Deductions for public interest litigation: See *New York Times,* October 10, 1970, p. 1; October 16, 1970, p. 44; November 13, 1970, p. 1.

185 Reapportionment order first announced in the case of Alabama's state legislative districts: *Reynolds v. Sims,* 377 U.S. 533 (1964). Advisory Commission: See *Reapportionment of State Legislatures.* Hearings before the Subcommittee on Judiciary Committee, 89th Congress, 1st Session (1965); testimony of William G. Colman, p. 481; testimony of Robert B. McKay, p. 455.

185–86 Colloquy: *Id.* at p. 379.

188 Brown quoted: from George H. Brown letter of May 22, 1970, to author. Soldiers' and Sailors' Civil Relief Act: 50 U.S.C. App. §501 *et. seq.*

189 Table: Source is U.S. Census Bureau, from Brown letter, *op. cit.*

191 Opinion of the Attorney General: 41 Op. Atty. Gen. 59 (1950). Brown quoted: Brown letter, *op. cit.* Footnote: *Borough of Bethel Park v. Bush,* No. 71-1007, No. 71-1063 (3rd Cir. 1971).

193 McGee: See Taylor Branch, "Courage Without Esteem: Profiles in Whistle-Blowing," *Washington Monthly,* May 1971, p. 34.

194 Welfare: John Rothchild, "The Culture of Bureaucracy: Washington's Other Crime Problem," *Washington Monthly,* August, 1970, p. 56. Many other agencies: See James S. Turner, *The Chemical Feast: The Food and Drug Administration* (New York: Grossman Publishers, 1970); Robert Fellmuth, *The Interstate Commerce Omission* (New York: Grossman Publishers, 1970); John C. Esposito,

Vanishing Air (New York: Grossman Publishers, 1970); James M. Fallows, *The Water Lords* (New York: Grossman Pubishers, 1971); Edward F. Cox, Probert C. Fellmuth, John E. Schulz, *The Nader Report on the Federal Trade Commission* (New York: Richard W. Baron Publishing Co., 1969). $100 billion: "Forward," 2 *Economics and Antitrust Law Journal* 1 (1969).

194–95   MTX and the FDA: *Washington Post,* May 3, 1971, p. A3.

195   Bureau of Mines: *New York Times,* June 1, 1971. Department of Labor: *New York Times,* January 2, 1970, p. 17, Walsh Healey Act: 41 U.S.C. §35 *et seq.*

195–96   FHA and Section 235: *New York Times,* January 6, 1971, p. 1.

196   Penn Central: *New York Times,* March 29, 1971, p. 1. Congressman Green: *Philadelphia Evening Bulletin,* April 20, 1971, p. H29. Chafee: *Washington Post,* December 8, 1970, p. A3.

197   Kenneth Culp Davis, *Discretionary Justice* (Urbana: University of Illinois Press, 1971), p. 12.

199   Attorney General Cummings quoted: *New York Times,* August 19, 1937, p. 9. Borah: *New York Times,* September 18, 1937, p. 17.

200   Kelly and Levitt: *New York Times,* October 5, 1937, p. 1.

201   Denial of petitions: 302 U.S. 633 (1937); 302 U.S. 634 (1937). Two more denials: 302 U.S. 729, and 302 U.S. 650. The Taylor denial is at p. 654. Reappointment of Black: 37 *Columbia Law Review* 1213 (1937).

201–02   North Carolina case: *Parker v. Morgan,* 322 F. Supp. 585 (W.D.N.C. 1971).

202   New York case: *Long Island Vietnam Moratorium Committee v. Cahn,* 437 F.2d 344 (2d Cir. 1970). American Legion and young housewife: *New York Times,* January 10, 1971, p. E10. South Carolina correspondent: Augustus T. Graydon letter in 56 *A.B.A. Journal* 1038 (1970).

202–03   Later response: William T. Stevens letter in 57 *A.B.A. Journal* 16 (1971).

203   Zambian zoning problem: *Washington Post,* October 16, 1970, p. D1. Illegally parked police cars: *New York Times,* April 24, 1971, p. 24. Lyndon Johnson: Drew Pearson and Jack Anderson, *The Case Against Congress* (N.Y.: Pocket Books, 1969), p. 289.

203–04   Doctoring documents: *Washington Post,* January 17, 1971, p. A3.

204   Mail censorship: *New York Times,* June 23, 1971.

205   Bacon quoted in Joseph Borkin, *The Corrupt Judge* (N.Y.: Clarkson N. Potter, 1962) p. 3. Quotations immediately following: Borkin, *op. cit.,* p. 5. For a sympathetic account of Bacon's difficulties, see Catherine Drinker Bowen, *Francis Bacon: The Temper of a Man* (Boston: Little Brown, 1963).

206   Burger and Douglas fees: *New York Times,* June 9, 1969. See also, Robert Shogan, *A Question of Judgment* (Indianapolis: Bobbs-Merrill, 1972). Quotation concerning Talbott: David A. Frier, *Conflict of Interest in the Eisenhower Administration* (Baltimore Penguin Books, 1970), p. 79.

207 Eisenhower as shameless recipient: See *id.,* pp. 206–12. Korth: *Ibid.,* pp. 214–15. Klotz: *Ibid.,* p. 317.

207–08 Rankin: *New York Times,* February 11, 1971, p. 44.

208 Celler: Jack Anderson, "Congressional Ethics—When?" *Parade,* March 17, 1971, p. 24.

208–11 The ITT affair: *New York Times,* March 1, 1972, *et seq.* and *passim.*

211–13 President Nixon's bribe: The account is based on Frank Wright, "The Dairy Lobby Buys the Cream of Congress," *Washington Monthly,* May 1971, pp. 17–21; *Washington Evening Star,* June 24, 1971, p. A10; *Washington Post,* September 27, 1971, p. A7; *New York Times,* January 25, 1972, p. 1; Complaint in *Nader v. Butz,* No. 148–72 filed January 24, 1972, in the U.S. District Court for the District of Columbia.

213 Kleindienst testimony: *New York Times,* November 17, 1971, p. 34.

214 Chicago 1960: Task Force Report "The Police," *op. cit.,* p. 210. Denver 1961: *Ibid.* Merger of bureaus and narcotics offenses: Clark, *Crime in America, op. cit.,* p. 80. 170 officials: John N. Mitchell, "The War on Organized Crime and Corruption," address to the Convention of the Associated Press Managing Editors Association, Philadelphia, October 20, 1971. Kerner: *New York Times,* December 16, 1971, p. 1. Walker: *New York Times,* December 19, 1971, p. E4. Armstrong: *New York Times,* October 24, 1971, p. E2.

215 Bottle Club: *New York Times,* June 21, 1971, p. 18. Police captain quoted: *New York Times,* December 19, 1971, p. E5. *New York Times,* December 18, 1971, p. 1. Walsh: *New York Times,* December 17, 1971, p. 1. Behan and Cornelius: *New York Times,* December 16, 1971.

215–16 Leary: *New York Times,* December 21, 1971, p. 32.

216 Kriegel: *New York Times,* December 21, 1971, p. 1. Powell: *New York Times,* January 15, 1971, p. 1. Turner: *New York Times,* May 11, 1971, p. 1. Diamonds and furs: *Washington Post,* November 3, 1971, p. A3.

216–17 Letter of December 31, 1970, from Senator Abraham Ribicoff to Secretary of Defense Melvin R. Laird.

217 Reorganization of CID: *New York Times,* April 8, 1971, p. 15. Kirk: *New York Times,* July 22, 1971.

219 Ninety percent: "The Challenge of Crime in a Free Society," Report by the President's Commission on Law Enforcement and the Administration of Justice, 1967, p. 134.

220 False charges in St. Louis: Jules B. Gerard, "St. Louis Plays Politics with Law," *Focus/Midwest,* vol. 6, reprinted in Becker and Murray, *op. cit.,* p. 345.

220–21 Ballew incident: *Washington Post,* July 14, 1971, p. C1; August 2, 1971, p. C1; August 3, 1971, p. A1.

222 Miller whitewash: *Illinois Bar News,* June 1968, pp. 6–7.

223 Mitchell quoted: Speech before Kentucky Bar Association, Cincinnati, Ohio, April 23, 1971.

224 Ever's Law: *New York Times,* September 24, 1970, p. 1. Department spokesman quoted: *New York Times,* May 16, 1971, p. 21.

225 Response to Lykken raid: *Minneapolis Star,* May 13, 1970, p. 7A.

226 Corwin quoted: Edward S. Corwin, *The Constitution and What It Means Today* (Princeton: Princeton University Press, 1947), pp. 60–61.

227 Hanrahan: *New York Times,* December 18, 1971.

228 Rumored Long indictment: *Washington Post,* April 27, 1971. Fulford quoted from letter of May 18, 1971, to the author.

229 Bercu testimony: May 3, 1971.

230–32 Nixon press conference: *New York Times,* June 2, 1971.

234 Davis' short quotation: *Treatise on Administrative Law, Supplement* (St. Paul: West Publishing Co., 1970), §4.13, p. 206. Long quotation: *Id.,* §1.02, pp. 4–5.

235 "One essayist": John H. Rothchild, "The Culture of Bureaucracy: Washington's Other Crime Problem," *Washington Monthly,* August, 1970, p. 57.

238 Mine Bureau rules: *New York Times,* January 18, 1971, p. 15.

239–40 Nixon remarks concerning Manson: *Weekly Compilation of Presidential Documents,* 1970, pp. 1018–20.

240 Nixon confession of error: *Weekly Compilation of Presidential Documents,* 1970, pp. 1653–54 (news conference of December 10, 1970). Marijuana statement: *New York Times,* May 19, 1971, p. 50.

241 Wilson quoted: *New York Times,* July 13, 1971. Policeman quoted: Task force report, "The Police," *op. cit.,* p. 209.

241–42 Texas Youth Council statistics: from testimony of Bill Payne, *op. cit.*

242 Official quoted: Adam Walinsky, *Official Lawlessness in New York State, op. cit.* reprinted in Becker and Murray, *op. cit.,* pp. 236–37. Advisory Committee: *New York Times,* February 12, 1971.

243 Mitchell: *Address to Kentucky Bar Association.* Cincinnati, Ohio, April 23, 1971. Footnote: Senator Lee Metcalf, "The Vested Oracles: How Industry Regulates Government," *Washington Monthly,* July 1971, p. 48.

244 Indian Affairs Manual: John H. Rothchild, *op. cit.,* p. 58.

245 Menuhin episode: *New York Times,* December 4, December 5, December 6, 1970. Professional civil service: See Theodore J. Lowi, *The End of Liberalism* (New York: W. W. Norton & Co., 1969), pp. 303–05.

246 Two narcotics inspectors: Ramsey Clark, *op. cit.,* p. 79. Geological survey: *Business Week Magazine,* April 4, 1970, p. 102. Admiral Rickover quoted by Jack Anderson, *Washington Post,* February 18, 1970, p. B15. Duncan quoted: *Washington Post,* February 13, 1971, p. A1.

247 Doubling welfare rolls: Rothchild, *op. cit.,* p. 57. Havelock Ellis, *Studies in the Psychology of Sex,* vol. I, pt. 1. (New York: Modern Library, 1936), p. 164. Thurmond Arnold, *The Symbols of Government* (New Haven: Yale University Press, 1935), p. 160.

248   Arrests for vague offenses: See James S. Campbell, Joseph R. Sahid, and David P. Stang, *Law and Order Reconsidered*, Task Force Report to the National Commission on the Causes and Prevention of Violence (New York: Bantam Books, 1970), Ch. 23. Gambling raids in Passadena: *People v. Harris*, 182 Cal. App. 2d 837, 5 Cal. Rptr. 852 (Super. Ct. 1960). Sunday closing laws: *McGowan v. Maryland*, 366 U.S. 420 (1961); *Gallagher v. Crown Kosher Super Market of Massachusetts*, 366 U.S. 617 (1961); *Two Guys from Harrison-Allentown, Inc. v. McGinley*, 366 U.S. 582 (1961); *Braunfeld v. Brown*, 366 U.S. 599 (1961). $6.2 million in bribes: *New York Times*, December 3, 1970, p. 54; Serpico: *Ibid.*

249   Prosecution of grocery stores: *Taylor v. City of Pine Bluff*, 226 Ark. 309, 289 S.W. 2d 679 (1956). "Overcriminalization": See Campbell, Sahid, and Stang, *op cit.*, Ch. 23.

249–50   Prayers: *Engle v. Vitale*, 370 U.S. 421 (1962); *School District of Abington v. Schempp*, 374 U.S. 203 (1963). See *New York Times*, November 23, 1969, p. 74.

250   Concentration camps: *Hirabayashi v. United States*, 320 U.S. 81 (1943). Steel mills: *Youngstown Sheet & Tube Co. v. Sawyer*, 343 U.S. 579 (1952). Habeas corpus: *Duncan v. Kahanamoku*, 327 U.S. 304 (1946).

251   Policeman of the Year: *New York Times*, October 7, 1970, p. 43.

252   Footnote: Philosophy professor, *Washington Post*, September 30, 1970, p. A16; McKneally, *New York Times*, December 21, 1971, p. 32.

253   De facto segregation: *New York Times*, March 24, 1971.

254   Quotation: Walinsky, excerpted in Becker and Murray, *op. cit.*, pp. 237–38. Hebert: *New York Times*, May 6, 1967, p. 1. Hebert, a few days later: *New York Times*, May 10, 1967, p. 21.

256   Ridgway: *New York Times*, April 2, 1971, p. 37.

256–57   Freedom of Information Act: 5 U.S.C. §552.

260   "Complicated specialty: *United States ex. rel. Chapman v. Federal Power Commission*, 345 U.S. 153, 156 (1953).

261   Massachusetts taxpayer case: *Frothingham v. Mellon*, 262 U.S. 447 (1923). Rule was partially overturned: *Flast v. Cohen*, 392 U.S. 83 (1969). *Reservists Committee to Stop the War v. Laird*, 323 F.Supp. 833 (D.D.C. 1971). "Logical nexus": *Flast, op. cit.*, at p. 103. "Zone of interests": *Association of Data Processing Service Organizations, Inc. v. Camp*, 397 U.S. 150, 153 (1970).

261–62   Gesell quoted: *Reservists Committee, op. cit.*, pp. 840–41.

262   British precedents: For the position that this is a mistaken view, see Louis A. Jaffe, "Suits against Governments and Officers: Sovereign Immunity," 77 *Harvard Law Review* 1 (1963). Holmes: *Kawananakoa v. Polyblank*, 205 U.S. 349, 353 (1907). Title to oil producing land: *Simons v. Vinson*, 394 F.2d 732, 736 (5th Cir. 1968).

263   1871 case: *Bradley v. Fisher*, 80 U.S. (13 Wall.) 335, 347 (1871). 1896 case: *Spalding v. Vilas*, 161 U.S. 483, 498 (1896). Secretary of Interior case: *Glass v. Ickes*, 17 F.2d 273 (D.C. Cir. 1940), *cert.*

den. 311 U.S. 718 (1940). Secretary of Treasury case: *Standard Nut Margarine Co. v. Mellon,* 72 F.2d 557 (D.C. Cir. 1934), *cert. den.* 293 U.S. 605 (1934).

264   Turnabout: *Bivins v. Six Unknown Federal Narcotics Agents,* 403 U.S. 388 (1971). Justice Blackmun: *Ibid.* at p. 430. Majority's answer to Blackmun: *Ibid.* at p. 381. The federal statute in question is 42 U.S.C. §1983. Cardozo: *People v. DeFore,* 242 N.Y. 13, 21, 150 N.E. 585, 587 (1926).

265   Burger: *Neuman v. United States,* 382 F.2d 479, 480 (D.C. Cir. 1967).

266   Burger (long quotation): *Ibid.,* p. 482.

267   Bingo case: *Society of Good Neighbors v. Van Antwerp,* 324 Mich. 22, 36 N.W. 2d 308, 310 (1949). Pasadena gamblers: Letter of June 1, 1971, from defendant's counsel, Don H. Terry, to author.

267–8   Goodrich: *Wall Street Journal,* April 16, 1971, p. 1.

268   Loitering law case: *Coates v. City of Cincinnati,* 402 U.S. 611 (1971).

269   Morton Mintz and Jerry S. Cohen, *America, Inc.* (N.Y.: Dial, 1971), Ch. 12.

270   Nixon and "minimal" busing: *New York Times,* August 3, 1971. Moore and Westmoreland: *New York Times,* March 10, 1971, p. 14.

271   Ombudsman: Walter Gellhorn, *When Americans Complain* (Cambridge: Harvard University Press, 1966). Footnote: Senator Lee Metcalf, "The Vested Oracles: How Industry Regulates Government," *Washington Monthly,* July 1971, p. 51.

279   General Sherman: 14 Opp. Atty. Gen. 200 (1873).

Index

Index